Fighter Pilot

AERIAL COMBAT ACES FROM 1914 TO THE PRESENT DAY

Revised Edition

Edited by
BRIG. GEN. STANLEY M. ULANOFF

Prentice Hall Press • New York

Front cover painting depicts a pair of U.S. Navy F-14 Tomcats shooting down two Libyan
Su-22 jets that attacked them over the Gulf of Sidra.

Published by Prentice Hall Press
A Division of Simon & Schuster, Inc.
Gulf + Western Building
One Gulf + Western Plaza
New York, NY   10023

PRENTICE HALL PRESS is a trademark of
Simon & Schuster, Inc.

This is a revised edition of a book originally published in 1962
by Doubleday & Co., Inc.

Library of Congress Cataloging-in-Publication Data

Fighter pilot.

   Reprint. Originally published: Garden City, N.Y.:
Doubleday, 1962.
   1. Air warfare.   2. Fighter pilots—Biography.
I. Ulanoff, Stanley M.
UG632.F53   1986   358.4'14'0922   [B]   82-16277
ISBN 0-13-314816-5

Manufactured in the United States of America

10 9 8 7 6 5 4 3 2 1

First Prentice Hall Press Edition

TO TOOTY

My loving wife (who is known by that name and would not allow me to dedicate this book to Bernice, her legal, given name), who has constantly encouraged me, relieved me of other responsibilities, and placated my four children when they wanted to know what Daddy was doing in that locked room—the converted garage—more kindly known as the "den."

Contents

Acknowledgments

I must express my gratitude to all of the wonderful people who contributed to the success of *Fighter Pilot*.

As always, Lt. Col. Nick Apple of the USAF Magazine and Book Division, and his successor Lt. Col. Eric Solander, gave their full cooperation in providing needed photos and materials, as did Mrs. Virginia Fincik of the Still Photo Depository Section, and the Operational Branch of the Naval Historical Center.

Inestimable assistance was provided by the USAF Academy Cadet Library, particularly by Duane Reed of the Special Collection, and Betsy Kysely.

To Col. J. G. Boulet and Capt. Paul Robinson of the Canadian Armed Forces, to Gen. Menachem Eini of the Israeli Air Force and Capt. Nurit Charlotte Rosen, Israeli Defense Forces Spokesman, go my appreciation for their efforts on my behalf; to the French Embassy, and to my long-time friends Ed Lieberman of Rockville Centre, N.Y., and Bill Hess of Houston, Texas, for the excellent photos they contributed to this volume.

I must also acknowledge the help of Revell, Inc.; Airfix of England; Joe Phelan, a "Cross and Cockade" buddy; and the U.S. Department of Defense for their fine three-view aircraft drawings and aviation art.

I am particularly grateful to Mike Krushinsky of *Der Dienst* in Lowell, Michigan, for the very authentic reproductions of German, Russian, British, and Japanese pilots' wings and badges he provided; and to the Fox Military Equipment Co. of Hinsdale, Illinois, for its beautiful, authentic reproductions of embroidered United States Air Service pilots' wings of the First World War.

Many thanks to *Air Force* magazine, to *Airman*, and to other USAF publications for their contributions. As ever, my profound appreciation goes to the helpful librarians of the Bryant Library in Roslyn, N.Y. and of the Grist Mill Library in Great Neck, N.Y.

And, of course, without the help and cooperation of those stalwarts at Prentice Hall Press—Bill Thompson, Andy De Salvo, and Hal Siegel—this book would not have been published.

Last and certainly not least, much appreciation to Bob Cunningham for his stirring jacket art depicting the "shoot-out" over the Gulf of Sidra off the coast of Libya.

Introduction

Some believed that the coming of the Space Age with its guided missiles and rockets may well have brought the closing chapter to the glorious story of the fighter pilot.

A number of years ago the British Government announced a policy of reliance on the mechanical missile as opposed to the manned-fighter plane. No doubt a great deal of emotion was involved in this momentous decision. For who can forget those brave men who went aloft time and time again (to the point of exhaustion) in their game little Spitfires and Hurricanes to beat back the might of the Nazi Luftwaffe? Who, indeed, can forget those immortal "few" who saved the free world and won the Battle of Britain? Moreover, British Sea Harrier jump jets proved their worth against Argentine forces during the Falkland Island fracas in the spring of 1982.

In the minds of some, the day of the champion, the bold knight who mounted his steed and sallied forth to meet the enemy in mortal combat, is fast waning. In all, these heroes flashed their deeds across the skies in the short space of some forty-five years. This period included two major wars, the Spanish Civil War, the Korean conflict, the Vietnam War, and some smaller conflagrations.

The mere achievement of flight—the mastery of the art of flying alone has captured man's fancy from time immemorial and set his mind to soaring far beyond the clouds. In the beginning, the man who flew was a brave and courageous individual, a man acclaimed and set apart, above the crowd! He was ten feet tall, comparable in stature to a Gagarin or a Shepard, those intrepid fliers who first ventured out into space.

But war brought a new breed of flier—a warrior who not only mastered the techniques of flight but who would also go forth to face an enemy, brave his guns, and kill or be killed. This was the fighter pilot whose deeds and exploits are recorded here.

The colorful air battles of World War I were fought at speeds of 100 to 120 mph in aircraft that, by today's standards, were rather frail and flimsy. An adventuresome lot, the fliers on both sides followed a code of ethics that rivaled the chivalry of the Knights of the Round Table. They formally challenged their adversaries to an aerial duel, wined and dined the captured enemy airman, and honored a fallen foe by dropping flowers at his aerodrome or returning his personal effects in the same fashion. Certain of the aces were allowed to "free-lance"—go out on their own and seek out the enemy. The favorite method of attack was to pounce on the enemy from out of the sun. But the customary combat was the "dogfight" with opposing squadrons or flights milling about, maneuvering to get the enemy in the gun sights, and firing at each other, with the unlucky ones crashing to the earth below.

The Spanish Civil War, though partially a carry-over from the "Great War," was nothing more than the proving grounds for the global conflict yet to come. The German "Condor Legion" tested and perfected their Me-109 and blooded future aces like Galland and Molders. The Russians and Italians did the same.

The Second World War saw the end of free-lancing. Aerial warfare was no longer on a personal basis. Big aerial battles were more the rule here— fighters protecting their bombers, the enemy fighters attack and the tail chasing begins, hurtling at each other at rates of 350 to 400 mph, machine guns blazing, and "the devil take the hindmost."

Even greater speeds marked the coming of the jet. In Korea, squadroms of MiGs and Sabrejets tore at each other at velocities upwards of 600 mph. This higher speed made long turns necessary for each "pass" at the enemy, and the rapid rate of fuel consumption limited the number of passes. The problem was further intensified when the UN Sabres had to fly all the way north to challenge and draw the Chinese Reds out from behind the political protection of the Yalu River.

Air-to-air missiles, drawn almost unalterably to the heat produced by the enemy aircraft or directed by other sophisticated guidance systems, were the standard operating procedure of the Vietnam War. The aerial victories gained by American Air Force, Navy, and Marine fighter pilots were scored with missiles fired from F-4 Phantoms, F-105 Thunderchiefs, F-8 Crusaders, and A-4 Skyhawks against North Vietnamese-flown, Russian-built MiG 17s, 19s, and 21s. On the other hand the Israeli Mirages, Mystères, and Ouragans annihilated the air forces of four Arab-nation adversaries in a few hours, by the unorthodox use of extremely accurate cannon fire. Both U.S. and Israeli Air Forces, however, suffered heavy losses from Soviet-built surface-to-air missiles (SAMs) fired by their respective enemies, until the American-developed countermissile—the Shrike, and other countermeasures were brought into action. Their effectiveness was proved when Israeli fighters wiped out the Soviet-built Syrian SAM-6 missile batteries in Lebanon's Bekaa Valley during Operation "Peace for Galilee" in June 1982.

Today's fighter plane is actually a bomber. It can carry a bomb far more devastating than the ones that destroyed Hiroshima and Nagasaki, and fly faster than twice the speed of sound. It can strike a single target and scoot for home, but it may not have the fuel to stay and fight. And it would be hard put to evade an air-to-air or surface-to-air missile.

Whatever the outcome, in the battle between the fighter plane and the missile, the fighter pilot, in the short space of time he has thus far occupied in history, has cut a colorful, blazing swath across the sky!

This volume is the story of the fighter pilot in his own words. Here are all of his feelings and emotions: fear, excitement, joy. He tells us why he became a fighter pilot; how he was trained; what he thinks of his comrades, his plane, the enemy; and what he thinks makes a good fighter pilot.

These are the breath-taking experiences of the courageous men, be they friend or foe, who flew out to do battle above the clouds. They are German, French, Canadian, Japanese, English, Belgian, Australian, Spanish, Israeli, American, Korean, and more. They are the heroes of the RAF, the Luftwaffe, French Armèe de l'Air, the Belgian Flying Corps, the Israeli Air Force, the Imperial Japanese Army and Navy Air Forces, the United States Army, Navy, Marine Corps, and Air Force, and others. They belonged to such fighting teams as the Lafayette Escadrille, Richthofen Flying Circus, Hat-in-the-Ring Squadron, Condor Legion, Eagle Squadron, Flying Tigers, and the Black Sheep.

The names of many of these immortals are legendary—Rene Fonck, Albert Ball, Billy Bishop, James McCudden, "Mick" Mannock, Eddie Rickenbacker, Elliott White Springs, Manfred von Richthofen (the "Red Baron"), and Max Immelmann. Here too, are Garcia-Morato and Orrin Bell of the Spanish Civil War. Johnnie Johnson, Dick Bong, Joe Foss, "Pappy" Boyington, Bob Johnson, Adolf Galland, and Saburo Sakai of the Second World War are of a later vintage. Of more recent history are Jabara, Thyng, and No of the Korean fracas, and Olds, Ritchie, Feinstein, and Cunningham of the Vietnam War.

These are the brave and gallant men who flew and fought in the Spad, Sopwith Camel and Fokker D-7; the Spitfire, Hurricane, Thunderbolt, Lightning, Corsair, Me-109, and Zero; the Sabrejet and the MiG-15; the Phantom, Mirage, and MiG-21; and other great fighter and pursuit planes (known in their native tongues as *Kampfflugzeug, appareil de chasse*, and *avion de caza*—but always connoting the "hunter")!

As I have stated previously, the adventures within these pages are the first-hand, true combat experiences of the fighter pilots themselves, recounting their own exploits and/or those of their comrades. In this fashion General Kenney wrote the chapter on Dick Bong, who served under his command; and Billy Bishop tells of his friend and fellow Canadian ace, Billy Barker. In several instances we have also included fictionalized versions of the author's experiences. For example Captain Elliott White Springs, who, together with other Americans, flew with the British, fictionalizes some of his own adventures in the excerpt from *Above the Bright Blue Sky*. William Lichtman also gives us his fictionalized version of combat in the Israeli Air Force.

The military ranks listed for the authors are generally the ranks they held during the particular war or period concerned. Some of these fighter pilots received higher ranks later and during other wars: i.e., Billy Bishop was a lieutenant colonel after the close of the first world war and was Air Marshal of the RCAF in World War II; Colonel Robert L. Scott was promoted to Brigadier General after World War II; Major Joe Foss became Commanding General of the South Dakota Air National Guard after that war; Colonel

Robin Olds was promoted to Brigadier General following the Vietnam War and served as Commandant of Cadets at the USAF Academy. I have also used the fliers' own national rank with the United States equivalent in parentheses, where necessary.

Another point I must make is that a good part of the verve and spirit which goes into the drive of the fighter pilot is—HATE! It is not the intent of this book or its editor to rekindle past animosities of "the heat of the moment" or to open old wounds. Many of the fighter pilots kept diaries, made notes immediately following their combats or wrote their books or articles shortly thereafter. They spent the venom of the heat of battle by indulging in name calling. The "Hun," "Amerikanischer Schweinhund," "Verdamter Engländer," "Nip," or "Sal Boche" of yesterday is the friend and ally of today.

But whatever their names, their nationalities, or even their political philosophies (repugnant as the Nazi or Communist might be), these men had much in common. You will learn what it is in the pages that follow.

STANLEY M. ULANOFF

Fighter Pilot

PART ONE

GENESIS—
THE GREAT WAR

It's a Long Way to Tipperary

Royal Flying Corps

TOP MAN

by Lieutenant Colonel William A. Bishop,
RFC and RCAF

On the fourth day of the Battle of Arras, I happened to be flying about 500 feet above the trenches an hour after dawn. It had snowed during the night and the ground was covered with a new layer of white several inches thick. No marks of the battle of the day before were to be seen; the only blemishes in the snow mantle were the marks of shells which had fallen during the last hour. No Man's Land itself, so often a filthy litter, was this morning quite clean and white.

Suddenly over the top of our parapets a thin line of infantry crawled up and commenced to stroll casually toward the enemy. To me it seemed that they must soon wake up and run; that they were altogether too slow; that they could not realize the great danger they were in. Here and there a shell would burst as the line advanced or halted for a moment. Three or four men near the burst would topple over like so many tin soldiers. Two or three other men would then come running up to the spot from the rear with a stretcher, pick up the wounded and the dying, and slowly walk back with them. I could not get the idea out of my head that it was just a game they were playing at; it all seemed so unreal. Nor could I believe that the little brown figures moving about

below me were really men—men going to the glory of victory or the glory of death. I could not make myself realize the full truth or meaning of it all. It seemed that I was in an entirely different world, looking down from another sphere on this strange, uncanny puppet show.

Suddenly I heard the deadly rattle of a nest of machine guns under me, and saw that the line of our troops at one place was growing very thin, with many figures sprawling on the ground. For three or four minutes I could not make out the concealed position of the German gunners. Our men had halted, and were lying on the ground, evidently as much puzzled as I was. Then in a corner of a German trench I saw a group of about five men operating two machine guns. They were slightly to the flank of our line, and evidently had been doing a great amount of damage. The sight of these men thoroughly woke me up to the reality of the whole scene beneath me. I dived vertically at them with a burst of rapid fire. The smoking bullets from my gun flashed into the ground, and it was an easy matter to get an accurate aim on the German automatics, one of which turned its muzzle toward me.

1

But in a fraction of a second I had reached a height of only 30 feet above the Huns, so low I could make out every detail of their frightened faces. With hate in my heart I fired every bullet I could into the group as I swept over it, then turned my machine away. A few minutes later I had the satisfaction of seeing our line again advancing, and before the time had come for me to return from my patrol, our men had occupied all the German positions they had set out to take. It was a wonderful sight and a wonderful experience. Although it had been so difficult to realize that men were dying and being maimed for life beneath me, I felt that at last I had seen something of that dogged determination that has carried British arms so far.

Lt. Col William A. Bishop and his Nieuport 17. Bishop, credited with seventy-two confirmed victories, was the leading surviving British ace of the war, and later became Air Marshal of the Royal Canadian Air Force. (Canadian Forces photo)

The next ten days were filled with incident. The enemy fighting machines would not come close to the lines, and there was very little doing in the way of aerial combats, especially as far as I was concerned, for I was devoting practically all of my time to flying low and helping the infantry. All of our pilots and observers were doing splendid work. Everywhere we were covering the forward movement of the infantry, keeping the troops advised of any enemy movements, and enabling the British artillery to shell every area where it appeared concentrations were taking place. Scores of counter-attacks were broken up before the Germans had fairly launched them. Our machines were everywhere back of the enemy lines. It was easy to tell when the Germans were massing for a counter-stroke. First of all our machines would fly low over the grey-clad troops, pouring machine-gun bullets into them or dropping high-explosive bombs in their midst. Then the exact location of the mobilization point would be signalled to the artillery, so that the moment the Germans moved our guns were on them. In General Orders commending the troups for their part in the battle, Field-Marshal Sir Douglas Haig declared that the work of the Flying Corps, "under the most difficult conditions," called for the highest praise.

We were acting, you might say, as air policemen. Occasionally one of our machines would be set upon by the German gangsters—they were "careful" fighters and seldom attacked unless at odds of four to one—and naturally we suffered some casualties, just as the ordinary police force suffers casualties when it is doing patrol duty in an outlaw country. The weather was always favorable to the German methods of avoiding "open-air" combats. Even the clearer days were marked by skies filled with clouds sufficiently large and dense enough to offer protection and hiding-places to the high winging Hun machines.

I had several skirmishes, but did not

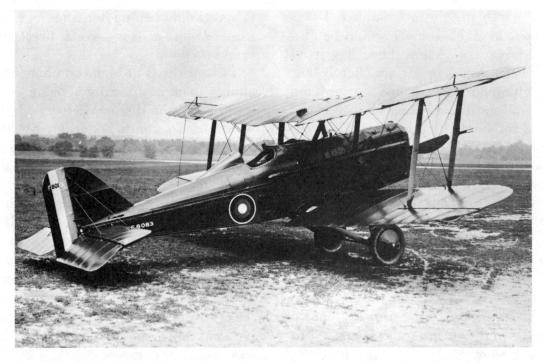

Flown by Bishop, as well as the RFC's two other top aces, McCudden and Mannock, the SE-5 was regarded as one of the war's great fighters. It was also favored by American ace George A. Vaughn, Jr. (USAF)

succeed in bringing down another machine until April 20th, when I was fortunate enough to begin another series of extremely interesting and successful fights. I was promoted to Captain at about this time and thought I was very happy; but the promotion was followed by another incident which really made me proud. The sergeants of my squadron had made me a round "nose" for my machine. It fitted on the propeller head and revolved with it. I had it painted a brilliant blue, and from that time on my machine was known as "Blue Nose." It was given to me, the Sergeant-Major explained, as a sign that I was an "Ace"—that I had brought down more than five machines. I was so pleased with this tribute from the men that I took old "Blue Nose" visiting to several other squadrons, where I exhibited my new mark of distinction to many of my friends and flying companions.

The machine I got on April 20th was the first I ever destroyed in flames. It is a thing that often happens, and while I have no desire to make myself appear as a blood-thirsty person, I must say that to see an enemy going down in flames is a source of great satisfaction. You know his destruction is absolutely certain. The moment you see the fire break out you know that nothing in the world can save the man, or men, in the doomed aeroplane. You know there is no "camouflage" in this, and you have no fear that the enemy is trying any kind of flying trick in the hope that he will be left alone.

I was flying over a layer of white clouds when I saw a two-seater just above me. We generally met the enemy in force during these days, but this German machine was all alone. Neither the pilot nor observer saw me. They flew along blissfully ignorant of my existence, while I carefully kept directly underneath them, climbing all the time. I was only ten yards behind the Hun when I fired directly up at him. It had been an exciting game getting into position underneath him, carefully following every move he made, waiting, hoping, and praying that he would not see me before I got into the place I wanted. I was afraid that if he did see me I would be at a distinct disadvantage below him. My hand must have been shaky, or my eye slightly out, because, although I managed to fire ten rounds, I did not hit anything vital. Even in this crucial moment the humor of the situation almost got the better of me. My machine seemed so little, carefully flying there under the big, peaceful Hun, who thought he was so safe and so far from any danger. Suddenly, from just underneath him, he heard the "tat-tat-tat-tat-tatter-tatter" of my machine gun almost in his ear, the range was so close. Then he must have seen my smoking bullets passing all around him. Anyway, there was consternation in the camp. He turned quickly, and a regular battle in the air began between the two of us. We maneuvered every way possible, diving, rolling, stalling; he attempting to get a straight shot at me, while my one object was

to get straight behind him again, or directly in front of him, so as to have a direct line of fire right into him.

Twice I dived at him and opened fire from almost point-blank range, being within two lengths of him before I touched the lever which set my gun to spouting. But there was no success. The third time I tried a new maneuver. I dived at him from the side, firing as I came. My new tactics gave the German observer a direct shot at me from his swivel gun, and he was firing very well too, his bullets passing quite close for a moment or two. Then, however, they began to fly well beyond my wing-tips, and on seeing this I knew that his nerve was shaken. I could now see my own bullets hitting the right part of the Hun machine, and felt confident the battle soon would be over.

I pulled my machine out of its dive just in time to pass about 5 feet over the enemy. I

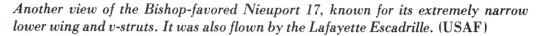

Another view of the Bishop-favored Nieuport 17, known for its extremely narrow lower wing and v-struts. It was also flown by the Lafayette Escadrille. (USAF)

could see the observer evidently had been hit and had stopped firing. Otherwise the Hun machine seemed perfectly all right. But just after I passed I looked back over my shoulder and saw it burst into flames. A second later it fell a burning mass, leaving a long trail of smoke behind as it disappeared through the clouds. I thought for a moment of the fate of the wounded observer and the hooded pilot into whose faces I had just been looking—but it was fair hunting, and I flew away with a great contentment in my heart.

This fight seemed to have changed my luck for the better. Everywhere I went for the next few weeks enemy machines were easily found, and I had numerous combats, many of them successful. Some days I could have been accused of violating all the rules of a flying men's union (if we had had one). I would fly as much as seven and a half hours between sunrise and sunset. Far from affecting my nerves, the more I flew the more I wanted to fly, the better I seemed to feel, and each combat became more and more enjoyable. Ambition was born in my breast, and, although I still dared not entertain hope of equalling the record of the renowned Captain Ball, who by this time had shot down over thirty-five machines, I did have vague hopes of running second to him.

Along with the new ambition there was born in me as well a distinct dislike for all two-seated German flying machines! They always seemed so placid and sort of contented with themselves. I picked a fight with the two-seaters wherever I could find one, and I searched for them high and low. Many people think of the two-seater as a superior fighting machine because of its greater gunpower. But to me they always seemed fair prey and an easy target. One afternoon, soon after this new Hun hatred had become a part of my soul, I met a two-seater about three miles over the German lines and dived at him from a very low height. As bad luck would have it, my gun had a stoppage, and while I turned away to right it, the enemy escaped. Much

disgusted, I headed away homeward, when into my delighted vision there came the familiar outlines of another Hun with two men aboard. I flew at this new enemy with great determination; but after a short battle he dived away from me, and although I did my best to catch him, I could not. He landed in a field underneath me. To see him calmly alight there under perfect control filled me with a towering rage. I saw red things before my eyes. I vowed an eternal vendetta against all the Hun two-seaters in the world, and, the impulse suddenly seizing me, I dived right down to within a few feet of the ground, firing a stream of bullets into the machine where it was sitting. I had the satisfaction of knowing that the pilot and observer must have been hit, or nearly scared to death, for, although I hovered about for quite a long time, neither of them stepped from the silent machine.

Half an hour after this occurrence I saw one of our machines in difficulties with three of the enemy. The Huns were so engrossed with the thought that they had a single British machine at their mercy, I felt there was a good chance that I might slip up and surprise them. My scheme worked beautifully. I came up to within 15 yards of one of the Huns, and, aiming my machine at him with dead accuracy, shot him down with my first ten bullets. He probably never knew where the bullets came from, not having the slightest idea another British machine was anywhere in that part of the sky. I turned now to assist with the other two Huns, but by this time my brother pilot had sent one of them spinning out of control, while the last remaining enemy was making good his escape as fast as his Mercédès engine could pull him through the air. It is surprising sometimes how much dead resistance there is in the air when you are in a hurry. Having nothing better to do under the circumstances, I dived down after my own victim to get a view of the crash. I was just in time. He struck the ground at the corner of a field, and what was one instant a falling machine was next a twisted bit of wreckage.

PRECISION FIGHTER

by Major James T. B. McCudden,
RFC and RAF

A Great Fight

We were just on the point of engaging six Albatros Scouts away to our right, when we saw ahead of us, just above Poelcappelle, an S.E. half spinning down closely pursued by a silvery blue German triplane at very close range. The S.E. certainly looked very unhappy, so we changed our minds about attacking the six V-strutters, and went to the rescue of the unfortunate S.E.

The Hun triplane was practically underneath our formation now, and so down we dived at a colossal speed. I went to the right, Rhys-Davids to the left, and we got behind the triplane together. The German pilot saw us and turned in a most disconcertingly quick manner, not a climbing nor Immelmann turn, but a sort of flat half spin. By now the German triplane was in the middle of our formation, and its handling was wonderful to behold. The pilot seemed to be firing at all of us simultaneously, and although I got behind him a second time, I could hardly stay there for a second. His movements were so quick and uncertain that none of us could hold him in sight at all for any decisive time.

I now got a good opportunity as he was coming towards me nose on, and slightly underneath, and had apparently not seen me. I dropped my nose, got him well in my sight, and pressed both triggers. As soon as I fired up came his nose at me, and I heard clack-clack-clack-clack, as his bullets passed close to me and through my wings. I distinctly noticed the red-yellow flashes from his parallel Spandau guns. As he flashed by me I caught a glimpse of a black head in the triplane with no hat on at all.

By this time a red-nosed Albatros Scout had arrived, and was apparently doing its best to guard the triplane's tail, and it was well handled too. The formation of six Albatros Scouts which we were going to attack at first stayed above us, and were prevented from diving on us by the arrival of a formation of SPADs, whose leader apparently appreciated our position, and kept the six Albatroses otherwise engaged.

The Death of a Brave Man

The triplane was still circling round in the midst of six S.E.s, who were all firing at it as opportunity offered, and at one time I noted the triplane in the apex of a cone of tracer bullets from at least five machines simultaneously, and each machine had two guns.

Major James T. B. McCudden; a skilled mechanic, superb flier, and expert marksman with 58 victories (USAF)

6

The Albatros Scout D-5, the prime German fighter before the introduction of the Fokker D-VII and Triplane. (USAF)

By now the fighting was very low, and the red-nosed Albatros had gone down and out, but the triplane still remained. I had temporarily lost sight of the triplane whilst changing a drum of my Lewis gun, and when I next saw him he was very low, still being engaged by an S.E. marked I, the pilot being Rhys-Davids. I noticed that the triplane's movements were very erratic, and then I saw him go into a fairly steep dive and so I continued to watch, and then saw the triplane hit the ground and disappear into a thousand fragments, for it seemed to me that it literally went to powder.

Strange to say, I was the only pilot who witnessed the triplane crash, for even Rhys-Davids, who finally shot it down, did not see its end.

It was now quite late, so we flew home to the aerodrome, and as long as I live I shall never forget my admiration for that German pilot, who single-handed fought seven of us for ten minutes, and also put some bullets through all of our machines. His flying was wonderful, his courage magnificent, and in my opinion he is the bravest German airman who it has been my privilege to see fight.

A Worthy Sentiment

We arrived back at the mess, and at dinner the main topic was the wonderful fight. We all conjectured that the enemy pilot must be one of the enemy's best, and we debated as to whether it was Richthofen or Wolff or Voss. The triplane fell in our lines, and the next morning we had a wire from the Wing saying that the dead pilot was found wearing the Boelcke collar and his name was Werner Voss. He had the "Ordre Pour le Mérite."

Rhys-Davids came in for a shower of congratulations, and no one deserved them better, but as the boy himself said to me, "Oh, if I could only have brought him down alive," and his remark was in agreement with my own thoughts.

The First in Our Lines

Nothing happened of interest that I am able to recall until the 27th, when I brought down my first Geman machine in our lines. I left the ground soon after lunch, and very soon saw a Hun two-seater flying round over Houthoulst Forest, apparently ranging. Whilst waiting for a favourable opportunity I saw a SPAD* attack this Hun, and I saw the Hun twisting

*The letters SPAD indicate that the machine was built by the "Société Pour Aviation et ses Dérives," a firm founded by M. Blériot on the wreck of the business of M. Armand Deperdussin. Originally the firm was called the "Société Pour les Appareils Deperdussin."

and swerving about with the French SPAD in pursuit, and then suddenly the SPAD appeared to be hit, and went down out of control. The Hun went off east a little and then came back, apparently very pleased at having shot the SPAD down.

He now came to within reasonable distance of where I was waiting, and after him I went. When I got to my two-seater position, the Hun was going due east, and I fired a good burst from both guns until I had to turn sharply to the right to avoid colliding with the Hun. As I turned I saw the Hun gunner at a range of twenty yards with his gun central to the rear waiting to see which way I would turn, for he had seen me overtaking him too fast, and knew that I should have to turn, and as I did turn I saw him turn his gun and fire just four shots, each "Cack, cack, cack, cack," two bullets of which I distinctly felt hit my machine. I half rolled, and got clear of him, and glanced round to see where he was.

When I did see him he was in flames going down in a vertical dive, after which he went past the vertical, and then onto his back, so that he was now falling towards our lines, into

which he fell near St. Julien, although when I had shot him he was flying east.

When the machine went beyond the vertical and onto its back, the enemy gunner either jumped or fell out, and I saw him following the machine down, twirling round and round, all arms and legs, truly a ghastly sight. A queer thing happened, the enemy gunner fell into his own lines, and the machine and the pilot in our lines.

I flew back to my aerodrome very pleased, for it is the wish of most pilots to bring Germans down in our lines, so as to get souvenirs from the machine.

Over Houthoulst

The next morning, September 28th, I led my patrol over the lines at 11,000 feet over Boessinghe, and before crossing the lines I saw a patrol of Albatroses going south over the Houthoulst Forest. I signalled to my patrol, who understood what I wanted, and down went our noses, and although I thought I was going down fairly slowly, my comrades afterwards said they were recording 180

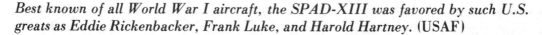

Best known of all World War I aircraft, the SPAD-XIII was favored by such U.S. greats as Eddie Rickenbacker, Frank Luke, and Harold Hartney. (USAF)

m.p.h. to keep up with me. I picked out the Albatros who was on the east of this formation and, opening fire at 200 yards, released my triggers about 50 yards short of the Albatros, whose left wings at once fell off, and then the whole machine fell to pieces at about 9000 feet. The enemy pilot also fell out and went down much quicker than the machine.

I then flew onto the leader, who was still in front of me, and having apparently seen me shoot his comrade he was very wide awake. Before I got to close range he had turned round, and we now started to do the usual circling, each trying to get behind the other. Meanwhile, all my comrades were also busily engaged with their partners.

My opponent and I continued to circle round from 8000 feet down to 4000 feet, when, as the German passed directly below me in the opposite direction, I did a steep Immelmann turn to get on his tail, but in doing so I lost a good deal of height and now I found the German above me. I continued to circle, but at last the German got behind me and commenced to shoot.

We were now 2000 feet over the Forest of Houthoulst, and things for me did not look very cheerful, for I had been out maneuvered by the German pilot, and was now over a mile behind his lines. I continued to maneuver to prevent the Hun from shooting at an easy target, and when we were down to about 1000 feet I dived with engine on almost to the ground, intending to contourchase back at a few feet when the silly old Hun turned off east and flew away just at a time when things were looking rather black for me.

I heaved a sigh of relief as I recrossed the lines, and then I went up to my rendezvous, to reform my patrol, but could not find them. So, after climbing up to 10,000 feet I flew towards Menin, and found Barlow leading them miles east of the lines, with dozens of Huns west of them. I flew towards them and fired two recall signals, and then they rejoined me, but there was nothing more that happened of interest to relate.

Reflections

This is peculiar. While the Hun who had outmaneuvered me was engaging me, at about 2000 feet, I happened to see one wing of the Hun whom I had shot to pieces floating down like a leaf quite near me, three minutes later.

Our patrol time being over we flew back to our aerodrome and had breakfast, and Mayberry, who was also having breakfast when we trooped in, remarked that I was becoming expert at turning Huns out of their aeroplanes. We chatted over breakfast and found that Rhys-Davids and Barlow had each got a Hun out of the first formation whom we attacked, so out of the five we attacked only two went home.

The Hun who outmaneuvered me was very good indeed, but I never have understood why he left me at a time when he could have most likely shot me down.

BILLY BARKER, FIGHTING CANADIAN

by Lieutenant Colonel William A. Bishop, RFC and RCAF

He was a Canadian and his name was Billy Barker. Like so many North Americans who have left their imprint on the pages of combat, he came from a midwest prairie farm and had no experience of war, or aviation, and little of the world itself, when he joined the Canadian forces in 1914 as a private soldier. In this respect at least he bears a marked resemblance to America's young Major Bong. It was 1916 before Barker transferred from the infantry into the old Royal Flying Corps. He joined, like myself, as an observer, in which role he had more experience than I, for by the time he went back to England from France to learn to fly he had already been wounded and had won the Military Cross.

Billy Barker went back to the war as a pilot early in 1917, this time as chauffeur of a two-seater artillery observation machine. After a tour of operational duty at the front he was sent back to England to be an instructor.

Barker felt completely frustrated in a Training Squadron, teaching other youngsters how to fly. He applied to be returned to operational duties, but the application was denied. Whereupon he took a most unmilitary and undisciplined step and decided to make himself a nuisance to the staff that they would be glad to see the last of him. Day after day he was pulled up on the carpet for low flying over towns, for stunting over headquarters, and for playing the fool generally. Called to account by his superiors he promptly informed them that he intended to misbehave and commit compound fractures of the rules until such time as the brass hats decided to post him back to the front.

So Barker was sent back to France by his irritated superiors, this time to fly a Sopwith Camel, that delicate piece of sudden death with which British pilots wrought so much havoc amongst the Albatroses in the later months of the war.

Barker was the originator of one great trick. That was to lure his enemies into battle as close to the ground as possible, for he had made the discovery that the Camel was infintely more maneuverable close to the ground than any airplane the Germans possessed.

The first great test of the Barker system came one day at dusk when he was leading his flight home, but was still deep in German-held territory. Suddenly ten planes appeared in the half-light heading east: German Albatroses on their way home. Barker and his friends went in to attack.

Early in the melee the Canadian pilot, while going to the assistance of one of his mates, found himself with a Hun on his own tail. This was his chance to try out the system. Zigzagging to keep out of range of the German's guns, Barker circled lower and lower, making no attempt to get into shooting position, coaxing the German pilot right up the garden path. He led the enemy almost down to the treetops, then suddenly—and suddenly is altogether too slow a word—went into a tight loop with his small, quick Camel. The slower Albatros could not cope with such activities. In a split second Barker was on the German's tail and with one quick burst destroyed him.

Almost before the first had crashed, a second pounced on Billy. Using the identical tactics he crashed the second German in flames, zoomed away, and made for home in the falling light. Such a master of low fighting did Barker become in the next few weeks and such a madcap devil was he in his sheer youthful exuberance that Headquarters hit on a brainy idea and formed a squadron of youngsters who were then trained to the Barker system and shipped to Italy to fight the Austrians and Germans in the mountain passes.

In Italy Barker's bunch ran wild. They blew Austrian captive balloons, hitherto unmolested, out of the sky far behind the lines. They strafed enemy aerodromes at grasstop height, pouring inflammable bullets into the open doors of hangars to set them aflame. They played particular and general hell with the easygoing Austrians.

The enemy, including German reinforcements sent to the Italian front to deal with this mad Canadian and his lunatic youngsters, tried bombing Barker's aerodrome with more than thirty German Gothas and on the first try lost almost half their force when Barker and his boys soared up into battle. Barker had now developed a new brand of attack much used in World War II. It is called the head-on system and it takes plenty of guts to be properly executed and get your man, because you must fly at him on his level, straight down his path toward him, and keep going until somebody weakens. I cannot remember ever having met a German who did not duck first. They certainly used to duck when they saw Barker coming.

That was Billy's way of dealing with the Gotha bombers, and on his first encounter he took two out of three by this device. That, in my opinion, must have been one of the great shows of the war. The three Germans were flying in line astern and Barker flew head-on to meet them. He nabbed the first when they were almost bow to bow, ducked under the second, came up head-on into the third, knocked it out of formation, turned on it, and plunged the big Gotha to earth a flaming wreck.

But it was in low flying where he always excelled. Most pilots preferred the more formal method of getting up high, between the enemy and the sun, and pouncing on him from that vantage point. Barker wanted them down near the ground and to find them near the ground meant he practically had to visit their aerodrome and lie in wait. His superiors

considered him completely mad, but the system worked and soon Billy was knocking enemy aircraft down like flies. Decorations came his way one after the other. The D.S.O. was soon added to the M.C., won as an observer. Then came a bar to his D.S.O. and a bar to his Military Cross. Early in May 1918 the Italians decorated him and Barker subsequently confided in me that, while it was nice to be honored by one's Allies, it was *not* nice to be kissed on both cheeks by a man with a beard.

Perhaps one of the funniest stories about this terrific fighting man is what his friends call the Spy Story.

The practice had come into vogue of flying Allied spies across the enemy lines and dropping them by parachute to do their jobs. At that time, of course, very few people knew much about chutes and extremely few thought highly of dangling under the silk to descend to the ground in the middle of the night. Consequently, it was often the case that a spy would set off in the rear cockpit of an aircraft to be dropped at an appointed place by the pilot, but prior to arrival would achieve

While a tough plane to master, the Sopwith Camel ended the war with the most enemy aircraft to its credit. Barker, as well as Elliott White Springs and Roy Brown flew it to great success. (Canadian Forces)

understandable frigidity of the feet and decide not to make the jump. To meet this problem Barker, who had had a couple of experiences with mind-changing spies, devised his own system, which was simply to equip the passenger seat with a trapdoor arrangement operated by a lever from the pilot's cockpit, the passenger being totally unaware of the arrangement. Then Barker would fly off with his spy for delivery behind the Austrian lines, keeping the nervous gentleman comforted with reassuring noises as they flew along. When the appointed destination was reached Billy simply sprang the trap. The spy fell out through the floor and died a thousand deaths while he waited for his parachute to open. Inasmuch as each passenger traveled on a one-way ticket, it was not difficult to keep the system secret from prospective riders. Thus for some time Billy operated a spy delivery service which won him high repute with the Intelligence staff.

The greatest Barker story of all relates to three famed Austrian pilots with whom Billy and his teammates sought combat but who had consistently ducked whenever Barker and his Camels appeared on the scene. They were looking for sitting birds, nice quiet artillery observing two-seaters, not maniacs who seemed to be able to do anything they liked with their midget fighting machines.

So Barker had thousands of leaflets printed, and dropped them behind the Austrian lines. The leaflets carried the following challenge:

Major W. G. Barker, D.S.O., M.C., and the Officers under his command present their compliments to

Captain, Brumowsky,
Ritter von Fiala,
Captain Havratil,

and the pilots under their command and request the pleasure and honor of meeting in the air. In order to save Captain Brumowsky, Rither von Fiala and Captain Havratil and the Gentlemen of their party the inconvenience of searching for them,

Major Barker and his Officers will bomb Godega Aerodrome at 10:00 A.M. daily, weather permitting, for the ensuing fortnight.

Barker and his young men carried out their schedule to the letter and the moment. They bombed Godega daily through the fortnight. Once or twice the enemy appeared. But they were face-saving appearances and Barker, as always, came out on top by a lopsided score.

Billy left Italy in the summer of 1918 and returned to Britain to pursue a new course in air-fighting tactics—a young man off to school to learn from the book he had practically written. As always he rebelled against the discipline and red tape of the war behind the lines. This time he evolved a new excuse to get back into combat and asked to be allowed a few weeks at the front in France before taking the course, to acquaint himself with new German tactics. There, on October 27, 1918, only two weeks before the Armistice, and on the flight which was supposed to take him back to Britain, he put on a show which stands as the greatest in the annals of World War I, and one which it would be hard to tie in the later to-do.

The official account states that Barker, having packed his kit and seen it shipped to England, climbed into the Sopwith Snipe he was to fly back, but couldn't resist taking one more look at the lines. He decided to do a little wandering and to have one last look at the war he was on the point of leaving. Instead of turning toward the Channel he swung off over the lines. In a few moments he saw a German machine at 22,000 feet and attacked. The German observer fired so accurately that the Canadian's own machine was badly hit. As Barker's journey was to have been routine and peaceful, the telescopic sight had been stripped off his guns before taking off, so Bill was equipped with ordinary peep-sights, nothing else. Twice he attacked the German before he was able to kill the observer. Then he closed in to short range and shot the pilot and airplane down. The enemy machine

In action for only the last three months of the war, the Sopwith Snipe was nonetheless regarded as the finest of all the conflict's fighters. Easier to handle than the Camel, it was designed for high-altitude fighting. Major Barker won his Victoria Cross in a Snipe. (Canadian Forces)

broke apart in the air and fell in a rain of small pieces. At this juncture a Fokker pounced on Billy, catching him by surprise, putting an explosive bullet into his right thigh and shattering it. That would have been enough to cause any ordinary fighting man to get out of there, but not Bill Barker. Billy was going to get even. He stayed with his German, finally brought him into the peep-sight for a split second, and sent him reeling down in flames.

Still Billy had not enough, although by then he was fighting to retain consciousness. He must have passed out because, as he told me afterwards, he suddenly found himself in the midst of a crowd of enemy machines, the number of which was estimated by people on the ground as being at least sixty, without having the slightest idea how he got there.

Germans jumped him from every corner of the sky. His machine was hit repeatedly and he was severely wounded again, this time in the left thigh. He fainted from loss of blood and fell thousands of feet out of control with the whole German circus after him. The rush of air in his wild dive brought him back to life and suddenly he turned on his enemies like a mad dog. By then any hope of survival must

have gone from his mind. He was simply going to wreak all the havoc possible before the enemy fliers polished him off. He charged head-on at an enemy machine, thinking to collide with it and take at least one more German with him where he was sure he was going.

But, as always, his bullets were right on the target. Before the collision could occur the German burst into flames and fell out of battle—and Barker had picked up an explosive bullet in his left elbow. To tally the score at this juncture, Barker was now sitting in his cockpit, with one thigh shattered, the other severely wounded, and his left arm limp and useless. He fainted again, and again fell out of control. Again he recovered and again swooped up into the melee. This time he fought the Germans all the way down the long hill almost to the ground and in the course of the battle shot down two more. By then he was close to the ground and still under attack from many German machines. A burst of explosive bullets perforated the gasoline tank under his seat, but by miraculous good luck—and there were no self-sealing gas tanks then—the machine did not take fire. Barely conscious, Barker switched to his auxiliary tank and kept the little Clerget rotary engine spinning. He fainted again and almost spun in, recovering consciousness and pulling out just in time. With the machine almost out of control he put its nose down and headed west, not knowing where he was, and piled his machine into a maze of barbed wire immediately behind the British lines. Five German aircraft had gone down in that tremendous melee between one man and God knows how many antagonists, a man who was supposed to be quietly flying across the Channel to Britain to take a course in air fighting! They gave Billy the V.C. for that one.

His wounds mended and soon after the end of the war he returned to Canada, where he and I were happy partners in one of the first and most amusing commercial aviation enterprises ever undertaken by foolish young men. The irony of life caught up with Billy Barker soon afterwards. He died by stalling and spinning into the ground just after taking off from Ottawa in one of the first Fairchild machines. So passed a man who, in my book, stands as the greatest air fighter the world has ever known.

THREE COMBAT REPORTS

by Second Lieutenant A. Ball, Captain E. Mannock, and Captain J. B. McCudden, RFC and RAF
Army Form W. 2368

Combats in the Air

Squadron: No. 11
Type and No. of aeroplane: Nieuport
  Scout A.134
Armament: Aerial Torpedoes & Lewis Gun.
Pilot: 2/Lt. A. Ball
Observer: _____
Locality: Pelves

Date: July 3rd 1916
Time: 2.15 p.m.
Duty: Special Mission
Height: 5000–3000 ft.

Remarks on Hostile machine: — Type, armament, speed, etc.

Observation Balloon

Narrative

Nieuport Scout A.134 crossed the lines at 5000 ft. and went towards Balloon. When within ¼ mile Balloon was being hauled down. Nieuport fired darts when within 16 yards and immediately afterwards emptied drum of Buckingham Bullets at Balloon. Darts missed, Buckinghams mostly hit but did not ignite Balloon, which was hauled down to ground apparently uninjured.

A. Ball
2/Lieut.
No. 11 Squadron, R.F.C.

Major,
Commanding No. 11 Squadron, R.F.C.

Combat report by Second Lieutenant A. Ball, July 3rd, 1916

W3042/M2233 50,000 6/17 [X373a] W. & Co. Army Form W. 3348
W7213/M2953 60,000 8/17 [X439a]

At the time of his death, 2nd Lieut. Albert Ball led the Royal Flying Corps with forty-four victories. He was nineteen years old. (USAF)

Combats in the Air

Squadron: No 74
Type and No. of Aeroplane:
    S.E.5a C. 6468
Armament: 1 Vickers 1 Lewis
Pilot: Capt. E. Mannock D.S.O. M.C.

Date: June 1st 1918
Time: 4.25-4.35 p.m.
Locality: Estaires
Duty: O.P.
Height: 13,500–11,000 ft.

Observer:＿＿＿   Result

Destroyed . . . . Two . . . .
Driven down out of control . . . . . One . . . . .
Driven down . . . . — . . . .

Remarks on Hostile Aircraft: — Type, armament, speed, etc.

Pfalz, Dark camouflaged with white tails

Narrative

Observed and engaged formation of E.A. Scouts East of Merville. Attacked from the front and above. The highest Scout being behind, S.E. opened fire with both guns at point blank range. The E.As bottom wings fell away and it crashed. Confirmed also by Lts. Giles and Birch.

Engaged another E.A. and after a short vertical burst at close range, this Scout burst into flames. Confirmed by all other members of patrol.

Engaged another E.A., which was turning towards me on the same level. Fired several short bursts at this machine whilst circling. This E.A. went into a spin, and disappeared from the fight.

> E. Mannock
> Captain
> R.E. attached R.A.F.
>
> Major
> Commanding . . . 74 . . . Squadron

Combat report by Captain E. Mannock, June 1st, 1918

Number 20.
(4 50 25) W6180—778 20,000 9/16 HWV(P1484/7)
Forms/W3348/2   Army Form W. 3348.
10432 M1979 30,000 11/16

Combats in the Air

Squadron: No. 56   Date: Nov. 30th, 1917
Type and No. of Aeroplane: S.E.5. No.B. 36.   Time: 11.5. a.m.
Armament: Vickers and Lewis Guns.   Duty: D.O.P.
Pilot: Capt. J.B. McCudden. M.C.   Height:
Observer: None.
Locality: S.E. of Havrincourt.

Remarks on Hostile machine: — Type, armament, speed, etc.

Two-seater

Narrative

Got to lines at Masnieres at 10.10 and patrolled from Gouzeaucourt to Bourlon. Clouds at 2000 feet. At 10.45 drove several E.A. Scouts away from Bourlon. E.A.A. very active and accurate. At 11.15 saw 2 E.A. two-seaters coming W. over Fontaine. I secured a good position behind front E.A. and fired a good burst from both guns. E.A.'s engine stopped and water streamed from radiator. *As E.A. glided W, I let him land O.K. and then landed myself,* as E.A. gunner had hit my radiator with explosive bullet. E.A. landed S.E. of Havrincourt intact with exception of bullet holes. The pilot badly wounded. Placed guard on E.A.

> J. B. McCudden
> Capt.

Occupants made prisoners by 59th Div. H.Q.

R. Malcomb Brown
Major,
Commanding No: 56 Squadron,
Royal Flying Corps.

Combat report by Captain J. B. McCudden, November 30th, 1917

Lafayette Escadrille

The First American Volunteers

BIRTH OF THE LAFAYETTE ESCADRILLE

**by Major Edmund Gros,
U. S. Air Service**

When the history of America's participation in the Great War is written, the earliest chapter should be given to a record of the services of the American volunteers who came to France while our country was still neutral. Animated by the finest spirit of patriotism, believing with all their hearts in the justice of the Allied cause, many young men joined the armies of France and England, and among them those who have since become pilots in the Escadrille Lafayette Flying Corps. I have been associated with this group of volunteer aviators from the very beginning. I have examined every candidate medically and morally. After their acceptance in the Corps I have kept their interests at heart, and my feelings toward them is almost a paternal one. Much has already been written of Chapman, Kiffen Rockwell, Prince, McConnell, McMonagle, Chadwick, Genet, Hoskier, Campbell, to speak only of a few of those who have met glorious deaths; and of those pilots, still living, still taking a splendid part in the aerial battles along the Western Front. To the example set by the American volunteers, perhaps more than to any other cause, was due the awakening of the national soul of America, the realization that this war is not a local conflict between European nations, but a world struggle between the forces of Good and Evil.

William Thaw, Kiffen Rockwell, and Victor Chapman joined the Foreign Legion at the beginning of the war. They were infantrymen before they became aviators in the French service. (So, too, were William Dugan, Robert Soubiran, and other men who were later to join the Franco-American Flying Corps.) Norman Prince had already flown in America.

After some delay these four men were sent to the French aviation schools, soon joined by Cowdin, Bert Hall, Masson, and our future "ace," Raoul Lufbery. They were distributed in various French *escadrilles*.

Thaw and Prince dreamed of a squadron of American pilots, which would be grouped together at the front, but for some time this suggestion met with no favor on the part of the French military authorities.

In the meantime the American pilots were being trained in the French schools. The idea came to several of us that this grouping of Americans at the front could and should be accomplished.

M. de Sillac, whose position in the Ministry

of Foreign Affairs peculiarly fitted him for approaching the Minister of War, was taking active steps to bring this about, and at the same time, and quite independently of him, whilst I was helping in the organization of the American Ambulance, I was dreaming of a *squadrilla* of American volunteers who would express their sympathy for France in a material form. I believed that these boys were to be but the vanguard of other great hosts that would come from America some day.

In the spring of 1915, Prince, M. de Sillac, and myself met at M. de Sillac's office, Thaw being heartily in accord with us, but obliged to remain on duty at the front. The plans of the future American *squadrilla* were then drawn up.

This grouping together of Americans at the front in a fighting unit, brought up a delicate question of international law, and in the face of America's jealous neutrality, the French Minister of War did not seem inclined to sanction this proposition.

It looked as though we should fail, when M. de Sillac arranged a luncheon at Senator Menier's home, to which were invited: General Hirschauer, then head of French aviation; Colonel Bouttieux, his assistant; Leon Bourgeois, French Minister of State; our ex-Ambassador, Robert Bacon; Dr. William White, of Philadelphia; and M. de Sillac, and myself.

Robert Bacon and General Hirschauer discussed the matter fully, and the conclusion was that there existed no international law which forbade Americans from enlisting in a foreign army—as long as the recruiting was not carried out in America.

General Hirschauer promised to give orders immediately that the various American aviators then in the French army should be grouped together in an *escadrille* commanded by a French captain; it was to be called the "Escadrille Américaine" (officially Escadrille N. 124), a name which we shall see later led to a diplomatic incident.

Now that we had succeeded in forming a squadron, it was necessary to appoint a com-

Norman Prince, who, with William Thaw and Dr. Edward Grox, dreamed of an all-American squadron flying in service to France. (USAF)

mittee and to obtain the necessary funds for monthly allowances, uniforms, distribution of prizes, printing of pamphlets, etc.

The financial question was quickly solved. I called with Robert Bacon on Mr. and Mrs. W. K. Vanderbilt. We spoke with warmth of our plans. Our enthusiasm must have been contagious, for when I appealed for funds, Mrs. Vanderbilt walked to her desk and wrote a check for five thousand dollars—and turning to her husband said: "Now, K., what will you do?" His check read, fifteen thousand dollars. With this sum in hand, it looked as though our dream was really coming true!

From that day to this, these generous people have never ceased to be the patron saints of the American boys, and have contributed to aviation alone, modestly as is their custom, what would be considered a small fortune.

The composition of the first *Escadrille*

(Escadrille Américaine) was as follows—authority, letter of Minister of War, March 14, 1916:

Captain Thenault   ⎫
Lieutenant de Laage de Meux   ⎬ French
Lieutenant William Thaw   ⎭
Seargeant Norman Prince
    ″   Elliott Cowdin
    ″   W. Bert Hall
Corporal Victor Chapman
    ″   Kiffen Rockwell
    ″   James McConnell

Raoul Lufbery came very soon after this, followed by Charles C. Johnson and Clyde Balsley, who, for several weeks, were attached to the aerial guard of Paris. Balsley was very severely wounded in an air battle soon after joining the Squadron. By great presence of mind he succeeded in planing down to the French lines. He was in hospital for more than a year, during which time his life was frequently despaired of. Following the first volunteers came Dudley Hill, Masson, Pavelka, Robert Rockwell, and, as they completed their training, other American who have done splendid service for the Allied cause and who have added steadily to the prestige of the Corps.

No sooner had this Squadron been sent to the front than it took a vigorous part in aerial activities, as the following report sets forth:

The American pilots who have enlisted in the French army are already distinguishing themselves by a series of exploits. The first "Escadrille" is composed of only seven Americans, and here are the results of the last seven days:

Sergeant Elliott Cowdin attacked twelve German planes and brought one down in our lines (Military Medal).

Sergeant Kiffen Rockwell a few days later brought down a L.V.G. enemy plane.

The next day Bert Hall used his machine gun on another airplane which fell in flames.

Finally two days later, Lieutenant William Thaw destroyed a Fokker.

It is not strange that the pilots of the Escadrille Américaine gained renown both in France and in America and were bitterly hated by the Germans.

The following letter of Victor Chapman, written on May 19, 1916, from Luxeuil, gives a vivid picture of the Squadron's activities:

Dear M. de Sillac:

The efficiency of the Escadrille has been temporarily reduced by several breakages of the unavoidable variety. Nevertheless, six of us are going to Bar-le-Duc tomorrow, where the unit will join us as soon as possible. On the 17th, two days ago, Thaw played a Boche in the most approved style over the Forest of Carspach. Dodging to the right, then to the left, he ended under the enemy's tail, where he emptied his machine gun. The bureau de tir at Souane telephoned and reported that all their observers saw the "appareil ennemi regagnant ses lignes en paraissant bien touché. Il est piqué à mort."

Yesterday, May 18th, Kiffen Rockwell, finding himself above another L.V.G., east of Thann, fell upon him. The mitrailleur emptied a multitude of cartridges on Rockwell as he sped down, but when the latter, from a distance of thirty mètres, gave one "rafale" [four or five shots], the mitrailleur threw up his hands and fell over on the pilot who likewise seemed to crumple up. Rockwell made a steep bank to avoid hitting the machine, but saw it fall smoking to the ground, where it continued to burn. The artillery signaled the fight and say the machine fell in the German trenches, vicinity of Uffhulz.

This morning, May 19th, two German machines in *revenge* came over the field before sunrise (3 o'clock and 3.30). I gave chase to the first, but lost him in the haze (I forgot to say one of his bombs missed our machines on the ground by ten metres). Thaw gave chase to the second one, overtook him at thirty-two hundred metres near the lines, exchanged several volleys at close range, but, with no extra height to maneuver with, was forced to desist on account of his machine gun jamming. Rockwell and myself are proposed for sergeant, he being also proposed for the Medaille. Thaw is also to be cited when the reports come in.

Yours sincerely,
VICTOR E. CHAPMAN

In the meanwhile a committee was appointed to handle the affairs of the Franco-American Flying Corps, which later became known as the Lafayette Flying Corps.

This committee was composed as follows:

Honorary President, W. K. Vanderbilt
President, J. de Sillac
Vice-President, Physician, Dr. Edmund Gros
Director for America, Frederick Allen
American representatives: Henry Earle, Geo. F. Tyler, Philip Carroll, Frank J. McClure

Treasurers: Laurence Slade, Colonel Bentley Mott
Assistant treasurer, Arthur G. Evans
Bankers, Bonbright & Co.
Secretary, Mrs. Georgia Ovington.

It was decided to give a monthly allowance of one hundred francs, later increased to two hundred francs, to each American volunteer.

Prizes were distributed as follows:

Francs 1500 ($300) for Legion of Honor
" 1000 ($200) for Military Medal
" 500 ($100) for War Cross
" 200 ($ 50) for each citation (palm)

This last item became a very important financial obligation which we were glad to meet.

For instance, the members of the Escadrille Lafayette alone have received over forty citations. Lufbery has brought down seventeen German machines—he ranks sixth in the list

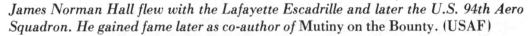

James Norman Hall flew with the Lafayette Escadrille and later the U.S. 94th Aero Squadron. He gained fame later as co-author of Mutiny on the Bounty. *(USAF)*

of living "aces" in the French army, and wears the Legion of Honor, Military Medal, the War Cross with sixteen palm leaves, and the English Military Cross.

Thaw has the Legion of Honor, Military Medal and War Cross with four palms, etc.

The greatest honor which can come to an individual or to a fighting unit is to be mentioned in the French daily official *communiqué*. The Escadrille Américaine has been mentioned several times, this leading early to a diplomatic incident which I learned of as follows:

On November 16,1916, I was paying a visit to the Escadrille when Colonel Barrès, chief of French aviation, at General Headquarters, walked into the tent. He said that he was sorry, but in the future the Escadrille could no longer be known as the Escadrille Américaine, but should henceforth be designated by its official military number, N. 124.

Kiffen Rockwell, who, along with Chapman, McConnell, and Prince, died wearing the uniform of France. (USAF)

He seemed reticent to give me an explanation, but I got this the next day at the Ministry of War. I learned that Bernstorff had protested to Washington that Americans were fighting on the French front—that the French *communiqué* contained the name, "Escadrille Américaine," and that these volunteer Americans pushed their brazenness to the point of having the head of a red Sioux Indian in full war paint depicted on their machines!

A few days afterwards I called at the Ministry of War and saw Captain Berthaud, who had always been a loyal friend to Americans. He told me that the name which they thought of applying to the Escadrille was "Escadrille de Volontaires." "Squadron of Volunteers" seemed to me such a colorless name that I protested, suggesting a name which could not lead to any diplomatic protest, "LAFAYETTE ESCADRILLE." Such is the origin of the title which has become celebrated, and which will be perpetuated through the war by being applied to the first American Squadron of our United States Air Service.

Attracted by the fame of the Lafayette Escadrille even before the United States entered the war, more than two hundred American volunteers have joined the Lafayette Flying Corps. Some have become pilots in the Lafayette Escadrille, to take the place of those who have fallen, others have served and are serving with equal brilliance in various French *squadrillas*.

Over twenty have lost their lives, the majority having fallen in combat.

The names of Chapman, Rockwell, Prince, McConnell, Genet, Hoskier, Barclay, Chadwick, Biddle, McMonagle, Campbell, Walcott, Trinkard, Spencer, Benney, Tailer, Loughran, who died at the front, and of Dowd, Meeker, Hanford, Fowler, Starrett, Palmer, Grieb, who were killed before they could fight, will not be forgotten.

Walcott, Spencer, Benney, Tailer, and Loughran were on the point of being taken over by the Air Service of their country when they died, and were still in the uniform of

The Lafayette Escadrille in May, 1917. (USAF)

France which they honored and glorified.

This brief outline is, in no sense, a history of the Lafayette *Squadrilla* and Lafayette Flying Corps. Much could be written of the wonderful exploits of these heroic pilots. They have paid a heavy toll, and many of them lie within the sound of the guns, side by side with the French soldiers whom they loved, and with whom they served.

They are not dead, their spirits will live, inviting us to higher ideals, nobler aspirations, and unwavering patriotism.

PARIS, *February* 3, 1918

A VOLUNTEER

by Lieutenant Norman Prince,
French Air Service
G.D.E. Div. Nieuport Secteur 92A,
February 19, 1916.

Dear Governor,

Enclosed is a letter from Freddy. Notice that he says the discipline at Pau is very strict.

I am a schoolboy again. I am training to fly the very fastest *appareil de chasse* — quite a different instrument from the *avion canon* which weighs three times more than these small chasing *appareils.*

I am busy pushing matters, in regard to the formation of the Escadrille Américaine. There is a possibility that St.-Saveur, now a captain in the aviation, may command us. Although but a short time on the front he has done finely as a pilot. We are all *disponible* to go to the front and are only waiting for a captain, the personnel—(chauffeurs, secretary, cook, etc.) our avions and the motor cars. Orders for our formation will be issued, I hope, next week. The weather has been very rainy and windy here for a week, which is to be expected, during the month of February. We are losing no time, however.

Those Lewis guns, if there is any way of getting hold of a dozen, would be much appreciated by us here. The more you can get for us the better, but I realize that it may be impossible even for you to get hold of any.

How are the horses? Don't overdo the schooling!

I hope you and Mamma are enjoying Aiken. The main thing is to care for your health.

With love to Mamma, who, I trust, is not too anxious about Freddy and me.

Your affectionate son,
NORMAN

PENGUINS LEARN TO FLY

by Sergeant James R. McConnell, French Air Service

France now has thousands of men training to become military aviators, and the flying schools, of which there is a very great number, are turning out pilots at an astounding rate.

The process of training a man to be a pilot aviator naturally varies in accordance with the type of machine on which he takes his first instruction, and so the methods of the various schools depend on the apparatus upon which they teach an *élève pilote*—as an embryonic aviator is called—to fly.

In the case of the larger biplanes, a student goes up in a dual-control airplane, accompanied by an old pilot, who, after first taking him on many short trips, then allows him part, and later full, control, and who immediately corrects any false moves made by him. After that, short, straight, line flights are made alone in a smaller-powered machine by the student, and, following that, the training goes on by degrees to the point where a certain mastery of the apparatus is attained. Then follows the prescribed "stunts" and voyages necessary to obtain the military brevet.

Training for Pursuit Airplanes

The method of training a pilot for a small, fast *avion de chasse*, as a fighting airplane is termed, is quite different, and as it is the most thorough and interesting I will take that course up in greater detail.

The man who trains for one of these machines never has the advantage of going first into the air in a double-control airplane. He is alone when he first leaves the earth, and so the training preparatory to that stage is very carefully planned to teach a man the habit of control in such a way that all the essential movements will come naturally when he first finds himself face to face with the new problems the air has set for him. In this preparatory training a great deal of weeding out is effected, for a man's aptitude for the work shows up, and unless he is by nature especially well fitted he is transferred to the division which teaches one to fly the larger and safer machines.

First of all, the student is put on what is called a roller. It is a low-powered machine with very small wings. It is strongly built to stand the rough wear it gets, and no matter how much one might try it could not leave the ground. The apparatus is jokingly and universally known as a Penguin, both because of its humorous resemblance to the quaint arctic birds and its inability in common with them to do any flying. A student makes a few trips up and down the field in a double-control Penguin, and learns how to steer with his feet. Then he gets into a single-seated one and, while the rapidly whirling propeller is pulling him along, tries to keep the Penguin in a straight line. The slightest mistake or delayed movement will send the machine skidding off to the right or left, and sometimes, if the motor is not stopped in time, over on its side or back. Something is always being broken on a Penguin, and so a reserve flock is kept at the side of the field in order that no time may be lost.

After one is able to keep a fairly straight line, he is put on a Penguin that moves at a faster rate, and after being able to handle it successfully passes to a very speedy one, known as the "rapid." Here one learns to keep the tail of the machine at a proper angle by means of the elevating lever, and to make a perfectly straight line. When this has been accomplished and the monitor is thoroughly convinced that the student is absolutely certain of making no mistakes in guiding with his feet, the young aviator is passed on to the class which teaches him how to leave the ground. As one passes from one machine to another one finds that the foot movements must be made smaller and smaller. The increased speed makes the machine more and more responsive to the rudder, and as a result the foot movements become so gentle when one gets into the air that they must come instinctively.

First Flights Alone

The class where one will leave the ground has now been reached, and an outfit of leather clothes and casque* is given to the would-be pilot. The machines used at this stage are low-powered monoplanes of the Blériot type, which, though being capable of leaving the ground, cannot rise more than a few feet. They do not run when the wind is blowing or when there are any movements of air from the ground, for though a great deal of balancing is done by correcting with the rudder, the student knows nothing of maintaining the lateral

*helmet.

stability, and if caught in the air by a bad movement would be apt to sustain a severe accident. He has now only to learn how to take the machine off the ground and hold it at a low line of flight for a few moments.

For the first time one is strapped into the seat of the machine, and this continues to be the case from this point on. The motor is started, and one begins to roll swiftly along the ground. The tail is brought to an angle slightly above a straight line. Then one sits tight and waits. Suddenly the motion seems softer, the motor does not roar so loudly, and the ground is slipping away. The class standing at the end of the line looks far below; the individuals are very small, but though you imagine you are going too high, you must not push to go down more than the smallest fraction, or the machine will dive and smash. The small push has brought you down with a bump from a seemingly great height. In reality you have been but three feet off the ground. Little by little the student becomes

James McConnell, one of the Lafayette Escadrille's charter members. (USAF)

accustomed to leaving the ground, for these short hop-skip-and-jump flights, and has learned to steer in the air.

If he has no bad smash-ups he is passed on to a class where he rises higher, and is taught the rudiments of landing. If, after a few days, that act is reasonably performed and the young pilot does not land too hard, he is passed to the class where he goes about sixty feet high, maintains his line of flight for five or six minutes and learns to make a good landing from that height. He must by this time be able to keep this machine on the line of flight without dipping and rising, and the landings must be uniformly good. The instructor takes a great deal of time showing the student the proper line of descent, for the landings must be perfect before he can pass on.

Now comes the class where the pilot rises three or four hundred feet high and travels for more than two miles in a straight line. Here he is taught how to combat air movements and maintain lateral stability. All the flying up to this point has been done in a straight line, but now comes the class where one is taught to turn. Machines in this division are almost as high powered as a regular flying machine, and can easily climb to two thousand feet. The turn is at first very wide, and then, as the student becomes more confident, it is done more quickly, and while the machine leans at an angle that would frighten one if the training in turning had not been gradual. When the pilot can make reasonably close right and left turns, he is told to make figure eights. After doing this well he is sent to the real flying machines.

There is nothing in the way of a radical step from the turns and figure eights to the real flying machines. It is a question of becoming at ease in the better and faster airplanes taking greater altitudes, making little trips, perfecting landings, and mastering all the movements of correction that one is forced to make. Finally one is taught how to shut off and start one's motor again in the air, and then to go to a certain height, shut off the motor, make a

half-turn while dropping and start the motor again. After this, one climbs to about two thousand feet and, shutting off the motor, spirals down to within five hundred feet of the ground. When that has been practised sufficiently, a registering altitude meter is strapped to the pilot's back and he essays the official spiral, in which one must spiral all the way to earth with the motor off, and come to a stop within a few yards of a fixed point on the aviation grounds. After this, the student passes to the voyage machines, which are of almost twice the power of the machine used for the short trips and spirals.

Tests for the Military Brevet

There are three voyages to make. Two consist of going to designated towns an hour or so distant and returning. The third voyage is a triangle. A landing is made at one point and the other two points are only necessary to cross. In addition, there are two altitudes of about seven thousand feet each that one has to attain either while on the voyages or afterward.

The young pilot has not, up to this point, had any experience on trips, and there is always a sense of adventure in starting out over unknown country with only a roller map to guide one and the gauges and controls, which need constant attention, to distract from the reading of the chart. Then, too, it is the first time that the student has flown free and at a great height over the earth, and his sense of exultation at navigating at will the boundless sky causes him to imagine he is a real pilot. True it is that when the voyages and altitudes are over, and his examinations in aeronautical sciences passed, the student becomes officially a *pilote-aviateur*, and he can wear two little gold-woven wings on his collar to designate his capacity, and carry a winged propeller emblem on his arm, but he is not ready for the difficult work of the front, and before he has time to enjoy more than a few days' rest he is sent to a school of *perfectionnement*. There the real, serious and thorough training begins.

Schools where the pilots are trained on the modern machines—*écoles de perfectionnement* as they are called—are usually an annex to the centres where the soldiers are taught to fly, though there are one or two camps that are devoted exclusively to giving advanced instruction to aviators who are to fly the *avions de chasse*, or fighting machines. When the aviator enters one of these schools he is a breveted pilot, and he is allowed a little more freedom than he enjoyed during the time he was learning to fly.

He now takes up the Morane monoplane. It is interesting to note that the German Fokker is practically a copy of this machine. After flying for a while on a low-powered Morane and having mastered the landing, the pilot is put on a new, higher-powered model of the same make. He has a good many hours of flying, but his trips are very short, for the whole idea is to familiarize one with the method of landing. The Blériot has a landing gear that is elastic in action, and it is easy to bring to earth. The Nieuport and other makes of small, fast machines for which the pilot is training have a solid wheel base, and good landings are much more difficult to make. The Morane pilot has the same practices climbing to small altitudes around eight-thousand feet and picking his landing from that height with motor off. When he becomes proficient in flying the single- and double-plane types he leaves the school for another, where shooting with machine guns is taught.

This course in shooting familiarizes one with various makes of machine guns used on airplanes, and one learns to shoot at targets from the air. After two or three weeks the pilot is sent to another school of combat.

Trick Flying and Doing Stunts

These schools of combat are connected with *écoles de perfectionnement* with which the pilot has finished. In the combat school he learns battle tactics, how to fight singly and in fleet formation, and how to extract himself from a too dangerous position. Trips are made in squadron formation and sham battles are effected with other escadrilles, as the smallest unit of an aerial fleet is called. For the first time the pilot is allowed to do fancy flying. He is taught how to loop the loop, slide on his wings or tail, go into corkscrews and, more important, to get out of them, and is encouraged to try new stunts.

Finally, the pilot is considered well enough trained to be sent to the reserve, where he waits his call to the front. At the reserve he flies to keep his hand in, practises on any new make of machine that happens to come out or that he may be put on in place of the Nieuport, and receives information regarding old and new makes of enemy airplanes.

At last the pilot receives his call to the front, where he takes his place in some established or newly formed escadrille. He is given a new machine from the nearest airplane reserve center, and he then begins his active service in the war, which, if he survives the course, is the best school of them all.

A FIGHTING FOOL

**by Adjutant Bert Hall,
French Air Service**

Diary note, July 21, 1916

Had a Heinie down to 300 meters this morning, and by God, he gave me the slip. He was flying a two-place fighter and I give him credit for being a hell of a good pilot. I had used up all my ammunition except about twenty rounds. I was saving this for the last dive, but when I got into position for the aforementioned maneuver, the Heinie left. He just went home like hell beatin' tanbark. So I said enough's enough, and I went home too. Leon was slightly miffed because I didn't bring home a victory. It's getting to be something terrible—you don't know whether you're fightin' the war for the French Government or the motor mechanics.

This afternoon I encountered Captain Boelke. He is flying a new type Fokker fighter. It is painted jet black with white crosses. All the other German planes are marked with black crosses on a white field. I recognised him at once, as I have encountered him before. And, as usual, I could not find a single opening in his defense. He, on the other side, could not find a convenient way of attacking me, so we stunted for each other and went on our way. A good pilot can always defend himself in a single-combat affair. Boelke, like many of the Germans with high scores, makes a specialty of popping off slow machines, photographers, recalage machines, day bombers, etc.

It was on July 23rd, that I marked up a score in my favor. It was three o'clock in the afternoon. That's the most I remember about the fight. I know this because I was wearing a new wristwatch. A wounded German prisoner had given it to an ambulance man and the ambulance man had sold it to me. I say sold, but it wasn't exactly that way. I took the watch in lieu of an I.O.U. Now that ambulance man was a gambling man; he believed he was what we call "right," but he wasn't quite as "right" as he thought he was; therefore, the new watch.

But to go on with the more important details. That victory on the 23rd wasn't much to crow about. At first I thought it might be interesting. It was one of the new type Fokker fighters, all decorated up like a new saloon. But that German began to shoot too soon and thereby gave himself away as a beginner, or a very nervous pilot. I waited, as usual, and made sure there was no one sitting in a back seat somewhere. The memory of that last

mouthful of loose teeth was still very clear. As soon as I was sure that I was attacking a single-seater I hopped in for all I was worth. I dived and he dived. He pulled a very tight *virage* and I did the same. He was firing all the time. As I came out of my *virage* I raised the nose of my plane a little bit and there before my sights was a perfect target. I only had time to give him two short bursts.

After that he turned over on his back, then slipped over on his nose and spun like a bastard for more than 10,000 feet. Altogether, the fight lasted about thirty seconds. I followed down as far as was necessary to see where he crashed. The remains of the plane hit the ground between Vaux and Daniloup. All the observers in France saw the fight and confirmation was an easy matter. Leon was much relieved at my success. It seems that the other mechanics had been giving him a slight raspberry on my ability to shoot down the Boche. I had been told that since the shot I got in the mouth the enlisted men had given me the soubriquet of "iron chewer." That made two good nicknames—the "Ozark snake-stomper" and the "flying iron chewer."

On July 30, 1916, Luf (Lufbery) brought down his first Boche since his transfer to N.124. It happened in the neighborhood of Etain. All I ever knew about it was that Luf claimed it and the French observers confirmed it and that night Luf wanted to lick Gitchy-Goomie again.

Now let's get that fellow Lufbery straight. Born in Connecticut. At eighteen he ran away from his parental home and started traveling. And as the old song goes, "he was some travellin' man." He'd been everywhere. Marc Pourpe said that Lufbery had hung his hat in more countries than any other man living, and Pourpe ought to know. Lufbery spoke a little bit of all the known languages and a lot of the important ones. He was not a big fellow in stature, but he was a powerfully quick lad in a fight—didn't matter much what kind of a fight it happened to be, as long as it was a good fight.

And Luf knew things, not in an educated

Raoul Lufbery topped the Lafayette Escadrille with seventeen confirmed kills. When the U.S. entered the war he was assigned to the 94th Aero Squadron, before his Nieuport went down in flames in May, 1918. (USAF)

way, but in the way of men who are always looking for information. Marc Pourpe said that Raoul Lufbery was a walking encyclopaedia. He could tell you about any city that amounted to a damn anywhere in the civilised or uncivilised world. He could tell you how to spell the name of the city, where it was located, when the train left, what the jails were like, how the police treated gang fighters, if the food was any good; in fact, he could supply any information needed by a soldier of fortune, and that's what Luf was.

His two years in the Philippines with the U. S. Army had taught him what the war was. He was a marksman long before he came to us.

So, on July 30th, he got his official victory in the Lafayette Escadrille. We were beginning to develop some excellent new fighting pilots.

Diary note, August 3, 1916

That fellow Lufbery has had two successes in two successive days, his two lucky days being July 30th and 31st. Some ambulance men told us yesterday that the handsome MacMonagle fellow (who is also an ambulance man) is going into aviation. Also, news comes from Paris that Carter Ovington, son of Mrs. Ovington, the secretary of the Lafayette Escadrille, is dead set on flying with us.

Diary note, August 4th, 1916

Jimmy McConnell, who crashed his ship between two trees and thought he was unhurt, is in the Hospital at Paris. After his crash, he went to Paris with Nimmie Prince. In Paris, Nimmie met his brother, Paul Prince, and together they took care of poor old McConnell. But his back got so bad that they finally appealed to the hospital authorities and now Jimmy is under the eye of the Medical Department. He thinks he can get back by October, but if the story Nimmie tells is true, Jimmy will be in a lot longer than this fall.

Lufbery had another victory today. That makes three now. He'll soon be in the "ace" class. His fight today was over Alancourt.

Saw two French pilots buried yesterday. They decorated the graves with the remains of the smashed airplane. Personally, I think this business of displaying the remains of airplanes on the graves of dead pilots is very bad. It's bad for the troops. Half-burned or otherwise demolished remains of airplanes belong on the junk heap, and if I had my way, that's where they would land.

Lufbery is a mushroom hound. Every time it rains he goes out and gathers some mushrooms. The French say he is going on a *reconnaissance de champignons.*

The reason we have so many visiting ambulance men and other hungry soldiers is possibly because Didier Masson, recently of C.18 and N.68, is our Chef de Popote. (This would correspond to Mess Officer.) Masson is a whizbang at getting up the kind of food that makes the troops want to fight, and he's a damn good aviator too.

Balsley will recover, but they tell us that he will possibly not fly again.

From what I have observed in air fighting, I believe that the rapid decisive attack is the thing that won oftenest in the long run. Nungesser, Lufbery, Guynemer, Dorme, Heurteaux, Deullin—I have seen them all in action and I am forced to admit that combating around one's antagonist is a very dull and exasperating procedure, compared with the quick dive, fire, and pull-away method. Usually, it's all over in twenty seconds—either it's a victory or you go down afire. For, if you live to pull away at all, you must have fired with great precision, and having fired, you must have pulled away with everything you had.

Collisions in the air were more frequent than one might think, and I do not refer to the many unfortunate collisions caused by inexperienced pilots at flying schools. I shall never forget one day in the early summer of 1916, while we were in the very middle of the Verdun offensive. I was flying along with a French captain—a man I had known in civilian days back in 1912. We were not so very far from Fort Douaumont, when we ran into two two-place Aviatiks. I took on one of them and after my first burst, something seemed to have happened to the engine on the Boche plane—at least, my antagonist dropped down as safe as he could with the propeller standing perfectly still. I lost him in some clouds and presently gave up the chase.

When I got back to where I had left my French captain friend, I saw that his ship had gone afire. Before I could do anything to help square the situation by attacking the victorious Boche, the French captain dived his burning ship full into the German plane. For a moment, the wings of the two planes held together. Then they fell apart and fell to the ground, a swirling mass of flames and smoke.

Back at the field I found that they had reported me down afire. How glad Leon was to see me taxiing up to the hangars for ammunition and gasoline. I tell you all this story to show you that collisions actually happened.

Now to go back to the business of attack. The reason the fight is often over in a very short time is because one pilot or the other gains the offensive. And the man with the offensive has most points in his favor.

I suppose that every military pilot who ever flew out to meet an enemy sooner or later developed a fighting technique of his own. Later on in the war, the Americans with their usual mania for standardization tried to teach their pilots a cut-and-dried formula—one they could follow at all times and be sure of success. But as soon as the American pilots got up to the front and tried out the cut-and-dried formula, they discovered that no two fights were alike. So the American who lived through the first half-dozen combats worked out something individual and thereupon came home to tell the story of how it happened. No two fights were ever alike. We met different situations every time we encountered the Boche. Altitudes altered situations slightly. In very high, thin air the Nieuports maneuvered very well, better perhaps than the SPADS did, because the SPAD was a heavier machine. At low altitudes they all handled about the same.

As soon as one gets above 10,000 feet, the thinness of the air becomes noticeable, but the air as a rule is very smooth at the higher altitudes. Earth bumps from heat waves are usually felt down nearer the earth. In early days these bumpy places in the air were referred to as "Swiss cheese air." The modern airplane is seldom bothered with this condition.

Captain Georges Guynemer used to say that the first fifteen to twenty seconds should turn the trick. He used to dive on his antagonist and hold his fire until the last possible moment. If his antagonist was firing all the while, Guynemer dived just the same. He had no idea of protecting himself. René Fonck, on the other hand, was a master of self-preservation. His ship was never shot up.

In fact, after countless combats, his SPAD was still intact, while Guynemer had to have an entirely new outfit every two weeks. His mechanics were working over "Vieux Charles" all the time.

René Dorme, or "Père" Dorme as we called him, was known as "the unpuncturable." He used the same tactics employed by Guynemer. Several times his SPAD held together by luck and the grace of God and brought him home to the landing field of the famous Cigognes (the Stork Escadrille, originally N. 3). But Dorme went down ultimately to the very same fate that caught the miraculous Georges Guynemer, and Dorme's loss was a great one to French aviation.

I admit that I seldom thought of protecting myself at the expense of a rapidly concluded contest, and for that reason, I came home time and time again with my plane full of holes, to say nothing of my body.

Nerve and a steady hand are what decided most air battles. I have found that the best tactics are to go straight at the Boche. While you're doing this, he of course gets a good chance at you, but if you have nerve enough, you might get in, or rather you will get in more shots from a more favorable position that when you maneuver around one another in an attempt to gain a good firing position. The reason I stick to this idea of rapid attack is because I have seen all the great ones in action and have spent many an evening listening to them discuss the details of air fighting.

Diary note, August 8, 1916

Lufbery had another success today. And Lieutenant de Laage de Meux did a very heroic thing. He was out on a patrol with Nimmie Prince and Kiffen Rockwell. Kiffen became disconnected from the patrol and Nimmie was attacked by three Boche. Lieutenant de Laage, although he had exhausted his ammunition, dived into the fight and saved Prince at a moment when there were two Boche on Prince's tail, each pumping a stream of lead into the poor boy. Of course, it was a bluff, but the Boche never knew that. They beat it back to Germany and Nimmie Prince lived to tell the story. Incidentally, Lieutenant de Laage never mentioned it and even now denies that it ever happened. Thereupon, de Laage goes up in our estimation.

This man de Laage de Meux has had a whale of a career as a soldier. He was a cavalryman in the early days and had several horses shot from under him during the first retreat and later during the battle of the Marne. He has wounds all over his body. Bravo, de Laage!

I'm going to visit Paris to get a new ship tomorrow, and I suppose I'll have to visit Doctor Gros and tell him all about poor old Victor Chapman.

In one of the hangars the other day I saw the remains of McConnell's ship. It is too badly busted up to repair, but they are keeping it in case they need any of the uncracked parts. On the side of the fuselage were the letters, "M.A.C.," and now the poor devil is up at Paris in the hospital. Christ! I wish he was with us! I like Jimmy.

There are rumors that a negro named Eugene Bullard, who comes originally from some out-of-the-way place in Georgia, has transferred from the Foreign Legion to the flying corps for training. He expects to join the Lafayette Escadrille. They say he made a great success as a *soldat à pied.* He is one of these big burly black boys who apparently came to France on a mule ship and couldn't keep out of a good fight.

Diary note, August 14th, 1916

My new Nieuport is a peach. The new ship we have been hearing about will be a SPAD, and from what they told me at le Bourget it will give us mastery of the air. (The SPAD outfit is the old Deperdussin Company taken over by M. Blèriot).

In spite of the fun I had on this trip, there was a note of sadness about it. The first afternoon I encountered Captain d'Harcourt who was at one time second in command of MS-38 back at Chalons.

Bertin's death—how Eugene had a premonition of what was going to happen to him. I hate to see men like Bertin bumped off, but as the saying goes, the best men are finished off first; that's why I've lasted so long.

Diary note, August 15th, 1916

A pilot of American origin named Pavelka joined us the 11th of this month. He was with Kiffin Rockwell in the Foreign Legion. Seems, according to Kiffin, that Pavelka saved Kiffin's life when the Legion was attacking up in the north end of the line, somewhere near Arras. That D'Harcourt told me all about Eugene was after Bill Thaw and Jimmy Bach and I left the Legion for the Flying Corps. Kiffin Rockwell had been very desperately wounded, and Pavelka carried him from the field, where he surely would have died, to a dressing station. And all the while, Pavelka was wounded too! So you see, we have a damned good man with us. Needless to say, he and Kiffin are most awfully good friends.

Lufbery wants to get leave to visit his girl in Chartres, but the Captain can't see it. Last time Luf damned near finished off the entire police force of that charming little town. So it seems that Luff will have to stay at Bar-le-Duc.

The French and Belgian Allies

THE AVENGER

**by Capitain Rene Fonck, French Air Service,
translated by Lt. Colonel Clovis R. Gagnon, USAR**

The 11th of September, 1917, must be remembered as a black day.

On that day the Air Corps lost its most glorious hero. In prose and in verse, others have praised his exploits, expressed all the sorrows of the nation. Parliament voted him the Honor of the Pantheon; but the best mark of admiration and of regret is the one which has remained engraved in the hearts of his fighting companions, who all became his avengers and among whom, many fell in this endeavor.

Guynemer left on patrol at the break of day. The first rays of sun, showing through the mist, sparkled on the foliage already turning brown because of the coolness of the nights.

While the mechanics were scurrying about his plane, the pilot, a bit nervous, as if a hidden fear was haunting him, was pacing feverishly, like a caged lion.

"Guynemer is in a bad humor this morning," observed someone, but none of us thought, at the moment, of attaching any importance to the remark.

Finally the motor started up and our comrade climbed quickly into the cockpit, the propeller whirred and like a great bird, the plane took off.

Lieutenant Bozon-Verduras left at the same time. What happened after that? . . . We never learned the facts, precisely. We only knew that they flew together and helped each other in several engagements.

Lieutenant Bozon, separated from his companion by an unexpected pursuit, lost sight of him and returned alone to the field.

Rene Fonck, a fellow member with Guynemer and Nungesser of the legendary French "Storks" fighter squadron. His 75 victories made him the leading Allied ace of World War I. (USAF)

It was not the first time that Guynemer had returned late, therefore no one even thought of worrying, but as the hours passed, his absence became the subject of all conversation. Commandant Brocard no longer hid his concern. Information was requested by telephone from the front lines and we were soon notified that a French plane had been seen falling behind the German lines.

Those who had observed the plane falling asserted, however, that it was not in flames and that the pilot might not be injured.

Two or three days went by and Guynemer's return became more and more doubtful. We hoped nevertheless that he had made out all-right and that escape or peace would bring him back to us, but an enemy newspaper deprived us even of this hope. It published, along with the news of the death of our national hero, the name of the man who had shot him down . . . Wissemann.

I was near the hangars when Commandant Brocard brought me the sad confirmation. Instantly I had my fighter plane brought out, determined to seek an escape from my deep sorrow, in the air.

Ten minutes after my departure, I spotted an airplane off in the distance. I realized immediately that it was a two-seater observation plane. Absorbed in their work, the two passengers had not seen me coming. As usual I climbed very high in order to dive on the enemy. This tactic, common to birds of prey and which is instinctive to them, has always seemed the very best to me.

I surprised them in an attitude of complete security, the pilot with his hands on the throttle and the observer in the process of taking pictures, leaning out over the fuselage.

I swooped down but waited until I was a few yards away before opening fire. With my eyes glued to the sight, I could see all details growing rapidly in size. Aiming directly for the center of the plane, my bullets swept across the motor and crew.

It wasn't long before I saw the results. Killed, no doubt, by the very first burst, the pilot must have slumped in his seat, jamming the controls in his agony, for the plane immediately began to spin. While I was avoiding a collision by making a rapid turn, I saw the live body of the observer fall from the upside-down plane. For a brief moment he had tried to remain in his seat. He passed by, his arms frantically clutching at the emptiness, a few yards from my left wing. . . .I will never forget this sight.

But the incendiary bullets had done their job, and the plane like a gigantic torch dropped at full speed towards the earth, preceded by the body of the observer.

A few days later our group left Flanders. There, in foggy regions, the never-ending rain and fog are likely to keep a squadron such as the "Cigognes" ("Storks") on the ground for an entire winter. At that time the retention of such a unit in this area would have been a real waste of power.

During autumn, we were hardly able to claim even a few victories for ourselves, and for my last success I brought down a large two-seater reconnaissance plane. On Sept. 30, 1917, I was up about 12,000 ft. with several comrades, when I saw this bold fellow making a turn below us. He continued his inspection calmly as if his position was completely free of danger.

Immediately I opened my throttle and my SPAD leaped forward. The enemy plane didn't seem to be worried, but upon approaching I saw the gunner at his combat post. The maneuver required close precision, but I was an old hand at this game. While closing on him, I made my plane rise and fall in a flitting manner similar to that which permits a butterfly to evade his enemies, and my tactics evidently seemed to disconcert him.

I do not subscribe to the historic chivalrous remark made by Fontency. That officer who was in command at the time thought it necessary to say: "Englishmen, you may fire first." This is a very archaic method. If the English had had machine guns at their disposal at that time, not one single Frenchman would probably have survived to report these gallant words. I believe that it is necessary to adopt a

The pilot identification card of celebrated French ace Georges Guynemer. (USAF)

middle course, not to waste your ammunition and to fire your bullets at the very instant where they have a chance to reach their target.

Therefore, without response, I accepted the fire of the Boche three times. But when my turn came I fired my machine gun and had the satisfaction of seeing the enemy plane turn. I made a few feints and rapidly broke off, having succeeded in placing myself under my adversaries' control surfaces. I hit the pilot and the gunner almost simultaneously.

From above, I watched their fall. Perhaps three thousand feet below me, one of the wings broke loose and the men were hurled out of their bucket seats. I always experienced a certain compassion for my victims at such a sight, in spite of the satisfaction, somewhat animal-like of having saved my own skin, and the patriotic joy of victory.

I would often prefer to spare their lives, especially when they have fought courageously but as I believe I've already said, in air battles there is generally no alternative but victory or death, and it is rarely possible to show mercy without betraying the interests of one's country.

Thus, these last Germans brought down had been admirable; neither the pilot nor the gunner had lost his composure for an instant, and upon seeing me approach from a distance, instead of abandoning their task of reconnaissance and going back to their lines with throttle wide open, they had waited for me solidly accepting battle without flinching. Immediately upon returning to the field I took a car to go and look at my victims and examine the remains of the plane to find out if they had any new technical devices. Some officers had preceded me and the first news that they announced was that one of the bodies carried identification in the name of Wissemann—the very one that the German papers had publicized as the pilot who shot down Guynemer.

BALLOON BUSTER

by Lieutenant Willy Coppens, Belgian Flying Corps

. . .An extraordinary joy seized me, a joy that grew and grew as I approached our lines where the enemy's shells would soon be unable to reach me. But before that firework display, put up in my honor, ceased, I thought of the excitement the event must have caused down below in our trenches, and began an aerial waltz, in the course of which I looped and rolled. Then, as a shell exploded close to me, I went into a long-drawn spin and heard in imagination the Teutonic *"Hochs!"* that would follow it, and felt the anguished silence that would accompany it on our own side of the lines. One turn—two turns—three (my stomach usually called upon me to stop at this stage!)—four—and five. Here my diaphragm rose in self-pity, and implored mercy. With triumphal conceit I came out of the spin and looped again. I always did enjoy those unprofitable gambols in and out among the shell-bursts.

My machine had become somewhat strained, and was flying left wing down. I landed, and at once gave orders for this to be put right. But my bracing wires had scarely been slackened off and the rigger, armed with his spirit-level, had not even begun to take his measurements, when I was summoned to the telephone. Another enemy kite-balloon, which was directing the German artillery fire, was causing our troops a lot of trouble. . . .

Had I cause to complain? After all, such confidence after my success of that morning was a very fine compliment. . . .

It gave me a wonderful sense of power—of confidence in my capability, that was to carry me from strength to strength, right up to the time of my wound, a few days before the Armistice. All that was needed to satisfy the demands of our men in the trenches was incendiary ammunition. . . .

I hurriedly had my bracing wires retightened, without much regard to accuracy, and took off again. Arrived on the lines, I found three German machines—two artillery airplanes and one little Hannoveraner* two-seater, watching over them from above. Once again I only had four "good" rounds in among the rest of ammunition. It would be necessary to use these against the airplanes and, for the time being, leave the balloon alone.

I dived at the Hannoveraner as it flew towards me, but I had counted without the Bowden control-cable of my machine gun, still fitted *à la mode de Calais!* Through continual flexing, the steel cable was frayed and stretched. This was not surprising, really; for the control left the hand-grip at what was vir-

*A business-like machine, built on up-to-date lines, and provided with an Opel Argus engine of 180 h.p. A feature of the Hannoveraners was their biplane tail, constructed largely of "moulded" three-ply (on a metal framework).

Willy Coppens, with thirty-seven destroyed German aircraft and balloons to his credit, was the Belgian ace-of-aces. (Coppens)

tually a right-angle, and when I squeezed the grip nothing happened. I was disarmed and furious, but the hostile two-seater already appeared inclined to retreat. I gave this inclination my moral support, taking care to fly from one side to the other so as not to give the enemy observer time to bring his machine gun to bear on me. Meanwhile I examined my Bowden cable, and found that by holding it straight with the left hand it appeared to work. I tried it, and it did in effect function; but I wasted one precious incendiary bullet in the process.

By this time, the two German artillery machines had vanished and the Hannoveraner was keeping at a respectful distance. Whenever I dived towards him he turned and fled, and then remained standing about well out of range. There was no reason to fear any interference from him while I tried to fire my remaining incendiary bullets at the kite-balloon that had been reported "active."

Holding the Bowden cable with my left hand and flying the machine with my right, without being able to touch the throttle-control—which made things extremely difficult—I dived upon the Houthulst kite-balloon, now flying at 3150 feet, and fired one or two rounds at point-blank range. Then the Bowden control broke and I was definitely disarmed. But the balloon was flaming. It was 9.55 a.m., and the Hannoveraner, ashamed, now returned towards me, but with so little determination that he did not succeed in cutting me off, and I reached the lines without trouble.

During lunch, I was called to the telephone to receive the King's congratulations. His Majesty expressed his appreciation of the fact that a Belgian should have shot down a kite-balloon and have followed up this success with another.

During the afternoon, I succeeded in obtaining at last a longer Bowden cable and in getting the firing control modified, while the machine itself was being adjusted.

On the following day, the 9th, I did two patrols, one with Gallez and Dubois and the other with De Meulemeester and Dubois. On the 10th, bad weather raged once more.

On the 11th, the weather was slightly better, but I was only able to do one flight. On this day we lost Degrauw. Degrauw, who had been my companion at the Ruffy-Baumann School at Hendon, had managed for several months not to fly over the lines. He had even tried to get himself invalided out of the Army, but, being declared fit for service in the infantry, he had preferred to come back to the Flying Corps; and our Command had accepted him! Today, he went out in a single-seater as escort to a two-seater; the two-seater had led him to the lines, it being his *first visit;* and, once there, he had contrived to lose the two-seater and disappear in some unexplained manner. We did not hear anything further concerning him until after the Armistice. He had landed, sound in limb, far inside the German lines, where he had been made prisoner.

On the 12th and 13th, the weather was again bad. I passed the afternoons at La Panne, where I saw *"Mon Bébé,"** the old success of Maz Dearly's, performed by the *Théâtre du Front.*

On the 14th, the weather cleared and I did a patrol. On the 15th, I attacked the Houthulst balloon at a height of 3900 feet. It was at 8.7 a.m. Although I fired three times at it at point-blank range, it did not catch fire. To make more certain, I slowed down, flying horizontally, and approached—firing at the last half-second. Then, as though relieved of a weight, it suddenly shot up and I collided with it. My wheels struck the gasbag, which gave under the shock, although it capsized my machine and my tail rose up into the air. My right wing also touched the envelope and for a second I pivoted on my nose, while the balloon sagged and sank under the weight. I had the presence of mind to switch the engine off with the control-lever switch, and my airscrew, which had been turning over slowly, stopped dead. At this moment, I said to myself (in the following actual words): "That's the end! It is bound to happen to those who risk too much."

The next instant my machine began to slide across the spongy thing that gave way beneath me as we advanced, until it plunged over the "side," nose-first, gathering speed as it fell. The propeller started spinning, like the wings of a windmill in a puff of wind; I took my thumb off the button-switch on the control-lever, opened the throttle, and—my machine scarcely any the worse for its experience—took to my heels for our lines, while the balloon, torn and leaking, fell to the ground, where it luckily burst into flames, to such good purpose that the conflagration was seen from our lines and the victory could be credited to me.

The tale of my adventure left many people unconvinced. It was necessary for me to point to the traces of white "down" from the side of

*"Baby Mine." (Tr.)

the gasbag on my lower wing and the front right-hand interplane strut, as well as the marks on the wood of my propeller of the outline of a cord, struck by one blade, before I could convince the unbelievers, of whom the most obstinate was Olieslagers. Finally, the observer posts in the line sent in their reports confirming the destruction.

My victory cost me eight of my incendiary bullets: I now had nine left.

On the 16th, Gallez, Dubois, and I had an indecisive engagement with three enemy single-seaters, and I did an escort flight for a photographic reconnaissance.

On the 17th, I was detailed for two patrols early in the day, but unfortunately I was absent from the squadron in the afternoon, when we received a visit from the King, who came on foot, unofficially and unannounced, in order to congratulate De Meulemeester and me.

On May 18, 1918, the weather was fine, and I did two flights. On this date Marcel Ciselet was brought down in the enemy's lines by antiaircraft fire. His brother, Robert, had been shot down on November 20, 1917, with a bullet through the heart. Their elder brother, Charles, likewise in the Flying Corps, had been seriously wounded several times; fate seems to have singled out this family of soldiers.*

For myself, I shall always believe in luck. It is, to my way of thinking, something that exists even as the magnetic currents exist, just as invisible as these, and yet just as potential, and I am not too sure that the one has no connection with the other . . . . At this period I felt that my luck was right in, and I wanted to make hay while the Sun shone. Had I not still a few magic bullets left? Robin had tried his but had fired from too great a range, and therefore without result; and, to make matters worse, had turned on his tracks in the center of the densest barrage area, and had been

severely "strafed,"** his machine being riddled by the enemy's fire. Robin had not tried again. As for Dubroux, he elected to abstain altogether. Other pilots now began to obtain this ammunition, but very few of them would succeed with their 7-mm. machine guns. Later, after the issue of the one that I should have, other 11-mm. guns would make the task easier.

Among those who were to succeed, in time, were De Leener, Georges Médaets, Jacques Ledure, each of whom accomplished the exploit that had previously been considered impossible in the Belgian Flying Corps—and certainly was a highly dangerous one.

Jan Olieslagers, the oldest member of our squadron, the rival of Pégoud before the War, who never showed jealousy towards the younger ones, wanted to see me rope in my fifth air victory, and urged me to shoot down another kite-balloon.

On the 19th, taking advantage of the fine weather and the presence of a balloon in the air over Houthulst, he suggested that he should accompany me with his youngsters to protect me from surprise attacks. Attacking a kite-balloon, unleashing as it does every antiaircraft gun in the vicinity and filling the sky with shell bursts, attracts the attention of every chase-pilot within range, and the low height of the balloon necessitating going down to a negligible height, exposes the attacker to surpise from behind at any moment.

I fell in with Olieslager's proposal, and we set out for the lines, which we reached to the north of Dixmude, and at once came upon a

---

*Another brother subsequently died of wounds, and Charles Ciselet himself lost his life, flying, on April 1, 1931. Thus, four brothers gave their lives to the service of aeronautics. (Author.)

**The verb, "to strafe," came indirectly from the German. At the beginning of the War, the Germans invoked divine assistance by means of the now almost-forgotten famous prayer: "Gott strafe England!" The British humourously adopted the verb "to strafe," and officially described as "Zepp-strafing" those flights made for the purpose of attacking Zeppelins. From the British slang the word found its way into the French. (Author).

"Ground-strafing," the low-flying attack of hostile troops, became condoned officially, as an operational term, in the British Royal Flying Corps and Royal Air Force in 1917–1918. (Tr.)

The French-made Hanriot Dupont HD-1 was Coppens' favored plane, as well as that of the Storks' Nungesser, and the leading surviving Italian ace, Scaroni. (USAF)

German single-seater patrol of equal strength. This patrol was flying southward, parallel to the trenches, and Olieslagers, evidently determined to deliver combat, turned towards it, setting a southeasterly course that duly brought us to the German side of the lines. But the enemy patrol had kept straight on, and had gained on us. We were now behind it and could not overtake it. As we were then over Houthulst, I dived at my balloon and set it on fire, at 9.45 a.m., right under the nose of the German single-seater fighter patrol. Olieslagers was so delighted that he forthwith executed a faultless aerial saraband. Dear old Jan!

Later, when I landed at Les Moëres, I found Jan already down waiting to shake me by the hand. Five victories spelled "ace" in the Belgian Flying Corps, as it had in the French Air Service up to 1916. I have by me, today, a snapshot showing me still seated in my little 120-h.p. Hanriot (a machine of the power of a light airplane of today), shaking hands with Olieslagers with almost all the squadron crowding round us. It includes Jacquet, Gallez, André De Meulemeester, Pierre Dubois, Georges Kervyn, Gusto de Mevius, and others, not to mention all the dogs, attracted to the spot as to all the events of our existence with which they were so closely linked. There are the fox terrier,

Biquet, lean and haughty, the Malines sheepdog, Black, affectionate and active, the cockerspaniel, Topsy, silky of coat and quite mad, and several more. Practically every squadron on the western front had its dogs; for the dog is man's friend, and the aviator is the friend of the dog.

It happened that Pageot, a pilot in the 2nd Squadron, was taken prisoner a little later on. There was a terrible mongrel fox terrier that for days afterwards literally cried its eyes out and ran sadly out to identify the crew each time an airplane of the type flown by its master, a Breguet XIV, landed at Les Moëres. It never came out for any other airplane; for it knew the note of the engine.

That same day, May 19, 1918, André De Meulemeester and I were summoned to Belgian General Headquarters at Houtherm, to receive the congratulations of General Gillain, the chief of the General Staff. In the course of a second flight at 6.30 p.m., with De Meulemeester and Mévius as my companions, my patrol put four single-seaters to flight.

I had the pleasure of reading in the official Belgian *Communiqué* that evening, the announcement of the sixth victory of Lieutenant Olieslagers and the fifth of Warrant Officer Willy Coppens; for this was the way in which the success of our "aces" were made public. The news was pasted up in the billeting areas, in the towns and villages, spread across the frontiers and appeared in the newspapers throughout the world!

I recollect the childish pleasure I used to experience in joining the crowd of soldiers in some public square, in La Panne, for example, to read the communiqué. The men would read aloud and I would hear my name pronounced. But that was in the beginning, before I became *blasé*, and, more particularly, before I was known; because my childishness never went so far as to go in search of public acclamation! When, later on, I came in for that sort of thing it was quite bad enough.

My flight over Brussels had robbed me of all fear, and, confident of my complete mastery in the handling of my faithful little Hanriot, I was prepared to fly anywhere. Alas, *not once* were we asked to undertake a special mission. The only thing I did fear was engine failure, that would have delivered me into the hands of the enemy, but I nevertheless had faith in my star and "the pride to consider myself invulnerable." At this period, when all that was asked of a man was that he be profligate of courage, I felt that I was the richest man on earth—and I have always loved spending.

Between April 25 and May 19, that is to say in a space of three weeks, I had won my five first victories, and I now realized that, as Thieffry, De Meulemeester, and Olieslagers had shown, success flourishes only in perseverance—ceaseless, restless perseverance.

The Yanks Are Coming

DECOY

by Captain Elliot W. Springs,
U. S. Air Service

Henry took off at exactly six next morning. They chose that hour because the Fokkers were sure to be out enjoying the advantage of the sun behind them, and still the sun wasn't high enough to let them get immediately above them.

Henry had four planes behind him. Johnny was a thousand feet above him with five planes and Tubby was a thousand feet above Johnny with six planes. Sixteen little Camels—going out to deliver an invitation to battle.

At 10,000 feet over a ruined town they made a rendezvous with the S.E.s. The S.E.s turned south and continued to climb. The S.E.s worked best at 15,000 feet so they were to stay high up. The Camels were no good above 12,000. At 18,000 were the Dolphins—how many, he couldn't see.

He crossed the lines at 12,000 and was greeted by a bombardment of Archie. Fine—good advertisement! The S.E.s were invisible now. Good! Mustn't let the Huns see them.

He steered straight into Hunland for ten miles, turning, twisting, and peering below and above. Nothing but Archie. Johnny was back three miles and 2000 feet above him. Tubby was 2000 feet above Johnny. Then there were the S.E.s and finally the Dolphins. Just like the steps of stairs. When the fight started the formation would collapse like a

house of cards. Woe to the Huns at the bottom!

Henry turned south and held his level. The wind was against him fairly strong so he turned back to the lines. Mustn't get too far over. That Hun leader knows his business.

In ten minutes he saw what he was looking for—four Fokkers 2000 feet below him. So that was it? The Hun leader wasn't going to take a chance of letting him slip out of his clutches this time. He was going to cut him off from below. He studied the sun, his finger covering the ball of it. There they were! Two layers of them—about ten in each layer several thousand feet above him.

The four were climbing and turning south underneath him. The nerve of it! What an insult—four Fokkers flying under fifteen Camels! He knew it was because they had other machines above him. They were decoys too! All right, a little closer to the lines and he'd give them the surprise of their lives. He'd nail those four first—before the others got down on him—he'd show them what to do with decoys!

The Huns above were drawing nearer, two traps were ready to be sprung. All right, he'd spring it. He warmed his guns, waved to his men, and raised his right arm. Then he put his nose down and throttled back. No zooming now—he was going to stay down

The Fokker D-VII, considered the finest enemy fighter aircraft of the war, was the mainstay of the German "Flying Circuses" at the time American flyers fought on the Western front. (USAF)

with them—dogfight those four; and he didn't need speed—too much speed and he couldn't shoot straight to get in a long burst.

The four Fokkers saw him coming and were ready. They closed up and turned. Henry took the leader head on. The leader turned and Henry was on his tail in a flash. But before he could get his sights on him another Fokker was firing at him. He saw the tracer bullets streaking by and had to turn quickly. The Fokker stuck on his tail. He circled and turned to shake him off. Where was Johnny? The Fokker was firing again. Pretty close, that! Here were the others! Down came five Camels, guns blazing tracer sparklets and phosphorus. Four Fokkers and ten Camels—but only for a second. Eight more Fokkers dived after the Camels! A Camel was firing at the Fokker on his tail. Good old Johnny! He could tell it was Johnny by his streamer. He saw the Camel go down out of control. Poor Johnny! Good-bye, Johnny. Henry was firing at a Fokker and a Fokker was firing at him when both guns jammed. Damn that gunnery officer. He turned on his side, loosed his shoulder yoke, and worked at the stoppages. One clear.

Where's that hammer? Bang! The other gun was clear. Where's that top flight?

Five more Camels plunged into the center of the whirling mass, each man taking a Fokker as he leveled off. Henry saw two planes go down in flames—burning like meteors. So swift was their descent that he could not tell friend from foe. All were firing, twisting, turning. Henry saw a Fokker beneath him and pounced onto its tail. The Fokker half-rolled, and he turned quickly onto another. There was that damn sickly yellow phosphorous again in front of him. He looked back. Then came the other eight Huns. Where were the S.E.s? He was too busy to look.

He looked at his altimeter—10,000 feet. He noted his position—ten miles over. A killing for the S.E.s. For God's sake, come on! He saw a Fokker explode and blaze up. Fine. Down went another plane, twisting dizzily and smoking badly. A Camel this time. God, what a fight! Greatest dogfight in history. He was proud that he had staged it. Beyond his control now—nothing to do but fight his own battle. Another jam—he cleared it and looked above him. There was a Fokker coming down

The Nieuport 28, the first fighter aircraft furnished to the fledgling U.S. 94th and 95th Aero Squadrons, had the annoying habit of shedding its wings in a dive. (USAF)

on him. He turned sharply and the Fokker roared by and turned back toward him. Henry noticed that he had a streamer on his ruddder—it was the Hun leader! All right—after this scrap one side or the other would have a new leader. Johnny was already gone. He must even up the score.

There were the S.E.s. We've won! My God, there're more Fokkers! Where'd they come from? What a fight! He saw an S.E. and a Fokker collide, head on. A horrible sight. An immediate death was kind—think of the seconds they had to wait as eternity rushed up at them. There were the other Fokkers. Must be fifteen of them. All right—every man for himself. The sky was black with planes and powder. The greatest fight of the war!

Henry and the Hun leader were to the southeast of the fight and five hundred yards from it now as they jockeyed for position. Twice they came at each other head on and pulled away in climbing turns at the last fraction of a second before colliding. Nerve the fellow had! Not a shot fired—both were too wary and too cool to waste a foot of altitude for a random shot. A burst of twenty at fifty feet on a man's tail was worth 300 random

shots. Henry didn't even glance through his sight. He was watching the Fokker—an ugly square plane with a white nose and a black and white checkerboard fuselage and tail. He made out a skull and crossbones on it. The same fellow! He'd give him a death's head all right. They had closed in now and were circling. The circle was not a hundred feet in diameter and each plane was at the nadir, flat on its side in a vertical bank. Occasionally one would hit the other's backwash and stagger dizzily for a moment, then get back its stride. Not a shot came from either pair of guns.

Henry glanced at the ground. The wind was blowing him farther over; this wouldn't do! All the Hun had to do would be to hold him in a turn, and the wind would do the rest. He must get out of this.

Henry was as cool as if he were playing chess. He had perfect command of every faculty—every resource. He was in the enemy's territory. He had a good plane but a poor motor. The Hun clearly had the better motor for he was gaining a little in height every time.

Henry was thinking calmly: this bird is too good for me—I'll never get him—got to get

America's fourth ranking ace, George A. Vaughn Jr., began his service with a group of American pilots flying for the British. He ended the war with thirteen victories, and went on to command air units of the N.Y. National Guard. (USAF)

out of this—can't run for it—he'd get me first crack—can't stay here—other Fokkers will see this fight and come down—then *fini*. Gotta get out of this—this fellow knows his job and he's gaining—he's gaining twenty feet a turn—we're at 7000—he'll run me into the ground at this rate—he'll get above me—then he's got me. I can come out of this turn, but he'll be on my tail above me. I can half-roll and loop, but he'll follow me. Everything I do, he'll do right above me. If I half-roll, he'll half-roll. Sooner or later he gets me. He'll never fire until he's sure of me. If I go into a spin, so does he. When I come out, he's still on my tail. He can do this all day—damn fine pilot. And he will! Well, I've got to get him. Got to get him! Only one way to do it. It's he or I now. Take a chance. Let him get on my tail—he's going to sooner or later—dive for it and see who can stand the gaff the longest.

Then pull the old trick on him. It might work. When I pull up, he'll pull up and wait for a shot. I'll take one when he isn't looking—worth a try—my only hope!

Henry looked at the sun and waited until his back was to it. Then he leveled off and dived toward the lines.

Come on, you sucker, I'll dive until I see your tracer!

He hadn't long to wait. The Hun finished his half circle and dived after him. Henry had a start of five hundred feet on him.

The Hun closed it up. Henry turned around as far as his shoulder yoke would let him and watched—three hundred feet—two hundred feet—one hundred feet. He must sit still and take the first burst. He was suddenly cold as he awaited the crack of the spandaus. How good a shot was this Hun? Cool and deliberate he was. Could he hit him with the first burst? He'd soon know. Gotta sit and take it.

Captain Fred Libby, an American, downed all of his 24 enemy aircraft while in a British uniform. (USAF)

140—150—160—175—his airspeed indicator told him. It broke. Crack—crack—crack! There it was—the Hun was making his killing. Now for it! Henry had both hands on the stick and he pulled it back steadily with all his force as he pressed his own trigger. The terrific pressure threw him back into his seat and pressed the breath out of him.

He was looking through his sight now— God what a noise from the wires! He heard one snap—good shot—would his wings stay on? The whole machine shook convulsively as his nose rose, pointed straight up, and continued backward in a loop. Would the Hun see him and pull up or would they collide? Crack! Something pierced his left shoulder. Good shot again!

Then he saw through his sight what he was looking for—the white nose. Both guns were going and he pushed the stick forward to hold

David S. Ingalls, who downed 5 enemy aircraft while attached to the RFC's 213th Squadron in Flanders, enjoys the distinction of being the war's only U.S. Navy ace. In 1929, he became Assistant Secretary of the Navy for Aeronautics, and later a Rear Admiral in the Naval Reserve. (USN)

Harold Hartney, a Canadian who had become an ace serving with the British Royal Flying Corps, later commanded the U.S. First Pursuit Group (the formidable 27th, 94th, 95th, and 103rd Squadrons). (USAF)

his sight on the Hun—just a second, oh God— just a second! He was upside down now— both guns playing on the white nose.

His nose started to drop—he half-rolled and turned quickly—thank God for that shoulder yoke—ouch—how his shoulder hurt! Where was the Hun? There he was— my God, what a zoom! The Fokker was going straight up like an elevator—he must be doing 250—there, he's half-rolling—he's—— An icy hand gripped his heart as the wings folded backward and the Fokker turned a somersault in the air and went roaring down not fifty feet from him. He watched it a second, and saw it fluttering downward. Too bad—he was losing a friend—a fine fellow—hell of a war!

He was diving toward the lines now with his motor wide open. He must get back quickly. Faster—faster—faster—nothing could catch him now but the angel Gabriel. He tried to look back, but when he moved his shoulder stabbed him. The pain made him sick to his stomach. How was his arm? He could move his arm all right—at least he could land—he could work the throttle. God, what pain! Would he bleed to death before he got back? Probably. He felt he was fainting.

There were the lines, two miles ahead. Should he land in the balloon line while he was still conscious? No. Go on—back where he came from—like Ben did. Die on his own field—that was the way to do it. He could feel the blood running down his back. Was his shoulder blade broken? He tried to move it—the pain made him wince. What about his lung? Pierced? He took a deep breath. More pain. Yes, shoulder and lung. *Fini la guerre!* He was through. He and Johnny—gone the same way! And Ben! Good way to go!

They'd died with their shoes on! All right.

What's the use of the whole thing? Been fighting five months. What for? To get plugged through the shoulder by a better man.

He wondered if he had hit the Fokker or if it had simply broken up from structural weakness. Nobody would ever know. At least, he was firing at the Fokker. He could get credit for it. Credit? What did he want with any credit? He couldn't take any credit with him where he was going.

He was tired, dog-tired. His mind burned him. Well, it was all over now—he could feel himself getting weak. Could he last it? God, what pain!

Well, this was the end. Suddenly he was frightened—panicky. He didn't want to die. He was young; the wealth of life called to him. He had never been afraid to die—damn it, he wasn't afraid to die now—never had been afraid—he knew he had to die—that was the bargain he had struck with himself as the price of his courage. But he wasn't ready yet to pay the forfeit. He wasn't afraid—only regretful. Now he would never enjoy the fruits of his labors. In the moment of victory he was

snatched away. He would die in torture like Ben. He recalled his shrieks of agony. No, he wasn't afraid to die but he was afraid of pain. He couldn't stand pain. They would probe and cut and sew. He couldn't stand it! Should he dive into the ground now and end it?

This was the end. Why? He had given his life. For what? He couldn't remember. War! A good joke on him. He was a soldier—well, soldiers got killed. Why? So somebody else could get the booty. So the Congressmen's sons could take their feet off their desks and go home and get elected to office eternally. So Wall Street could get 8 per cent. So our grandchildren could be taught a fresh bunch of lies. This was glory. This was the end!

Was this what happened to a drowning man? God, he was so lonely. He didn't want to die. He wanted to scream it so loud that Johnny would hear and yell back to him. Think of the wine he would never drink—the girls he would never kiss—the books he would never read—the music he would never hear! A big monument at home—taps—he felt sorry for himself and the tears came. No, he didn't want to die—he wasn't going to—he must pull himself together! He must fight for his life.

There was the aerodrome. He throttled back and sideslipped in. He landed in a daze. How tired he was!

He taxied up to the hangar. A lot of serious faces—his sergeant at attention—come here—help me out—send for a doctor—shot through shoulder—Hun leader did it—then pulled wings off. He noticed all his flying wires were loose and flapping—a narrow escape from crumpling. All right, get me out.

They lifted him out tenderly and laid him on the ground.

"There it is," exclaimed the sergeant; "drilled clean through. Look at the blood."

He was dizzy. They were taking off his helmet and boots and overalls, then his shirt and undershirt. Why didn't they hurry? Here was the doctor. The doctor bent over him and put his hand on his shoulder—he was wiping away the blood—

Henry saw the bloody cloth—blood from his shoulder—his life's blood! Then he fainted.

When he came to he was lying in the shade. The sergeant was sitting beside him fanning him with his hat and holding a wet piece of cloth on his forehead. The pain was all gone and a piece of canvas was thrown over him.

"There, you're all right," the sergeant soothed him. "Those yellow-bellied Heinies can't kill you. We got ten of 'em this morning—five of our men missing. Lie still a minute. You're all right. Your plane's no more good. Every wire loose—full of holes too."

Henry groaned. Why, he didn't know. He was in no pain. He was just tired.

"I guess you got to get a new sergeant," he went on. "I blacked an eye for that damn medical sergeant. He laughed at you. And I nearly busted the doc one too. Damned old sawbones!"

"Laughed at me?" Henry asked, trying to think what he had done that was funny.

"Why was he laughing at me?"

"Cause you thought you were hit and weren't. If somebody took a shot at that medico he'd run all the way to Calais."

"Not hit? What about my shoulder?"

"You must have reared back something fierce 'cause you jabbed the buckle tongue of your shoulder yoke plumb through your flying suit and dug it an inch under you skin. Must have stayed in the flesh because it's all torn loose. All right, let's go down and get doc to plaster it up. I'd better let one of the other men take you down. I ain't popular in the medical tent right now."

"All right, my boy," the doctor told him as he worked with tape and gauze. "I'm glad it's no worse. But you're through here. No more flying for you for a while. I've been expecting you to break—you can wear out any machine. You had a fine case of dementia. You go to Boulogne this afternoon. I don't know what they'll do to you there—probably two weeks' leave. Good for you—spend all that money you won—all right—trot along, now."

BY THE SEAT OF
OUR PANTS

by Lieutenant Douglas Campbell,
U.S. Air Service

I have been asked to write a few words about the pilots of World War I. This is a broad term, taxing both my knowledge and the possiblity of accurate research on short notice, since it comprises pilots of many nationalities, in each of which group there were pilots who engaged in action against the enemy, pilots who were stuck with frustrating training and administrative assignments, and a very few who, by talent or assignment, really contributed to the technical development of aircraft and the art of operating them. I must perforce confine my remarks to the group of World War I pilots in which, by a combination of accident and design, I found myself at the time—namely, the American pilots who were directly engaged in the various forms of aerial warfare after the United States entered that conflict as a belligerent. We numbered only about 600, and because of the then appropriation of about $600,000,000 for the Air Service (as it was then called), were sometimes referred to—not always as a compliment—as "the million-dollar babies."

Whatever our contribution to the first 50

Doug Campbell, with Alan Winslow, scored the war's first U.S. aerial victories from an American squadron, on April 14, 1918. The distinctive insignia on Campbell's plane denotes the 94th "Hat-in-the-Ring" Squadron, to which Winslow also belonged. (USAF)

years of aviation may have been, it was certainly not of a technical nature. Nobody could every have accused us of being scientists; in fact, by present-day standards, we were hardly even pilots. Precision flying was something we knew nothing about, and how could we? Equipped with an altimeter, which, if functioning, was accurate within perhaps a couple of hundred feet, and had no adjustment for changes in barometric pressure (which we had no way of knowing anyway); with maps which showed with fair accuracy the location of roads, rivers, woodlands, cities, and other topographical features

but which indicated no terrain altitudes; with compasses (if any) which when most needed would more often than not be found spinning round and round in the most disturbing fashion; it is no wonder that "by guess and by God" was the order of the day. Unknown and unborn were today's standard blind-flying instruments and instrument-flying techniques which were to appear a few years later, largely as a result of the combined genius, courage, and perseverance of Lawrence Sperry and Jimmy Doolittle, and which constitute perhaps the most important single contribution to the development of aviation in the last thirty-five years. Meteorology was not one of the subjects on the curricula under which we were trained (to which we were exposed, is a more accurate expression). Airborne radio

While Frank Luke was an undisciplined "maverick," he was also America's second highest ace, with twenty-one victories. Had Luke, known variously as "The Arizona Cowboy" and "Balloon Buster," returned from his last flight he'd have been courtmartialed. Instead, he died a hero and won the Medal of Honor. (USAF)

Eddie Rickenbacker, a former Indianapolis Speedway driver and chauffeur to General Pershing, became a fighter pilot and rose to command the 94th Aero Squadron. In less than six and a half months he scored twenty-six victories to become the U.S. ace-of-aces. (USAF)

equipment in 1918 was, I believe, being experimented with by a few "screwballs" here and there, but if any World War I aircraft was equipped with it on a combat mission, I never heard of it, and it must have been exceedingly rare. Fortunately, and owing to a few centuries of research, we had one very reliable instrument—the clock, which at the same time was (hopefully) our fuel meter.

Even our military equipment and facilities were of a similar quality as compared to present-day standards. As a "chasse" pilot (later called pursuit pilot, now called fighter pilot), my gun sights were quite rudimentary, and although I cannot speak with authority on the bomb sights of that era, I believe they were of similar character. Getting about 50 yards behind the adversary's tail—above it if he was a one-man crew, and below it if there was a rear gunner—before opening fire, and then correcting the aim by watching the tracer bullets, seemed to offer the best chance of

hitting him. There were, of course, some tricks which did not depend upon airborne equipment, which one learned if one lived through enough encounters to build up some experience. Clouds were useful for ambushing purposes or to hide in at altitudes where the direction or attitude of one's exit from them was of minor importance; coming at the adversary from the direction of a bright sun was often a surprise to him; and although once one was off the ground the location of enemy aircraft was completely an unknown quantity because of lack of communication with the ground or with other friendly aircraft, certain deductions could be made from the shape and pattern of the bursts of shells fired by friendly or enemy antiaircraft batteries, which would often pay offensive or defensive dividends when their aircraft target was too far away to be seen.

But don't get the idea that we felt let down by the aforementioned deficiencies in our training or the equipment we had to work with, or even that we were particularly aware of them. There were some, I know (and they were the real heroes), who pushed themselves into the cockpit for every patrol feeling that their chance of coming back from it was quite slim; but I think most of us, having been cast at an early age into what, up to then, was undoubtedly the most exciting adventure of all time, regarded it as exactly that, and the future was non-existent. We had the best aircraft and equipment there were at the time, we thought, and better ones were being developed. True, we were lucky if the engine did more than about about 50 hours before overhaul, and overhauled engines were not considered good enough to be used in combat aircraft, but we had been trained always to be on the lookout for a likely-appearing cow-pasture in case we suddenly needed it, so what? True, there were few parachutes—some elected to jump without one as an alternative to sitting behind a fuel tank set on fire by an enemy incendiary bullet—but that was the situation, up to that time, in the business we were in. Most of us were too young, I guess, or too wrapped up in our adventure, and too oblivious of anything beyond the next few hours, to demand that something be done

about it. True, many of us, like myself, entered out first combat with a total of about fifty flying hours in our logbooks, including perhaps three hours of aerial gunnery practice, but that was pretty normal too, and in the case of some of our allied colleagues it was said that the figure was somewhat less. In short, we were enthusiastically doing the job we wanted to do, and those were just the normal conditions in 1918.

To get back to the question of what were our contributions to the history of flight, I suggest that they were three in number, and all rather indirect in nature. First, the activity itself was so spectacular in that day that it caught the public fancy to an extent that the prewar aviation exploits never had. Second, the positive results obtained by the adventurous enthusiasm of this group of youngsters removed any doubt that air power would be an element essential to successful military operations. Third, the technical limitations to real efficiency which were made evident by our experiences clearly pointed the way to the vast and varied fields of research, development and training necessary to make the airplane and its crew the effective instrument in war and peace which it has subsequently become.

Knights of the Black Cross

THE MASTER

**by Leutnant Max Immelmann,
Imperial German Air Service**

The Seventh

Yesterday, Lieutenant Immelmann shot down his seventh enemy aircraft, an English monoplane, in an airfight over Valenciennes.
Excerpt from the official military communique of December 16th, 1915.

The next day it was fairly foggy. The clouds appeared to hang pretty low. But you can never trust an Englishman, and so I took off in spite of the uncertain weather. It was fairly dark when I started, but half an hour later it was quite bright. I was up to about 200 meters when I saw the flashes of bursting shells or shrapnel in the far distance. They came from the direction of Lille, and the flare of the bursting shells stood out quite clearly against the dark sky. So off I went to Lille. When I was 10 kilometers away from the town I saw the enemy high above me to northward and on my right. I was only 1200 meters up then, and he was 2800, so that I was not able to attack him at the moment.

I am making you a little sketch of my pursuit. If you have a map, you will be able to follow it more exactly. I am sketching the whole thing from memory, so I make no claim to accuracy.

When he saw me, he did not fly southward, as was probably his original intention, but bore away from me in an eastward direction. I went into a turn and flew alongside him, although still much lower. He tried to reach the salvation of the lines by a right-hand turn. I promptly flew towards him, although still somewhat lower and so unable to attack. I had climbed to 2600 by then, but he was at 2800. The feint attack I made on him misled him into abandoning his westward course and flying further southeast. Again he tried to reach his lines, but with a similar lack of result.

Now we were both at the same height, but I nevertheless let my machine climb a bit more. He did the opposite, for he put his machine down and thus obtained such a great speed that he almost disappeared from my view. I could only see him as a faint grey smudge on the distant horizon. He certainly hoped I had lost him, because he went into a right-hand turn and headed for Douai.

I was now 3200 meters up, while he might have been 2600–2700. As his line of flight was now about perpendicular to my own, my greater height enabled me to approach him at very fast speed. When we were still 500–600 meters apart, he opened a furious fire on me. The distance was too great for him to have any chance to succeed. He fired at least 500 rounds while I was coming up from 500–150 meters of him.

Max Immelmann, German hero and the first ace of World War I. Though a poor marksman he was a superb pilot, and the combat maneuver the "Immelmann Turn" was named for him. (National Archives)

Then I too began to shoot. First I gave him a series of 40 rounds. The enemy flew gaily on; why not? Now there was only 100 meters between us, then 80 and finally 50. I saw the enemy observer fiddling at his machine gun. Probably he had a jam.

I had to use the moment. Without allowing the pause of even a fraction of a second, I let off 150 rounds. Suddenly the enemy monoplane reared up; with its propeller pointing skyward and its steering surfaces earthward, it stood on its tail for several seconds. Then it turned over by the right wing and whirled down in a nose-dive.

My efforts to catch another glimpse of it during the fall were useless. I flew a circle around the scene of the fray and then went off home.

Then I received a jubilant welcome, for a

telephone message had already come through: "In an airfight over Valenciennes a Fokker monoplane shot an enemy monoplane down. The latter turned over several times and crashed near Raismes, northeast of Valenciennes. Further details are lacking. The German monoplane went off in the direction of Douai."

The section knew who was the victor, because I was the only one who had been up.

I asked our section-leader for permission to proceed to Valenciennes at once, which he granted. When I arrived there, I learnt that the wreckage had been cleared away and the bodies (Lieutenants Hobbs and Johnston) already buried.

I ascertained the following detail from eye-witnesses. After dropping vertically for some distance, the machine turned over several times. In one of these turns the observer fell out when the machine was about 100 meters from the ground. He fell onto a tree. The branches pierced his body, which then dropped to the ground. There were several bullet wounds in his head and neck, so that his death must have been instantaneous.

The machine and the pilot were found about 500 meters away from this tree. The pilot had a couple of bullet wounds in his head, in addition to one in his chest and another in a leg. The machine crashed on to the wall of a house and was smashed to bits.

No gun was found in the machine. But I induced the men to make a further search, because I had heard the enemy's shots. Finally they discovered the machine gun a long way to one side; it had fallen out.

Then it became clear to me why the Englishman ceased fire. One of my bullets went through his barrel, while another destroyed the loading mechanism. These facts I naturally could not know when I was still in the air. After receiving congratulations from all sides, I returned to Douai.

There you have in brief the events of the last few days. Did you hang out your flags when the news of No. 7 came?

You hope I may be home for Christmas,

but it is quite impossible. Yesterday I sent you two large photos, taken by P. They will have to be our Christmas surprise.

I am sending you 100 marks. I am sure you want something and would gladly buy it if you had the money. I really would have liked to buy something for you with it, but if I did so, the business would go to the French. And any tradesman at home would surely be glad to take the 100 marks. I am enclosing 50 marks for Elfriede. She must buy herself something sensible with it. I know it seems funny to be sending you money, but I find it foolish to buy French vases or that sort of rubbish, as so many do, and send them home.

I shall hardly write again before Christmas, because there won't be much happening up to then. So I wish you today a real good Christmastide!

The Eighth

Lieutenants Boelcke and Immelmann each shot down an English machine, to the northeast of Turcoing and near Bapaume. In recognition of their manificent achievement His Majesty the Emperor has been pleased to confer the Pour le Mérite Order on these two dauntless officers.
Excerpt from the official military communique of January 13th, 1916.

Douai, January 29th, 1916.

I believe there is no need to assure you that my correspondence obligations have risen to something immeasurable. I receive 30–40 letters and postcards every day. Terrible. All the same I am going on well.

I don't remember where I got up to in my last letter. I certainly wrote you that I had received a silver cup, inscribed 'To the Victor in Aerial Combat' and that your parcel arrived somewhat late. But that hardly matters at all. Everything was in good condition and everything except the Christmas-tree decorations could be used.

A bombing squadron came along on January 5th. One enemy belonging to it was shot down. Boelcke shot one opponent down in the morning. When the squadron arrived, I jumped hastily into Boelcke's 160-h.p. machine. I did not know how much petrol there was in it, and it was all gone by the time I climbed to 2500 meters.

The two-seater FE-2b English Night Bomber, with which the RFC's Lieutenant George R. McCubbin downed Immelmann. McCubbin had to dispatch Immelmann with his machine guns, as his gunner's weapons had jammed. (USAF)

About 8:30 a.m. on January 12th when dawn was just giving place to daylight, news came through that enemy machines had crossed the lines in various places. So Osterreicher and I climbed into our Fokkers in the hope of catching one or other of them. When I was up to 500 meters, I saw Boelcke also getting in his machine. Then I saw no more of him, and didn't know where he had flown to. In any case we didn't hang about Douai, because we knew no more would turn up there. Osterreicher and I flew to Arras, and then bore off southwards.

I was halfway between Arras and Bapaume when I saw shell bursts in the direction of Cambrai and stretching away to northward, so that apparently someone was trying to fly from Cambrai to Douai. I promptly turned eastward.

Osterreicher also appeared to have seen the shell bursts. We were both about 3200 meters up, while, judging by the shell bursts, the enemy seemed to be between 2600 and 2800. We could not see the enemy aircraft at all, and the shell bursts only with difficulty, because we were flying right into the sun, which was still very low. I had some trouble to keep on the right course. Osterreicher went off southwards.

That was the only reason why I reached the enemy machine before him; it was flying a west-to-east course. Before I could recognise the type he went into a sudden turn and headed due west. I was 3000 meters up and he was 2800. He appeared to have seen me. Why otherwise this sharp turn?

Now I recognised him. A Vickers biplane, with both pilot and observer in front of the engine. I dived steeply onto him, as he was now coming straight towards me. The observer fired at me from in front.

I could see their leather helmets quite plainly. The observer was kneeling behind his machine gun. So now it was up to me to get my machine round quicker than the enemy.

I went completely round before the Englishman started to go into a right-hand turn. I was now firing like mad, but without re-sults, for he completed his turn. But I went round again at once, so that I had him in the same position. I gave him about another 100 rounds.

Then all of a sudden a reddish-yellow flame shot out from his engine, leaving a long trail of smoke behind him. I ceased fire, and the Englishman went down in steeply banked turns, with his machine all ablaze.

I saw the machine make a smooth landing and someone jump out. Men who had been working a threshing machine in the neighborhood hurried up. I landed in a meadow about a kilometer away.

The machine was set alight by spurting petrol, because I hit the tank several times. It caught fire at 2200 meters, and was still burning when I arrived.

The observer was killed, but the pilot escaped with a slight wound in the head. He told me his observer lost his head completely and only fired 5 rounds, after which he was incapable of offering further resistance. I introduced myself and told him he was my eighth victim.

"You are Immelmann?" he then inquired. "You are well known to us. Your victory today is another fine sporting success for you."

I then handed the wounded man over to a doctor, while a section stationed in the neighborhood took charge of the machine and its contents. I climbed in my cockpit; as the weather had grown worse, I flew straight home. I proudly reported my new victory to my captain. He congratulated me cordially and said: "You are a fine fellow, and Boelcke also got one, somewhere near Lille, you know."

I was never so pleased at one of Boelcke's victories as I was that day. Unfortunately, he had landed at Lille and was not yet back, so that we were unable to congratulate one another.

In the afternoon our captain put a car at my disposal, so that I could fetch the machine gun, ammunition, etc. I also took along a photographer, who made several snaps. We were accompanied by a very dear comrade,

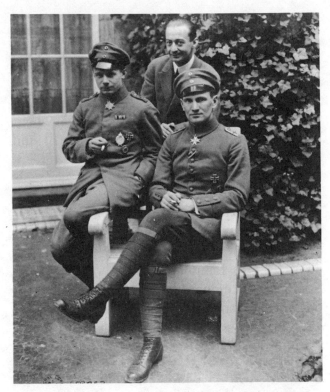

Two other of the Imperial German Air Service's aces were Ernst Udet (left), whose sixty-two victories made him second only to von Richthofen, and Bruno Loerzer (right), who had forty-five. They are pictured with friend Sigmund Abel. (U.S. Signal Corps)

who, I regret, to say, was killed several days later in an airfight.

On our way to Bapaume, whither the debris and armament of the machine had been taken, we ran over three fowls, which we took along with us, and they made us a nice meal the next day when cooked with rice.

We got home fairly late, about 9 p.m. In view of the double victory it was not surprising to find champagne on the table and every-one in high spirits. But they had all dined, and only we latecomers were hungry.

The "Pour le Mérite" (The "Blue Max")

As is the custom when the section celebrates a joyful event, our leader spoke a few words, but this time his speech was livelier and gayer than usual. I cannot remember everything he said, because I was too excited with my pleasure. I did not really listen until at the end of his short speech. He said something about a milestone in the history of aviation and a turning point and recognition in high places, but finally the big word came out: "His Majesty the Emperor has been graciously pleased to confer the highest war order, the "Pour le Merite," on the two victors in aerial warfare."

I was dumb. I should have thought it a joke if my section-leader had not said it in front of all our officers. I couldn't eat or drink anything that day; I didn't know whether I was awake or dreaming.

The next day congratulation followed congratulation, by telephone and telegram.

Those were days I can never forget. We were invited to dinner with the King of Bavaria, and a couple of days later with the Crown Prince of Bavaria, who gave us the Orders. The King of Saxony, the Crown Princes of Prussia and Saxony, Prince Sigismund, the Chief of War Aviation, etc., sent me telegrams of congratulation. They sent them to Boelcke as well. My mail swelled to 50 letters a day, and my batman became my "private secretary." At last, after a fortnight, things grew a bit quieter.

BLOODY RED BARON

by Rittmeister Manfred von Richthofen, Imperial German Air Service

My First Double Event

The second of April, 1917, was a very warm day for my Squadron. From my quarters I could clearly hear the drumfire of the guns which was again particularly violent.

I was still in bed when my orderly rushed into the room and exclaimed: "Sir, the English are here!" Sleepy as I was, I looked out of the window and, really, there were my dear friends circling over the flying ground. I jumped out of my bed and into my clothes in a jiffy. My Red Bird had been pulled out and was ready for starting. My mechanics knew that I should probably not allow such a favorable moment to go by unused. Everything was ready. I snatched up my furs and then went off.

I was the last to start. My comrades were much nearer to the enemy. I feared that my prey would escape me, that I should have to look on from a distance while the others were fighting. Suddenly one of the impertinent fellows tried to drop down upon me. I allowed him to come near and then we started a merry quadrille. Sometimes my opponent flew on his back and sometimes he did other tricks. He had a double-seated chaser. I was his master and very soon I recognized that he could not escape me.

During an interval in the fighting I convinced myself that we were alone. It followed that the victory would accrue to him who was calmest, who shot best and who had the clearest brain in a moment of danger. After a short time I got him beneath me without seriously hurting him with my gun. We were at least two kilometers from the front. I thought he intended to land but there I had made a mistake. Suddenly, when he was only a few yards above the ground, he once more went off on a straight course. He tried to escape me. That was too bad. I attacked him again and I went so low that I feared I should touch the roofs of the houses of the village beneath me. The Englishman defended himself up to the last moment. At the very end I felt that my engine had been hit. Still I did not let go. He had to fall. He rushed at full speed right into a block of houses.

There was little left to be done. This was once more a case of splendid daring. He defended himself to the last. However, in my opinion he showed more foolhardiness than courage. This was one of the cases where one must differentiate between energy and idiocy.

He had to come down in any case but he paid for his stupidity with his life.

I was delighted with the performance of my red machine during its morning work and return to our quarters. My comrades were still in the air and they were very surprised, when, as we met at breakfast, I told them that I had scored my thirty-second machine.

A very young Lieutenant had "bagged" his first airplane. We were all very merry and prepared everything for further battles.

I then went and groomed myself. I had not had time to do it previously. I was visited by a dear friend, Lieutenant Voss of Boelcke's Squadron. We chatted. Voss had downed on the previous day his twenty-third machine. He was next to me on the list and is at present my most redoubtable competitor.

Manfred von Richthofen, the Red Baron (right), was the war's high-scoring ace with eighty kills. He was well known for his all-red fighter planes and "Flying Circus" Jagdstaffel (fighter squadron). At left is his brother Lothar. (USAF)

The Fokker DR-1 Triplane, though slower than the SPAD and Camel, was more maneuverable. It was flown by such high-scoring aces as von Richthofen, Udet, and Werner Voss. (the latter downed twenty-two Allied aircraft in three weeks with it). (Revell)

When he started to fly home I offered to accompany him part of the way. We went on a roundabout way over the Fronts. The weather had turned so bad that we could not hope to find any more game.

Beneath us there were dense clouds. Voss did not know the country and he began to feel uncomfortable. When we passed above Arras I met my brother who also is in my squadron and who had lost his way. He joined us. Of course he recognized me at once by the color of my machine.

Suddenly we saw a squadron approaching from the other side. Immediately the thought occurred to me: "Now comes number thirty-three." Although there were nine Englishmen and although they were on their own territory they preferred to avoid battle. I thought that perhaps it would be better for me to repaint my machine. Nevertheless we caught them up. The important thing in airplanes is that they are speedy.

I was nearest to the enemy and attacked the man to the rear. To my greatest delight I noticed that he accepted battle and my pleasure was increased when I discovered that his com-

rades deserted him. So I had once more a single fight.

It was a fight similar to the one which I had had in the morning. My opponent did not make matters easy for me. He knew the fighting business and it was particularly awkward for me that he was a good shot. To my great regret that was quite clear to me.

A favorable wind came to my aid. It drove both of us into the German lines.* My oppo-

*It is well to note how often von Richthofen refers to the wind being in his favor. A west wind means that while the machines are fighting they are driven steadily over the German lines. Then, if the British machine happens to be inferior in speed or maneuverability to the German, and is forced down low, the pilot has the choice only of fighting to a finish and being killed, or of landing and being made prisoner. The prevalence of west winds has, for this reason, cost the R.F.C. a very great number of casualties in killed and missing, who, if the fight had occurred over territory held by the British, would merely have landed till the attacking machine had taken itself off. For similar reasons, the fact that the R.F.C. has always been on the offensive, and so has always been flying over the German lines had caused many casualties. Under all the circumstances it is surprising that the R.F.C. casualties have not been a great deal heavier.

The Bristol F2b Fighter proved effective as a scout, although it was badly defeated by Richthofen in its first action. Andrew McKeever shot down five of the enemy in one battle flying a "Brisfit," and totaled a score of 30 by war's end. (Renwal)

nent discovered that the matter was not so simple as he had imagined. So he plunged and disappeared in a cloud. He had nearly saved himself.

I plunged after him and dropped out of the cloud and, as luck would have it, found myself close behind him. I fired and he fired without any tangible result. At last I hit him. I noticed a ribbon of white benzine vapor. He had to land for his engine had come to a stop.

He was a stubborn fellow. He was bound to recognize that he had lost the game. If he continued shooting I could kill him, for meanwhile we had dropped to an altitude of about nine hundred feet. However, the Englishman defended himself exactly as did his countryman in the morning. He fought until he landed. When he had come to the ground I flew over him at an altitude of about thirty feet in order to ascertain whether I had killed him or not. What did the rascal do? He took his machine-gun and shot holes into my machine.

Afterwards Voss told me if that had happened to him he would have shot the airman on the ground. As a matter of fact I ought to have done so for he had not surrendered. He was one of the few fortunate fellows who escaped with their lives.

I felt very merry, flew home and celebrated my thirty-third airplane.

My Record Day

The weather was glorious. We were ready for starting. I had as a visitor a gentleman who had never seen a fight in the air or anything resembling it and he had just assured

Canadian ace Arthur Roy Brown is credited by the Royal Flying Corps with shooting down the Red Baron. (Canadian Forces)

me that it would tremendously interest him to witness an aerial battle.

We climbed into our machines and laughed heartily at our visitor's eagerness. Friend Schäfer* thought that we might give him some fun. We placed him before a telescope and off we went.

The day began well. We had scarcely flown to an altitude of six thousand feet when an English squadron of five machines was seen coming our way. We attacked them by a rush as if we were cavalry and the hostile squadron lay destroyed on the ground. None of our men was even wounded. Of our enemies three had plunged to the ground and two had come down in flames.

*Schäfer was also shot by Lieut. Rhys-Davids, R.F.C., later in 1917.

The good fellow down below was not a little surprised. He had imagined that the affair would look quite different, that it would be far more dramatic. He thought the whole encounter had looked quite harmless until suddenly some machines came falling down looking like rockets. I have gradually become accustomed to seeing machines falling down, but I must say it impressed me very deeply when I saw the first Englishman fall and I have often seen the event again in my dreams.

As the day had begun so propitiously we sat down and had a decent breakfast. All of us were as hungry as wolves. In the meantime our machines were again made ready for starting. Fresh cartridges were got and then we went off again.

In the evening we could send off the proud report: "Six German machines have destroyed thirteen hostile airplanes."**

Boelcke's Squadron had only once been able to make a similar report. At that time we had shot down eight machines. Today one of us had brought low four of his opponents. The hero was a Lieutenant Wolff, a delicate-looking little fellow in whom nobody could have suspected a redoubtable hero. My brother had destroyed two, Schafer two, Festner two, and I three.

We went to bed in the evening tremendously proud but also terribly tired. On the following day we read with noisy approval about our deeds of the previous day in the official communique. On the next day we downed eight hostile machines.

A very amusing thing occurred. One of the Englishmen whom we had shot down and whom we had made a prisoner was talking with us. Of course he inquired after the Red Airplane. It is not unknown even among the

**It is possible that the figures are correct. Early in 1917, before the advent of the British fighters and de Havilands in quantities, the R.F.C. was having a very bad time. One April 7, for example, it was reported in the G. H. Q. Communique that twenty-eight English machines were missing.

The Fokker D VIII, "The Flying Razor," was the last of the WWI Fokker fighters. It joined the Western Front conflict in October, 1918, and was the last German plane to shoot down an Allied aircraft before the Armistice. (USAF)

troops in the trenches and is called by them "le diable rouge." In the Squadron to which he belonged there was a rumor that the Red Machine was occupied by a girl, by a kind of Jeanne d'Arc. He was intensely surprised when I assured him that the supposed girl was standing in front of him. He did not intend to make a joke. He was actually convinced that only a girl could sit in the extravagantly painted machine.

PART TWO

SPANISH CIVIL WAR

Scrimmage for the Big Show

A RETREAD FROM THE
FIRST WORLD WAR

by Teniente Orrin D. Bell, Spanish Loyalist Air Force

So far I had been flying and fighting in a blue serge suit. Now I got 500 more pesetas and spent it on a snappy double-breasted blue uniform and cap. But that was all. In the end I went off to the Huesca front a *teniente* (lieutenant) only because they said I was. The last evening with Noka made many things worth while.

The Huesca front was very quiet and damnably cold until midday, when the sun warmed up sufficiently to make loafing possible. Out of the mountains blew, every day almost, a steady thirty-mile-an-hour breeze. We could have patrolled despite it. The *escuadrilla* leader did not think so and kept the ships on the ground. We billeted in the Commercial Hotel in Sariñena, about three miles from the airdrome, and bussed to the field every morning at six a.m. Then we'd sit around all day.

Rick and I belonged to the Las Rojas squadron, supposedly a crack outfit; but for a week we never left the ground. And neither did the Insurgents. In the first week Rick took off once on an offensive patrol, and I got away once—in Nieuports, God save the mark!— and never saw a black-tipped pair of wings in the sky.

Queerly enough, this was an efficiently organized *aerodromo*. Being only fifteen kilometers behind the Huesca-Zaragoza front, it had posts planted ready for barbed wire, machine-gun emplacements, and dugouts. But most of our time was spent entertaining the high officers who came swanking in. General Luis Aguillia, commandant of the district, was one. We drank wine, ate well, and gave the *salud* so much, clenched fists at the forehead, that it got to be like a setting-up exercise.

And then, on a morning in February, an electric shock went through the Sariñena. The Spanish government army was going to assault to break the deadlock around Madrid. The big push at last.

Rick came in excitedly. "This time it's the McCoy, O.D. We're going to Madrid front and we're going to fly the P ships."

"Ah, man!" I jumped out of bed and into my clothes.

"It'll be tough going." he warned. "Franco's got a hundred Heinkels and Fiats r'aring to go."

We went to Valencia that night on a troop train. In the morning I went to the Air Ministerio about a real contract. As usual, nobody in authority was there. I saw Noka for a precious few hours and went to the Inglése Hotel. I stuck my head in the dining room.

A familiar voice said, "Damn, boy, don't I call my shots? I said we'd be sittin' here and in would walk O.D. to buy us a drink. José, damn your pink eyes, get back in your little white box—here's company."

It was like a letter from home. There was Tex Allison, 'Napolis (an Annapolis grad who had resigned from the navy after a pal cracked up trying to land on the Lexington). Kid Sol (I knew no other name for him), Manuel Gomez, Stolke the Swiss, Tiny Koch, the young Spaniard Barbieri, and finally Harold "Whitey" Dahl.*

I had the news from them between drinks. A group of young Spaniards were just back from Russia, where they had undergone intensive training in combat tactics. There would be two of these youngsters to one of us older, more experienced men. Thus we would have a fighting squadron of twenty-seven men.

"And plenty to do," concluded Tex. "It's a hot front and I hope we can all be drinking together like this a month from now."

We went to Madrid that night; and none of us Americans had a line of writing to confirm our commissions or our jobs.

But what was that now? We were to be in a major battle; we would have the best fighting ships; we had the most active front. My spirits soared.

The next morning we were bussed out to Huete, where the aerodrome was. There they were on the dead line, the snub-nosed Russian P ships built exactly like our beautiful Boeing Fighters. How splendid they looked, lined wing to wing! And how deadly! Not only were two machine guns prop-synchronized to shoot through the propeller, but there was a Vickers mounted on each wing; the four guns lined up to converge their tracer fire 150 feet ahead. And what guns! The latest vickers models; their combined power was 3200 shots a minute!

---

*Harold "Whitey" or "Blondy" Dahl was afterward captured by the Insurgent troops and sentenced by court-martial to be shot. Through the pleas of his wife, Edith Rogers Dahl, to General Francisco Franco, the sentence commuted, and at this writing Dahl is to be exchanged and finally repatriated.

Our experiences on the first training patrols were funny. These P ships were so sensitive, so speedy. I started to throw the crate into a snap roll. I was used to the Nieuports and gave her too much stick. The ship went through the air like a corkscrew and made three and a half turns before I could level her out.

Landing them was the big laugh to the onlookers. Cruising at 280 miles an hour, we became accustomed to high speed and would come back to the field and start to sit down at 120 or so, and would float clear across. Then we had to gun all out and zoom up and make another circle to try it again. I made two circles trying to get in, and finally dipped down to the field edge as close to a stall as I could come, then cut the gun and brought her in—an engine-stall landing, I supposed you'd call it. We all worked this method of landing and finally got to be good at it. Say this much in praise of all Americans—flying in Spain we never so much as blew a tire on our equipment. The only planes lost were those that were shot down.

Life was perfect for a while. Noka came to Madrid, where I lived. We commuted to the field by bus. And there were grand flying ships and the thrill of flying at 14,000 feet to greet the sun.

And so I arrive at our first combat on the Madrid front. I was never to forget it!

I came out of a sound sleep with Manuel shaking my shoulder. "What eet ees, camarada, the bus she come queeck!"

It was still dark, bitter cold. He shivered even more than I as I got dressed. I tried to cheer him up.

"Hey, Manuel," I grinned, "you damned son of a theesa and thatta, don't shiver that crate of yours into my tail this morning."

"No, camarada," he said. "Eet ees not I am afraid, no. But thees cold—eet goes into my veree soul. Ah, Mexico City—she ees so warm."

"We'll go up to the sun; it will be warm there. And remember, try to keep them off my tail and I'll try to do the same for you."

The Russian Polikarpov I-16, called "Rata" by the Spanish Civil War insurgent forces who flew against it, was supposed to have resembled the U.S. Boeing P-26. I-16s fought against the insurgents' Henschel HS-123s, Fiat CR-32s and later, Messerschmitt Me-109s. The I-16 was also employed by the Soviet Air Force at the start of World War II. (Revell)

He nodded absently. "They are wrong—all those black flyers. . . . O.D., lend me your new goggles—mine hurt my eyes."

Going out in the bus, I broke down and loaned them to him. I had bought them myself because the truck drivers grabbed most of the government issue, and those we got were not lined and hurt the flesh around the eye sockets. We had no breakfast, of course, nor wanted any. I was in the mess hall, drinking a *café con Americano* because the cognac warmed me inside.

I had the jitters again, a warning, I suppose, that something was going to break loose. So far it had been a nice war, nobody hurt much on our side, and all the boys together in the evening.

Whitey Dahl stuck his head in the door. "Come on," he said, "snap out of it—we're going upstairs."

"Keep your shirt on," I said.

"Nuts. Let's get going."

"Nuts to you. I'll finish this cigarette."

He gave me an odd, quick look. All this must have been nerves, because actually we were fair friends. When he went to another front I escorted his wife, Edith Rogers Dahl, around Valencia, and I'm pleased to hear she saved his life when Franco was going to stand him against a wall.

Finally my shakes stopped a little and I went out to the crate. Vicente, my mech, said in Spanish, "She is ready to do miracles, *Señor Teniente*. I, Vicente, so say."

We took off in a climbing turn, Tiny Koch and myself behind and above as rear protection, assigned there, I suppose, because of our World War experience. Offhand it looked like a routine patrol, and when the sun blazed brightly I shouted into my slip stream and gloried in the sharp thin air of 12,000 feet.

I saw the enemy planes—Fiats and twenty of them—flying at 8000 feet. They made no move to come up or prepare for attack. I lifted my head and put a thumb in front of my eye so as to see into the sun. Certainly enough I saw specks up there—more Insurgent planes. Lots of them. I knew then that the Fiats below were decoys to lure us into a dive, and when we were into them, the gang would drop on our necks with fistfuls of bullets. It was an old World War trick, but I couldn't stop it succeeding. Our squadron leader waggled his wings, fell off on his right wing. We all followed, nosed down and, full out, dived on to the Fiats.

Tiny and I had the job of breaking the leading wedge. Tiny was leading, and almost subconsciously I saw him whip on to his man in a stalled Immelmann, and the Fiat burst into flames. I went for their Number Two. The poor guy turned away, but he never had a chance. I pointed that crate of mine as you point your finger.

That Fiat pilot was right in the bead. I tripped the triggers. The converging fire of four guns slammed him as if he had been hit by a truck. He went straight down and I was behind him. The pilot's head turned slightly, sun glint on the goggles. Then, in a most agonizing movement, he put his hands up behind his head as if he would ward off the bullets that knocked at his back.

He left me there and his Fiat went down in a tight spin and never came out of it. For a moment I was shocked. Reality penetrated the veils of illusion. This was no game. I saw this man die. I saw his helmet turn from black to strawberry red. I saw him fall against his instrument panel.

The realization made me sit there motionless, and while I idled, thirty-six Heinkel Fighters came down out of the sun with a roar like doomsday, and flashed around us like skittering silverfish, filling the air with a thousand javelins of tracer fire.

Just why I wasn't cold meat I'll never know. I turned in a vertical and came on a sight that wiped the other from my mind. I saw Manuel Gomez going down with two Heinkels raining a crossfire on his cockpit.

I went in on the right-hand Heinkel, and Tex, I think it was, dived on the tail of the other. But we were too late. Manuel's ship turned upside down and he fell out the length of his safety belt, and although the crate righted itself, he remained outside, his body flapping limply back and forth on the safety belt. I was crying—I guess yelling, "God, they got Manuel!" and piling the bullets into the Heinkel, and he was going down, fighting his controls, and I was blasting his motor apart. He was still fighting his controls when I nosed up, but a black streamer like a woman's hair in the wind was coming from his motor. Fire!

I was probably insane with anger then—shouting, cursing, and saying silly things. I

tried to pick a target out of the wheeling circle of diving, zooming ships. But I never did. Something struck me a sharp blow in the head. That's all I knew then.

"You went into a tight spin," Koch told me later, "nosed straight down, and two Heinkels were potshooting at you from both sides. I came down a bit, but a Heinkel jumped me, so I said to myself, "There goes Bell, poor devil,' and went to bat with him. The last I saw of you, you were still spinning at a thousand feet, so I figured you were gone since you didn't bail out."

Well, the devil looks after his own, I guess. Less than 500 feet up I regained consciousness. I thought I was blind in one eye because I couldn't see out of it. I pushed up my goggles to make sure. Automatically I came out of the spin and leveled off about 100 feet up. My head ached as if a hammer were hitting it, and when I wiped up there, my hand was all bloody, and blood kept running down on my coat. But I found I could see out of the eye if I wiped the blood away.

For maybe a minute I rode along, trying to pull myself together. A fistful of bullets that popped by my head helped considerably. I looked over the cockpit edge. It seemed that all Franco's army were firing their rifles as fast as they could pull the bolt, and a machine gun in a trench emplacement was tearing off a half belt.

Insurgent territory! And I was flying deeper into it with the passing seconds.

I made a tight bank and headed back—and then I lost my head. The pain of the wound, the shooting, the sudden recovery from bewilderment, all contrived to make a case of frothing insanity. I thought about Manuel, and I nosed the crate down and cut loost with the machine guns. I flew back over the same ground; and no one had ducked for cover because I hadn't shot them up on the way in. So now, despite my red wingtips and tail (standard coloring for government aircraft), I had plenty of targets, and I gave them fifty or more short sharp bursts. The gun on the starboard wing jammed, but the other three threw bullets until I reached no man's land. The soldiers scattered and fell like ninepins—not human beings to me, but toy soldiers such as you knock over with rubber cannon balls on the playroom floor.

To show how groggy I was, I climbed for altitude after reaching our side of the barbed wire and ran into the dogfight, which had fought down from 12,000 to 4000 feet. Or rather the dogfight ran into me, because I wasn't looking for it. The scrap was about ready to break off by mutual consent; that is to say, pilots were running short of ammo, gas, and enthusiasm. As a matter of fact the Insurgent planes were pulling out to reform and go home when I blundered into the situation.

I didn't realize this at the moment. All I knew was that suddenly out of nowhere, in front of me and coming up with his guns flashing, was a black-wingtipped Heinkel, and I cut in my guns as instinctively as you wink your eyelid. I shot my way right through him. I never knew then what happened to him. He simply wasn't there any more. I kept on going, and another that tried to crawl my back was outdistanced because I was all out at 280, heading for home.

Rich and Tiny must have seen how I wobbled, because I found out later they fell in behind me to protect my tail to the field. Myself, I don't know how I reached it. Every so often the world would do a spin and I'd clamp down on the stick and say, "Hang on, guy, just a minute now."

The blood still ran from my head and was weakening me every second. Once or twice I wobbled down and finally gritted my will to last just a little longer. When the field was reached I didn't think I could come in. Neither did anyone else, because the whole squadron veered and stayed back out of the way and gave me a clear shot to crack up by myself.

I saw the ground coming up and reached for the throttle. I cut it, pulled back on the stick. The wheels hit—and I passed out cold.

The next thing I knew I was in the infirmary and the medical officer was working on me. The bullet had scooped out a gutter of flesh along my right temple. As usual, the M.O. washed it with iodine—the universal Spanish remedy for wounds.

Later Tiny came in with the news: Tex had got a mushroom bullet through his leg that left a tiny place where it went in and a hole as big as a meat platter when it came out. Whitey Dahl had been shot down, but bailed out and was seen to land safely. Stolke was killed. Two of the Spanish youngsters copped it.

"We shot down fourteen of them," Tiny said. "Your three have been confirmed."

It was the first I knew that the Heinkel which got in my way at the end had cracked up. He told me then that we'd lost five ships and four men—Gomez making the fourth.

"But we fought them to a finish, O.D., and they hauled air."

That night I did a lot of thinking. I kept seeing Gomez' grave, vivid face; I kept seeing that Heinkel pilot throw up his hands to the back of his neck as bullets—my bullets—tore him to pieces. I rubbed the scalp wound I had; what a difference a quarter of an inch would have made right there! I kept thinking of that wild strafing I'd given the Insurgent lines. Killer! That was me—killer.

I was glad they put me on the wounded list for a week. I didn't feel like fighting any more just then. The soldier-of-fortune idea was tarnished with blood, and I didn't like the reality I saw.

At the end of the week I went to the hospital to see Tex. He was in bad shape and worried me.

"Do you know what that so-and-so did?" he groaned. "He took a piece of gauze, soaked it in iodine, and passed it through the bullet hole and drew it back and forth like a shoe-black polishing your shoes. Then he sewed it up."

"Sewed it up?" I repeated. "Sewed up both holes? How does the wound drain?"

"It don't. Look."

His leg was as big as an elephant's and about as black. While I was there the medico came in and looked at the leg.

"Ah, Señor Jeem, she not so good today, eh?"

Tex's answer was unprintable.

"I theenk, Señor Jeem, we take her off—about here, eh?" The medico drew his forefinger across Tex's leg just above the knee.

Tex gave a yell. "O.D., get me some pants and some crutches! These butchers ain't going to whittle on me."

I saw him on the train to Barcelona, whence he went to the American Hospital in Neuilly, where they saved his leg. But he, too, was gone for good, Tex and his phantom white mouse José. And Gomez was dead. Out of the four who had sailed on the Normandie, two were left. This might be a second-class war, but you died just as thoroughly as if it were a first-class one.

There were other incidents during that week besides Gomez' funeral. One of the young Spaniards, Luis Muñoz, shot down an Insurgent plane and the Franco pilot bailed out. Muñoz shot up the poor devil's parachute. The man landed fast and quite dead. In the World War the machine-gunning of an observer dropping by chute was not considered cricket, although I understand such target shooting is official orders in modern tactics. In any case, this shooting of a helpless man was seen from the Insurgent lines. Towards the end of the week one of our chaps made a forced landing behind Franco's lines.

The next day a Heinkel four-bomber slid over the field at Huete and tumbled out a box hanging from a chute. The box landed near the aerodrome. It was opened, and there was our pilot, his arms and legs torn off, his head twisted from his body. Behind a hangar I was good and sick.

One by one these episodes smashed the stupid pictures of my mind. And while I was still bewildered, Noka disappeared! Vanished between two days. One evening she was there, her eyes brimming with laughter; the next she was gone.

Not of her own volition, I knew, because we had an engagement that was important. I made inquiries at her hotel. I asked her friends. Finally I asked government officials. No one knew anything.

One louse among the officials put his tongue against the roof of his mouth and made it vibrate like the stutter of a machine gun. That was all.

I never saw her again, and it was small consolation then to hope and wish she had escaped safely to the frontier.

I was glad then to go back to patrol duty. While I was flying I could avoid unpleasant thoughts.

Shortly after I went back to duty, Loyalist infantry made a raid and brought in some prisoners. These babbled about the red devil with horns who had flown so quietly among them and blasted his way out with bullets. The devil was I, of course, because bloody goggles pushed up do look like horns. Out of this talk the squadron leader got an idea. I poured mercurochrome on some bandages and flew without a helmet. With me leading, we took off for a ground strafe, half the squadron on the carpet with me, the other half on the ceiling to protect us upstairs.

I mention this only because the Heinkels were looking for revenge and hopped down on us, to be squeezed between two halves of our squadron. And this enabled me to shoot down my sixth plane. In the scramble of fifty Heinkels and Fiats, the crate with the black wingtips slid in behind me. I made a stalled Immelmann and came down on him. I don't think I fired eight shots. It was as simple as that.

Doubtless many of you are asking yourselves why it seemed so easy to knock off the Insurgent pilots, particularly for the Americans. I'm not certain I can answer the point properly, but I'll try. In the first place, our snub-nosed P planes were swifter, more maneuverable, so they gave us a decided advantage. Secondly, the Americans seemed to think—how shall I put it?—think more swiftly on their feet. They had more initiative; they saw openings and seized them before the opponent realized what was up. In my case and Tiny's, we had had World War experience on Camels, and 'Napolis had United States Navy training in combat tactics.

I know that on this particular day we shot down thirteen Heinkels and Fiats as against losing only two of our young Spanish lads, with several others slightly wounded. Despite their lack of actual combat experience, the Spanish lads more than held their own, due to the superior speed of the ships.

And then again, we may have been having a great run of luck. We were not always so fortunate. . . .

FRANCO'S AIR HERO

by Comandante Joaquin Garcia-Morato y Castaño, Spanish Nationalist Air Force, translated by Brigadier General Stanley M. Ulanoff

Remembering incidents of the war, for a pilot who had taken part in quite a number of combats, is a task loaded with interest, because in delving again into these actions, we relive intensely those unforgettable exciting moments.

When the Nationalist troops advanced toward Badajoz, the large number of fighter planes gathered by the Reds in the aerodromes of Getafé and Los Alcázares hampered the advance. It was at that time, for a short period, that the enemy had mastery of the air. Under such conditions, my squadron of "Fiats" arrived at the Talavera front. And practically on top of that city we came face to face with the enemy for the first time, with his undeniable superiority in fighter planes. The Reds didn't want to give up their mastery of the air; but we were bent on attaining it. For the first time, the enemy found himself with opponents that were ready to give battle, and to defeat him. A substantial number of Red fighter planes fell mortally wounded, and after this the battle lasted only some few seconds. The enemy forces retreated, and the Nationalist Air Forces once again had control of the air. In the days that followed, the Nationalist infantry advanced free from attack by enemy aircraft. We knew that the Reds had asked France for more modern and powerful matériel. And their petition was immediately answered. On finding ourselves in combat, a short time later, and still shooting down Red planes without losing any of our own, we saw, checking the identification plates on the doomed enemy planes, that the date they left the factory was only ten days from the day they were shot down. From this time until the arrival of the Nationalist troops at the gates of Madrid, air superiority belonged to us. Red aircraft were in the air only when ours weren't flying. Our main activity, during this period of the war, was limited to the ground support, attacking retreating enemy troops, machine-gunning them. The day the Nationalists entered Illescas, I was entrusted with the protection of a column. Suddenly, far below me, I discovered a squadron of Red bombers, escorted by three fighters. They were in an excellent position to strike a mortal blow against our infantry. Taking account of their imminent danger, I immediately attacked the lead bomber. It was a difficult target; but in spite of it. I had enough good luck to hit the pilot in my first burst. His plane burst into flame, falling behind our lines. On pulling out of the dive I attacked the second bomber and this one also fell in flames. The rest of the squadron turned tail and retreated at full speed, without dropping their bombs. Rapidly, I gained altitude to face the enemy fighters; but it wasn't necessary. They followed the lead of the bombers.

On this day I witnessed one of the most stirring actions that I can recall. The Nationalist cavalry, quartered in the Mocejón sector, were trying to close an enveloping maneuver that would enable them to capture a concentration of militiamen who were in the town. A large number of these militiamen had begun a retreat towards Madrid. Sizing up the situation, I decided to help our cavalry. Diving, I machine-gunned those that were fleeing, again and again, noting that each time I passed over them, they threw themselves on the ground, continuing their flight in the interval that I had to gain height and begin my new dive. The cavalry, who also noted the result of my tactics, began a pincer movement. Attacking, they closed the circle, not only around the fugitive militiamen, but also the town. More than 200 prisoners were taken in this military action, that to me was most moving.

The Government of Valencia was not disposed to ceding the control of the air without a fight. At their request, the Russians sent a new type of fighter plane that we knew by the nickname of "Ratas" and others by the name of "Chatos." These were manned by experienced, aggressive Russian pilots. The first encounter we had with them, or better said, the first time we were aware of their presence on the Madrid Front, was by the loss of one of our planes that had run into one of their squadrons and was shot down in flames. As soon as we learned of the death of our comrade we made up our minds to avenge him. My squadron of new Fiats, in combat formation, took off in the direction of Madrid. We flew over the lines, passing into enemy territory. Suddenly we saw the silhouettes of thirteen of the new enemy fighters, in

the distance, flying to meet us. The battle began over the roof tops of Madrid giving the inhabitants an unforgettable spectacle. Without preoccupying ourselves whether or not to gain altitude, we launched ourselves against the enemy fighters. Together we dived, then climbed at blackout velocities, trying all the time to avoid the bullet that might shoot us down. The first victim was one of our planes, downed by a Red fighter. The pilot bailed out and we saw his parachute open. The Red machine gunners on the ground opened fire on him and I don't think he got down alive.

We continued the battle, at that moment pledging ourselves to vengeance and victory. For some time we despaired of gaining the victory; but we continued with the fervent wish to avenge our fallen comrades. Suddenly my bullets struck a Red fighter that exploded in the air only a few meters from me. A little below, another enemy aircraft fell in flames; its pilot bailed out by parachute, finding death from the fire of his own machine gunners on the ground, who mistook him for a Nationalist flyer, the same as our comrade. In the minutes that followed four enemy fighter planes fell mortally wounded, plummeting toward the earth. And those that were left decided on a prudent retreat. We remained sole masters of the sky over Madrid; we flew there for awhile and returned to our base. That defeat, however, was not enough for the Red fighters. Hence, several days later we met again in battle over the houses of Madrid. But this time we were thoroughly familiar with the enemy's new fighter; we changed our tactics and were able to down six Red fighter planes in a few minutes, without loss of a single one of ours.

The Reds, knowing that we were otherwise engaged in battle, tried to bomb our infantry who were at the edge of the city. I was battling two Red fighters when I saw the enemy bomber squadron approaching our ground forces. Knowing their intentions, I immediately broke off the combat and headed for the bombers with a vengeance to prevent the attack on our infantry. Realizing what I had in mind, the bombers broke their formation and tried to escape; one, however, moved too slowly and my bullets caught up with one of his motors. I barely had time to see him start his spin, because four of the Red fighters jumped me and I had to struggle desperately to save myself. When we finally left the aerial battlefield, I looked and saw that the bomber had plummeted to the ground. And when we arrived at our base I was able to add two more notches to my leather belt—two more Red planes that had been knocked down by the bullets from my machine guns.

PART THREE

GLOBAL WAR—
WORLD WAR II, EUROPE

Yanks in the RAF

EAGLE SQUADRON

**by an Unidentified Pilot Officer,
RAF**

October, 1940

The Eagle Squadron is a squadron composed of pilots from the United States who have come to this country to help in the Battle of Britain. The story following is by a young pilot officer who hails from California. He took part with a British squadron in the great air battle on September 15th when the German Air Force lost 185 aircraft. He has had many adventures since he left his peaceful sunny California.

I expect it must seem a long hop from guiding visitors round the movie studios in Culver City to fighting in an eight-gun Spitfire over London. But that's just how it happened to me, and all within a little more than a year, with some exciting adventures in between.

It was only my second air fight when I helped rout Goering's mass attack on September 15th. And I had the good luck to shoot down my first raider.

During the battle, the air over Surrey, Kent, and Sussex, was full of bombers and fighters. At 20,000 feet I met a formation of Me-110s. I gave one a burst and saw him giving out smoke. But I lost him in the cloud before I could press home my attack.

Then below me I saw a big Dornier 215 bomber trying to seek the safety of some clouds. I followed it down and gave it a long squirt. Its left motor stopped and its right aileron came to bits. Smoke was pouring from it as the bomber disappeared in a cloud. I followed. Suddenly the clouds broke and on the ground I saw a number of crashed aircraft. It was an amazing sight. They had all crashed within a radius of about twenty miles from our fighter station. My Dornier was there too. I was quite sure I could see it. A little later I learned that the Intelligence Officer's report on the damage to the crashed Dornier agreed with my own, so I knew I had claimed my first definite German victim.

That was a great day for England. I thought this little island was going to sink under the weight of crashed enemy planes on that day. And was I proud to be in the battle! It was the fulfilment of a year's ambition.

But let me go back and tell you the story of this momentous year.

My home is in Hollywood. It was in the wonderful Californian climate that I was born, educated, and learnt to fly. I don't suppose there are more than seven days in a year when you can't take the air in California. I learnt to fly at the Mine Fields, Los Angeles. I was always pretty keen on flying and whenever there were no classes at school I hurried out to the airfield to put in all the time I could learning about aircraft and their vices. My instructors were mostly army people. I went through the various graduations and by July

The Messerschmitt Me-109 got its baptism of fire in the Spanish Civil War, and later became the Luftwaffe's work-horse in WW II. Adolf Galland's Condor Legion gave the Allies an early taste of the Nazi air-war in the skies over Spain. (Monogram)

last year I was a fully qualified charter pilot.

For nearly two months last year I flew parties up to the High Sierras in California on hunting and fishing expeditions. It was pretty tricky flying, because you get some fierce downdrafts and you can't be too careful.

I had a civilian job of course in the M.G.M. studios at Culver City; I finally acted as guide for visitors to the studios. I used to meet all the film stars and found them nice ordinary folk. But my studio jobs didn't keep me from flying and in the winter of 1939 I took a course in aerodynamics at evening school.

Then a number of us met Colonel Sweeney, whose name you will know from his association with the Escadrille Lafayette in the last war. With him we decided it would be a grand idea to form a flight and go out and fly for Finland. But, I guess, that war was over before we could get going.

In May of this year we decided to form a squadron of all American flyers, another Escadrille Lafayette. The adventure was off.

Several of us went by train from Los Angeles, through the States to Canada. Final-

ly we finished up at Halifax, Nova Scotia, where we got split up. I joined a large French motor vessel, which was part of a big convoy sailing for France. My boat could do about sixteen knots but she had to travel at only six. In front of us was a boat with 400 mules on board. The stench from the mules was something awful and so was the weather. We had pursuit planes, bombers, and munitions of all sorts on board, cargo worth in all about seven and a half million dollars. We rolled and pitched all the way across the Atlantic and were mighty thankful after seventeen days to tie up at St. Nazaire.

All our plans went haywire at St. Nazaire. I had no passport and had lost my birth certificate. Naturally the French treated me with suspicion.

Incidentally, there's a story about that birth certificate. In all my journeys up and down France, I stuck to an old shirt just in case I wanted a spare one any time. Only last week I took out that shirt and from it dropped my birth certificate.

The next thing was to get to Paris and meet

the rest of the boys. I took three and a half days to reach the capital and there I met my friends who had disembarked at Bordeaux. Just outside Paris while in the train I had my first experience of being bombed. The scream of the bombs dropping on the suburban houses from about 20,000 feet was awful.

We made our way to the French Air Ministry, saw high officials there, and were given our physical examination. The French didn't hurry, and we were in and out of the Ministry for three days. They kept telling us that all would be well and that we would be flying any day soon. Actually we spent a whole month in Paris, doing nothing, for nothing could be done for us.

Then suddenly one day we realised that Paris was going to be evacuated. As the Air Ministry had gone, we made up our minds to get going as well—to Tours. A pall of smoke—which might have been a smoke-screen—covered the city and you couldn't see more than a block away. There must have been 10,000 people at one station, all patiently waiting for trains to take them to safety—staunch solemn queues all around the station—men, women, and children.

It took us a day and a half to reach Tours and it was an awful journey. Sometimes we had to ride between the cars to get a breath of fresh air. But there was no panic among the refugees, just fear and depression. We didn't lose a bit of luggage on this journey. We spent a week at Tours and were bombed by Heinkels and Dorniers every day. There was a pretty big party of us by now, most of them belonging to the French Air Force. We left Tours by bus for Chinon, about an hour's ride away. We got away just in time, for the Nazis bombed and machined-gunned the main bridge out of Tours just as it was packed with refugees. The bridge was completely destroyed and very many refugees were killed.

Things weren't looking at all good. We were tired and food was getting scarce. We set out for Arcay about four hundred of us of all ranks, and from there walked another fifteen miles to Air Vault. Our boots were completely worn out, and we had no food and no water. Dog-tired, we lay down in some fields at Air Vault, but not for long. At nearly midnight we were ordered by an elderly French officer to get going once again, this time to Bordeaux. It took us three and a half days in a packed train to reach Bordeaux, and when we got there we found that the French Air Ministry could do nothing for us. We Americans were pretty sore by this time and thought that the best thing we could do would be to take some aircraft and fly to England. But that little plan didn't come off and we began our travels again determined to get out of the country.

Our little bunch went by bus to Bayonne. The British consul had left. We had no money and were starving. Eventually we made our way to St. Jean-de-Luz and were lucky enough to get the American consul. He was a fine guy and treated us pretty handsomely. But he told us the situation was pretty bad and advised us to quit. There was a crowd pouring into St. Jean-de-Luz and the quayside was crowded with refugees. They came any old way they could, in cars, on motorcycles and cycles. The cycles they did not bother to park, but simply threw them in the water.

We boarded a British ship, *Baron-Nairn*, a little old-timer of seven knots. We were a mixed crowd on board. Our number included seven hundred Polish refugees. A tragedy occurred as we were going on board. We had only one suitcase between our little bunch. The handle came off and into the water she went with all our belongings. All the extras I had then were a pair of shorts and a couple of shirts. We sailed across the Bay of Biscay. It was a three-day journey and all we had to eat was a dog biscuit—even the one dog on board wouldn't eat them. The boat had no cargo and rolled pretty badly. But the crew were rather kind and did all they could for us.

Eventually we made Plymouth, although I thought at one time we were bound for South Africa judging by the ship's course.

I guess we weren't too popular at Plymouth. We had no papers and we were evacuated straight away to London. We were put in an ice-skating rink and had to stay there for three days. We weren't allowed out at all. We rang up the Air Ministry, who sent round an officer to see us. He was very kind but didn't hold out much hope that the Air Force could use us at the moment.

We talked it over between us and made up our minds to return to America. We rang the Embassy who sent round a representative to see us. He got our particulars, checked them over with Washington, fixed us up with passages to America and lent us £15 for food and clothing. It looked as if the adventure was over.

Then, I forget how, we met a very fine English lady, who after hearing our story told us she was sure that a friend of hers, a well-known member of Parliament, could do something for us. We met him next day in the Houses of Parliament and he sent us to the Air Ministry. We were given our physical examination at once. All passed, and so we were in the Volunteer Reserve of the Royal Air Force for the duration of the war.

We felt pretty good when we went to the American Embassy. The officials there were mad with us at first for upsetting all the arrangements, but we soon smoothed that out. Things moved rapidly. Three of us, all in RAF uniforms, were sent north to an Officers' Training Unit. I had not flown for two months, but after twenty minutes in an advanced trainer I was put into a Spitfire.

After twenty hours' flying in Spitfires I was attached to a station in the south, just in time for the opening of the big Blitz. But I had several weeks' training before I became operational, that is, fit to fight. And I guess my first fight was lucky.

I was patrolling high over an English port on the South Coast when I saw some Me-110s. I went into them and hit the first guy with my first burst. He was quickly lost in a cloud. Then another Me-110 shot ahead of me. I gave him a long burst and saw my stuff entering his fuselage. He climbed steeply then, and then as steeply dived in a sort of

spin. I couldn't turn on oxygen and suddenly had what they call over here a blackout. I went into a sort of dream from which I awakened when I was only 1000 feet from the ground. I think I heard myself say "you'd better come to, you're in trouble." Anyway, I landed safely with two probables in my "bag."

And now, we Americans are a separate squadron. We wear RAF uniforms with the American Eagle on the shoulder. It's a grand idea this Eagle squadron of all American flyers. We must try and make a name for ourselves, just like the famous Escadrille Lafayette. After all, we're all on the same side and all fighting in the same cause. The fellows in the squadron come from various parts of America—New York, Idaho, Minnesota, Oklahoma, Illinois, and California. We're all flyers and very keen. We have got a lot to learn yet, of course, and that is why I'm so glad to have been with an English fighter squadron, first. These English pilots certainly know their fighting tactics. My old squadron has brought down at least one hundred German aircraft. The German airmen may be pretty good formation flyers, but the British pilot has got the initiative in battle. He thinks quickly and gets results. He knows how to look after himself.

And are we lucky with our fighter planes? I guess the Spitfire is the finest fighter aircraft in the world. It's rugged and has no vices. I'd certainly rather fight with than against one.

We like England and its people who are cheerful and very easy to get on with. I miss the Californian weather, of course, and if I could only have the English people and the Californian weather combined, everything would be grand. Everyone in the Royal Air Force is most kind to us all. They somehow seem to understand us and go out of their way to be helpful.

It's grand to say hello to everyone on behalf of the Eagle squadron. You can be sure we will do our very best, because we're in this business to try and do a little job of work for England.

The Supermarine Vb Spitfire, war-wagon of the RAF. Outclassed by the Luftwaffe's F.W.-190, the more powerful Spitfire IX helped to somewhat even the balance. (USAF)

The Few to Whom So Many Owe So Much

WING LEADER

by Group Captain J.E. "Johnnie" Johnson, RAF

. . . And so the Royal Air Force came back to France for the first time since our abrupt departure in 1940—almost four years to the day.

After a leisurely snack I walked to the edge of the orchard, which was flanked by a narrow secondary road. Here a continuous nose-to-tail procession of trucks, tanks, armored vehicles and the like made a slow progress to the front lines after disgorging from the various ships on the coast, little more than one mile from the airfield. For some time I watched this unending stream of vehicles, and the incalculable value of our complete air superiority was clearly demonstrated to me. Had a similar scene been enacted in the enemy's territory, then the column would have been gutted immediately by our fighter-bombers which ranged to and fro over Normandy seeking such a target. In fact, we could always tell which side of the lines we were on by noting the remarkable contrast in the activity and spacing of road traffic.

We took to the air again after lunch, and although our patrol was again uneventful we felt reasonably satisfied with the day's work. We had landed and refuelled in France, which made an important milestone in our progress. Even if the assault on the Normandy coast had failed to flush the Luftwaffe, perhaps the ensuing battle for France, which was yet to come, would produce some reaction.

Soon we took off from Ford for the last time. Our ground crews and equipment had arrived safely in Normandy, had established themselves at St. Croix and were ready to operate the wing. We stuffed our meager belongings, consisting of a spare shirt, a change of underclothes and shaving-tackle, into various odd corners of our Spitfires, thanked the ground crews who had serviced our Spitfires at Ford, and thirty minutes later were on the strip at St. Croix. I was very pleased to join forces once more with Varley and my Labrador, Sally, who had also arrived on the scene. Varley had sited my caravan alongside the clutch of operations vehicles in the orchard, and he greeted me with a cup of his special brew of tea.

I did not fly again on this day, but spent my time on the ground checking the small group of vehicles which formed the nerve center of the wing. The two army liaison officers were hard at work marking up the various friendly and enemy ground positions on the large-scale maps which hung on the sides of our briefing tent. Our spies were busy with the many reports and summaries of enemy activity, and I was delighted to hear that the expected Luftwaffe reinforcements had arrived and were now based on various airfields to the south and southeast. Intelligence estimated that more than 300 enemy fighters had been flown in to oppose us, and *Jagdkorps 2* could muster about 1000 aircraft of all types. I gave instructions for the various Luftwaffe dispositions to be carefully plotted on an appropriate map, for we would pay them a social call at the very first opportunity. The signals personnel had established good communications with 83 Group, which would control our activities in the air. It was apparent to me that the many tactical moves we had rehearsed continually in England had paid a handsome dividend. The machinery of the control organization was working smoothly and efficiently. We were the very first wing to be based in Normandy: as such we possessed a far greater radius of action over France than those Spitfires still operating from southern England. We should be able to strike deep into enemy territory, and if the enemy squadrons did not take to the air we should seek them out in their lairs and write them off on the ground. Highly satisfied, I jumped into my jeep to inspect the airfield. After making certain that the three squadrons were well prepared for a spell of intensive flying. I returned to my caravan, where Varley and I unpacked my personal belongings.

Varley had already spent two or three nights in Normandy and repeatedly told me that the customary evening barrage was quite unpleasant. According to him, a few enemy reconnaissance and bomber aircraft put in an appearance immediately it was dark and every gun on the beachhead opened up at the intruders. Varley suggested that perhaps the safest place for my bed would be in a narrow slit trench, but I am afraid that I paid little heed to his advice and was determined to sleep in the caravan—a decision I was to regret before many hours had elapsed.

I turned in quite early, as it had been a strenuous day and I wanted the benefit of a good sleep for the activities of the morrow. I was rudely awakened by the loud staccato chatter of a Bofors gun situated some twenty

J. E. "Johnnie" Johnson led the RAF with a score of 38 German planes destroyed. (Bill Hess)

yards from my caravan. Faintly I could hear the typical unsynchronized drone of a few enemy aircraft, and so great was the clamor of our barrage that sleep was quite impossible. I might as well get dressed and see what it was all about. To the southeast the sky was bright from some large fires, but the enemy pilots were directing their attentions against the mass of shipping lying offshore. The naval gunners opened up with everything they possessed, and orange tracer ripped across the sky in fantastic crisscross patterns. Pieces of hot shrapnel fell upon my caravan, and the thousands of anti-aircraft guns concentrated in the relatively small area made the general din almost unbearable. Searchlights swept the sky but were hampered by the low cloud base, and occasionally the earth reverberated to the impact of bombs. Deciding that the tin roof of my caravan offered little protection against this sort of thing, I went in search of Varley, so that together we could move my bed to a more secure position; but the wise fellow had long since gone to earth, and the Labrador with him.

I dragged my sleeping bag from the bed and struggled into it underneath the rear axle of the caravan. This would at least afford me some protection from the shrapnel. But sleep was quite out of the question, as the Luftwaffe sent over sporadic raids until the small hours and, to my regret, our gunners did not appear to suffer from any lack of ammunition! The dawn found me cold and miserable—I crept out of my damp sleeping bag and walked across the soaking grass to the mess tent for a hot drink. I wondered how my three squadron commanders, Browne, Russel and McLeod, had fared during the firework display, and went in search of them. I had some difficulty in tracking them down, but eventually I found them, warm and snug, in a stoutly constructed underground dugout which had been built in the orchard by the Germans. I watched them for a few seconds as they lay in a deep slumber and resolved that the coming night would find me alongside.

Twelve of us were sitting at readiness in the cockpits of our Spitfires prepared for a quick scramble. I had decided to fly with Wally McLeod's squadron and he was leading the other flight of six aircraft. Should the enemy show any activity in the air, his movements would be picked up by 83 Group's radar and plotted on the operations table at the group control center. 'Kenway,' the code name for the center, would then telephone through to our operations caravan and order the readiness squadron into the air. The signal to take off would be a Very light fired from the operations caravan. Once we were airborne we should receive our instructions over the radio direct from Kenway. After half an hour in the cockpit, gloved and masked ready for an immediate takeoff, I was rather drowsy as a result of my lack of sleep, but my cramped uncomfortable position sufficed to keep me awake. Suddenly a red Very light soared into the air from the orchard. Switches on, my fingers pressed the starting button, and the Merlin roared into life. Then I was travelling down the narrow taxi-track and made the right-angled turn on the steel planked runway at too high a speed, for the starboard wing tilted down at a dangerous angle. A few

The RAF's Hawker IV Hurricane, hero of the Battle of Britain. Together with the Spitfire, this gallant little fighter, flown by "the few to whom so many owe so much," beat back the might of the Luftwaffe. (Airfix)

seconds later and the twelve of us were airborne in a ragged, straggling gaggle, but the boys were already picking up their battle formation.

"Greycap to Kenway. Airborne with twelve Spits. What's the form?"

"Kenway to Greycap. Bandits active five miles south of Caen at low level. Please investigate."

"Greycap to Kenway. Roger. Any definite height on bandits?"

"Kenway to Greycap. No, but they're below 5000 feet. Out."

There was scattered cloud between five and six thousand feet, and above the sun blazed from a clear sky. If Kenway's information was correct, they were probably a raiding party of fighter-bombers. I eased the Spitfires through a gap and flew immediately below the cloud base.

"Stay down sun, Wally, and keep as near to the cloud base as you can. I'll drop down a few hundred feet."

Greycap from blue three. Bandits at nine o'clock, 2000 feet below."

"Roger, blue three, I have them. They're heading towards us. Turning port."

The bandits were a mixed gaggle of Focke-Wulfs and Messerschmitts. About a dozen all told. Now they were immediately below me, heading towards Caen. They were not higher than 2000 feet, and the sun was behind us. We had all the makings of a perfect bounce.

"I'm going in, Wally!" I exclaimed. "Cover my section. Take any of the bastards who climb above me."

My section was streaking but still well out of range when the Huns saw us, probably because we were conspicuous against the background of white cumulus cloud. They broke round into our attack in an experienced manner and I realized they were led by a veteran.

"Get in, Wally. These brutes are staying to fight."

Now twenty-four fighter aircraft twisted and jockeyed for an advantageous position. My number two called up:

"Greycap! Keep turning. There's a 190 behind!"

I kept turning and saw the ugly snout of the 190 over my shoulder. But he couldn't draw a bead on me and soon he was driven off by a Spitfire. I made a mental note to buy my number two a drink back at St. Croix.

The enemy leader must have given the order to withdraw, for his aircraft dived towards the ground and set course for the south. Then I spotted four 190s flying in a wide, evenly spaced finger formation, but the starboard aircraft was lagging badly and, in this position, could not be covered by his colleagues.

"Red two. Cover my tail. I'm going to have a crack at the starboard 190."

"O.K., Greycap. You're clear. Nothing behind."

Flying a few feet above the bocage country, I narrowed the gap between my Spitfire and the 190. His three comrades were still well ahead of him and he was an easy target. I slid out to one side so that I would have a low line-astern shot and pulled slightly above him to avoid some high trees as I concentrated on firing. I hit him with the first burst on his engine cowling. More cannon shells ripped into his cockpit and the 190 plunged into the ground only a few feet below. We were over a strongly defended area, for as I pulled up into a steep climb we were engaged by a considerable amount of flak. Gaining altitude, I spiralled my Spitfire and caught a last glimpse of the remaining three 190s. Oblivious of the fate of their comrade, they continued to streak away at low level, and after making quite certain that they were not going to return, the two of us flew back to St. Croix in a wide abreast formation.

Back at our airfield I learnt that Wally had smacked down a 190 and that Don Walz had accounted for a third victim. It was a pity that the Huns had seen us launch the initial attack: if we had achieved complete surprise, we could have knocked down half a dozen. Still, three victories were better than none, and the engagement marked our first success from St.

The Focke-Wulf F.W.-190, appearing in action for the first time over France in early 1941, immediately demonstrated its superiority over the sluggish Spitfire. The 190 supplemented the Me-109 and held its lead over the RAF fighters through 1943. (USAF)

Croix. My own personal score now stood at twenty-eight.

Most unfortunately Walz, together with three other pilots, was shot down later that day. At the time we knew nothing of the circumstances, only the bare fact that a complete section of four aircraft had failed to return from a scramble. The four aircraft had taken off late in the evening and eventually located a force of Focke-Wulfs, which they attacked. In the fading light they were not aware that they had engaged a far superior force. The Germans, realizing their advantageous position, stayed to fight, and all four Spitfires were shot down. Walz's own aircraft was hit in the engine and the petrol gas exploded. He lost little time in baling out and landed safely in a field. After some adventures on the ground he was eventually assisted by the local peasants and returned with the tragic story. The incident was specially grievous for Dal Russel, whose young brother was one of the three pilots killed on this mission.

Once again the weather clamped down with low cloud and rain. Flying was quite out of the question, and we took the opportunity to make ourselves comfortable at St. Croix. Our dugout was warm and dry, and offered ample protection from the nightly barrage, which continued unabated in its intensity. The mayor of the local village came to see me and, with one of the French-Canadians acting as an interpreter, told me that the Germans had abandoned a number of sound cavalry horses in the locality. He had also "collected" some saddles and bridles, and suggested that we might care to take over two or three of the steeds for our recreation. One of my pilots, Johnny Irwin, had some knowledge of horseflesh, so together with the mayor and Varley we drove into St. Croix to inspect the animals. They were not exactly the type of immaculate charger one would see at a Trooping, but from my Yeomanry days I knew something of the subject and they appeared to be sound in wind and limb. Irwin confirmed my diagnosis. He and I rode back to the airfield in some style, whilst Varley drove the jeep. With these animals we enjoyed a lot of amusement and some hard exercise. On one occasion I astonished our senior army liaison officer, who belonged to a crack cavalry regiment, when I turned up at 83 Group for a conference on my steed. Wally adopted the pastime with some zeal and rode as he flew—flat out. He soon discovered that it is far easier to stay on a horse's back at a gallop than in a canter, and proceeded across the Normandy pastures either flat out or at a sedate walk.

Our mess was located in a large tent on one side of the orchard. We lived exclusively on the tinned compo rations and soon became bored with this monotonous but adequate diet. The Canadians deplored the absence of fresh meat, milk and fruit juices, and wanted good fresh bread instead of the hard biscuits. Each day a twin-engined Anson landed at St. Croix from Tangmere carrying mail, newspapers and urgently required small spares. I sat down in my caravan to write a note to Arthur King back at the "Unicorn" in Chichester. I told him of the dreariness of our food and asked him if he could arrange to deliver to Tangmere a supply of fresh vegetables together with bread and perhaps some meat. If he could get this stuff to Tangmere, the pilot of the Anson would do the rest and we should be very grateful.

The following day the Anson turned up with a crate of tomatoes, loaves of new bread, fresh succulent lobsters together with a reasonable supply of stout. Arthur maintained this private supply organization until we moved out of the narrow confines of the beachhead area and were able to purchase what we considered to be the necessities of life from local sources. One day a small party of press correspondents came to see the wing and I invited them to stay for lunch. They were somewhat reluctant to accept my offer as they had considered driving to Bayeux, where a reasonable meal could be obtained. However, they took keen interest in the proceedings when the lobsters and local wine were set before them. Naturally, they enquired as to our arrangements for the supply of such essentials and I told them of our base organization in Sussex which centered upon Arthur King.

Some few days later, the story was published in one of the national newspapers. It had an amusing sequel, since Arthur was visited by a representative of His Majesty's Custom and Excise, who solemnly told him

The Bristol Beaufighter gained fame as a night fighter, though it was first designed as a long-range escort fighter. It was flown with marked success by the RAF's top night-fighter team: Cunningham and Rawnsley. (USAF)

that an export license would be necessary if he persisted in this sort of thing!

Since its introduction to the Service in 1939, the versatile Spitfire had participated in many diverse roles and had fought over a variety of battlegrounds. It had appeared as a fighter, a fighter-bomber and as a tactical-reconnaissance and a photographic-reconnaissance aircraft. Now it fulfilled yet another role, perhaps not so vital as some of the tasks it had undertaken in the past, but to us of supreme importance. Back in England, some ingenious mind had modified the bomb racks slung under each wing so that a small barrel of beer could be carried instead of a 500-pound bomb. Daily, this modern version of the brewers' dray flew across the Channel and alighted at St. Croix. The beer suffered no ill effects from its unorthodox journey and was more than welcome in our mess.

Now we met and fought the Luftwaffe daily over the Normandy countryside. Whenever the weather permitted, they were active over the battle area, and we ranged far to the south so as to cut them off before they could attack our ground troops. They generally operated in small formations—rarely of more than a dozen aircraft. Consequently we resorted to sweeps and scrambles in squadron strength and the wing seldom flew as a complete formation. Thirty-six aircraft would be unwieldy and too conspicuous. I flew once or twice each day, leading the various squadrons in turn so that I did not lose my intimate association with all the pilots. The wing's total score of confirmed victories now stood at a pleasing figure and my own personal score at twenty-nine, all of which were single-engined fighters. There was a widespread speculation about how long it would be before I equalled the Sailor's* record of thirty-two victories, but I refused all discussion on the subject and would not countenance it in my own mind.

*"Sailor" Malon.

Should we continue to be successful in our fights with the Luftwaffe, and should they still operate at the same intensity, then I should have many opportunities for combats in the immediate future. My job was to lead the pilots into combat and to make sure that our team knocked down the maximum number of enemy aircraft. My personal score and any records attached to it were quite a secondary consideration. I did not intend to take undue risks and was quite content with our present rate of progress. Nevertheless, on a sweep on June 23rd I missed a golden opportunity of adding a further scalp or two to my belt.

It was an excellent flying day and I was at the spearhead of Wally's squadron. He was leading a section of two aircraft on my starboard side. High in the heavens the sun blazed down from a blue sky, but there was a great deal of fluffy white cumulus cloud at 6000 feet. This cloud was broken, and covered about half the countryside. Sometimes it continued unbroken for five or six miles, and then we would fly over a clear expanse where we could see the ground below. After crossing the enemy's flak belt, just south of the Caen–Bayeux road, I dropped the squadron to the base of the cloud, for I didn't want to be silhouetted from above against such a telltale white background.

We had just left Alençon on our port side when I saw a bunch of bandits at three o'clock. They were a formation of Focke-Wulfs and travelling in the same direction as ourselves. Like me, their leader had elected to fly just below the cloud base so that he could not be bounced from above. Under these circumstances I had only two methods of attack to choose from. I could take the squadron down to ground level and try to creep up on them from below with an attack into their vulnerable bellies, or I could climb through the cloud, fly on the same course as the enemy and strike from the sun when they appeared from the broken cloud cover. I adopted the high tactics, and with throttles wide open we climbed through the cloud and swung high into the sky. Now we were on the same course as the enemy formation and I could see that five or six miles ahead the cloud ceased in a ragged line. If my timing was right and if the Huns continued to fly a straight course, then we should reach the edge of the cloud at the same time.

Obligingly, the enemy leader held his original course, and twelve of fourteen Focke-Wulfs swept into view. Telling blue leader to attack the aircraft on the port side, I took the six Spitfires of red section down in a fast dive on the starboard Focke-Wulfs. As the range closed I glanced back over my shoulder, a thing I did automatically, to make certain no enemy aircraft were above us. The sky was empty, but as I focused my eyes back on the enemy I saw they had commenced a turn to starboard. Wally was on my starboard side some two hundred yards out and the 190s were now nearer to him than to me. He was well within range and hit a turning 190 with his very first cannon shells. Flames leapt from the cockpit; the aircraft fell over on to its back and dived vertically into the ground. Surprise was now gone, but the Germans were confused by our sudden arrival and remained turning and twisting in the air. There was yet another 190 ahead of me. He was swinging to port, but not too steeply. An easy shot. Just a little deflection. One glance back to make sure no one was on my tail. All clear. Eyes back on the 190. Thumb on the firing button. But already cannon shells are tearing into his engine cowling and wing root. Mortally damaged, the 190 joins some of its comrades in their funeral pyres below, but I have not fired a shot! The 190 was attacked from below, and a Spitfire, the killer, zooms into the air a hundred yards ahead of me. Another search, as I had not fired my guns. But the enemy aircraft had either fled or were burning in the fields. I gave the order to reform, and

The De Havilland Mosquito, with its light wood construction, was originally planned as a highly-maneuverable bomber. As a night fighter it supplanted the Bristol Beaufighter. (Monogram)

feeling more than a little frustrated, set course for St. Croix. I had spotted the bandits, had brought them to account, several had been destroyed, but I, the leader, had not fired a single shot. Back at St. Croix, I walked over to Wally's Spitfire. The armorers were already rearming it.

"That 190 of yours was a piece of good shooting, Wally. I suppose you clobbered the second?"

"Yes, I got a couple of them. Did you see the second one, chief?" This last with a disarming grin.

"I not only saw it, Wally, I was about to shoot the —— down," I replied.

"Hard luck, sir! I saw a Spitfire behind the 190, but I thought I'd better make sure of it. Of course, I didn't know it was you!"

"Anyhow, the great thing is for someone to hack them down. I've never seen better shooting. Just how many rounds did you fire?"

"I don't know yet. Let's see what the armorers say."

We learnt that Wally had only fired thirteen rounds from each of his two cannon. Each gun carried a total of 120 rounds, so that Wally had use about one-tenth of his ammunition. It was a remarkable display of both flying and shooting skill and, as far as I know, the performance was never equalled.

Once more the Luftwaffe changed their tactics and we began to meet fairly large formations of enemy fighters. Sometimes they numbered as many as fifty aircraft, but their leaders could not control such unwieldy formations and we were quite content to operate in squadron strength. One of the enemy leaders was easily identified in the air as he invariably flew a long-nosed Focke-Wulf when leading his gaggle of Messerschmitts. From various pieces of information available to them, our spies deduced that the pilot was a fairly well-known veteran known by the un-Teutonic name of Matoni. We met him in the air on several occasions, but he was an elusive sort of character, skillful, dangerous and diffi-

cult to bring to combat unless the affair was of his own choosing.

The presence of Matoni was something of a challenge, and we would have welcomed a joust with him. Once airborne, we formed the habit of calling Kenway and asking whether there was any news of Matoni today. Some of my Canadians made rude remarks over the radio in the hope that the German listening service, which doubtless monitored our radio conversations, would pass our comments to the enemy pilot. But I was never successful in having a crack at him.

The story of Matoni and our vain quest for him came to the ears of the eager beavers of the press. They were ever alert for a personal human story of this type, and several of them can to see me. I gave them the facts as set down in this record and went to some pains to explain that the old-fashioned "duel to the death" epics of the First World War were just not possible under the conditions imposed by our type of team fighting. Despite my explanation of the affair, the story was suitably garnished and published in the popular press. It was front-page news, and its substance was that I had challenged Matoni to a personal combat over Normandy. This breach of faith on the part of certain war correspondents meant that I was subjected to a great deal of unmerciful chaffing by my comrades. It also caused me some personal unhappiness, for Paula wrote to say she thought I was taking quite enough risks without sticking my chin out any further.

The Matoni episode had an interesting sequel. The story found its way into the German newspapers and was brought to the attention of the enemy pilot. But by this time he had been shot down, wounded and lay in hospital. I heard from him shortly after the war was over, when he wrote from an address in the Ruhr and regretted that he had been unable to accept the "challenge." But perhaps it was not too late for him to pay his respects? In my reply I asked him to dine with us, but he never turned up.

BATTLE OF BRITAIN

by an Unidentified Sergeant Pilot, RAF

August, 1940

The story of a sergeant pilot of a Fighter Command Spitfire squadron who shot down five enemy aircraft in three air battles on one day. On the same day fifty raiders altogether were destroyed, and two days later the sergeant pilot brought down two more. He is a north countryman—Yorkshire born and bred. His father lives in Harrogate.

Saturday was certainly a grand day. It started as most days for fighter pilots start—with the dawn. We were up at a quarter past four. I felt in my bones that it was going to be a good day. We were in the air just after five o'clock. Shortly before half-past eight we were in the air again looking for enemy raiders approaching the South Coast from France. We saw three or four waves of Junkers 88s, protected by a bunch of Me-109s above them. We were flying at 15,000 feet, between the bombers and the fighters. The fighters did not have much chance to interfere with us before we attacked the bombers. I attacked one of the waves of bombers from behind and above. I selected the end bomber of the formation which numbered between fifteen and eighteen. I gave this Junkers a burst of fire lasting only two seconds, but it was enough. It broke away from the formation, dived down, and I saw it crash into the sea.

I then throttled back so that I would not overtake the whole formation. I was getting quite a lot of crossfire from the other bombers as it was, though none of it hit me. If I had broken away after shooting down the first bomber, I should have exposed myself to the full force of the enemy formation's crossfire, so I throttled back and stayed behind them. I didn't have time to select another bomber target, for almost immediately an Me-109 came diving after me. As I had throttled back he overshot me. He simply came along and presented me with a beautiful target. He pulled up about 150 yards in front of me, so I presssed the gun button for two seconds. He immediately began to smoke and dived away. I followed him this time and saw him go straight into the sea. When the sky was clear of German planes, we went home for breakfast. We had a nice "bag" in that combat before the other Germans escaped.

As a matter of fact, I didn't get any breakfast at all. I only had time for a hot drink before we were ordered to stand by again and by half-past eleven that morning we were patrolling the Southeast Coast. We were attacked by half a dozen Me-109s, and, of course, we broke up to deal with them individually. I had a dogfight with one, both of us trying to get into position to deliver an attack, but I outmaneuvered him. I got on his tail, and he made off for the French coast as hard as he could go. The fight started at 10,000 feet, and we raced across the Channel like mad. As were going like that, I saw one of our fellows shoot down another Me-109, so I said to myself: "I must keep the squadron's average up and get this one." I didn't fire at him until we were actually over the French coast. Then I let him have it—three nice bursts of fire lasting three seconds each, which, as you may imagine, is an awfully long time! I started that final burst at 8000 feet, and then he began to go down, and I followed until I saw him crash into a field in France. Then I went back home without seeing any enemy at all. I carefully examined my Spitfire when I landed, certain that I must have been hit somewhere. But, no, not a mark. It was very satisfactory.

Our third show began just before four

With a tally of 34 enemy planes, Marmaduke T. St. J. Pattle was second only to Johnson in the U.K. ace ranking. (Bill Hess)

Robert Stanford Tuck had an official kill record of 29 German aircraft during the Battle of Britain. The "immortal" Tuck survived two air collisions, crash landings, and dogfight defeats. (Bill Hess)

o'clock in the afternoon. We were flying towards the Thames estuary at 5000 feet, when we saw antiaircraft shells bursting in the sky to the northeast. We changed course, and began to climb for the place where we thought we should meet the enemy. We did. They were flying at 12,000 feet—twenty JU-88s in tight formation accompanied by about twenty Me-109s, above them. They were flying towards the London area and we could see the balloons shining in the sun. When we spotted the fighters we pulled up towards them. I got under one Me-109 and gave him two bursts. Smoke started to pour out of him, and he went down out of control. Suddenly, tracer bullets started whizzing past my machine. I turned sharply, and saw an Me-109 attacking one of our pilots. I turned on the attacker and gave him a quick burst. Immediately he began to slow down and the aircraft began to smoke. I pressed the gun button a second time, and he caught fire. I fired a third time, and the whole machine became enveloped in flames and pieces began to fly off. Finally, as it went down, more pieces came off, all burning. As it tumbled down towards the Thames estuary it was really a bunch of blazing fragments instead of a whole aircraft. It was an amazing sight. That was my fifth for the day, and the squadron's ninety-ninth! The squadron brought the score over the century the next day, as a matter of fact. The squadron has damaged a lot more, of course.

There is a lot of luck about air fighting—by which I mean it's a matter of luck whether you get into a good scrap or not. I was right through the Dunkirk show, and didn't get a thing. But recently I seem to have been lucky. These fights are over so quickly that unless you are there right at the beginning, you are liable not to see anything at all. None of the fights on Saturday lasted more than five minutes each.

Cross of Lorraine—
The Free French

"ALSACE" IN ACTION

by Commandant René Mouchotte,
Free French Air Force

March 17th, 1943

The incredible signal came yesterday evening: we are moving south to relieve and replace old 340 at Biggin Hill. We are beating all records: we began flying on February 1st and we go on operations on March 18th . . . . My boys are wild with delight. Martel and Farman, who came to England together after crossing Spain as far as Portugal on foot, simply cannot contain themselves. I have managed to get young Lafont, a friend since the first days in England. He was sick for a long time, then went to Libya, where he distinguished himself—brilliantly. Once he returned he never stopped trying to get back to me. He is always spoiling for a fight. Boudier and Bouguen, veterans from 340, are here too, one as a flight commander, the other for health reasons, but really, I think, for sentimental reasons, as he has been under me since he first went on operations. Also, veterans of the first 'Alsace' Squadron, among the best: Raoul Duval, Chevalier, Bruno Bourges, to mention no others. These young pilots, meticulously selected from British units, have at last come to 341, though there was an uphill fight to get them. The phone calls I've made over them! I even threatened to throw my hand in if I did not obtain satisfaction. I do not know how many officials I've given my two famous lists to, the golden list of the pilots I wanted and the black list of the ones I wouldn't have at any price, being ready, as I swore, either to let them take my place or to send them back to London. And what a result! Here I am at the head of a squadron I can boast about, with some chance of it being the most famous in all Fighter Command. Wait till they see us on the job. I mean to go very carefully for the first month, to give my whole mob a quiet initiation and perfect the new kind of formation I have invented. No breach of discipline in the air will be tolerated; no individual attack allowed without my order. We shall not try at first to shoot down the Boche but to learn our business, improve our form, make it perfect as that of a fine, well-oiled machine. We shall let the enemy come and sniff at us, merely showing him our strong teeth; they will keep him at a distance. The day of the offensive which is fast approaching will find us a young force, terribly armed with a science of warfare and discipline. We shall put our whole soul into this holy war of liberation and the octopus shall perish, even if it costs us our lives . . . .

April 18th

A month at Biggin Hill now. 341 Squadron has begun its sweeps over France at a faster rhythm. We have moved into the still-warm beds of 340, who have gone up to rest at Turnhouse. They certainly needed it, poor devils. The veterans were terribly worn, and deserve not only physical and mental rest but also health-giving peace of mind. They had a lot of success lately but they paid dearly for it, losing more pilots than they shot down Boches. Happily, a fortnight after being shot down, their C.O., Schloesing, sent news of himself from Switzerland; a fortnight later their next C.O. was shot down in his turn . . . .

Group Captain Malan and Wing Commander Deer got some of the Biggin Hill people together and asked me to explain the principles of my formation to them. They had a few criticisms to make, but I must admit that on the whole they seemed to like it for its maneuverability and its rational use of each unit, giving the maximum of security. The weak point, they say, is that I have to count on the blind discipline of each of my pilots for it to be successful . . . .

Today, which brings us up to twenty sweeps, I can affirm the complete triumph of my theories. Never, the wing commander is saying to anyone who cares to listen, has a squadron kept formation so well and shown so much flexibility in maneuver.

As far as operations go, we have resumed our flying over our poor France. The young members of my squadron who went off "to the war" with their hearts racing said, "So that was all," when they came back.

The sky seemed pretty empty for the first fortnight. We tried to set traps for the Boche to attract him to us and make him fight. The radio often announced a squadron of the enemy at one point but when we went after them they disappeared at once. We despaired of ever seeing them, and one day I said to General Valin, "We shall soon have to land on aerodromes in France and give the Ger-

mans a boot in the backside to make them get into their planes and fight." I was taken up on this imprudent remark. The very next day a shower of 200 Boche fell on a mere twenty-four of us. They tackled it like beginners. We took "evasive action." They dropped out of the sky on us like stones, miraculously passing through us while we went round like circus horses . . . for the most part, they hardly ever followed up their attacks. When the last of them had vanished and was undistinguishable from the sea, we regained formation and confirmed, with relief, that no one was missing.

The operations which followed taught us that the enemy's effective strength has tripled since last year and that he accepts battle only when he is sure of numerical and tactical superiority. Whereas we, unlike last year, rarely take off in numbers greater than twenty-four.

The operation immediately after that one was unfortunately less favorable to us. Fate would not have it that "Alsace" should register a victory in the first battle. In consequence of a mistake on Flying Control's part, we found ourselves in a whirlwind mass of Spitfires and F.W.-190s or Me-109s coming from above and below. All my pilots stayed prudently close to me but one and he got himself shot down before we could even try to help him. Poor Raoul Duval! Ardent, enthusiastic, he made us all share his good humor. Béraud, one of the best, did not come back either, victim of engine trouble. Powerless, we watched him leave us quietly, long after the battle, heading his plane for the south. He vanished from our eyes, soon lost against the carpet of fields on which he meant to land if some overcurious Boche did not put an end to his schemes. A mysterious disappearance, which the future may perhaps explain. . . .Duval was engaged to be married and lived in peacetime in the same Le Havre region over which he was shot down in flames. Béraud was married and not a little proud of a delightful little girl of four, whose photograph he loved to display.

These two first losses of the squadron, cruel

and unjust as they are, far from discouraging us, have stimulated us all the more.

Operations resumed tomorrow. Nothing to report. The Boche gets to hell out of it. Impossible to engage him when he has the advantage of either altitude or numbers.

May 15th

To retrace this last week's events and describe them in all their detail with the color, the reality, that made them so "exciting" for us all would take time I haven't got and moreover would need literary talents I am far from possessing.

So I will sketch them quickly, mentioning that as the fine weather continued we went on making sweeps on an average of one of two a day. Furthermore, those who order them and give them to us to do seem to be getting bolder and bolder. Never have we flown so far with so little petrol; the prospect of prolonged aerial combat leaves us with the further prospect of a dip in the North Sea. . . . One day we went to Antwerp, escorting some American bombers; the day after, to Courtrai; then to Méaulte, near Albert; yesterday, from Cornwall, we went on a visit to Brittany, over the pretty town of Morlaix. How much water, water, there is to cross!

Thanks to the generosity of our godmother, Mme. Ida Rubinstein, I organized an enormous ball on the occasion of our squadron's baptism. It took up a lot of my time, especially on account of wartime difficulties in getting gin, whisky, etc., and providing a suitable buffet to satisfy 350 people's hunger and thirst. Its scene was the ballroom of one of the finest London hotels and I proposed to invite some celebrated people—the Air Minister, his wife and his daughter Catherine, the head of Fighter Command, the Air Marshal commanding 2 Group, General de Gaulle, etc. Other invitations were sent to his personal staff-officials, General Valin, General d'Astier de la Vigerie, General Bouscat (Giraud's representative), a dozen officers from the diplomatic mission,

nearly all the officers from General and Air Headquarters, some of the personalities from the Comité National Francais, and the rest I forget. Before the ball, the announcement made a tremendous stir, for London no longer sees balls of such a scale and in such style. But it was exactly what I needed to launch the "Alsace" Squadron in London society . . . (victories being conspicuous by their absence!). I dreaded to add up all the figures circulating in my head, I was so afraid of being thunderstruck by the terrifying total. Poor dear godmother!

The Biggin Hill station, where we are, has the highest total of enemy aircraft destroyed by squadrons from its aerodrome. There is competition between the Fighter Command stations, and Biggin Hill was winning with 995. It had long been anticipated that the day when Biggin Hill got its 1000th Boche would see some choice parties and celebrations. A sweepstake had been on the go for over a month. Whoever so desired could buy a ticket which might correspond, after the draw, to the name of some pilot on the station. The ticket bearing the name of the pilot who shot down the 1000th plane would win a very large sum of money. It was also understood that the pilot himself would get £ 300, a good round sum, enough to make those least greedy for gain think twice. . . .

On the 10th, a pilot of 611 Squadron, which flies with us, shot down the 996th Boche. People began to get excited. On May 14th we were over Belgium—Courtrai—and we were engaged by F.W.-190s. I attacked two of them, but being unable to get nearer to them than 350 meters, in a vertical dive, in spite of the terrifying speed of 540 m.p.h., I thought it better to save my ammunition and return to my squadron. During this time, Martel, after another engagement, suddenly found himself on his own and climbed back like lightning towards what he thought were three Spitfires until he saw the black crosses under them. He opened fire and saw one of them explode and disintegrate in the air. The two others thought it best to make off . . . . Well done,

Christian! The squadron's first victory, which brought Biggin Hill's total to 997 . . . . Pilot society was getting noisily excited.

Our party was this evening, May 15th. No sweep in the morning. At two o'clock we were hoping that nothing would disturb us and prevent us from bathing, scenting ourselves and getting ready.

No luck! Take-off at four o'clock for a small and apparently inoffensive operation . . . . We all got ready with a bad grace. We took off. First, we had to fly at sea level until the French coast was in sight, then do a breathtaking climb, so uncomfortable that your feet were almost in the air. You had the feeling that if the engine stopped you would fall, tail first. The radio anounced the Boche, lots of Boche. We checked the sight contacts and made sure instinctvely that the button was in the firing position . . . . Le Havre slid past to port, here was Trouville, 22,000 feet below. And, all at once, battle. Shouts over the radio, the other squadron was attacking. I noticed one parachute already. I gave the order to turn, intending to help them by getting the sun behind me and thus drop more easily on the offered prey.

Hardly had I begun to turn to starboard when a nice little job slid under my starboard wing. I turned on my back without even trying to identify it. I went at terrific speed, giving the plane all it had. As I dived after my National Socialist, for I could see his black crosses shining now, I gave rapid orders over the radio so that my faithful troops would cover my attack. The other plane went on diving vertically. "Too bad, I'm having a go." Yesterday's experience had been too mortifying . . . . I got the nose gently into position and opened up. The great distance between us gave me little hope. But I was somewhat startled by what I saw: there was a violent explosion in the fuselage of the Focke-Wulf, followed by a huge flame. The plane rose in the air, then burst into bits, seeming to disintegrate in the air. It is a miracle I got through without damage. The return to the aerodrome would have made all the gossiping *concierges* of Paris pale with envy. Never was the radio so loud with useless chatter. We were all exultant, for Squadron Leader Charles, of 611 Squadron, had shot two of them down, thus bringing to 1000 the total of planes shot down by Biggin Hill. After we landed there was a great problem as to which of us, Charles or I, had got the third Boche . . . . I immediately said I had seen the parachute of Charles's first victim, about two or three minutes before I shot mine down. Charles had shot his down consecutively, one after the other. I remembered having said, immediately after firing, "Hello, boys, I've got one too!" The Operations Room then confirmed that mine was the third.

But the wonderful coincidence in all this was that our party was this very night. What a gift for the baptism of our squadron! It was a magnificent ball, the kind of thing we hardly ever see nowadays. Lots of top brass, generals, etc., and vast numbers of pretty women. The open windows at the beginning of the evening overlooked the park and the mild temperature of the end of a splendid spring day allowed elegant ladies to show off their toilette to the curious. In addition to a British orchestra (obtained by a miracle) I had a French accordion band. It was wildly successful. The cocktails also gave satisfaction. I, as was understood, had to do the honors, and my success of a few hours before, in addition to the fact that it was the celebrated "1000th" at Biggin Hill, meant that I had to shake twice as many hands; my sweet modesty was put to the test. The writer Joseph Kessel was there: he plans to spend a few days with us; Germaine Sablon would not give us the pleasure of hearing her. A famous producer, some well-known English film stars, politicians, Giraud's military mission, journalists, etc. . . . A French radio announcer told me he meant to speak of the "1000th" that same night on the radio, at 2 a.m. . . . In short, everyone seemed to be enjoying themselves and getting on well together.

One thing gave me great pleasure which

Pompéi told me: the Conseil de l'Ordre de la Libération has just admitted me as a Companion. I am terribly proud of getting this decoration, so sparingly awarded. This is for my family, who will read this in time to come, if I am no longer here: Pompéi added, "If they had been as severe two years ago as they are today, I certainly should not have received it. Let me tell you that when they had been through Commandant X's file they rejected him, but, my dear fellow, I had the pleasure of seeing unanimity over you."

May 16th

We are resuming our sweeps, no pity for our sleepless night. Rapid takeoff, landing an hour and a quarter later at the extreme west point of Cornwall. After lunch we took off to escort some bombers over Morlaix. Four and a half hours' flying after only three hours' sleep last night.

May 17th

Caen again. Last year I damaged an Me-109 at Caen; the day before yesterday the F.W.-190 was at Caen again. Today I shot down an Me-109 at Caen.

It was midday, 23,000 feet. There was the usual radio news of Boche all round. Lower down, at about 12,000 feet, the twelve Boston bombers, in two groups of six, were flying in close formation, crossing the coast in a dive directly at their target. Starboard and port, rising towards us, five or six squadrons of Spitfires were escorting them like sheepdogs. Then, with brutal suddenness, battle. . . . Some turns, and after passing above us, the Boche escaped without any chance of being pursued . . . .

A few minutes later, when I had succeeded in reforming my Spitfires, I spotted four suspicious planes astern. I took them for Spitfires at first, on account of their manner of flying being exactly like that of our forma-

tions. Nevertheless, I gave the order to attack and swung my plane. It was well and truly a group of Fritzes, protected, I noticed much later, by a much greater umbrella of their colleagues. An exciting battle began, during which I began by choosing my victim. But just as I was letting him have my first burst, unfortunately deflected to one side, my attention was caught by cries of "Hello, number one Red, hello, number one Red, I've a Messerschmitt on my tail." Turning my head to try and spot the poor unfortunate was enough for my prey to get away for good. But I had the luck to pick out my poor sick bird straight away. Still followed by my faithful number two, I turned over and dived above a queer succession of planes composed of two Spitfires turning desperately, pursued at equal distances by a Messerschmitt and two Focke-Wulfs. I went for the former while the other two, seeing me, turned over and vanished. The Boche, finding himself attacked in his turn, abandoned his pursuit and fled as best he could with me on his tail. I learned after I landed that the two F.W.s came up behind to try and help their leader, and but for my number two's presence of mind in facing them and making them scatter they would have set about me while I was so busy getting the Fritz in my sights . . . and would probably have shot me down.

I began by giving my fugitive a visiting card from about 250 meters, without seeing any other result than a sudden slackening of his speed; I was obliged to throttle back my engine quickly so as not to overrun him. He was getting so unnaturally large that I thought I was going to crash into him. The film gives an astonishing impression of it, so close was the distance at which it was taken. Unfortunately only one of my cannons was working, with the result that each time I fired my plane swung to starboard. Little accuracy. The ground was getting dangerously near, for we were in a nose-dive. I soon had to think about pulling out to avoid feeling the hardness of French soil. I relinquished my prey regretfully, trailing a thin thread of black smoke behind him. Following him with my eyes, I saw him crash in a ball of fire. The devil of a Fritz did not expect to finish the war so soon. To harden my heart, I thought of the wretched convoys of defenseless French peasants machine-gunned on our roads when they were fleeing the savages' bombing and unheroic advance. If, tonight, I say a more heartfelt prayer than usual, it is for all our unhappy fellow-countrymen who fall each day beneath their blows, and it is to implore Heaven to leave me enough life as a fighter pilot to avenge, to avenge over and over again, the whole martyred, starved generation of French youth which is longing to fight and all those, too, who suffer in France, chained like slaves . . . .

What awaited me on landing made me pay dearly for the feeling of pride which had momentarily taken possession of me. The news of this future success had reached Biggin Hill before our return. Thirty reporters, who had come on the occasion of the 1000th plane, were waiting for me, bold and well-armed . . . . Strategic retreat to my office, where I learned that "Alsace" had distinguished itself brilliantly: Boudier and Bouguen each had a Boche too. A loss to regret, unfortunately—young Sergeant Bourges, whom a witness saw baling out. Three for one . . . .

I escaped to lunch. I was called to the phone. I scented the enemy and had them say I wasn't there. Unable to find me, the camp loudhailer tore its lungs out calling me twice. No way out, it had to be faced. I went to the Intelligence Room where the reporters, sucking their pencils, were waiting for their victim. Two ravishing young women were among the fiercest of them. On the way out photographers on the watch shot us pitilessly. I was accompanied by Malan, Deer and Charles. At last, naively, I thought it was over and was off back to the mess when Malan took me by the arm: "René, it's the price of success. It's the cinema's turn now, and I'm

very much afraid you'll have to say a few words . . . ." That was the limit! All this for one poor Boche who had the bad luck to be in my sights. . . .

For nearly an hour we had to play the film star, say stupid things and repeat them interminably, for each time something went wrong. I had to shake Charles's hand theatrically at least ten times while saying, "Yes, let's share it (the 1000th). I think that would be fair."

Then it was the B.B.C's turn. Once more we had to improvise and recount our brief battles and finally repeat the comedy of "We're going to share the 1000th sportingly." Then we simulated and lived over the battle and the famous return, talking from our planes, as if our conversation of the other day had really been recorded at the time, etc . . . . That went on until tea, when we were set free again.

The following days I received numerous telegrams of congratulation, some really moving. One of them, addressed to "Monsieur le Commandant René," said, "Our most cordial congratulations on your magnificent exploit. Love. Austin family."

Also got a very lovely telegram from Lady Sinclair: "All my congratulations to you personally and to our magnificent Squadron. My husband and I thank you from the bottom of our hearts for this new proof of France's fighting spirit. Long live 'Alsace.' Marigold Sinclair."

It is incredible how keen the English are on autographs. I noticed this when I had to answer many letters from unknown people sending my photograph, found in a paper, to be signed.

North Africa is free at last . . . . Thousands of prisoners and an enormous amount of booty. Tunis delirious. Will Tunisia be the springboard for a forthcoming landing on the Continent?

Duperier is back from America, where he has been on a tour visiting American factories

An Me-109 bites the dust, photographed by the gun-camera of the victorious U.S. 8th Air Force fighter. At first the Messerschmitt attempts a hedgehopping escape. Flames burst from the enemy plane as bullets strike the wings and fuselage, and disintegration soon follows (pieces of the destroyed fighter were later found in the American plane's wings). (USAF)

and flying schools. I am taking him into my squadron to fly on some operations again.

The parties, fetes and dinners in celebration of the famous 1000th follow one another. The last party was here in the mess; about midnight the draw of the sweepstake took place, after which Air Marshal Saunders gave Charles and me each a cheque for £ 90.

We are continuing our sweeps regularly. Nothing very exciting to report, except that I look at France with fierce determination to return there soon as a conqueror. I have more than once wondered how many French lives the landing will cost. But the Boche will pay dearly for his attempt to enslave the world.

I have already led the wing ten times and I have confided to Wing Commander Deer my ambition to command it the day we land for the first time on the other side. To my great contentment he promised me this, which will give me the honor of being the first Frenchman to lead the first squadron to set foot on our poor soil.

I have just been testing a new plane of a very recent type, which our squadron may be among the first to get. Its performance is stupefying: by my watch it climbed to 6500 meters in 4 minutes 30 seconds. And I think it can do better. The angle of ascent is such that in the pilot's seat the legs are as high as the head (I was going to say higher). The same sensation when beginning a loop. To see the ground, you have to look behind you. The diving speed is clearly superior to that of our Spitfire IXs and in trying a nose-dive from 18,000 feet I touched 560 m.p.h. without pushing the plane. I had to pull out, my ears were giving me an unbearable sharp pain.

The famous ball given in London by Biggin Hill in honour of the 1000th plane shot down has just been given in the biggest hotel, Grosvenor House. By general consent this was "the most gigantic reception of the war." It cost a mere £ 1500! If German prisoners could have been brought to the buffet they would not have believed their eyes. Hundreds of ducks, chickens, lobsters, perfectly prepared, were offered to the gourmandise of some 2000 guests. Gorgeous side dishes, beer, cocktails, champagne, all generously served. Vickers, the maker of the Spitfire, paid the evening's expenses. The legendary Windmill Girls, in on all the Biggin Hill parties (for some mysterious reason), gave one of their little numbers. Numerous aviation celebrities crowded among the guests. Besides top brass, like Leigh Mallory, Saunders, etc., there were Jimmy Rankin, Malan, Screwball McMullen, Johnny Walker and Appleton. The photographers have had another go at me, obviously stupid!

FRENCHMAN IN A TEMPEST

by Lieutenant Pierre Clostermann, Free French Air Force and RAF

The Messerschmitt 262s were becoming a distinct nuisance. These blasted jets were appearing on our front in ever-increasing numbers. Every day at dawn and at twilight they came over, singly, at ground level, to take their photographs. Every now and again, just for a change, patrols of six, or even twelve, came and machine-gunned or bombed our lines.

For Kenway's controllers they were a difficult proposition. Radar couldn't pick them up properly as the posts swept the 360 degrees of the horizon too slowly to follow and fix the echo of a 262 batting along at nearly 600 m.p.h. at treetop level.

The 21st Army Group G.H.Q. didn't understand these technical subtleties and bombarded G.C.C. with peremptory notes, demanding immediate steps to have these armed reconnaissances stopped. Poor Wing Commander Lapsley cudgelled his brains to find some means of intercepting the 262 with Tempests capable of only 490 m.p.h. Finally, he and Brooker worked out the "rat code" (later called the "bastard code" by the pilots).

The principle of the thing was as follows. Two pairs of Tempests were permanently kept at a state of immediate alert—i.e. the planes were actually in scrambling position on the runway, with the pilots ready strapped in their cockpits, their finger on the starter, engine warmed up, radio switched on.

As soon as a 262 crossed the Rhine towards our lines, Lapsley sent out a warning in clear from his control post straight to the pilots, as follows:

"Hallo, Talbot Leader, scramble, rat, scramble, rat!"

The engines were immediately started up, 3 red Very lights went up to clear the circuit and give the rat-catchers priority. The quarry being too speedy for any attempt to catch it to be worthwhile, the two Tempests immediately made for Rheine/Hopsten, the jet-fighters' base. Exactly 8 minutes from the sounding of the alarm the Tempests would be patrolling the approaches of Rheine at 10,000 feet, and trying to catch an Me-262 returning from his trip, when he would have to slow down to let down his undercart and his flaps before landing.

In one week we brought down eight "rats" in this way. I was out of luck and missed two, who slipped through my fingers. The second one provided a complete triumph for the Volkel ack-ack boys. The "rat-scramble" had just been given out. I was taking off, followed by my No. 2, when the 262 whizzed over the field about a hundred yards behind me. By the merest chance, and by an extra-special

dispensation of Providence, the two Bofors of posts S.E.4 and 5 were pointing in the right direction with the crews in position. Each gun fired one clip, with the odds about a million to one, and the Me-262 stopped a 40 mm. and disintegrated into the air.

The Germans soon found the answer to "rat-catching" The Me-262s were told to return home at full speed and at ground level—which made them very difficult to spot, owing to their camouflage—and not to slow up until they got to the flak lane. Once there, they could land at leisure and in complete safety. In line with the main east-west runway at Rheine, over a distance of 5 miles there were 160 quadruple 20-mm. mountings in a double line. These could put up an impenetrable curtain of steel and explosive, under which the Jerry could slip and land perfectly peacefully.

In one week we lost 3 Tempests which tried to attack an Me-262 in this flak lane. There was no point in persisting. Strict orders came out, absolutely forbidding any attack on a 262 within a radius of 6 miles of Rheine; which considerably reduced our chances of bringing any down.

On the 7th of March, 3rd Corps of the 1st American Army reached the Rhine at Remagen and by an extraordinary stroke of chance found the Ludendorff bridge intact. The 9th Armored Division seized it in double quick time and General Bradley began to exploit the bridgehead. Within a couple of days this enclave on the right bank of the Rhine had become such a threat to the Germans that they made desperate efforts to cut the bridge. The Luftwaffe was hurled in and the American fighters, who had no suitable bases within reasonable distance, were soon overwhelmed. The RAF was called in to help and, as Tempests were the only aircraft with a sufficient range to cover Remagen while operating from Holland, this task too fell to our lot.

I led the first of these protective missions, at twilight. Our 8 Tempests flew up the

The Messerschmitt Me-262 was the first jet fighter actually flown in combat, in mid-1944 (though flight testing had begun in 1941). Thanks to Hitler's insistence that the plane be developed as a bomber, the Allies were saved from facing what could have been a history-changing fighter. (Revell)

Rhine, through Cologne, and reached Remagen, where we were greeted by virulent American ack-ack. The Yanks were in such a state of nerves that, even after we had made the usual recognition signals and they had been acknowledged, they continued to let off an occasional burst of Bofors at us. By the third salvo, which didn't miss me by much as I collected some shrapnel in the wing, I felt I didn't particularly want to go on giving these gentlemen target practice. I got my formation to do a 180° turn to make for home, when horrors!— We found ourselves face to face with an absolute armada of seven or eight Arado 234s escorted by thirty or so Me-262s, diving down on that miserable bridge.

At full throttle I fell in behind them. Just as I was opening fire on an Arado 234 at over a thousand yards' range, forty "long-nose" Ta-152s emerged from the clouds on my left. To hell with it! I warned my formation over the radio and kept straight on. The speed shot up frighteningly—420 m.p.h.—450—475. I was hurtling down at an angle of about 50°; the 7 tons of my plane, pulled by 3000 h.p. had terrific acceleration. The Arado levelled out gently, insensibly, following a trajectory which would bring it down to the level of the Rhine a few hundred yards short of the

bridge. I was 800 yards behind, but I daren't fire. At this speed, I felt that firing my guns would certainly wreck my wings. Still behind my Hun, I flew into a frightful barrage of 40 mm. and heavy M.G. I saw the two bombs drop from the Arado quite distinctly. One of them bounced over the bridge and the other hit the bridge road. I passed over the bridge, 40 yards to the left, just as it exploded. My plane was whisked up like a wisp of straw and completely thrown off her balance. I instinctively closed the throttle and pulled the stick back. My Tempest shot up like a bullet to 10,000 feet and I found myself upside down right in the clouds, sweating with funk. A violent vibration—my engine cut out, and a shower of mud, oil, and ironmongery fell on my face. I dropped like a plummet and then my plane went into a spin. A spin in a Tempest is the most dangerous thing on earth—after one turn, two turns, you get thrown about helplessly, you cannon into the walls of the cockpit in spite of the harness straps.

In a complete flap, I wrenched at the hood release; it came away in my hand. I tried to get up on my seat to bail out, but forgot to unstrap myself and succeeded only in giving myself a terrific bang on the head. When I came out of the cloud I was still in a spin—there was the ground, less than 3000 feet below. I pushed the stick right forward and opened the throttle wide. The engine coughed and suddenly fired again, practically jerking itself out of the fuselage. The spin turned into a spiral; I gently tested the elevators, which responded all right—the fields however were rushing towards my windshield. I levelled out at less than 100 feet.

A close shave. I raised my helmet and felt my hair soaked with sweat.

I pinpointed my position quickly. I was on the right bank of the Rhine to the north of the American bridgehead. I set course 310° for home and over the radio gave my patrol a rendezvous over Cologne at 13,000 feet. Just at that moment Kenway called me:

"Hallo, Talbot Leader, Kenway calling. What's your position? Over to you."

I replied briefly: "Hallo, Kenway, Talbot Leader answering, my approximate position is 20 miles north of Remagen, along Rhine. Out."

It was Lapsley personally controlling at Kenway today, I could recognize his drawl.

"O.K. Pierre. Look out, there are a couple of rats around. Out." Right, I'd keep my eyes open. I was O.K. for juice and decided to do a quiet 360° turn under the clouds to try and spot the two rats in question.

A few seconds later some ack-ack tracers started coming up along the Rhine and I made out two long slender grey trails weaving just above the ground.

It was a 262. It looked superb with its triangular fuselage like a shark's head, its tiny arrow-shaped wings, its two long turbines, its grey camouflage spotted with green and yellow. This time I wasn't too badly placed, I was between him and his base. Once again I dived hell for leather, to accumulate the greatest possible speed. He hadn't seen me

yet. A slight turn on the ailerons and I got up to him at a tangent. I was making careful allowance for speed and bullet drop when suddenly two long flames spurted from his jets. He had seen me and opened up. I was in perfect position, 300 yards away. I fired a first burst. A miss. I increased the correction and fired again quickly, for he was gaining on me. This time I saw two flashes on his fuselage, then one on the wing. The range was now 500 yards. An explosion on the right turbine which immediately vomited an enormous plume of black smoke. The 262 skidded violently and lost height. Our speeds evened out, with about 600 yards between us. The smoke got in my way and I missed him again. Curious red balls floating in this smoke dazzled me. Jesus! My two port cannon jammed. I aimed more to the right to correct the skid, and my two other cannon jammed too. The Me-262 flew on on one engine. I was mad with rage. There seemed to be a leak in my pneumatic system—no pressure showing on the gauge. I was simply livid with fury. I went on after the 262 in the hope that his second turbine would overheat.

After a few moments it was my own engine which began to heat. Regretfully I gave up, swearing to have that idiot's scalp who had written in the Air Ministry technical bulletin that an Me-262 couldn't fly on only one turbine.

Through all this I had clean forgotten my section, which must be getting somewhat restive over Cologne. Over the radio I handed over to MacCairn and we returned to Volkel separately at nightfall.

I was in a vile temper. Just to improve matters one of my tires burst as I landed. I had to wait in an icy wind until it was changed before I could taxi to the parking place and get off to dinner.

Nothing Can Stop the Army Air Corps

RUGGED

by Major Robert S. Johnson,
USAAF

More than fifteen years have passed since I flew that mission. Fifteen years since the most critical moments in my life, eternal seconds of flight, of roaring guns and searing flame, the horrifying sound of cannon shells and bullets flashing, seeking—me. A tumbling stream of emotions, exultation, pain and despair, the grip of terror and Death anxious and expectant. Fifteen years past, and yet every moment is still alive, still painted vividly in my mind. It is easy, so easy, to turn back the years to that warm and sunny morning at Manston. . .

. . . into the Manston briefing hut, walls clouded with maps and charts, with recognition sheets and colored symbols, the travel posters of a fighter group. This morning especially I am attentive. The words are the same as other briefings, and yet they are different. Details are vital; details of what to expect can save your life, prepare you for the worst: ". . . to be a maximum effort . . . expect heavy and determined opposition." More words on clouds and winds aloft and rendezvous points with the Big Friends: ". . . protect the bombers, at all costs." The latest intelligence reports on escape and evasion tactics, on contacting the underground, how to wiggle past tens of thousands of Nazi troops, how to work your way down to Spain. *If* you're shot down, and *if* you remain alive. No one wants or expects to be shot down, to tumble unsuspectingly before a Focke-Wulf's or a Messerschmitt's guns. But we all check, carefully, our maps, chart courses, vital data, our knives and guns, and escape kits.

This isn't an ordinary mission. Too much preparation. Too much careful planning. Details usually accepted as a matter of routine are studied exhaustively; nothing is taken for granted. The Thunderbolts roar sweetly, alive and tense, seemingly as taut as their pilots for a mission everyone knows is our most important to date. There is a feeling in the air, a tenseness that crackles invisibly among the pilots, that is transferred to our ground crews. There's little joking this morning, the usual levity is replaced by somber self-reflection.

We are tense, excited, thinking of the imminent battle miles above the ground when the Germans race after the bombers. No doubt today of a maximum interception. The black-crossed planes will be out in force, and as always flown by skillful and courageous pilots, flying fighter planes the match of those anywhere in the world. I love the Thunderbolt, glory in its power and strength, in its incredible, unsurpassed durability and its tremendous armament—but I am not so foolish as to lack a keen appreciation of the flashing speed and agility of the opposition. And they are rugged, those boys out there!

I run through the fighter's cockpit check almost by instinct, my eyes and hands and feet moving in response to habit drilled into me. I forget nothing, miss nothing, but it is almost rote. I cannot keep my mind off the mission. I know that, more so than on previous Ramrods, I am excited and tense. I wonder what will happen today, and I wonder if I will come home. That quivery feeling. Scared? I try to be honest with myself, and yet I'm not sure! Can I distinguish between the slight tremors of excitement and those of fright? I'm not certain; yet, I am aware, as are the other pilots, that this is the ultimate test. We have been warned so many times and with such emphasis of the opposition today that we are expecting half the Luftwaffe to scream at us. There is no question that we must fly our best—or many of us will not come home today.

This quiver of excitement, the anticipation, I had experienced before. The trembling of knees, the undue clarity of vision and of mind. I remember back even further into the years: clad in boxing trunks, taped fists clenched and taut within the leather gloves, waiting the eternity of seconds before the bell rings, waiting to shuffle forward, to have my head rocked back by a stinging jab, waiting for the fear to leave me, for the opponent's blow to wash my fear away, until I could rush into him, swinging, alive with the moments of the fight. I can never explain these feelings better. I knew them more intimately after this mission, and with every succeeding fight against the Luftwaffe I failed to escape these moments of fear. To deny these feelings, even to myself, would be a lie. Fear was with me as it was with the other men. And it was healthy, a provider of respect and caution, not to be denied, but to be welded into what is de-

The famed 56th Fighter Group of the Eighth Air Force in 1944. From left to right are Lt. Col. Francis S. Gabreski, Captain Walter Cook, Bob Johnson, Lt. Col. David C. Schilling, Captain Walker M. "Bud" Mahurin, and Col. Robert B. Landry. (USAF)

scribed as a fighter pilot's "killer instinct." Fear could also be a friend; it speeded up my reactions.

Thunderbolts moving out from the perimeter, propellers drenched in the sun, grass flattened by airblast. Pilots leaning out of cockpits to see beyond those giant engines, weaving their way along, moving into position for takeoff. Orders from the tower, brakes released, throttle forward, go! Hard on the rudder to counteract torque, the needle climbs around, back pressure on the stick. Grass and trees fall away magically beneath my wheels, I work the controls, hydraulics surge in tubes, the gear folds up and inward and tucks away into the Thunderbolt's broad wings.

Left turn, stick and rudder working smoothly, tilting the earth sharply, back on the stick, climb out, and meet in the air. Forty-eight Thunderbolts in formation, sliding and wheeling into neat and precise patterns. No one aborts, no engine fails, the pilot of the forty-ninth Thunderbolt, our standby, mutters unhappily and peels off to return to Horsham St. Faith. We lead today; the 61st Fighter Squadron holds the low and leading position for this mission. I swivel my head. High to my left, bunched together, the sixteen fighters of the 63rd labor for altitude. To my right, slightly higher than my own formation, wings the 62nd. I am Blue 4 in Blue Flight, stuck on the end slot. My element leader is to my left; sliding smoothly through the air into his left ride our fight leader and his wingman.

It is a tight, well-drilled team. Each flight of four Thunderbolts holds tight formation, four finger tips greasing through the air. Manston falls far behind as the forty-eight fighters drone southward, all climbing at an indicated 170 miles per hour. Our throttles are held back, allowing the Thunderbolts to ascend in a shallow, fuel-saving climb.

Dover below, the cliffs melting into the Channel waters. A day of crystal clarity, scattered clouds far below us, miles between the puffy white. There is absolutely no limit to visibility; the earth stretches away forever and forever. A strange world—made for solitary flight, and yet made also, it seems, of three-dimensional movement, the gliding through space of forty-eight fighters, each alone, each linked also by the unseen thread of metallic, radio voices.

Over the Channel, only a mile or so off the French coast. Still climbing, the altimeter winding around slowly, clocking off the hundreds, the thousands, past ten thousand, reaching for twenty. The coastline drifts by, quiet and almost sleepy in the rich sun, unrevealing of gun batteries and listening posts and radar scanners already reporting of our position, number, height, and course, data flashed back to German antiaircraft batteries, to fighter fields, to command posts. From this altitude, France slumbers, beautiful and green.

Le Treport beneath our left wings, the mouth of the Seine River clear and sharp. "Blue Flight, stay sharp. Nine zero degrees. Let's go." Blue Flight wheels, banks and turns in unison with its squadron, the 61st matching flawlessly the wheeling of its two sister squadrons. Below the formation, the Seine River, occupied territory.

"Open up, Blue Flight." Our radio call, orders to the other flights. Move out, separate into combat formation. Pilots work stick and rudder; the Thunderbolts ease away from one another. Now Blue Flight is in its combat position, each Thunderbolt 200 yards apart. Between each flight of four fighters stretches a space of 500 yards and, even further out, holding a distance of 1500 yards, ride the squadrons. Almost constantly I turn and look, turn and look, watching the position of my own planes, seeking out strange black specks in the sky, alert for plunging Focke-Wulfs or Messerschmitts.

Marching in precision, the 63rd Squadron flies to the north, very high, in down-sun position. I turn my head, and see the 62nd Squadron, to our south, and slightly above our own altitude. Other things to check as I divert my attention to the cockpit. Gun switch "On." Gunsight "On." Check the chute harness. Shoulder and leg straps tight, cat-

The heaviest single-engine fighter of the war, the P-47 Thunderbolt was fondly known as "the Jug." Depicted here is Gabreski's P-47. (USAF)

ches secure, the harness fastened. Don't make it easy for the Jerries—check the "elephant trunk." I inspect the oxygen tube, start to count: "3-6-9-12-15-18-21-24-27-30." Oxygen okay; the count by threes to thirty clear and sharp, no faltering. Escape kit secured. If—that big "if"—I go down, I want to be sure of my equipment, my procedures, my position. It's a long walk through France and Spain, *if* luck holds.

The Thunderbolts move into the skies of Europe. A moment to myself. Alone, yet not alone, I pray. If He allows, a moment of thanks on the way home. There won't be time to pray once the black-crossed fighters rush in.

Keep looking, keep looking! It's that moment of carelessness, the second of not paying attention, when the fighters bounce. Occasionally I glance ahead, but I am in the end slot, exposed in the Blue 4 position. At all times my head swivels, my eyes scanning every inch of the sky from my right wingtip, rearward, and above, over my canopy, and down. The silk scarf around my neck isn't a hotrock decoration; without the silk to protect my skin, my neck by now would be raw and

bleeding from rubbing against the wool collar of my shirt.

Out of the corner of my eye—a speck. There, far to the right! I catch my heart with my teeth, swallow, snap my head to the right. I squint, study the sky. A speck of oil on the windshield, not a fighter. Gratefully, my heart drops back where it belongs.

Fifteen miles inland, the Thunderbolt phalanx due north of Rouen, still over the sparkling Seine. My head continues to swivel, my roving gaze stops short as I notice a formation of sixteen fighters, directly behind and slightly above us. They're coming in fast, flying a duplicate of our own formation. Thunderbolts? I look to the left; the sixteen fighters of the 62nd Squadron are rock steady. To the right; there, the sixteen fighters of the 63rd Squadron. Who the hell are these other people? For several seconds I stare at their silhouettes—they're Focke-Wulfs!

Slow, Johnson, take it slow, and be clear. I press the radio mike button on the throttle, and make an effort to speak slowly and distinctly. "Sixteen bandits, six o'clock, coming in fast, this is Keyworth Blue 4, Over." No one replies, no one makes a move. The

Thunderbolts drone on, utterly oblivious of the sixteen fighters streaking in. Am I the *only* man in the Group who sees these planes? I keep my eyes glued to the fighters, increasing in size with every second, trailing thin streaks of black exhaust smoke as they rush toward us under full power.

"Sixteen bandits, six o'clock, coming in fast—this is Keyworth Blue 4—*Over!"* Now I see the enemy fighters clearly—Focke-Wulfs, still closing the gap. Again I call in—I'm nearly frantic now. My entire body seems to quiver. I'm shaking, I want to rip the Thunderbolt around and tear directly into the teeth of the German formation. It's the only thing to do; break into them. For a moment, a second of indecision, I lift the P-47 up on one wing and start the turn—no, dammit! I swore I wouldn't break formation; I would act only on orders and not on my own. I jab down again on the button, this time fairly shouting the warning of enemy fighters.

What the hell's the matter with them? I glance quickly at the other Thunderbolts, expecting the leader's big fighter to swing around and meet the attack. The P-47 drones on, unconcerned, her pilot apparently oblivious to the enemy. My finger goes down on the button and I call, again: "Sixteen bandits, six o'clock, coming in f—"

A terrific explosion! A split-second later, another. And yet another! Crashing, thundering sounds. WHAM! WHAM! WHAM! One after the other, an avalanche smashing into my fighter, heavy boulders hurtling out of nowhere and plunging with devastating force into the airplane. A blinding flash. Before my eyes the canopy glass erupts in an explosion, dissolves in a gleaming shower. Tiny particles of glass rip through the air. The Thunderbolt shudders through her length, bucks wildly as explosions flip her out of control. Still the boulders rain against the fighter, a continuing series of crashing explosions, each roaring, each terrifying. My first instinct is to bail out; I have a frantic urge to leave the airplane.

Concussion smashes my ears, loud, pounding; the blasts dig into my brain. A new sound now, barely noticed over the crashing explosions. A sound of hail, rapid, light, unceasing. Thirty-caliber bullets, pouring in a stream against and into the Thunderbolt. Barely noticed as they tear through metal, flash brilliantly as tracers. The Thunderbolt goes berserk, jarring heavily every time another 20-mm. cannon shell shears metal, tears open the skin, races inside and explodes with steel-ripping force.

Each explosion is a personal blow, a fist thudding into my body. My head rings, my muscles protest as the explosions snap my body into the restraining straps, whip my head back against the rest. I am through! This is it! I'm absolutely helpless, at the mercy of the fighters pouring fire and steel into the Thunderbolt. Squeezed back in my seat against the armor plating—my head snaps right and left as I see the disintegration of my '47. A blow spins my head to the left as a bullet creases my nose. Behind me I can feel the steel being flayed apart by the unending rain of cannon shells.

I notice no pain. I have only a frantic feeling—an explosive urge to get out!

I am not frightened; I am beyond any such gentle emotion. I am terrified, clutched in a constricting terror that engulfs me. Without conscious volition my finger stabs down the radio button and I hear a voice, loud and piercing, screaming, "MAYDAY! MAYDAY! MAYDAY!" The words blur into a continuous stream. The voice goes on and on, shouting the distress call, and not until I have shrieked for help six times or more do I recognize my own voice.

I have no time to think, almost no time to act. Moving by sheer force of habit, by practice become instinct, my hands fly over my body. Without conscious thought, without even realizing what I am doing, I wriggle free of the shoulder harness and jerk open the seat belt.

Another explosion. A hand smashes me against the side of the cockpit; for a moment acceleration pins me helplessly. The Thunderbolt breaks away completely from my control. Earth and sky whirl crazily. I'm suddenly aware that the fighter has been thrown nose down, plunging out of control. The smashing explosions, the staccato beating of the bullets, blur into a continuous din. A sudden lunge, the fighter snaps to the right, nose almost vertical. The Thunderbolt's wild motions flip me back and forth in the cockpit. . .

Fire! A gleaming tongue of flame licks my forehead. It flickers, disappears. Instantly it is here again, this time a searing fire sheet, erupting into the cockpit. The fire dances and swirls, disappears within a thick, choking cloud of smoke. Intense, blinding, sucked through the shattered canopy. The draft is terror. The draft of air is Death, carrying the fire from the bottom of the cockpit, over me, crackling before my face, leaping up and out through the smashed canopy.

The terror is eternity. Burn to death!
GET OUT!

I grab the canopy bar, gasping for breath, jerk it back with maniacal strength. The canopy jerks open, slides back six inches, and jams.

Trapped! The fire blossoms, roars ominously. Frantic, I reach up with both hands, pulling with every bit of strength I can command. The canopy won't budge.

Realization. The fighter burning. Flames and smoke in the cockpit. Oxygen flow cut off. Out of control, plunging. Fighters behind. Helpless.

New sounds. Grinding, rumbling noises. In front of me, the engine. Thumping, banging. Bullets, cannon shells in the engine; maybe it's on fire!

I can't see. I rub my eyes. No good. Then I notice the oil, spraying out from the damaged engine, a sheet of oil robbing me of sight, covering the front windscreen, cutting off my vision. I look to the side, barely able to look out.

Great, dark shapes. Reeling, rushing past me. No! The Thunderbolt plunges, flips crazily earthward. The shapes—the bombers! The bomber formations, unable to evade my hurtling fighter. How did I miss them? The shapes disappear as the Thunderbolt, trailing flame and smoke, tumbles through the bombers, escaping total disaster by scant feet. Maybe less.

GET OUT!

I try, oh God, how I try! Both feet against the instrument panel, brace myself, grasp the canopy bar with both hands. Pull—pull harder! Useless. It won't budge.

Still falling. Got to pull out of the dive. I drop my hands to the stick, my feet to the rudders. Left rudder to level the wings, back pressure on the stick to bring her out of the dive. There is still wind bursting with explosive force through the shattered canopy, but is less demoniacal with the fighter level, flying at less speed.

Still the flame. Now the fire touches, sears. I have become snared in a trap hurtling through space, a trap of vicious flames and choking smoke! I release the controls. Feet firmly against the instruments, both hands grasping the canopy bar. It won't move. *Pull harder!*

The Thunderbolt rears wildly, engine thumping. Smoke inside, oil spewing from the battered engine, a spray whipping back, almost blinding me to the outside world. It doesn't matter. The world is nothingness, only space, forever and ever down to the earth below. Up here, fire, smoke.

I've got to get out! Terror and choking increases, becomes frenzied desperation. Several times I jerk the Thunderbolt from her careening drops toward the earth, several more times I kick against the panel, pull with both hands. The canopy will not move. Six inches. Not a fraction more. I can't get out!

A miracle. Somehow, incredibly, flame disappears. The fire . . . *the fires's out!* Smoke boils into the cockpit, swirls around before it answers the shrieking call of wind through the shattered glass. But there is no flame to knife into flesh, no flame . . . . Settle down! *Think!* I'm *still* alive!

The terror ebbs, then vanishes. At one moment I am beset with fear and frenzy, with the uncontrollable urge to hurl my body through the restraining metal, anything, just to escape the fire. Terror grips me, chokes my breathing and thinking and, in an instant, a moment of wonder, it is banished. I no longer think of other aircraft—enemy or friendly. My mind races over my predicament; what I must do. I begin to relax.

The cessation of struggle, physically and within the mind, is so incredibly absolute that for long seconds I ponder. I do not comprehend this amazing self-control. It may be simply that I am overwhelmed by the miracle of still being alive. Perhaps it is the loss of oxygen at five miles above the earth. The precious seconds of relief flee all too quickly. I must still get out of the stricken airplane if I am to live.

Feet on the instrument panel, hands on the bar. Pull. I pull with all my strength until I am fairly blue in the face. I feel my muscles knotting with the strength of desperation, my body quivers with the effort. Not even this renewed struggle avails me. Cannon shells have burst against the canopy, twisted and curled metal.

The fighter heels sickeningly over on her side, skids through the air, flips for earth. I barely pay attention to the controls; my feet and hands move almost of their own accord, coordinating smoothly, easing the airplane from her plunge. Out of the dive again, the desire to survive becoming more intense.

I *must* get out. I hunch up in the cockpit, desperation once again rising about me like a flood. The canopy, the canopy. Life or death imbedded within that blackened, twisted metal. Again, and again! Hard blows that hurt. Steel slams into my shoulder, hard, unyielding. I cry out in frustration, a wordless profanity. My hands ball into fists and I beat at the canopy, throwing punches, hard, strong blows. But I am not in the ring, not striking at flesh and bone. The steel mocks me, unyielding, triumphant. I sit back for a moment, level the P-47 and wonder.

There is another way out. The canopy is shattered, atop me, to both sides. I stand up in the seat, poke my head and shoulders and head through the broken canopy. I hardly notice the heavy force of the wind and cold. I ignore it. My shoulders are through, I stand to my waist—I can get out!

Despair floods my mind. The parachute snags against the ripped canopy. It can't clear; there's not enough space between the shattered cockpit for both my body and the chute. I'm not going without it! I crawl back to the seat, right the spiraling airplane, and think.

All through the struggle to escape the fighter, I have been talking to myself. Over and over again I have been repeating, "You can get out, you can. If you have to, you can get out!" Again and again the words formed, until finally reality ruled. And after each attempt: "You just must not have to."

I settle back in the seat, the terror and desperation vanished, caught by the wind shrieking through the cockpit, whisked away and scattered forever. I relax, a deliberate move to enable me to think clearly, to study my problem and to seek the solutions. My mind is clear, my thoughts spinning through my brain. I think of everything, a torrent of thoughts that refuse to be clouded, thoughts of everything imaginable.

I am absolutely unconcerned at the moment about enemy aircraft. I know the sky about me is filled with the black-crossed fighters, with pilots eager to find so helpless a target as a crippled Thunderbolt, trailing a greasy plume of smoke as it struggles through the sky, descending. There is no fear of death or of capture. The terror and desperation which so recently assailed me have been born of fire, of the horror of being burned alive. Now the fire is gone, the terror flung away with its disappearance. Solve the problems, Johnson, find the answers. You can't bail out.

A sound of danger snaps me back to full awareness. The engine is running very rough. Any moment, it seems, the giant power plant will tear itself free of its mounts to tumble through space, trapping me in an airplane unbalanced and uncontrollable. I turn my attention fully to flying, realizing that the Thunderbolt is badly crippled, almost on the verge of falling out of my control. Oil still bursts from the holes and tears in the cowling, a thin spray smearing itself against the windscreen, making vision forward almost impossible.

I cannot get out; I must ride this potential bomb to the very ground. My left hand moves almost automatically, easing the throttle back, a move made to keep the engine from exploding. Again—good fortune! The grinding, throbbing noise subsides; much smoother now. My chances are getting better.

I keep thinking of all the intelligence lectures we have sat through, buttocks sore on benches, about how to avoid capture, how to escape to Spain, to return to England. Intelligence officers, reading reports, after a while dull with repetition. Then the actual escapees, pilots who bailed out or crashed, who hid and ran and survived by their wits, who *did* walk out of France, aided by the underground to reach Spain and, eventually, to return to England. It could be done; it had been done. I could do it as well as any. My mind wanders; strangely, I seem to be looking forward to the challenge. It is a thought wholly ridiculous; to anticipate and savor the struggle to escape a land swarming with quick-fingered troops.

One entire B-17 crew had been shot down and lost not a moment in hustling their way out through France and into Spain. In just three weeks from the moment they bailed out of their burning Fortress and fell into space, they were in England. A record. *I* can do that—three weeks and I'll be back. Each time I dwell on the matter my mind tricks me, returns to me pictures of Barbara and my family.

What am I doing? I have been flying toward England, an instinctive move to fly toward the Channel. I remember words, lectures. "If you're going down, if you can't make the Channel, far out into the Channel, turn south. The coast is thick with Germans, and you won't have a chance if you go down there. Head south, head south, south . . . ."

The words flash by in my mind. Obediently, I work the controls, change my course. I look down. Twenty thousand feet to the earth. There—I can see them. They're so clear and sharp. In my oxygen-starved brain, I *see* the Germans. They are like ants, hordes of ants, each carrying a gun and a sharp, glittering bayonet. For twenty miles inland the horde is thick, impenetrable, inescapable. I can't land *there*; I can *see* the German soldiers.

The Thunderbolt turns, heads for Paris. I will fly over the sprawling city, continue flying south, try to get as close as possible to the Spanish border.

This means a crash landing, evasion, escape. I think about my procedures once I am on the ground, the Thunderbolt stopped. My plans are clear—I'll belly the crippled Thunderbolt in, slide the fighter wheels up along an open field. I will land as far south in France as the crippled airplane will take in the continuing descent. I plan to make the walk in Spain as short as possible, to get out quickly. I will *not* be captured. I'll evade them; others have—*I will!* The thought races through my mind; it stays with me through all the moments of considering the crash, the evasion, the escape back to England.

There, clipped to the right side of the cockpit near my knee, an incendiary grenade. Check it! Procedure! Words and method are habit by now. I hold the bomb, grip it tightly. This is the way you do it. The moment the ship stops its sliding across the ground. . .get out. Fling the bomb into the cockpit. Turn the fighter into flames and smoke and ashes.

My mind begins to wander; there is still clarity, but now there is less concentration. The thoughts flit in and out, they appear and flee of their own volition. One instant I think of escape procedures, then my mind dwells on the pilots after they return to Manston. I picture them in my mind, talking about my missing airplane, listing me as missing, probably dead, victim of the sudden bounce by the sixteen determined German fliers. I think about Dick Allison, victim of a fatal crash caused by vertigo. Dick was married, and my thoughts hover about his wife. I remember her, pretty, wonderful; I think of her holding their new-born child. I think of her, never again seeing Dick; the child never to know the father.

I cannot escape the thoughts. Dick's face looms before me, a face dissolving into a Thunderbolt spinning through clouds, a gout of flame, mushrooming smoke. His widow, the child. Then it disappears, the pictures are gone. Barbara. Thoughts only of her. That last sight of my wife, tearful, trying so bravely to smile as the train carried her away. How many months since I've seen Barbara? Seen home? Barbara back home, at Lawton, learning that I was missing. She knew enough of fighters, knew enough to realize the odds were that I would not survive.

In brief seconds the pictures flash into being, a kaleidoscope of people and thoughts and emotions, a world marching in accelerated time before my vision. I can't do this to them; I can't go down. I've *got* to get back!

My mind reels drunkenly; for several moments I think of the Thunderbolt burning while I flee. I do not realize the truth. Hypoxia is upon me. My body and brain clamor for oxygen; desire, covet the life-giving substance. The hypoxia becomes worse as I stagger through the air, thin and cold at 19,000 feet. The symptoms are drunkenness, a hypoxic intoxication, giddy in its effects, lethal if it is sustained. And yet, through this dangerous moment, I plan with all seriousness my crash landing, plan to shed the parachute and escape through the shattered canopy.

Barbara. My folks. Again I think of them. Again their presence invades the fog of hypoxia, struggles to the fore. Visions of loved ones; my concern for them forcing upward through the mists, the false sense of confidence. Again the thoughts are safety, are mental clarity, are the key to survival. The thoughts of their pain, their anguish. Sharp, clear. I *can't* go down.

My head is clearing. The fog is breaking up, dissolving. All this time I have been con-vinced that the fighter is incapable of flight, that it can only glide. I have been flying in a shallow glide, descending gently, losing altitude, at 160 miles per hour. Go for the Channel. Fly over the water, far enough out from the French coast to avoid detection by the Germans. Fly as close as possible to England, ditch the ship in the water, crawl through the hole. Air-Sea Rescue will pick me up, will race out to the scene of the ditching in boats or in planes, to rescue me, bring me back to England. Barbara and the folks may never even know that I've been in trouble.

Stick and rudder, still descending gently. The fighter wheels around in a graceful turn, almost ludicrous for a smoking, badly shot-up machine. But the Thunderbolt is still true, still responsive. She obeys my commands. I head for England, a goal, a place to fly, a home to return to.

I stare at the instrument panel. A shambles. Smashed glass, many of the instruments broken. The Thunderbolt descends, nose slightly down, settling gradually, at about 160 miles per hour. I have no air-speed indicator, but I know this fighter, know her feel.

My mask seems to choke me. Strapped to my face, it had been unknown to me, useless, unable to supply oxygen from a source shot away. I bank the fighter, stare down. At a height I estimate to be ten thousand feet, I un-hook the mask from one side of my face, suck deeply the good clean air, air now richer with oxygen, oxygen to clear my head, to return to me my full senses.

With the newly returned clarity comes soberness, a critical evaluation of my predicament. I am in trouble, in serious, dangerous difficulty. Not until this moment do I realize that I have been flying almost blinded. My eyes burn, a stinging sensation that increases every moment in pain.

I touch my face with my hands. No goggles, and memory comes to me. Yesterday I broke a lens, I turned the goggles in for repair. This morning I took off on the only combat mission I ever flew or was to fly with-out goggles. It was a foolish move, and now, over occupied France in a crippled, smoking fighter, I am paying the penalty for my own stupidity.

In the opening moments of attack a 20-mm. cannon shell had ripped through the left side of the cockpit, exploded with a deafening roar near my left hand, and wreaked havoc with the hydraulic system. The blast sheared the flap handle and severed the hydraulic lines. Since that moment the fluid had poured into the cockpit. Then several more shells exploded, blasted apart the canopy. Wind entered at tremendous speed and, without respite, whipped the fluid into a fine, stinging spray.

Now the wind continues its devastating work. The fluid sprays into my eyes, burning and stinging. I fail to realize during the flight through thin air the effect on my eyes of the fluid.

My hand raises to my face, and I flinch. The pain is real, the source is evident. My eyes are swollen, puffed. Around them the skin is raised, almost as if I have been beaten with fists. It's hard to see. Not until now, not until this moment, do I realize that I am seeing through slits, that if my face swells any more, the skin will close over my eyes.

The moment this happens, I am finished. Half the time I fly with my eyes closed, feeling out the struggling, crippled fighter. It is now that my sense of balance, my sense of flight, comes to my aid. I can *feel* the Thunderbolt when she begins to skid, to slip through the air. I can feel a wing lowering, feel the sudden change of wind draft in the cockpit. I listen carefully, strain with eyes closed to note labor in the engine, to hear the increase in propeller revolutions, in engine tone, when the nose drops. This is how I fly, half-blinded, eyes burning.

When I open my eyes to see, I must stick my head through the hole in the cockpit in order to look ahead. For the windscreen is obscured by oil. I do this several times. The wind stabs my eyes with ice picks, and the pain soars.

My attempts to clean my face, to rub away the fluid from my eyes, are pitifully hopeless. I pull a handkerchief from a pocket, wipe at my burning eyes. The first time I find relief. But the cockpit is filled with spray. My hands, my face, my clothes, are bathed, soaked in hydraulic fluid. In a moment the handkerchief too is drenched. Each time I rub my eyes I rub blood from my nose and the fluid deeper into my skin, irritating the eyes.

And yet, incredibly, I am calm and resolved. A succession of miracles has kept me alive, and I am not about to fret anxiously when only calmness will continue my survival. The pain in my eyes is nothing to the pain I have felt; certainly nothing against the past few minutes. Each time I open my eyes to check the flight, I scan the entire sky. My head swivels, I stare through burning eyes all about me. I am over enemy territory, heavily defended country, alone, in a crippled, smoking airplane, half-blind. I have no company, and I do not savor the sight of other aircraft. I wish only to be left alone, to continue my slow, plodding pace through the air. I've got to get as far out over that Channel as possible.

Again I look around. My head freezes, I stare. My heart again is in my throat. A fighter, alone. I am close to the Channel, *so* close, as I stare at the approaching machine. Slightly behind the Thunderbolt, closing from four o'clock at about 8000 feet, the fighter closes in. I squint my eyes, trying to make out details. The fighter slides still closer.

Never had I seen so beautiful an airplane. A rich, dappled blue, from a dark, threatening thunderstorm to a light sky blue. The cowling is a brilliant, gleaming yellow. Beautiful, and Death on the wing. A Focke-Wulf 190, one of Goering's Boys on the prowl after the raging air battle from which I have been blasted, and slicing through the air—at me. I stare at the airplane, noting the wax coating gleaming on the wings and body.

What can I do? I think of waving my handkerchief at him, then realize the absurdity of such a move. That's silly! I'll rock my wings. But what good will this do? I'm at a loss as to my next move—for I don't dare to fight in the disabled Thunderbolt. I've got to get out over the Channel, continue my flight toward the water and a chance at safety and survival.

I simply stare at the Focke-Wulf. My eyes follow the yellow nose as it closes the distance. The moment the nose swings on a line that points ahead of the Thunderbolt—all hell will break loose. That can only be the German's move to lead my fighter with his guns—the moment before he fires.

All I can do is sit, and watch. Closer and closer he slides the sleek fighter. I begin to fidget, waiting for the yellow flashes to appear from his guns and cannon. Nothing. The guns remain silent, dark. The Focke-Wulf nose is glued on a line to the Thunderbolt. Damn— I'll bet he's taking pictures of me! Rare photographs of a crippled American fighter completely at his mercy.

The yellow-and-blue fighter glides in, still closer. I wonder what he has in mind, even as the Focke-Wulf comes to barely 50 yards away. I think of what I have always wanted to do, to close in to point-blank range, to stick my four right guns almost in his cockpit and the four left guns against his tail—and fire. That would really scatter him! And that's just what this bastard wants to do—to *me*.

He's too close. I shove the stick forward and to the right, swerving the Thunderbolt beneath the Focke-Wulf. I've got to get to the Channel; every move, every maneuver leads to that destination—the Channel water. As the fighter drops earthward, I bank and turn back to my left, heading directly out toward the coast. I glance up as the Focke-Wulf passes over me to my left, swings beautifully in an easy curve, and slides on my tail.

Thoughts race through my mind. I know he's going to work me over, just the second he feels he is in perfect position. I can't stop him, I can't fight in the crippled Thunderbolt; I don't even know if the airplane will stay together through my maneuvers. Every moment of flight since I was shot up has been in a long and gradual descent, a glide, easy enough even for a disabled airplane. But

now . . . I can't slug it out with this Focke-Wulf.

I look the Thunderbolt over. For the first time I realize just how severe a battering the airplane has sustained. The fighter is a flying wreck, a sieve. Let the bastard shoot! He can't hurt me any more than I've been hurt!

I push back in the seat, hunching my shoulders, bringing my arms in close to my body. I pull the seat adjustor, dropping the seat to the full protection of the armor plate. And here I wait.

The German takes his time. He's having a ball, with a helpless pigeon lined up before his guns. When will he shoot? C'mon let's have it! He waits. I don't dare move away from the armor plating. The solid metal behind me is my only chance for life.

Pellets stinging against the wings, the fuselage, thudding into the armor plate. A steady, pelting rain of hailstones. *And* he's not missing! The .30-caliber bullets pour out in a stream, a rain of lead splashing all over the Thunderbolt. And all I can do is to sit there, crouched behind the armor plating, helpless, taking everything the Kraut has to dish out.

For several seconds the incredible turkey shoot continues, my Thunderbolt droning sluggishly through the air, a sitting duck for the Focke-Wulf. How the P-47 stays together is a mystery, for the bullets continue to pour into it.

I don't move an inch. I sit, anger building up. The bullets tear metal, rip into spars, grinding away, chopping the Thunderbolt. My nerves grate as if both hands hold a charge of electricity. Sharp jolts against my back. Less than an inch away, bullets crash against the armor.

To hell with this! My feet kick right and left on the rudder pedals, yawing the P-47 from side to side. The sudden movement slows the fighter to a crawl, and in that second the Focke-Wulf overruns me and bursts ahead.

My turn. I may be almost helpless, but there are bullets in the guns! Damn him—I can't see the Focke-Wulf. I stick my head out of the window, wince from the pain of wind stabbing my swollen eyes. There the bastard is, banking away. I kick right rudder, skid the Thunderbolt, squeeze the trigger in anguish. Eight heavy guns roar; my ship shudders as steel splits through the air. The moment of firing is more gesture than battle, for I cannot use my sights, I can barely see. The bullets flash in his direction, but I hold no hope that the Focke-Wulf will falter.

It doesn't. The sleek fighter circles lazily to the right, out of range. I watch him closely. Blue wings flash, the F.W.-190 swoops up, sweeps down in a wide turn. He's boss of the situation, and I simply fly straight and level as the German fighter slides into a perfect, tight formation with me! This is ridiculous, but I'm happier with the Jerry playing tag off my wing that sitting behind me and blazing away at the Thunderbolt.

The Focke-Wulf inches in closer, gleaming blue wing sitting over mine, the top so close that I can almost lean out of the cockpit and touch the waxed metal. I stare across the scant feet separating our two planes. Our eyes lock, then his gaze travels over the Thunderbolt, studying the fighter from nose to tail. No need to wonder what he is thinking. He is amazed that my airplane still flies; I know his astonishment that I am in the air. Each time his gaze scans the Thunderbolt he shakes his head, mystified. For at such close range he can see the tears and holes, the blackened and scorched metal from the fire, the oily film covering the nose and windscreen, the shattered canopy.

The Kraut stares directly at me, and lifts his left hand. He waves, his eyes expressionless. A wing lifts, the Focke-Wulf slides away. A long-held breath explodes from my lungs, and relief floods my mind. I watch the yellow-nosed fighter as he turns to fly away. But . . . he doesn't! The German plane keeps turning . . . he's on my tail again! "That son of a bitch!" I duck.

I cower again behind the armor plate. The Focke-Wulf is directly behind me, .30-caliber guns hammering. Still the bullets come, per-

fectly aimed. He doesn't miss, not a single bullet misses. I *know* they don't! Frantic, I kick rudder, jerk the heavy Thunderbolt from side to side, cutting my speed. The German waits for the maneuver; this time he's not sucked in. He holds back as the P-47 skids from side to side, and then I see the yellow nose drawing closer to me.

He pulls alongside tight to the P-47. Perfect formation, one battered, shot-up Thunderbolt and the gleaming new Focke-Wulf. By now we are down to 4000 feet, passing directly over Dieppe, our speed still 160 miles per hour. Over Dieppe! The realization makes me shudder, for below my wings lie the most intense antiaircraft concentrations along the entire coast.

They don't fire! Of course! The Focke-Wulf pilot is saving my life! *He* doesn't see Dieppe as a horror of flack. This is, to him, friendly territory, an area over which to fly with impunity. Unknowingly, he gives me another lease on life, is the unwitting party to the succession of miracles which, through one cumulative disaster after the other, are keeping me alive. Even his presence, his attacks are in a way miraculous. For the German has laced me over with his .30-caliber guns, and it is only the smile of fortune that he found me after his four heavy cannon had expended their explosive shells.

Water below . . . the Channel beneath my wings! Still in perfect formation, the dappled blue F.W.-190 glides slowly downward with me. Then we are at 3000 feet. The coast two miles from me, hope flares anew. There is a chance now, an excellent chance to make it into the Channel where I can be rescued! I stare at the German pilot. His left hand raises slowly to his forehead in an informal salute; he waves, and his fighter lifts a wing as he slides off to the right.

Relief, the gasp of pent-up breath. Oh, no! Here he comes again! Nothing to do but to crouch within the armor plating. The enemy fighter sits behind me, perfectly in the slot. He's extra careful this time. A series of sharp bursts ripple from his guns. Again the hail-

Like Bob Johnson, Douglas Bader became legendary for his miraculous escapes from death. Although he lost both legs in combat, Bader continued to fly and amassed a score of 22 enemy planes. Captured three times, he made two successful escapes. (Bill Hess)

stones pelting the tin roof, the P-47 takes the punishment, absorbs the terrible beating. I have long given up hope of understanding why this machine continues to stay in the air. The German is whipsawing his bursts, kicking rudder gently as he fires. A stream of bullets, swinging from left to right, from right to left, a buzzsaw flinging bullets from one wingtip across the plane, into the armor plate, straight across. The firing stops.

Here he comes again. The yellow nose inching alongside, the gleaming Focke-Wulf. The German pilot again slides into formation, undesired company in the sky. For several minutes he remains alongside, staring at the wreck I am flying. He shakes his head in wonder. Below my wings the Channel is only a thousand feet away. A blue wing lifts, snaps down. I watch the salute, the rocking of wings. The sleek fighter accelerates suddenly and turns, flying away in a long climbing turn back to the coast.

Free! England ahead, the Channel lifting to meet the crippled P-47. How far, how far

can I drag the Thunderbolt with her smashed and laboring engine before she drops into the waves?

All this time I have been so tense that my hand gripped the throttle and held down the mike button, transmitting all the things I had called the Jerry pilot, as well as the gunfire and the smashing of bullets into the Thunderbolt. And again, an inadvertent move comes to my aid. The moment the Focke-Wulf disappears, I release the throttle knob and begin my preparations for ditching. My plan is to belly into the Channel, nose high, tail down. As the fighter slows to a stop in the water, I will crawl out through the shattered canopy, dragging my folded dinghy life raft with me. Then, inflate the raft, move away from the sinking plane, and pray that Air-Sea Rescue will find me before the Jerries do, or before I drift long enough to starve. I am ready for all this, calm and prepared for the impact into the water.

And then . . . a voice! The moment my finger lifts from the mike button, I hear a voice calling urgently. "Climb if you can, you're getting very faint, climb if you can, you're getting very faint!" It's the Air-Sea Rescue radio—homing on me and giving instructions. At this instant I realize that it really is true—I'm still alive! The rugged old 'bolt, she'll *fly*, she'll bring me home yet!

I call back, exultation and laughter in my voice, nearly shouting. "Okay, out there! I'll try. I'll do everything I can, but I'm not sure what I can do. I'm down to less than a thousand feet now." And finally I discover that the battered and crippled Thunderbolt really *can* fly! I have been in a steady glide, convinced all this time the fighter is on the verge of falling out of control and now—only now—I discover that she'll fly. It is too good to be true, and I shout with glee.

I ease back on the stick. The Thunderbolt answers at once, nose lifting, and hauls upward in a zoom climb. I hold the fighter with her nose high until the speed drops to just above stalling.

Now, level out. Hold it, increase speed to at

least 160 miles per hour, back on the stick again. And climb! Again I repeat the maneuver, a crippled series of upward zooms, each bringing me higher and higher. Each zoom—a terrific boost to my morale. Clouds above me, a scattered overcast at 5000 feet. Just below the cloud deck, nose level, more speed, and back on the stick. She goes! The big fighter rears upward into the clouds. Another levelling out, another zoom, and I'm on top. From less than 1000 feet to more than 8000! I'm shouting happily to myself, so cocky and confident and joyous that I'm nearly drunk from the sensation. Everything is wonderful! *Nothing* is going to stop me now! I nurse the fighter, baby the controls, and the crippled airplane responds, slides through the air, closer and closer to safety.

"Blue 4, Blue 4." The voice is clearer, sharper. "We have you loud and clear, Blue 4. Steer three-four-five degrees, Blue 4, steer three-four-five degrees."

"Hello Control, hello Control, this is Blue 4. I can't steer your heading. Most of my instruments are shot out. I have a general idea of my direction, but I cannot follow your exact heading. Direct me either left or right. Direct me either left or right. I will correct in this manner. Over."

Mayday Control stays with me every moment, sending flight corrections. I think the Channel is only forty miles across, but I am far south, and long miles stretch ahead of me. At my laboring speed, it seems I'll never get across the water! The minutes drag. How long can this airplane keep flying? I listen for any change in engine sound, for a faltering of the thunder ahead of me. But the engine sings true, maintaining power, and at 160 miles per hour we drone our way above the clouds, guided by an invisible voice through space, drawn inexorably toward home.

Time drags. Thirty minutes. Below the clouds, only the Channel. Thirty-five minutes, forty minutes. And then, a break in the clouds, the overcast becomes broken white cumulus and there . . . directly below me, the stark white cliffs of Dover! I'm too happy to

keep radio silence, I whoop joyously. "Control, this is Blue 4. Those white cliffs sure look wonderful from up here!" No one can imagine just how wonderful they look!

The Controller seems to share my joy. In the next several minutes he guides me unerringly through the clouds and steers me to the Hawkinge air base. I can't find the field. The Controller tells me I am directly over the base, but this doesn't help. My eyes are too swollen, the field too well camouflaged. I pass directly over the hidden airfield, circle the field under the direction of the Mayday Controller, but cannot see a thing.

I check the fuel gauges: about a hundred gallons left. I call the Controller. "Hello, Mayday Control; hello, Mayday control, this is Keyworth Blue 4. I'm okay now. I'm going to fly to Manston. I'd like to land back at my outfit. Blue 4, Out."

Immediately a call comes back. "Roger, Blue 4. If you're sure you can make it, go to B Channel and give them a call. Mayday Control, Out." He signs off. I switch radio control, and call Manston. The field is less than forty miles away, almost in sight. The Thunderbolt chews up the miles, and soon I begin to descend, heading directly for the field.

"Hello, Manston Tower, this is Keyworth Blue 4, Pancake, Over." The reply comes at once. "Hello, Blue 4, Hello Blue 4, this is Manston, Pancake Number One, zero-six-zero, Over."

"Hello, Manston. Blue 4 here. I'm shot up. I will have to make a belly landing. I do not know the condition of my landing gear. I have no hydraulics for flaps or brakes. Over."

"Blue 4 from Manston. Make a wheels-down landing if you possibly can. Repeat, make a wheels-down landing if you possibly can. We are very crowded, and have other crippled airplanes coming in. Over."

"Okay, Manston, from Blue 4. I'll try it. Check my wheels as I come over the tower. I cannot bail out, repeat, I cannot bail out. I have no hydraulic system to pull the wheels back, no brakes, no flaps. Over."

I move the landing-gear control to "Down"

position. Fate still smiles on me. The wheels drop down, lock into position. With all the holes and gaping tears in the Thunderbolt, the wheels and tires have come through unscathed. I circle the field with my eyes almost closed, at 500 feet and less than 150 miles per hour.

This is it; now or never. I descend, turn into a long gliding turn for the runway so that I can see my point of touchdown. I cannot see through the oil-covered windscreen. Carefully, carefully, not enough power for an emergency go-around. I fly every inch toward the runway, nursing the Thunderbolt down. Over the very end of the field, just above stalling speed, I chop the throttle, drop the heavy fighter to the grass. It is one of the best landings I have ever made!

The fighter rolls down the hill to the center of the Manston field. On the rough, grassy landing strip I fight to keep her headed straight. Without flaps or brakes the big fighter rolls freely, barely losing speed. In the center of the field the strip slopes upward and the Thunderbolt charges along the grass. Ahead of me is a line of parked Spitfires and Typhoons; if I don't stop I'm going to slam into them!

At the last moment I kick left rudder, letting the ship turn freely with the wind. The wing tilts, the heavy machine slews violently about, slides backward into a slot between two Typhoons almost as if I'd planned it that way.

The Thunderbold has brought me home. Battered into a flying wrecked cripple, she fought her way back, brought me home. It's almost too much to believe! I feel a great wonder settling about me. My hand moves of its own accord. Engine off, switches off. My hands move over my body. Chute harness undone, straps free.

I crawl out through the hole in the canopy, dragging my parachute behind me. A grin stretches from ear to ear as I stand on the wing, stretch gratefully.

I jump to the ground, kneel down, and plant a great big kiss on Terra Firma. Oh, how good that solid earth feels!

The meat wagon is on hand, and the medics rush to me. I imagine I'm quite a sight, with blood from my nose smeared over my face, mixed with hydraulic fluid. The doctor shakes his head in wonder, and I don't blame him.

A .30-caliber bullet has nicked my nose. Splinters from 20-mm. cannon shells are imbedded deeply in both hands. A bullet has shot away the wrist watch from my arm; only the strap and face rim remain. Burns streak the skin on my forehead. My eyes are swollen, burning, and the flesh starting to blister. And on my right thigh they discover two flesh wounds from .30-caliber bullets, that I hadn't even known about.

They insist on taking me to the hospital at once. Not yet; I want to look over the Jug. And this airplane is not a pretty sight. My awe and respect for the fighter increase as I walk around the battered machine.

There are twenty-one gaping holes and jagged tears in the metal from exploding 20-mm. cannon shells. I'm still standing in one place when my count of the bullet holes reaches past a hundred; there's no use even trying to add them all. The Thunderbolt is literally a sieve, holes through the wings, nose, fuselage and tail. Every square foot, it seems, is covered with holes. There are five holes in the propeller. Three 20-mm. cannon shells burst against the armor plate, a scant inch away from my head. Five cannon shell holes in the right wing, four in the left wing. Two cannon shells blasted away the lower half of my rudder. One shell exploded in the cockpit, next to my left hand; this is the blast that ripped away the flap handle. More holes appear along the fuselage and in the tail. Behind the cockpit the metal is twisted and curled; this had jammed the canopy, trapping me inside.

The airplane had done her best. Needless to say, she would never fly again.

The doctors hustle me into the meat wagon, and roar off to the hospital for a thorough checkup and repair job. They look at me with misgivings, and cannot understand why I am not shaking and quivering. Not any more—all that is behind me! I'm the happiest man on earth, bubbling over with joy. I'm back, *alive*. A dozen times I thought I'd had it, thought the end had come. And now that I am back—with wounds and injuries that will heal quickly—I'm too happy to react physically.

I feel like a man who had been strapped into the electric chair, condemned to die. The switch is thrown, the current surges. Then, miraculously, it stops. Again the switch closes, the current.... Then, another reprieve. Several more times the closing of the switch, the imminence of death, and the reprieve, the final freedom.

But not all are reprieved.

Captain Eby is gone. Captain Wetherbee is gone. My close friend, Lieutenant Barron, is gone. Captain Dyar also is never to return.

All four men were last seen in the vicinity of Forges. All four men, we learn later, are dead.

Foster comes home with a huge hole in his right wing. Johnny Eaves staggers back to Manston in a Thunderbolt shot to ribbons. Charley Clamp barely manages to reach the field in another battered fighter. Ralph Johnson makes it back with his plane shot up, his hydraulic system gone, his right wing ripped, and one elevator in ribbons. His ship is so badly crippled he cannot land. Zemke orders him to bail out, and Air-Sea Rescue fishes Ralph out of the Channel.

It is not a good day. The 56th Fighter Group loses four men killed. A fifth fighter is abandoned. Mine will never fly again. Many others are badly damaged. We claim only two kills.

Our debt grows larger; we intend to pay in full.

WINGMAN

by Major John T. Godfrey, RAF and USAAF

On March 8, our group struck off for Berlin again. For this mission Don* received the DSC and I was awarded the Silver Star. Of all the stories written about Don and me, this was to be the most widely published.

I was now flying section leader occasionally. It doesn't sound like very much, leading three planes, when you consider that the CO assumed the responsibility for forty-seven flying behind him. Oftentimes I was envious of his role, but I was still grateful to be able to command these few planes because it gave me more opportunity of attacking on my own. Today was not the day for this however, for one by one White Two, Three, and

*Don Gentile was John Godfrey's wing man.

Four left me to return to base for various reasons. Don, who was leading Red section, found himself in a similar situation when his planes left him. The other two sections fared no better, and when the bombers were sighted, only four remained from the squadron. I flew Red Two to Don, but there were so few of us, call signs were omitted and we were using each other's first names.

From our very first sighting of the bombers we could see Jerry fighters reeling and diving onto the mass formation. It was a picture that only the devil could have enjoyed. Planes were rent by fiery explosions; white blossoms of parachutes could be seen here and there as the victims of the air battle drifted to earth. We threw ourselves into the melee in a desperate attempt to stem the slaughter of the Fortresses.

"Johnny, cover me. I'm diving on the Jerry at three o'clock."

"Right behind you, Don."

I followed Don down, my excitement at fever-pitch. I watched in fascination as Don closed on the 109. Then, taking my eyes away from Don's plane, I cleared my tail, looking up, down and around. We were O.K.

"Go to it, Don, your tail is cleared."

Don was at the most critical stage of shooting down an enemy plane. During these moments there was always a fear as to what was happening behind; with my assurance, Don closed in and literally blew the 109 apart. I didn't have time to study the spectacle, for off to the right I saw another 109 start its headlong attack onto a Fortress that was straggling behind the middle box.

"Cover me, Don. I'm breaking right." Banking my plane I wheeled on the 109, attacking him at 90 degrees.

"I'm right behind you, John. You're clear."

As Don's words snapped through my earphones I banked left and maneuvered onto the 109. He had seen me, and started to pull up from his dive. Don's voice reassured me once more. "You're still clear, Johnny—nail him!" As the German pulled out from his dive he was fully outlined in my right sight. I pressed the tit and saw strikes. Clinging tenaciously on his tail I kept firing, and after an explosion in the cockpit the 109 turned on its back, ever so gently, and, trailing smoke, started its earthward plunge to join the wreckage that was now strewn over the German countryside.

"Good show, Johnny. Let's climb upstairs."

Don and I, flying abreast, climbed to 28,000 feet. We now had the advantage of height over the 109s that were diving in and out of the Fortress formation. Two 109s pulled below us and were gently turning into the Forts.

"You take the one on the right, Johnny,

and I'll take the one on the left."

I dove down with Don, and we positioned ourselves to the rear of the 109s. So intent were they on their attack that neither one of them saw us approach. Don and I simultaneously opened fire; mine exploded in midair and I could see hits on the plane that Don was firing at. We had attacked with no cover, so I swung my plane around to insure Don protection.

"You're clear, Don. Belt him again." Don calmly blanketed the 109 with fire; it started smoking and burst into flames.

"You got him, Don" I yelled excitedly. I could see the pilot make a desperate attempt to free himself from his fiery coffin. Then the flames enveloped him, and I sickened with revulsion.

We had lost altitude with this latest attack and were now flying parallel on the same level with the bombers. There were no longer any planes attacking the Forts. We had lost the other two pilots of our squadron: Sel Edner, the new CO of 336, had called over the RT to tell us he was bailing out; the other pilot had not been seen or heard from.

The Forts were dropping their bombs, but the sky was so black with flak that only occasionally could we see them as they flew through the solid wall of sooty explosions. Don was the first to see the Me-109.

"Johnny, at six o'clock high there's a single bandit."

I looked back, and there he was high above us. I gazed in disbelief as his nose dropped and he plummeted down on us.

"Don, the crazy son of a bitch is bouncing us."

"I know. When I yell, 'Break,' you break right and I'll break left."

I watched as the 109 dropped closer and closer. "Break, Johnny."

I pulled sharply to the right, and thought at first I had broken too late as the 109 pulled on my tail. I tightened my turn and met Don halfway around as he tried to fire on the 109 in a head-on attack. I went around twice more with the Jerry on my tail, before Don could

John Godfrey originally enlisted in the RCAF and trained in Canada and England. In April, 1943, he transferred to the USAAF, where, with wing man Don Gentile, he became one of our leading European theater aces. (USAF)

reverse his turn and swing down for a rear attack. But this German pilot was a smart, capable flyer. As Don brought his guns to bear, he split S and dove to the ground. Don and I followed him, our motors roaring in pursuit. He pulled out of his dive and banked left, which brought him close to me. I followed him and fired. He wasn't one to sit still, however, and changed his turn to swing into Don. I followed, firing intermittently. Don, meanwhile, had climbed for altitude, and I kept the Jerry busy in a tight turn. As I fired, I saw flashes on the wing, fuselage and even his motor, but the pilot wouldn't bail out. Turning all the time and losing height, we were now just above the treetops, and the 109's engine was spewing smoke. I had no forewarning that the ammunition was running out, but as I prepared for the final burst

only silence came as I pressed the tit.

"Finish him, Don. I'm all out of ammunition."

Don, who had been maneuvering above us waiting for the Jerry to break out of the turn, zoomed down in front of me and made one pass at the courageous German flyer. His shots hit home, and the 109 crashed into the ground. We circled the wreckage, but it would have been impossible for any man to come out of that alive.

It was time to head home, so we climbed westward, hoping to meet friends on the way. Up ahead we could see one plane flying alone at 15,000 feet. As we approached we recognized it; it was a B-17 with one of its motors conked out.

"There's a big friend that needs company, Don. How's your ammunition?"

"I still have some left, but don't know how much. Let's throttle back, and maybe our presence will scare off any attacker."

"Roger."

Don flew off to the left, and I to the right, occasionally over the top of the Fortress as we weaved back and forth in what we hoped was a very convincing show of strength. As we hovered over the Fort our nerves were still on edge, for single planes such as this one were easy prey for eager German fighters; the strength of the B-17s lay in their group firepower.

By now we had flown around them enough for them to know we were their little friends. Usually we never flew close to Fortresses because they had a bad habit of shooting at anything that came in their range; their fear of enemy fighters caused them to be trigger-happy when any small plane appeared. Slowly, ever so slowly, I joined in formation with the Fortress.

Tucked in next to its wing I looked the plane over. In the waist gunners' positions I saw first one man and then another throwing kisses at me; the pilot was all smiles up front as he gave me the thumbs-up sign. I wondered how they would have felt if I'd told them I had no ammunition. For one hour we flew with them, and didn't leave until the Fortress entered the cloud covering that extended to England.

We opened our throttle in our hurry to return. Arriving over the field I followed Don down over the dispersal hut, where we both pulled up into a victory roll. On landing I taxied to where Larry was waiting with Lucky, relishing the word "ace" as it formed on my tongue.

That evening I borrowed five pounds from Don, to finance drinks for the house. After all, a pilot doesn't become an ace every day. If I bragged a little bit, no one held it against me. I was buying and entitled to my say.

Mar. 21, VF-P—White Three—Fighter sweep into Bordeaux. Weather wasn't so hot so went under clouds at 20,000 feet all the way from Bordeaux to two air-dromes south of Rouen. We went down to strafe and I was hit by a 40 mm. that exploded in radio compartment and also hit my leg. Bad scare. Group destroyed twenty-one Jerries. Time—3:50.

I climbed out of my Mustang and walked over to Larry, who was standing there gaping at the huge hole to the rear of the cockpit. We walked silently around the plane, and on the other side we saw where the shell had entered before exploding. Larry put his thumb by the hole and spread out his fingers; I knew what he meant. If the shell had entered four inches forward, instead of just in back of my armor-plated seat, it would have exploded in the cockpit, and blown me to smithereens! He unscrewed the section which held the radio, and reaching in, brought out jagged pieces of metal. How lucky can a fellow get? Only one piece of the exploding shell had hit me. There was a small wound on my right knee, from which a small bit of shrapnel protruded—my only injury.

In addition to "Reggie's Reply" and a fast growing number of swastikas painted next to the cockpit of my plane, I (along with Don) had painted the bottom half of my engine cowling with red and white checkers; this

The P-51 Mustang, originally designed for the RAF before the U.S. entered the war, bore the brunt of the USAAF action against the Luftwaffe (together with the P-47 Thunderbolt, which it replaced). Godfrey and Gentile both flew Mustangs. (USAF)

stood out beautifully, and we hoped that in this fashion we could distinguish each other's planes more easily. Don's score had been climbing steadily and he was up with the top-scoring pilots in the ETO. Regardless of how a plane was destroyed, the magical number of twenty-seven was the goal of all our pilots. Captain Eddie Rickenbacker had had twenty-six victories in World War I, and the first American pilot to beat his record would gain lasting fame. This was Don's ambition.

Some time back, the USAAF had issued a directive stating that all German planes destroyed on the ground would be given as credit to a pilot's score. I often think, now, that they were wrong in doing this, for due to strafing, the Air Force lost the cream of its pilots. Skill was not necessary and often blind luck was the principal factor in a successful strafing. The 20-mm. and 40-mm. fire of the Germans who were protecting their aerodromes was deadly. Against these insuperable odds we continued at every opportunity to attack the aerodromes. Yet I suppose the risk could be justified at Air Force headquarters; after all, if we could destroy a plane on the ground that would be one less to meet our bombers on the next raid. There was only one fighter pilot's life at stake compared to twelve men in a Fortress. The ruling was like throwing a bone to a pack of hungry dogs. The Air Force threw us the bait, and when the German fighters were not in the skies we went down on the ground to look for them.

Mar. 23, VF-P—White Four. Escort Forts to Brunswick. They were thirty minutes early, so picked them up at Munster. They were being bounced by forty plus. We engaged and I covered Don Gentile while he shot two. He then covered me while I got an Me-109. Another one escaped me in the clouds. Time—3:30. Claim: one Me-109 destroyed.

Don and I did our brother act again. Our teamwork was excellent, and the results were gratifying.

I gained in experience with every plane shot down, and now was able to fire in a calm, deliberate manner. Each attack was made in a precise manner. Distance and deflection were carefully judged before firing. This is not something that comes by accident; only by experience can a pilot overcome feelings of panic. A thousand missions could be flown and be of no use if the pilot had not exchanged fire with the enemy. I saw this happen on my February 15 mission. At that time I wrote in my logbook, "A major in our section panicked."

He had just come to our group, fresh from the Pacific—where he had flown countless missions without destroying a Jap. He led our section down on a bounce, and was just about to fire when he looked behind him and saw us on his tail. All reason left him; he became so excited he mistook the three men in the section that was protecting his rear for Jerries. He turned on his back, leaving the F.W.-190 flying on its merry way. Dumfoundedly the three of us followed the panic-stricken major down in a power dive, wondering what it was all about.

This was a prime example of the excitement that seizes a pilot while shooting down his first enemy plane. My present calm manner didn't mean that I wasn't scared when I saw an enemy plane; that feeling never left. On the first sighting of a German plane I always got the sensation a person would feel if his speeding car hit a slippery surface and slid out of control.

Don and I were fast becoming good friends, not only in the air, but on the ground. His roommate had bailed out over Germany. Both of us had lost our buddies, and we spent more and more time in each other's company. I didn't want to leave my room and Don was very happy in his; for that reason we didn't bunk together. My new roommate was Lieutenant Robert S. Tussey, from Altoona, Pennsylvania. Robert had joined the squadron a month before and was already showing promise of being a good fighter pilot, having shot down two Jerries the previous week.

Apr. 5, VF-P—Blue Two—Sweep to Berlin district. Did not see any Jerries, so went on deck. Strafed aerodrome. Missing: Beeson, Bonte, Carr, Hobert. Time— 4:45.

Claims: one locomotive destroyed
       one JU-88 destroyed
       one Me-110   "
       one JU-88   "   shared
       four Me-110s damaged
       one JU-52   "
       one JU-88   "
       one Me-410   "

It was a busy and successful day for me, but it was Don who deserved all the congratulations. His claim of five enemy aircraft destroyed at Stendal Aerodrome brought his score up to twenty-seven planes destroyed, making him the first to beat Eddie Rickenbacker's score in World War I. But the Air Force requested that all news of Don's score be kept confidential.

A big argument was now going on over the treatment of air and ground credits for planes destroyed. After they had thrown us that bone, they were now looking for a way to retrieve it. Of the four pilots shot down over the aerodrome, Beeson was by far the tops. He had been giving Don stiff competition, and before he was shot down, his score was twenty-five planes destroyed—eighteen in the air, and seven on the ground. It seemed ironic that some German gunner could shoot him down when the best German fighter pilots had been unsuccessful.

I aborted on the mission of April 8; four boys were shot down in a big dogfight and Don came through with high honors, shooting down three more planes. With his score now at thirty, news of his victory could not be squelched. The Air Force threw up its hands, and newspapers all over the U.S.A. proclaimed the ace of aces.

Seven days' leave, the medical officer said. Each squadron had its own MO. It was his duty to keep an eye on the pilots for signs of nervous strain. I had come down with what the MO called a bad case of shakes. He had been watching me for some time. The twitching about my eyes and mouth was now quite noticeable and my hands trembled. It was nothing serious if caught in time. A week's rest away from the base, away from its tense excitement, was what the doctor recommended. If I would like to spend my time in a "flak" home, arrangements would be made. That wasn't for me; most of the boys there were from bomber crews, who suffered more from shakes than fighter pilots. They were the ones who had nicknamed the rest home.

Debden hadn't missed me; the war had continued and twelve pilots had been shot down during my absence.

Don was the big news. He had, as the boys aptly worded it, "goofed" while buzzing the airfield for the benefit of cameramen. In trying to make an unusual showing, he had dipped so close to the ground in front of the cameras that his propeller had picked up tufts of grass. When he tried to pull up, the plane mushed into the ground and slithered for a thousand feet on its belly before stopping.

It was a chagrined Don who had climbed from the cockpit. He was uninjured, but the MO had felt it would be wise to remove him from Debden to a nearby hospital, to escape the wrath of Colonel Don Blakeslee ("Horseback").

To say that Colonel Don was fuming would be an understatement. He had made it quite clear that if any pilot damaged a plane while buzzing, he would never again be allowed to fly combat for the Fourth Fighter Group. Don Gentile was no exception, and was grounded.

The Air Force was mum over the story; even the films from the newsreel cameras of AP and INS were confiscated. That must have been a sad blow to the cameramen, for it was a one-in-a-million film of a plane "worth $50,000" cracking up.

As more fighter groups were formed, our group didn't have to stay with the bombers; we only had to fly around their vicinity to insure against penetration. On our April 22 mission Colonel Don brought the group down to 12,000, instead of flying a normal altitude of 26,000 feet. I was flying his wing in Number three position, with a new boy flying my wing. We stooged around for fifteen minutes, during which no enemy fighters were seen. I was the first to spot the bandits way down below us.

"Hello, Horseback, this is Shirt Blue White Three. I see two, three"—there seemed to be hundreds flying in a very loose formation—"eight, ten—God, there's a million of them!"

In my excitement I didn't think of giving the location of the enemy planes. Horseback reminded me of this, "Shirt Blue White Three, this is Horseback. Tell me exactly where they are, and all other planes keep flying in your original positions."

"Hello, Horseback, White Three here. Just on the deck, around two o'clock to us. There's a small batch of clouds, they seem to be grouping around there."

I could see Colonel Don's plane weaving like mad as he tried to find them.

"This is Horseback here. Johnny's right. I want no plane—I repeat—no plane to attack by himself. We have a perfect bounce. 336 and 335 will let down following me. 334 stay around 5000 feet to give us cover. If no more Jerries come in on us, you will be free to come down."

The thirty-two planes started into a shallow turning dive so as to position ourselves to the rear of the enemy fighters. It was a perfect bounce. Dead ahead of us and slightly below were forty Me-109s and F.W.-190s. As we dove into them I separated form Colonel Don. A four-section attack was of little use in this melee of planes. Don had his wingman for protection, and I had mine.

The first two minutes of fighting were a mad ordeal of twisting, firing planes. It was impossible for me to shoot because my wingman continually yelled to break when I'd position myself behind a plane. The Germans were now following each other around in a Lufbery circle. That was why I couldn't get a decent shot; there was always one in back of me. I broke away from this merry-go-round, gained a little height, and flew on the outside of the circle. My wingman was sticking to me like glue. What I'd hoped for happened: a 109 swinging wide on the turn just down below me. I dove, and with a 30-degree deflection shot, hit him. It was perfect firing, and the plane's engine burst into fiery smoke as it plunged to the ground.

I pulled up again and waited, continually circling above the conglomeration of planes below me. Another Jerry made the fatal mistake of pulling out wide. This one was a little harder to shoot down, for he spotted me on my attack; but he was too late. I hit him and his engine stopped, but there was no smoke. Coming in closer I opened fire again and must have hit his gas line, which spilled raw gas over his hot motor—he started to burn. I didn't watch his fall, but pulled up as I saw another 109 above me. This one was trying to escape from the milling planes and head for the ground; I followed. When he straightened out over the treetops, I had him full in my sights and pressed the tit. Strikes showed on his tail. A little more pull up on my part and I saw flashes around his cockpit. The pilot must have been killed, for the motor still running, the plane fell off on its wing and crashed into the treetops. This third Me-109 carried me away from the big fight. When I arrived back, it was all over.

Horseback called us over the RT that it was time to return to Debden.

I had just finished handing my combat report to Mac, the intelligence officer, when the phone rang by his side. He picked it up and then handed it to me, "It's for you, Johnny."

I picked the phone up and said, "Hello."

"Hi, Johnny, this is Gibby, J.J.'s buddy at 356. J.J. had tough luck today and was clobbered."

My heart jumped into my throat, and I asked, almost desperately, "Did he bail out okay?"

"No, he managed to make it here, even though his plane was pretty badly shot up. He had just destroyed a 190 and a JU-88, but they nailed J.J. right in the cockpit. J.J. caught a 20 mm. in his leg. They're operating on it now at DISS Hospital. If you call there tonight they'll give you more information. I thought you'd want to know."

"Thanks, Gibby, I appreciate the call. Have you written to Virginia yet?"

"Yeah, I just finished and sent the letter out air mail. I figured that J.J. would want me to tell the true story and make it sound better than the telegram the War Department will send."

I talked to the hospital that evening, and found out that even in all that blood-and-thunder, J.J. had somehow managed to apply a tourniquet from his first-aid kit—that's what saved his life. The operation had been successful, but they advised me against seeing him right away. Two or three days would be fine. Then I placed a call to London and gave Mrs. C. the news. We agreed to meet at the hospital at two o'clock on the afternoon of the twenty-fifth. There'd be no problem, I could fly up there—and together we might be able to cheer J.J. up.

> Apr. 24, VF-P—Red Leader. Our group went down again to 10,000 feet on the other side of Frankfurt. We bounced a gaggle of thirty plus who were forming. A hell of a dogfight ensued. Had to break every few minutes. Time—4:10. Claim: one F.W.-190 destroyed and one F.W.-190 damaged.

The twenty-fifth was a beautiful clear day, maybe for this reason I decided to give Lucky his first plane ride, and took him along with me to see J.J. After I had strapped myself in the cockpit, Larry handed me Lucky, who sat patiently on my knee as I tied his leash tightly on my harness strap. He was so used to engine noises that the take-off didn't faze him in the least. Just to see what would happen I climbed and then dove down, pulling my plane up fast. He shook his head and looked

up at me, and I'm sure his thoughts weren't printable.

I landed at a nearby B-17 field, only five miles away from the hospital. A fighter plane was a novelty here, especially one with twenty swatikas painted on its side. There were fifteen GIs standing around my plane as I parked it beside the control tower. I must have shocked them as I stood up in the cockpit and placed Lucky over the side onto the wing. One of the boys piped up, "No wonder he shot down so many planes. He carries a seeing-eye dog with him."

Sounds of laughter were coming from J.J.'s ward as we walked toward it. Lucky licked J.J.'s hands when I put him on the bed, but then jumped off to make the rounds of the beds of the boys who were calling to him. It was good to see J.J. again, but sad under the circumstances. He was out of the war now, and expected to be flown home very shortly. Sitting by his bedside, I wondered about my fate: first Bob, now J.J. How soon would it be before my number came up?

Two days later Tussey, my roommate, flew my plane (VF-P) and was killed when it crashed into the Channel.

Millikan, 336's new CO, and I were arguing at the bar as a result of the day's mission. I had called in the enemy fighters over the RT and dove to attack. Millikan had had plans of his own, but it had been too late for me to stop my attack, and I had gone into the enemy fighters—and got one—disregarding his order to pull up. (I liked Millikan personally and admired his keenness in the air. His flying in combat was precise and measured, and he had made other plans for attacking the 190s). My arguments over this bounce were centered on one theme—at least the attackers broke off from the Fortresses when they saw me. True, the squadron might have shot more planes down if careful planning had taken place, but how about the fate of the bombers?

In the middle of this argument the adjutant and the base public relations officer approached me. "Wonderful news, Captain Godfrey. You're leaving tomorrow for the U.S.A.," the adjutant said.

I stared at him, dumfounded. What was this, some kind of joke, being called Captain and going to the U.S.A.? "What gives?" I asked.

"We just received your orders from Washington—you've been promoted to Captain, and are to meet Don Gentile at Chorley, England. He's still there waiting for transportation back to the States. Both of you will return as the top combat team of the Air Force. When you arrive in Washington the Air Force Public Relations will brief you on what to say. Until then, keep mum."

The old saying of "Ours not to reason why" kept buzzing through my head. Evidently the Air Force didn't want Don to return alone as a hero—bad for the morale of the Air Force, probably, which continually stressed teamwork in all of its branches. If Don and I returned together, it would stress the fact that it was as a team that we had achieved success.

The Air Force was right, of course, but the teamwork had become only a means to a personal end. In the race of honors, I—and no doubt Don—had not forgotten the sole purpose of war. The "Reggie's Reply" written on my plane had become a mockery of my former purpose. So much had happened since I made that pledge to myself. Now it was no longer revenge I was seeking, nor was I fighting for the way of life which millions of Americans were struggling to protect. My battle was for my own personal glory. My own ambition was to be the top fighter pilot of the war. Where or how I lost my ideals I cannot say. Maybe it was the atmosphere of Debden, with its photographers and newsmen continually searching for heroes.

This much I knew; my flying and firing were at their peak. I was hot, real hot, and every combat film showed evidence of this when the German planes disappeared under a fusillade of machine-gun bullets. My claims for enemy destroyed were now up to twenty-nine, and at the rate I was knocking them down, fifty was not an impossibility. But orders were orders.

Heroes of the Soviet Union

RED STARRED COBRAS

by Major Vassily Kolibelnikov, Soviet Air Force

In his speech on March 11, 1943, at a breakfast given by Mr. Stettinius on the occasion of the second anniversary of the Lend-Lease Act, Soviet Ambassador Maxim Litvinov said that one Soviet air force guards group using "Airacobra" fighter craft, during the past three months' action on the Voronezh front and later in the Demyansk region, had downed thirty-three enemy planes, themselves losing only three aircraft.

Since June 22, 1941, the group has seen intense action in defending Leningrad against the German Nazi and Finnish invaders. Equipped with 1-15 aircraft the fighter pilots successfully repulsed attacks by superior enemy forces, downing thirty-five planes in the air and destroying twenty-nine on the ground.

In June 1942, the group was outfitted with new material—Airacobra fighters—and was ordered to the Voronezh front. On the first day they piloted Airacobras—June 29, 1942— in the first air battles, against superior German forces, the fliers in this group shot down 14 enemy planes. One Airacobra was hit but the Soviet pilot escaped safely.

The next day another 7 enemy craft were downed—one Heinkel III, three Junkers 88s and three Messerschmitt Me-109Fs. The Soviet pilots suffered no casualties. Altogether, during the period of action at the Voronezh front from June until August 1942, the fliers in this aircraft group piloting Airacobras shot down 64 enemy planes, of which 15 were Junkers 88s. Two Soviet fliers perished in these engagements, one of whom was killed when ramming an Me-109F. At that period the group was commanded by Hero of the Soviet Union, Colonel Sergei Mironov. He himself led fighter-craft into the attack, teaching the pilots to utilize all the advantages offered by an Airacobra as compared with an Me-109F, and deliver crushing blows to the enemy craft. Colonel Mironov shot down five German planes singlehanded.

During this period of fighting on the Voronezh front the Airacobras showed splendid fighting qualities, and in the able and experienced hands of the "Stalin Falcons" they were dreaded by the German fliers. As testified by most of the Soviet fliers in action in this region, whenever the Germans encountered Airacobra fighters, they would not enter battle unless they had numerical superiority. It was only in individual cases that arrogant German fliers would attack Airacobras—unexpectedly, and even then, only from behind clouds or from the direction of the sun.

Here is one episode, told to me by Hero of the Soviet Union, Senior Lieutenant of the Guards Ivan Grachev, who took part in an air battle on July 16th of last year. Sixteen Aira-

With a cannon in its nose, the P-39 Airacobra carried a rather potent sting. Manufactured by Bell Aircraft, the fighter was used effectively by the Soviet Air Force. (USAF)

cobras under the general command of Group Commander Colonel Sergei Mironov, took off to accompany bombers heading to strafe the enemy. Returning to our aerodrome post, having accomplished the task set, our fliers encountered 20 Me-109F aircraft proceeding in small groups of six or eight planes each. The German fighters tried to attack our bombers, but by a bold maneuver the Russian fighter pilots cut off the enemy fighters and, tying them into isolated groupings, opened battle.

The engagement lasted over thirty minutes. As a result of this battle, six enemy craft and also one Junkers 88 bomber which happened to be passing, were downed by our fighter craft. Mironov's aircraft suffered no losses. The battle was waged with vertical-banked turns. Incidentally, the vertical was a favorite stunt of the German fighters, but the Airacobra was fully equal to the German fighter in this figure.

"In the banked turn," says Ivan Grachev,

"the Airacobra has great advantages over the German fighter. Of this I became convinced myself."

Soviet fliers employed an original tactical method in another air battle over Voronezh on July 7, 1942. At the "Alert" signal, 13 Airacobras took off. At an altitude of 8000 feet, Soviet fighters encountered 50 enemy bombers and 20 fighters. The group, commanded by Hero of the Soviet Union, Major Makarenko, boldly attacked the bombers, breaking up the latter's battle formation, and then allotted a group of fighter craft to tackle the Messerschmitts, while a second group was ordered to open fire on the enemy bombers. The Commander's plan was brilliantly effected. In this engagement Soviet pilots downed 7 enemy planes, Major Makarenko shooting down two single-handed. He was badly wounded in this battle, but despite this he safely brought his machine back to the aerodrome.

In August 1942, a number of Airacobras was allocated from this aircraft group, under the command of Major Oleg Rodionov, to a sector of the front near Rzhev. Here, within a short period of time, Rodionov's aircraft engaged in several successful air fights. Altogether, in the battles at Rzhev, there were 68 planes on our side and 116 of the enemy's. Notwithstanding this ratio of forces, Soviet fliers downed 13 enemy planes—9 Junkers 88s and 4 Me-109Fs, themselves losing only 2 machines.

During September and October 1942, the aircraft group was held in reserve by the army command.

In November, 1942, a whole group was transferred to the northwest front, in the region of Demyansk. Winter set in early that year. The group personnel had had no experience in flying Airacobras under winter conditions. Despite this the ground crews, headed by Group Engineer Major Fedor Krasnovsky, did everything to ensure the fliers the possibility of maintaining normal battle activities. Airacobras are adapted for service on cement or asphalt runways, but the latter were not available at all frontline aerodromes. At Major Krasnovsky's suggestion, the fuselage leg nodes were reinforced, and after this there were no more cases of these nodes snapping. Winter battle experience with American fighter-craft showed that oil radiator thermostats deformed and fairly often were put out of commission. In order to avoid this, and keep the material in constant readiness for battle, special covers were made—as a result of which the oil was kept at a normal temperature.

Other difficulties were also met with—for instance, at low temperatures the hydro mixture employed for guns grew viscid. This could cause the gun to jam. The aircraft group then decided to use Soviet "MVP" oil, which has a low temperature. The results were good.

Major events were ripening on the northwest front. Conditions of battle work here turned out to be exceedingly complicated. Woody, swampy terrain made it very difficult for fliers to keep their bearings, and the limited landing fields forced the fliers, in case of emergency, to land wheelless, with landing gear retracted. But the pilots in this Guards aircraft unit paid small heed to such inconveniences.

Trying to retain at all costs their tactically advantageous positions in the region of Lychkovo Zaluchye and Lake Seliger, the Germans were painstakingly reinforcing strong points, primarily with artillery. The 53rd German fighter squadron, in action in this sector of the front, was urgently reserviced with Focke-Wulf 190 aircraft. And it was with these aircraft that a Soviet Guards air unit engaged in battle during February and March 1943. The very first engagements showed the Soviet fliers that both the Me-109 and the Focke-Wulf 190 are suited mainly for engaging in battle on the vertical, showing inferiority to the Airacobra, which simultaneously possesses good vertical and horizontal maneuverability. The Germans then employed the tactics of combined groupings of Focke-Wulf and Me fighters for use against the Airacobras. But this combination had no success.

On February 17, 1943, a formation of four Soviet fliers engaged a numerically superior enemy in an air battle at an altitude not exceeding 400 feet. The Airacobras encountered four Messerschmitts and two Focke-Wulfs in head-on parallel courses. The Messerschmitts proceeded in pairs on the right, with the two Focke-Wulfs bringing up the rear. As soon as the Germans discerned the outlines of the Airacobras—only too familiar to them—two of the Messerschmitts immediately sneaked off into the clouds. Formation leader, Senior Lieutenant of the Guards, Alexei Smirnov, deployed his group to the left, and with his leader—Junior Lieutenant of the Guards Ouglyansky—circled behind the tails of the enemy craft bringing up the rear. Meanwhile our second pair—Senior Lieutenant of the Guards Vassily Savin and Junior Lieutenant of the Guards Kryukov—described a smaller circle, heading to attack the second pair of Messerschmitts. All four Messers straightway made for the clouds, with both Focke-Wulfs following suit, to elude the four Soviet fliers. The battle initiative was instantly taken by Smirnov's quartet. One Messer which had darted out from the clouds, was quickly caught up with by Senior Lieutenant Savin. His Airacobra's speed in this particular situation was more than good and, to avoid colliding, Savin had to step on the gas. Choosing an opportune moment Savin opened point-blank fire on the German plane, which crashed to earth. The Germans then tried launching a sudden attack on the Soviet fliers, but all their efforts were in vain.

Knowing that Airacobras possess good horizontal maneuverability, Smirnov decided to lead his quartet at a low altitude, sharply banking. And it was here that he gave the Germans battle. This headlong but remarkable air duel between the four Airacobras, and four Messerschmitts and two Focke-Wulfs, ended in complete victory for the Soviet fliers. Three Messers were shot down, and one Focke-Wulf also failed to return to its aerodrome.

German propaganda shouts from the roof-tops that Focke-Wulfs are "invulnerable." But if you walk through the hills and woods of the Ilmen region, everywhere you will find the debris of these planes. Our pilots quickly learned both the strong and the weak points of this new German machine, and soon learned the knack of downing Focke-Wulfs.

During an air fight, Senior Lieutenant of the Guards Alexei Smirnov encountered a Focke-Wulf under equal conditions—at halfway bank. Smirnov reduced the radius of his bank to the uttermost limit. His Airacobra banked at a lower speed, and yet did not break into a corkscrew (tailspin). Controlling his machine with consummate skill, at its minimum possible speed, keeping his craft from breaking into a corkscrew by means of foot controls, Smirnov maneuvered his machine behind the Focke-Wulf's tail and shot down his opponent.

Piloting Airacobras, Soviet fliers force the Germans to fight in conditions unfavorable to the latter, and crack them on vertical figures, dragging them up to high altitudes where the Focke-Wulfs lose their fighting power.

The Yak 9d of the Soviet Air Force's heavily-used Yak series. The 9d also saw action in the Korean conflict. (Airfix)

The Germans were particularly anxious to put into effect their practice of combined groupings of fighters at the moment when our troops of the northwest front were liquidating the last enemy strong points in the region of the "Ramushevsky Corridor."

A formation of Soviet dive-bombers headed off to bomb enemy artillery and trench-mortar positions in the region south of Lake Ilmen. Two groups of four Airacobras each, were detailed to escort these bombers. The leaders were Hero of the Soviet Union, Senior Lieutenant of the Guards Ivan Grachev, and Senior Lieutenant Vladimir Bozrodny. German anti-aircraft guns raised a solid barrage of fire in front of our bombers and fighters, but this did not help the enemy. German fighters then appeared from the direction of Lake Ilmen—more than thirty of them. The Messers proceeded in pairs, higher up, while the Focke-Wulfs flew at about five to six thousand feet in echeloned pairs. This German tactical method was nothing new to Soviet fighter pilots. The Germans thought to entice the Airacobras into a pincer, disarrange the firing interrelationship of our fliers, and settle with them singly.

Taking due account of this maneuver, the leader of the righthand shock group, Bozrodny, was the first to force battle on the Germans and, darting ahead, he attacked the Focke-Wulf pair bringing up the rear. Flying in pairs, during the whole of this engagement, the Messerschmitts resorted to waiting tactics and pursuit of our three planes which had broken from formation. But the Germans' hopes were futile. Acting in mutual coordination, the Guards fighter pilots scattered the Focke-Wulfs and Messers all over the skies, and what is more, shot down three without losing a single machine of their own.

Nazi pilots show particular zeal in hunting for our landing fields, trying to spot and block them. Soviet Guards pilots gave them such a hot lesson that the enemy for a long time lost all desire to attempt to block this aircraft group's aerodrome.

On December 30, 1942, the German command equipped a special group of "Freehunter Aces" to block this unit's aerodrome. This enemy group was headed by Major Heinrich Bruno. Eight German aces were intercepted enroute by a formation of five of our Airacobras under command of Guards Captain Anatoly Kislyakov. The Germans as usual proceeded in groups of twos echeloned altitudewise (vertically). Our pilots, who were the first to spot the enemy, made use of the unexpectedness of the attack. Before the Germans even knew what had hit them, two of their craft were downed by Captain Kislyakov, one in his stride (in passing), and the other on a banking turn. The third enemy plane was bagged by Kislyakov's leader plane—piloted by Junior Lieutenant of the Guards Pasko—while the fourth Messerschmitt was set aflame by Guards Sergeant Lorent. From passive defense, the four remaining Messers soon turned tail and scurried off.

In this engagement, three German aces who had bailed out on parachutes—Paul Grothoff, Emil Koppelberg, and Heinrich Bruno—were taken prisoners. During the interrogation, all three declared they were powerless to stand up against the onslaught of the Soviet pilots, and the heavy fire and high maneuverability of the Airacobras. Their testimony is worth quoting.

"How were you shot down?" N.C.O. Paul Grothoff was asked.

"I didn't see the Soviet fighter. He had evidently come up so cunningly behind my tail that in this case my experience proved inadequate. He was apparently a good marksman—he downed me with his first volley. But I can't tell you very much because I recovered consciousness only when I was already at the war prisoners' transit station."

Sergeant-Major Emil Koppelberg stated, "I didn't see the Soviet fighter. He attacked me when I was escaping the antiaircraft fire, and when I caught sight of him it was already too late—my machine was hit and hurtling to the ground. Seeing that I've spent about five thousand hours in the air, it can be said that I was downed by a big Soviet Ace."

Only N.C.O. Heinrich Bruno had time to see how Captain Kislyakov shot him down.

"I found myself up against an opponent with whom I couldn't do anything, although I attacked him twice. Once I've been shot down—then that means that Soviet flier surpassed me in fighting skill and in piloting. So far I've been in over seventy air battles."

Grothoff, the youngest, had eight hundred hours on his flying record.

The interpreter asked Koppelberg. "You arrived on the eastern front a long time ago?"

"December 29th I reported for duty at the aerodrome. December 30th I was shot down."

Koppelberg had been flying since 1935, and in action since September 1939. In Holland, RAF pilots had fractured his skull and broken his jaw. His fingers are mangled. He spent a long time in different hospitals, and was away on a long furlough. He was a semi-invalid flier, and after being wounded piloted transport planes. Then he was appointed a flying-school instructor, and now had been reposted with the active army. He is typical of the scrapings that Goring is today obliged to send into battle.

"Have you received letters from your comrades that you started with when you began the war?" Koppelberg was asked.

"No, nobody else but me is left alive, excepting those who have been taken prisoners."

During their eight-month piloting of Airacobras, remarkable cadres of fighter-pilots have advanced in this unit, fliers who have superb command of their machines. Among these men the first to be named is Senior Lieutenant of the Guards Alexei Smirnov. Smirnov shot down eight German fighters and two bombers single-handed. He is a rank-and-file Russian fighter-pilot of which the Red Army numbers thousands.

Before being called to the Red Army he worked in Paltsevo Collective Farm, in the Kalinin Region. This Airacobra pilot has been awarded the Order of Lenin.

Junior Lieutenant of the Guards Nikolai Pasko, born in Kharkov, is 21. Before the war against the German invaders, Pasko was engaged as a flying-club instructor. He has been piloting the Airacobra since January 1943, and has brought down 6 Nazi planes single-handed. On the glorious anniversary of the Red Army—February 23rd—he shot down 2 German planes. Pasko wreaks vengeance on the Nazis for the torment and sufferings of his native Ukraine and his birthplace, Kharkov.

Since the war started, Hero of the Soviet Union Ivan Grachev has advanced from a rank-and-file pilot to assistant Squadron Commander. He is a real Soviet ace. Coming from a family of workers of several generations' standing, Grachev brought with him into the army his inherent determination, persistency and tenacity of purpose. He skillfully pilots all classes of Soviet fighter craft. He learned to pilot an Airacobra in two days. Grachev has accounted for 13 enemy aircraft single-handed, plus 8 more shot down in group engagement.

Ivan N. Kozhedub; Hero of the Soviet Union and the Red Air Force's World War II ace-of-aces. His total tally: 62 Nazi aircraft. (Bill Hess)

Group Commander Lieutenant-Colonel of the Guards Oleg Rodionov has been decorated with three orders of the Soviet Union. He has downed 5 enemy craft single-handed, 4 while piloting his Airacobra.

Since June 1942, when this aircraft group was equipped with Airacobras, and up to March 27, 1943, this unit has shot down 142 enemy planes in air battles. Of these there were 29 Junkers 88s, 2 Heinkel 111s, 1 Dornier 217, 8 Focke-Wulf 198s, 1 Messerschmitt 210, 72 Messerschmitt 109Fs, 21 Focke-Wulf 90s, 4 Macchi 200s, 4 Heinkel 126s. Besides this, 19 more enemy planes were hit. The group's losses were 20 Airacobras.

Altogether, forty members of the air crews, and forty-six members of the ground crews of this group have been awarded orders of the Soviet Union.

Such are the deeds and such are the men of this aircraft group—men who know no mercy for the foe. Into each battle flight, into each fight with the Nazis, these men carry their unquenchable hatred, their deep faith in the triumph of our righteous cause, in the inevitable defeat of Nazi Germany.

These Were the Enemy

LUFTWAFFE ACE

by Hauptmann Heinz Knoke,
Luftwaffe

April 28, 1944

A steady stream of new pilots arrived on posting to us during recent weeks. With the exception of a Flight Sergeant who came from the Eastern Front, where he had been awarded the Iron Cross, they are all young NCOs without experience, posted to us directly upon completion of courses at training schools which are altogether inadequate for operational requirement.

In personal character and physique, however, they are an exceptionally fine bunch of carefully selected youngsters. I myself take them up for about 120 training flights. Two veteran combat pilots also give them instruction in blind flying. In addition, they receive advanced instruction in bombing and gunnery.

In the middle of April, Barran, our good old Methuselah, rejoins us after his discharge from hospital.

Brand-new aircraft arrive straight from the factory. They are equipped with supercharged engines and the new methane device. The latter is something which I myself tested. It makes it possible for us to obtain from the engine a power boost of as much as 40 per cent for several minutes in case of emergency. This power boost is obtained by the injection into the cylinders of a mixture of methyl alcohol and water.

A camera is also attached to my plane. Several extracts from my latest films appeared in the *"Deutschen Wochenschau"* (German Weekly Review) newsreels in movie theaters everywhere in Germany.

"The Fifth" is back!

From April 15 to 20, I was attached to the Experimental Station at Lechfeld, where I flew for the first time a jet aircraft, the Me-262. In an ordinary standard model in level flight I reached a speed of 580 miles per hour. One thousand of these planes are to be on operations before the end of the year. God help the Tommy and the Yank then!

A few weeks ago at Zwischenahn I watched Major Späthe fly a Me-163. In three minutes he had climbed to 25,000 feet. This plane is rumored to be capable of a speed of more than 750 miles per hour. As far back as 1941 it was already doing over 600 miles per hour.

Development of other new types goes ahead rapidly. The German aircraft production industry is certainly operating in high gear now.

On the other side of the picture, however, are the American bombs which day after day come raining down on the factories. Will they succeed in bringing German aircraft production to a standstill before the new models can be produced in quantity? The answer to that question will decide the outcome of the air war over the Reich: it has become a sort of murderous race against time. The outlook is dark.

Day after day the Eastern Front has to be withdrawn. Africa was written off in March: 120,000 German soldiers there became prisoners, all of them well-trained and experienced combat veterans. The situation in Italy has become critical. The Italians as allies are utterly useless and unreliable and have never been anything else.

In the west we must expect an American landing on the Continent. For several months the Squadron has been making preparations down to the last detail for "Operation Doctor Gustav Wilhelm." Every pilot has received extensive theoretical training in preparation for operations against landing craft and transports.

The press of a button at the first alarm is sufficient to set the entire vast organization in the west rolling into action.

This morning Major Specht is appointed Commanding Officer (*Geschwaderkommodore*) of No. 11 Fighter Wing. A few days ago he was awarded the Knight's Cross.

I am appointed to succeed him as Commanding Officer of the Second Squadron of No. 11 Fighter Wing (II/JG. 11). I am also advised of my accelerated promotion to the rank of Captain (*Hauptmann*), owing to "bravery in the face of the enemy." At 23 years of age I seem to be for the moment the youngest Squadron Commander in the German Air Force.

Little Specht smiles as he shakes hands with me three times and congratulates me: one, on my promotion to Captain; two, on my appointment as Commanding Officer (*Kommandeur*); and three—because Lilo has just presented me with our second daughter.

It is a marvelous day; the sun is shining, and the lowering clouds are still far away on the horizon.

The P-38 Lightning, nicknamed "forked-tail devil" by the Germans. It also saw heavy action in the Pacific, where it was flown by such pilots as Dick Bong, Tommy McGuire, and Tom Lanphier. (USAF)

April 29, 1944

"Concentrations of enemy aircraft in Dora-Dora!" Here we go again! The reorganized Squadron is ready for action.

Three Bomber Divisions are launching an offensive from the Great Yarmouth area. Our formations in Holland report strong fighter escorts. My orders are to engage the escorting fighters in combat with my Squadron, draw them off and keep them occupied. Other Squadrons of Focke-Wulfs are thus to be enabled to deal with the bombers effectively without interference.

1000 hours. "Stand by, the entire Squadron!"

I have a direct ground line from my aircraft to the control room at Division. Enemy situation reports are relayed to me all the time.

They pass over Amsterdam . . . the south tip of Ijssel Bay . . . north of Deventer . . . crossing the Reich border . . . west of Rheine.

At 1100 hours the spearhead of the formation is over Rheine.

1104 hours. "Entire Squadron to take off; entire Squadron to take off!" The order booms forth from the loudspeakers across the field. Signal rockets and Very lights are sent up from the Flight dispersal points. Engines roar. We are off! The Flights rise from the field and circle to the left, closing in to make up a single compact Squadron formation.

I turn on the radio and contact base. "Heavy babies in sector Gustav-Quelle. Go to Hanni-eight-zero."

"Victor, victor," I acknowledge.

I continue climbing in a wide circle to the left up to the required operational altitude . . . 20,000 . . . 22,000 . . . 25,000 feet.

North and south of us other Squadrons are also climbing. They are mostly Focke-Wulfs.

"Heavy babies now in Gustav-Siegfried; Hanni-eight-zero."

"Victor, victor."

I have now reached 30,000 feet. The new superchargers are marvelous.

1130 hours. Off to the west and below I spot the first vapor trails. They are Lightnings. In a few minutes they are directly below, followed by the heavy bombers. These are strung out in an immense chain as far as the eye can reach. Thunderbolts and Mustangs wheel and spiral overhead and alongside.

Then our Focke-Wulfs sweep right into them. At once I peel off and dive into the Lightnings below. They spot us and swing round towards us to meet the attack. A pack of Thunderbolts, about 30 in all, also come wheeling in toward us from the south. This is exactly what I wanted.

The way is now clear for the Focke-Wulfs. The first of the Fortresses are already in flames. Major Moritz goes in to attack with his Squadron of in-fighters (*Rammjaeger*).

Then we are in a madly milling dogfight. Our job is done; it is a case of every man for himself. I remain on the tail of a Lightning for several minutes. It flies like the devil himself, turning, diving, and climbing almost like a rocket. I am never able to fire more than a few pot shots.

Then a flight of Mustangs dives past. Tracers whistle close by my head. I pull back the stick with both hands, and the plane climbs steeply out of the way. My wing man, Sergeant Drühe, remains close to my tail.

Once again I have a chance to fire at a Lightning. My salvos register at last. Smoke billows out of the right engine. I have to break away, however. Glancing back, I see that I have *eight* Thunderbolts sitting on my tail. The enemy tracers again come whistling past my head.

Evidently my opponents are old hands at the game. I turn and dive and climb and roll and loop and spin. I use the methanol emergency booster, and try to get away in my favorite "corkscrew climb." In only a few seconds the bastards are right back on my tail. They keep on firing all the time. I do not know how they just miss me, but they do.

My wingman sticks to me like glue, either behind or alongside. I call him to "Stay right there!" whatever happens. "Victor, victor," he calmly replies.

In what I think could be a lucky break, I get a Yank in my sights. I open fire with all guns. The crate goes up in a steep climb. Then all his comrades are back again on my tail.

In spite of the freezing cold, sweat pours down my face. This kind of dogfight is hell. One moment I am thrust down into the seat in a tight turn; the next I am upside down, hanging in the safety harness with my head practically touching the canopy roof and the guts coming up into my mouth.

Every second seems like a lifetime.

The Focke-Wulfs have meanwhile done a good job. I have seen nearly 30 of the Fortresses go down in flames. But there are still several hundred more of the heavy bombers winging their way eastward undaunted. Berlin is in for another hot day.

My fuel indicator needle registers zero. The red light starts to flicker its warning. Ten more minutes only, and my tank will be empty. I go down in a tight spiral dive. The Thunderbolts break away.

Just above the clouds, at an altitude of 3000 feet, I slowly level off. I estimate that I am probably somewhere in the vicinity of Brunswick or Hildesheim.

I look at my watch. Perhaps in another 45 minutes I shall be over the bomber alley again. Perhaps then I shall be able to get a fat bomber in front of my guns. . . .

Overhead, the sky is still streaked with vapor trails, stamped with the imprint of that infernal dogfight. Suddenly the wingman beside me flicks his aircraft round and vanishes into the cloudbank.

What the hell . . . ?

In a flash I glance round, and then instinctively duck my head. There is a Thunderbolt sitting right on my tail, followed by seven more. All eight open fire. Their salvos slam into my plane. My right wing bursts into flames.

I spiral off to the left into the clouds. A shadow looms ahead: it is a Thunderbolt. I open fire. Its tail is soon in flames.

Now I can see the ground. I jettison the canopy and am ready to bail out. There is another rat-tat-tat sound of machine guns close to my ear and more hammer blows hit my flaming crate. That Thunderbolt is there again, not 100 feet behind me.

Damn! I will be chewed to mincemeat in his prop if I try to bail out now. I huddle down and crouch low in my seat, trying to make myself as small as possible. The armor plate at my back protects me from the otherwise fatal shots. Wings and fuselage are riddled. A large hole gapes beside my right leg. The flames are licking closer now: I can feel the heat.

Crash! The instrument panel flies into splinters in front of my eyes. Something strikes me on the head. Then my engine stops: not a drop of fuel left.

What chance have I now?

My forward speed, of course, rapidly decreases. This causes my opponent to overshoot and pass me. For a few seconds only he is in my sights; but it is a chance to take him with me. I press both triggers. I feel myself trembling all over from the nervous tension. If I can only take him with me!

My salvo scores a perfect bull's-eye right in the center of his fuselage. He pulls up his smoking plane in a steep climb. In a moment he is in flames. The canopy opens and the body of the pilot emerges.

The ground comes up with a rush. Too late for me to bail out now. I cross some large fields. Down goes the nose and the plane settles. The flames come up, reaching for my face. Earth flies into the air. There is a dull, heavy, thud. The crate skids along in a cloud of dust, then digs its own grave in the soft earth. I throw up my arms to cover my face, and brace my legs against the rudder bar. It is all over in a split second. Something crashes with stunning force on to my head.

So this must be the end! It is my last thought before losing consciousness. . . .

I have no recollection of getting clear of that burning wreck, but I suppose I must have done so. Coherent thought is beyond me: there is only that dreadful pain in my head. I remember bullets flying past my ears as the ammunition explodes. I stumble and fall, and somehow stagger to my feet again. My one idea is to get away before the final explosion. The bright flames consuming my aircraft contrast vividly against the dark smoke pall rising into the sky behind it.

A second wreck is burning only a few hundred yards away. Dimly I realize that it must be my Yank. If only the pain would stop! My head! my head!—I hold it in both hands and sink to my knees. The world spins crazily in front of my eyes. I am overcome by recurrent nausea, until only the taste of green bile remains.

I finally roll into a shallow ditch and pass out again. I am at the end of my tether. . . .

When next I recover consciousness, I become aware of a man standing motionless and staring down at me. He is as tall as a young tree—an American!

I try to sit up on the edge of the ditch. The big fellow sits down beside me. At first neither of us speak. It is all I can do to prop my elbows on my knees and hold my splitting head in my hands. Then the Yank offers me a cigarette. I thank him and refuse, at the same time offering him one of mine. He also refuses; so we both light up our own.

"Was that you flying the Messerschmitt?"

"Yes," I answer in rusty English.

"You wounded?"

"Feels like it."

"The back of your head is bleeding."

I can feel the blood trickling down my neck. The Yank continues: "Did you really shoot me down?"

"Yes."

"But I don't see how you could! Your kite was a mass of flames."

"Don't I know it!"

The tall American explains how he spotted me above the clouds and went down after me with his men. "It sure seemed like a bit of luck," he added.

I ask him in turn: "What was your idea in getting out in front of me when my engine died?"

"Too much forward speed. Besides, it never occurred to me that you would still be firing."

"That is where you made your mistake."

He laughs. "Guess I'm not the first you bagged, am I?"

"No; you are my twenty-sixth."

The American tells me that he has shot down 17 Germans. In a few more days he was due to go home. He notices the ring on my finger and asks if I am married."

"Yes; and I have two little children." I show him a picture of Lilo and Ingrid.

"Very nice," he remarks, nodding in appreciation, "very, very nice indeed."

I am glad he likes them.

He also is married. His wife over there will have to wait for him in vain now. Rather anxiously, the big fellow asks what is going to happen to him.

I explain that he will be sent to a special POW camp for American airmen. "Are you an officer?"

"Yes; a Captain."

"In that case you will go to a camp for officers. You will be well treated. Our prisoners are just as well treated as yours."

We have a friendly chat for about half an hour. He seems like a decent fellow. There is no suggestion of hatred between us, nor any reason for it. We have too much in common. We are both pilots, and we have both just narrowly escaped death.

A squad of soldiers from a nearby searchlight battery arrives, and we are covered with raised rifles.

"Put away that damned artillery, you clods," I call over to them.

On the highway there is a truck waiting for us. Six Yanks from a Fortress are huddled in the back. They look rather gloomy. My Captain and I sit beside them. Although feeling like death myself, I try to cheer up the party with a few jokes.

On the road we collect more Yanks who were shot down. One of them is badly wounded in the leg. I see that our men lift him up carefully into the truck.

We are driven to the Brunswick Airfield at Broitzum. There I say farewell to my fellow-sufferers, and we all shake hands.

"Good luck!"

"All the best!"

"*Auf Wiedersehen!*"

One hour later Barran flies over and collects me in an Arado. The Squadron all returned without further casualties. I am the only one who was caught.

Later, in the operations room, I collapse, unconscious again. They first take me to my quarters, where I develop a raging fever. During the night I am admitted to the hospital.

ON THE RUSSIAN FRONT

by Leutnant Hermann
Graf, Luftwaffe

"5th August, 1941. Relative calm last night. A few enemy aircraft fired flares near our camp. Nothing else.

"We are sleeping under canvas in a great tent pitched in the middle of a magnificent field. Straw to sleep on. There are ten of us. We sleep with our clothes on.

"Near my head are two field telephones. I received the orders for tomorrow. Our Captain, who has been recalled to replace the Station Commander, has appointed me Group Commander. This is the first time I have been given this responsibility.

"Eight fighters will escort an important Stuka formation to attack enemy positions at Kiev. That is the mission. My chief mechanic will warm up the engines at the required time. He has to wake me up a quarter of an hour before take-off.

"It is two o'clock in the morning. I have written down the orders on my writing pad. My Irish setter is asleep on the floor at my side. It is all very romantic. The nervous expenditure of energy during the past few days is having its effect. Some of the pilots talk and rave in their sleep. They re-fight desperate air battles. I try to make out their indistinct words but eventually I fall asleep.

"A rap on my soles woke me up. 'Take-off in a quarter of an hour, *mein Leutnant.*' We put on our fur boots and lined up beside the aircraft. The engines were already revving.

"I gave the pilots their orders: 'Take off in ten minutes to escort the two groups of Stukas. We fly in sections of two, fifty yards apart. We are to stick to the Stukas and intercept anything that attacks them. The Stukas, heavy and slow with a full bomb load cannot defend themselves.'

"We shook hands irrespective of our rank. We were comrades about to fight together. All watches were synchronised with mine. An-

other three minutes. We climbed into our aircraft and our mechanics waved.

"The Stukas were already over the airfield gaining height. I raised my hand, full throttle and away.

"Once in the air I checked the formation order and took up my position. We were flying at 9000 feet.

"Slowly we approached the front line. While we were in Roumania we had been promised that the war in the east would be over in a few weeks. But now we saw the true nature of things. The soil was riddled and pitted with bomb and shell craters. Visions of the 1914–18 war returned to my mind. Were we too condemned to interminable static war with fuel and food becoming ever more hard to obtain?

Erich "Bubi" Hartmann, with an incredible 352 victories, was both the Luftwaffe's ranking ace, and the highest-scoring pilot of all time. (Bill Hess)

"The Russian ack-ack went into action. *Zum Teufel!* They fire well. Always just ahead of us which upsets the nerves. Fortunately the Stukas advanced imperturbably without bothering about the enemy fire. I could see them banking slowly away to the left. Their leader must have recognised his targets. We continued to give them cover at close quarters.

"The Commander of the Stukas dived on to the enemy positions followed by his two formations. They tumbled out of the sky one after the other in a vertical dive. A whirlwind of dust arose and the antiaircraft went on firing.

"Now the Stukas pulled out and were making their way westwards on the home journey. At the start they broke off and avoided the enemy fire as best they could. Then they returned to their close formation.

"I scanned the sky to the east. Suddenly some dots appeared, shining in the sunlight. Russian fighters. For a brief moment I felt excited and then I controlled myself. I gave my orders over the intercom. We maneuvered to get in the sun and attack.

"The first engagement was very short and the attackers immediately dispersed in all directions. Since some of them seemed about to return we dived on them. A few seconds' fighting and they turned back eastwards. We were unable to shoot any down but the Stukas were now safely over our lines. Our mission was completed.

"A few minutes later we landed. The Stuka pilots shook our hands and their Commanding Officer thanked us. We returned to our own camp. A report and a criticism of the operation. . . . Everyone, irrespective of rank, was allowed to give his opinion. Even a private soldier can have an inspired or interesting idea."

THE LAST

by General Adolf Galland, Luftwaffe

On February 26, 1945, Berlin experienced its fortieth large-scale raid; actually the four-hundredth raid this sorely tried city had suffered. From above the clouds, 1112 American bombers dropped 2879 tons of bombs. During March the American and English raids increased, delivering an almost continuous shower of bombs. Night after night, day after day, death and destruction descended upon the ever-diminishing area of the Reich. Hardly a town remained untouched. On March 12 the largest amount of bombs ever dropped during a night raid on a German town was registered as 4899 tons on Dortmund. The last week in March is entered as a record in the statistics of the RAF with a total weight of bombs dropped at 67,365 tons. On April 6, Harris stated that there were no worthwhile targets for his strategic bomber fleet in Germany. A day later the large-scale RAF air raids stopped. The bombing commission that functioned in London under the code name "Jockey" telegraphed to the Allied headquarters: "Jockey has unsaddled." Three days later, on April 10, American four-engined bombers raided Berlin for the last time. A fortnight later the Eighth AAF was transferred to Okinawa in order to bomb Japan in conjunction with the Twentieth AAF, already stationed in the Far East, until she was ripe for capitulation.

The last air battle of this war was over Germany in which the Americans suffered impressive losses was delivered by the German fighter arm on March 18, 1945, over Berlin. The capital of the Reich was attacked by 1200 bombers that had an escort of 14 fighter squadrons of P-51s. Although many flak batteries had already been removed to the nearby eastern front, 16 bombers were so heavily hit that they had to make emergency landings behind the Soviet front line. The enemy suffered much greater losses at the hands of the jet fighters of the JG7. From American flight reports one can see that the Me-262 broke again and again with ease through the American fighter screen and shot down one bomber after the other from the tightly closed formations despite an inferiority of 100 to 1. Besides those shot down by flak, the Americans had to report a loss of 25 bombers and 5 fighter planes. The next day the Americans again suffered losses from German jet fighters, while our piston-engined fighters could achieve nothing against the mass of the Allied fighter escort. Doolittle and Tedder now demanded decisive measures to prevent the operation of German jet fighters, without stating what these measures should be.

In January, 1945, we started on the formation of my unit that Hitler had ordered. It spread quickly through the fighter arm that our 44th Squadron was taking shape at Brandenburg-Briest. Our official nomination was a JV44.

Steinhoff was in charge of retaining the pilots. Lützow came to us from Italy. Barkhorn, who had scored more than 300 kills in the east, Hohagen, Schnell, and Krupinski were coaxed out of hospital. Many reported without consent or transfer orders. Most of them had been in action since the first day of the war, and all of them had been wounded. All of them bore the scars of war and displayed the highest medals. The Knight's Cross was, so to speak, the badge of our unit. Now, after a long period of technical and numerical inferiority, they wanted once more to experience the feeling of air superiority. They wanted to be known as the first jet boys of the last fighter pilots of the Luftwaffe. For this they were ready once more to chance sacrificing their lives.

Another Luftwaffe Ace, Walter Nowotny, had a mere 258 victories—good enough for only fifth place. (Bill Hess)

Soon after receiving the first planes we were stationed at Munich-Riem. In the early hours of the morning of March 31, 1945, the JV 44 took off in close formation, and 42 minutes later the planes landed in Munich. They had covered the distance of about 300 miles in record time.

Here in Munich the unit took on its final shape. The Squadron of Experts, as we were called, had as pilots one lieutenant general, two colonels, one lieutenant colonel, three majors, five captains, eight lieutenants, and about the same number of second lieutenants. None of us imagined that we were able to give to the war the much-quoted "turn." The magic word "jet" had brought us together to experience once more *"die grosse Fliegerei."* Our last operation was anything but a fresh and gay hunting. We not only battled against technical, tactical, and supply difficulties, we also lacked a clear picture of the air situation of the floods coming from the west—a picture absolutely necessary for the success of an operation. Every day the fronts moved in closer from three sides. But worst of all our field was under continuous observation by an overwhelming majority of American fighters. During one raid we were hit three times very heavily. Thousands of workers had to be mobilized to keep open a landing strip between the bomb craters.

Operation orders for the Me-262s now changed daily. Conditions in the armament industry were also turbulent. The time of commissioners, special commissioners, ambassadors of the Fuhrer, commissars, and special commissariats had started. All who were to increase production of the industry or to coordinate operations were appointed subordinate to each other, equal to each other, and over each other. From February until March the jet-fighter command went partly over to the SA. From their ranks came the so-called Commissariat of the Fuhrer for Jet Aircraft, a general of the Waffen SS. Hitler had appointed him although Goring in his turn had appointed a Special Commissioner for Jet Aircraft.

Surprisingly I was called by Göring to the Obersalzberg—it must have been somewhere around April 10. To my amazement he received me with the greatest civility, inquired after the progress of our initial actions, and gave me a restricted confirmation that my prediction concerning the use of bombers with the Me-262 in the defense of the Reich had been correct. This indicated that the Reichsmarshal had begun to realize that after all I had been right throughout all those sharp clashes of opinion of the last months. This was the last time I saw Göring.

Four weeks before the collapse of the armed forces, the fighter arm was still in a position to represent a factor that could not be overlooked. Operations from Riem started despite all resistance and difficulties. Naturally we were able to send up only small units. On landing, the aircraft had to be towed immediately off the field. They were dispersed over the countryside and had to be completely camouflaged. Bringing the aircraft onto the field and taking off became more and more difficult; eventually it was a

matter of luck. One raid followed another.

In this situation the safety of the personnel was paramount and came before any orders to clear the airfield. Each pilot was responsible for his own cover on the airfield and had to dig his own foxhole. When it came to physical work you cannot imagine anything more lazy than a fighter pilot in his sixth year of service. My pilots moaned terribly about the stony ground at Riem. Returning from a mission, I was standing with them on our western airstrip, watching the bombers attacking railway stations in Munich in single waves. Suddenly somebody called, *"Achtung! Bombenangriff!"* Already the ugly finger of death, as we called the markers of the daylight raiders, were groping for our aerodrome. I chased after one of my pilots, who slithered into a nearby hole he had dug for himself. Hellishly narrow, I thought . . . oh, a single foxhole. It was very shallow. Then the first carpet of bombs roared down, passed over our heads. Nauseating, the whistle, the explosion, the blast, the tremor of the ground. A brief pause occurred after the attack of the first formation. I was lying on top of a sergeant. It was Knier. He was shaking, but in answer to my question he insisted that he was no more afraid than I was.

Our hole had a cover. A few splinters had flown off this lid with a loud metallic clang. My back was pressed against it. "Knier, what's this on my back?" "100-pound bombs, Herr General," was the prompt reply. I certainly began to shake. Another five salvoes followed at short intervals. Outside there was smoke, debris, craters, fire, and destruction. All Germans had experienced this during the last years of the war: In the cities, in the factories, on the battlefield, on ships and U-boats: Bombs, Bombs, Bombs! But it was an awkward feeling to be in the middle of a raid and, what is more, to be sheltered by one's own bombs.

During these last weeks of the war we were able to fit out some aircraft with additional weapons, which gave a greater firing power to the Me-262: R4M rockets of 3-cm. caliber, and 500-g. explosives. A single hit from these was enough to bring down a multi-engined bomber. They were fixed beneath the wing in two racks that carried 24 rockets. In a feverish hurry our mechanics and servicing crew loaded up a few jet fighters. I took off in one of them.

In the district of Landsberg on the Lech I met a formation of about 16 Marauders. We called these twin-engined bombers *Halbstarke*. I opened from a distance of about 600 yards, firing in half a second a salvo of 24 rockets into the close flying formation. I observed two certain hits. One bomber immediately caught fire and exploded; a second lost large parts of its right tail unit and wing and began to spiral earthward. In the meantime the three other planes that had taken off with me had also attacked successfully. My accompanying pilot, Edward Schallmoser, who once over Riem had rammed a Lightning because in his excitement he could not fire, waded into the Marauders with all his rockets. That evening he reported back to his quarters, parachute under his arm, and a twisted leg.

Our impression of the efficiency of this new weapon was indescribable. The rockets could be fired outside the effective range of the defensive fire of the bombers. A well-aimed salvo would probably hit several bombers simultaneously. That was the way to break up formations. But this was the end of April, 1945! In the middle of our breakup, at the beginning of our collapse! It does not bear thinking about what we could have done had we had those jet fighters, 3-cm. quick-firing cannons, and 5-cm. rockets years ago—before our war potential had been smashed, before indescribable misery had come over Germany through the raids. We dared not think about it. Now we could do nothing but fly and fight and do our duty as fighter pilots to the last.

Service in action still demanded heavy and grievous losses. On April 18, Steinhoff crashed on a take-off but managed to free himself from the burning wreckage of his jet plane with very severe burns. A few days later

Gunther Lützow did not return from his mission. Long after the end of the war we were still hoping that this splendid officer might not have left us forever. In the same spirit and with the same devotion many more young pilots of our unit fell.

But the fate of Germany was sealed. On April 25 the American and the Soviet soldiers shook hands at Torgau on the Elbe. The last defensive ring of Berlin was soon penetrated. The Red flag was flying over the Ballhausplatz in Vienna. The German front in Italy collapsed. On Pilsen fell the last bomb of the 2,755,000 tons which the Western Allies had dropped in Europe during five years of war.

At the moment I called my pilots together and said to them, "Militarily speaking the war is lost. Even our action here cannot change anything . . . I shall continue to fight, because operating with the Me-262 has got hold of me, because I am proud to belong to the last fighter pilots of the German Luftwaffe . . . Only those who feel the same are to go on flying with me . . . "

In the meantime the harsh reality of the war finally decided the question: "Bomber or fighter action by Me-262?" in our favor. The leaders were completely occupied with themselves in Berlin and at other places. Numerous departments, which up to now had interfered with allocation and the operation of jet fighters, ceased to function or did not come through any more. Commanders of the bombers, reconnaissance, combat fighters, night fighters, and sundry testing units that had been fitted out with the coveted Me-262 passed their aircraft on to us. From all sides we were presented with jet fighters. Finally, we had 70 aircraft.

On April 26, I set out on my last mission of the war. I led six jet fighters of the JV 44 against a formation of Marauders. Our own little directing post brought us well into contact with the enemy. The weather: Varying clouds at different altitudes, with gaps, ground visible in about only three-tenths of the operational area.

I sighted the enemy formation in the district

of Neuburg on the Danube. Once again I noticed how difficult it was, with such great difference of speed and with clouds over the landmarks, to find the relative flying direction between one's own plane, and that of the enemy, and how difficult it was to judge the approach, This difficulty had already driven Lutzow to despair. He had discussed it repeatedly with me, and every time he missed his run-in, this most successful fighter commodore blamed his own inefficiency as a fighter pilot. Had there been any need for more confirmation as to the hopelessness of operations with the Me-262 by bomber pilots, our experiences would have sufficed.

But now there was no time for such considerations. We were flying in an almost opposite direction to the Marauder formation. Each second meant that we were 300 yards nearer. I will not say that I fought this action ideally, but I led my formation to a fairly favorable firing position. Safety catch off the gun and rocket switch! Already at a great distance we met with considerable defensive fire. As usual in a dogfight, I was tense and excited: I forgot to release the second safety catch for the rockets. They did not go off. I was in the best firing position, I had aimed accurately and pressed my thumb flat on the release button—with no result. Maddening for any fighter pilot! Anyhow my four 3-cm. cannons were working. They had much more firing power than we had been used to so far. At that moment, close below me, Schallnoser, the jet-rammer, whizzed past. In ramming he made no distinction between friend or foe.

This engagement had lasted only a fraction of a second—a very important second to be sure. One Marauder of the last string was on fire and exploded. Now I attacked another bomber in the van of the formation. It was heavily hit as I passed very close above it. During this breakthrough I got a few minor hits from the defensive fire. But now I wanted to know definitely what was happening to the second bomber I had hit. I was not quite clear if it had crashed. So far I had not noticed any fighter escort.

Above the formation I had attacked last, I banked steeply to the left, and at this moment it happened: a hail of fire enveloped me. A Mustang had caught me napping. A sharp rap hit my right knee. The instrument panel with its indispensable instruments was shattered. The right engine was also hit. Its metal covering worked loose in the wind and was partly carried away. Now the left engine was hit too, I could hardly hold her in the air.

In this embarrassing situation I had only one wish: to get out of this crate, which now apparently was only good for dying in. But then I was paralyzed by the terror of being shot while parachuting down. Experience had taught us that we jet-fighter pilots had to reckon on this. I soon discovered that my battered Me-262 could be steered again after some adjustments. After a dive through the layer of cloud I saw the Autobahn below me; ahead of me lay Munich and to the left Riem. In a few seconds I was over the airfield. It was remarkably quiet and dead below. Having regained my self-confidence, I gave the customary wing wobble and started banking to come in. One engine did not react at all to the throttle. I could not reduce it. Just before the edge of the airfield I therefore had to cut out both engines. A long trail of smoke drifted behind me. Only at this moment I noticed that Thunderbolts in a low-level attack were giving our airfield the works. Now I had no choice. I had not heard the warnings of our ground post because my wireless had faded out when I was hit. There remained only one thing to do: straight down into the fireworks! Touching down, I realized that the tire of my nosewheel was flat. It rattled horribly as the earth again received me at a speed of 150 mph on the small landing strip.

Brake! Brake! The kite would not stop! But at last I was out of the kite and into the nearest bomb crater. There were plenty of them on our runways. Bombs and rockets exploded all around; bursts of shells from the Thunderbolts whistled and banged. A new low-level attack. Out of the fastest fighter in the world into a bomb crater, that was an unutterably wretched feeling. Through all the fireworks an armored tractor came rushing across to me. It pulled up sharply driven by one of our mechanics. Quickly I got in behind him. He turned and raced off on the shortest route away from the airfield. In silence I slapped him on the shoulder. He understood better what I wanted to say than any words about the unity between flying and ground personnel could have expressed.

The other pilots who took part in this operation were directed to neighboring airfields or came into Riem after the attack. We reported five certain kills without loss to ourselves.

I had to go to Munich to a hospital for treatment of my scratched knee. The X ray showed two splinters in the kneecap. It was put in plaster. A fine business!

The enemy advancing from the north had already crossed the Danube at several places. The JV 44 prepared its last transfer. Bär, who had come to us with the remnants of his Volksfighter test commando, took over the command in my place. About 60 jet fighters flew to Salzburg. Orders came from the Reichskanei and from the Luftwaffe Staff in Berchtesgaden for an immediate transfer to Prague in order to pursue from there the completely hopeless fight for Berlin. The execution of this order was delayed until it became purposeless.

On May 3, the aircraft of the JV 44 were standing on the aerodrome of Salzburg without any camouflage. American fighters circled overhead. They did not shoot, they did not drop any bombs: they obviously hoped soon to be flying the German jet fighters that had given them so much trouble. Salzburg prepared for the capitulation. The advanced units of Devers' army approached the town. As the rattle of the first tank was heard on the airfield, there was no other possibility left: our jet fighters went up in flames.

PART FOUR

GLOBAL WAR— WORLD WAR II, PACIFIC

Flying Tigers

BUILDING THE AVG

by Major General Claire Lee Chennault, AVG and USAAF

The bombings began again and went on almost without interruption, day and night for seventy-two hours. Phone and electricity lines were cut. There was no water and only cold rice to eat. The second day a stick of bombs smashed nearby, scattering steel splinters into the compound and driving us into the dugout on a nearby hillside. I sat there listening to the intermittent thunder of the bombs, more angry than ever before as I thought of the delays that had made it impossible to hurl the American volunteers into this battle and prevent what turned out to be the final ordeal of Chungking. There was small satisfaction then in knowing that the planes and pilots capable of smashing the Japanese air effort in China were already in Asia. It was August 22 before I could get clear of bomb-spattered Chungking and return to Toungoo to meet most of the American volunteers for the first time. The camp at Kyedaw was seething with griping and unrest when I arrived. My first business was to accept the resignations of five pilots who were eager to return to the United States and airline jobs.

Toungoo was a shocking contrast to the peacetime Army or Navy post in the United States. The runway was surrounded by quagmire and pestilential jungle. Matted masses of rotting vegetation carpeted the jungle and filled the air with a sour, sickening smell. Torrential monsoon rains and thunderstorms alternated with torrid heat to give the atmosphere the texture of a Turkish bath. Dampness and green mold penetrated everywhere. The food, provided by a Burmese mess contractor, was terrible, and one of the principal causes of group griping.

Barracks were new and well ventilated, but along with the air came every stinging insect in Burma. There were no screens or electric lights and not a foot of screening to be bought in all Burma. We learned that the RAF abandone Kyedaw during the rainy season because Europeans were unable to survive its foul climate. Thanks to the abundance of medical supplies authorized by Dr. Soong and the work of our three-man medical staff—Doctors Tom Gentry, Lewis Richards, and Sam Prevo—we survived training in this pesthole without serious illness. When Brooke-Popham inspected the AVG at Kyedaw, his

Maj. General Claire Lee Chennault, commander of the 14th Air Force, took inexperienced ex-Army, Navy, and Marine pilots to China and whipped them into one of the world's greatest fighting teams—the AVG, or Flying Tigers. (USAF)

147

first concern was for our sick list. He inspected the large RAF-built hospital before he looked at the planes and was amazed to find only a single patient—a mechanic who had had his tonsils removed the day before.

Pawley finally provided three Americans and some Chinese mechanics from his Loi-Wing factory to assemble the AVG P-40s at Mingaladon aerodrome near Rangoon, but all radios, oxygen equipment, and armament had to be installed by group mechanics at Toungoo.

During one of the periodic British inspections of Kyedaw, Air Vice Marshal Pulford visited me and exclaimed, "This is incredible. Less than a month ago you arrived on the docks at Rangoon with only a briefcase, and now you have a fighter group ready to fight."

I assured Pulford that we were far from ready to fight. Ahead lay an arduous training period during which I had to teach my pilots all the tricks of their enemy—how to use their own equipment to the best advantage, and how to fight and live to fight again another day. This last factor was extremely important since, with a group so small and replacements so uncertain, we simply had to reduce our own combat losses well below average, at the same time boosting the enemy's high above what he was prepared to absorb. It was no easy task.

While the planes were being readied for combat, we began final pilot training. It was a rude shock to some of the AVG pilots when they matriculated in my postgraduate school of fighter tactics at Toungoo. Most of them considered themselves extremely hot pilots. After a long sea voyage bragging to fellow passengers about their prowess as fighter pilots, many of them were convinced they were ready to walk down the gangplank at Rangoon and begin decimating the Japanese Air Force. Some were highly skeptical of what a "beat-up old Army captain" who had been "buried in China" for years could teach youths fresh from official fonts of military knowledge. But I had been working on my

plans to whip the Japanese in the air for four years, and I was determined that, when the American Volunteer Group went into battle, it would be using tactics based on that bitter experience.

Pilots looked far from promising as they checked in at Kyedaw. The long boat trip and Dutch shipboard menus had left many flabby and overweight. They all appeared wilted during their introduction to the humid monsoon heat. Field transportation was cut to a minimum to keep them walking and sweating; regular schedules of baseball, volleyball, and calisthenics were instituted to whip them back into good physical condition.

Their flying records were not impressive. I wanted pilots between twenty-three and twenty-eight with at least three years of experience in fighter planes. Only a dozen met these standards and had ever seen a P-40. More than half the pilots had never flown fighters. We had everything from four-engine Flying Fortress pilots to Navy torpedo bombers. Louis Hoffmann, the oldest, was a forty-three-year-old Navy veteran and had almost as much fighter time as I had. Henry Gilbert, the youngest, had just turned twenty-one and was fresh from Army flying school. Of the hundred and ten pilots who reached Toungoo, four were Marines, with the rest about equally divided between Army and Navy. There was always some joshing about the respective services but never any of the bitter interservice rivalry in the AVG that was so evident later in the war.

We began at Toungoo with a kindergarten for teaching bomber pilots how to fly fighters. Some learned fast and well. Bob Neale and David "Tex" Hill, both Navy dive-bomber pilots, had the best combat records in the AVG. George Burgard and Charley Bond, both Flying Fortress pilots, ranked among the first ten. For others it was a long, tedious, and unsatisfactory process. Many multi-engined pilots had trouble getting used to the hundred-mile-per-hour landing speed and violent maneuvers of the P-40. One morning I watched them crack up six P-40s in landing—heavier losses than the AVG ever suffered in a day's combat. It reminded me of the Italian-trained Chinese pilots. While I was issuing orders to cancel flying for the rest of the day, a mechanic, bicycling while watching a wreck, crashed into a parked plane, tearing a piece off the aileron and putting the seventh plane of the day out of commission. Kindergarten got a long lecture on landings that afternoon. To emphasize the point, a white line was chalked marking one third of the runway length and a fifty-dollar fine slapped on any pilot who touched his wheels beyond the line. Our training program went on long after combat began. As late as March 1942, after the group had been fighting for nearly four months, we still had eighteen pilots classified as not ready for combat. No matter how pressing the immediate needs of combat I refused to throw a pilot into the fray until I was personally satisfied that he was properly trained. That is probably one of the main reasons Japanese pilots were able to kill only four

AVG pilots in six months of air combat.

Our Toungoo routine began at 6 a.m. with a lecture in a teakwood classroom near the field, where I held forth with blackboard, maps, and mimeographed textbooks. All my life I have been a teacher, ranging from the one-room schools of rural Louisiana to director of one of the largest Air Corps flying schools, but I believe that the best teaching of my career was done in that teakwood shack at Toungoo, where the assortment of American volunteers turned into the world-famous Flying Tigers, whose aerial combat record has never been equaled by a group of comparable size.

Every pilot who arrived before September 15 got seventy-two hours of lectures in addition to sixty hours of specialized flying. I gave the pilots a lesson in the geography of Asia that they all needed badly, told them something of the war in China, and how the Chinese air-raid warning net worked.

I taught them all I knew about the Japanese. Day after day there were lectures from

The Curtiss P-40, to which General Chennault's Flying Tigers brought notoriety. Variously known as the Warhawk and Tomahawk, the P-40 also saw some service with the RAF and in North Africa. The craft destroyed more enemy planes than any other Allied fighter. (Monogram)

my notebooks, filled during the previous four years of combat. All of the bitter experience from Nanking to Chungking was poured out in those lectures. Captured Japanese flying and staff manuals, translated into English by the Chinese, served as textbooks. From these manuals the American pilots learned more about Japanese tactics than any single Japanese pilot ever knew.

"You will face Japanese pilots superbly trained in mechanical flying," I told them. "They have been drilled for hundreds of hours in flying precise formations and rehearsing set tactics for each situation they may encounter. Japanese pilots fly by the book, and these are the books they use. Study them, and you will always be one jump ahead of the enemy.

"They have plenty of guts but lack initiative and judgment. They go into battle with a set tactical plan and follow it no matter what happens. Bombers will hold their formations until they are all shot down. Fighters always try the same tricks over and over again. God help the American pilot who tries to fight them according to their plans.

"The object of our tactics is to break up their formations and make them fight according to our style. Once the Japanese are forced to deviate from their plan, they are in trouble. Their rigid air discipline can be used as a powerful weapon against them."

I went into detail on the construction, performance, and armament of the Japanese planes, filling in many of the blanks in the War Department manuals. Mimeographed sheets containing drawings, specifications, and performance data on the famous Model Zero navy fighter (Zeke) were passed out to each pilot. Shortly thereafter a few more pilots submitted their resignations. I drew diagrams of the Japanese planes on the blackboard, circling vital spots—oil coolers, oxygen storage, gas tanks, and bomb bays—in colored chalk. Erasing the colored circles, a pilot would be asked to step up and redraw them from memory. My methods were simple

and direct, with plenty of repetition to make the lessons stick. In a fight you seldom have time to think, and it is training and reflexes that count.

Then I went into the tactics I had devised to put the P-40 against the Japanese fighters and bombers.

"You must use the strong points of your equipment against the weak points of the enemy. Each type of plane has its own strength and weakness. The pilot who can turn his advantages against the enemy's weakness will win every time. You can count on a higher top speed, faster dive, and superior firepower. The Jap fighters have a faster rate of climb, higher ceiling, and better maneuverability. They can turn on a dime and climb almost straight up. If they can get you into a turning combat, they are deadly.

"Use your speed and diving power to make a pass, shoot and break away. You have the

The Flying Tigers' second-highest ace was former Navy Pilot David "Tex" Hill, with twelve-and-a-quarter victories. He added five more after transferring to the Air Force. (USAF)

edge in that kind of combat. All your advantages are brought to bear on the Japanese deficiencies. Close your range, fire, and dive away. Never stay within range of the Jap's defensive firepower any longer than you need to deliver an accurate burst."

I harped on accurate gunnery.

"You need to sharpen your shooting eye. Nobody ever gets too good at gunnery. The more Japs you get with your first burst, the fewer there are to jump you later. Accurate fire saves ammunition. Your plane carries a limited number of bullets. There is nothing worse than finding yourself in a fight with empty guns."

Day after day I drew diagrams, lectured, and always repeated, "Fight in pairs. Make every bullet count. Never try to get all the Japanese in one pass. Hit hard, break clean, and get position for another pass. Never worry about what's going to happen next, or it will happen to you. Keep looking around. You can lick the Japanese without getting hurt if you use your heads and are careful. Follow them home. They are usually low on gas and ammunition when they break off and head for home. If they maneuver or open full throttle, they will not get back."

The AVG tactics of shooting and diving away were the subject of considerable amusement. At Rangoon the RAF 221st Group posted a notice that any RAF pilot seen diving away from a fight would be subject to court-martial. In the Chinese Air Force the penalty for the same offense was a firing squad. Many of the American pilots had been educated in the tail-chasing dogfight and had little enthusiasm for the shoot-and-dive tactics until after their first fight.

Later there was ample opportunity for comparison. The AVG and RAF fought side by side over Rangoon with comparable numbers, equipment, and courage against the same odds. The RAF barely broke even against the Japanese, while the Americans rolled up a 15 to 1 score. In February 1942, the Japanese threw heavy raids against Rangoon and Port Darwin, Australia, in the same week. Over Rangoon five AVG pilots in P-40s shot down 17 out of 70 enemy raiders without loss. Over Darwin 11 out of 12 U.S. Army Air Forces P-40s were shot down by a similar Japanese force. A few weeks later a crack RAF Spitfire squadron was rushed to Australia from Europe and lost 17 out of 27 pilots over Darwin in two raids. The Spitfire was far superior to the P-40 as a combat plane. It was simply a matter of tactics. The RAF pilots were trained in methods that were excellent against German and Italian equipment but suicide against the acrobatic Japs. The only American squadron in China that the Japanese ever liked to fight was a P-38 squadron that had fought in North Africa and refused to change its tactics against the Japanese.

During the first year of the war the AVG tactics were spread throughout the Army and Navy by intelligence reports and returning AVG veterans. At least one Navy commander in the Pacific and an Air Forces colonel with the Fifth Air Force in Australia were later decorated for "inventing" what were originally the AVG tactics.

To polish these tactics, every pilot went through sixty hours of specialized flying. Most of the flying was done immediately after lectures in the cool of the morning before the monsoon thunderstorms swept up the Sittang Valley. Pilots went aloft to dogfight while I watched from a rickety bamboo control tower with field glasses and microphone. I coached each pilot as though he were the star halfback on our football team. Over the field radio I gave him a running commentary on his flying and dictated additional notes to my secretary, Tom Trumble of Lincoln, Nebraska, who served me well in China for four years. On the ground I went over these notes with the pilot, giving him a detailed critique of his flying and tactics and prescribing specific practice methods to bolster his weak spots.

Later I sent pilots up in pairs flying together to give mutual support with one plane always protecting the other's tail. Finally we did squadron formation work, practicing attacks on bombers and strafing against ground targets. I still planned to use the AVG as a group with one squadron for initial attack, the second for support, and the third for the decisive airborne reserve to enter battle at the critical moment. There had never been an air battle in which airborne planes were used as reserves in the manner that ground forces poised their reserves to try for decisive blows. I was sure I could do it with my fighter group against the Japanese. Unfortunately I never got the chance.

During the training period at Toungoo we lost our first plane and buried our first dead in the cemetery of St. Lukes, Church of England. Jack Armstrong of Hutchinson, Kansas, was killed in a mid-air collision with another P-40, while dogfighting. Max Hammer, of Cairo, Illinois, crashed to his death in a monsoon storm while trying to grope his way back to the field. Peter Atkinson of Martinsburg, West Virginia, died when his propeller governor gave way and tore his plane apart in a screaming power dive.

The pilots had as little regard for Curtiss-Wright's P-40 at Toungoo as I did, but for different reasons. My main complaints were the vulnerability of its liquid-cooled engine in combat and its lack of droppable auxiliary fuel tanks and bomb racks. Before the pilots left the United States, the P-40 had acquired a reputation as a killer in the hands of relatively inexperienced pilots. The pilots' knowledge of the plane was based almost entirely on the crop of rumors then sprouting at military flying fields on the erratic flying qualities, hot landing speeds, and inferior power plant of the P-40. Most of them were convinced it was a "no-good" combat airplane. When they passed through Surabaya, Singapore, and Rangoon and saw the Dutch and British equipped with American-made Brewster Buffaloes they muttered darkly that "it was a helluva note that Americans had to fight in second-rate planes because all the best were going to the British and Dutch under lend-lease." When RAF pilots flew Buffaloes to Toungoo there was little enthusiasm for mock dogfights with them. Actually the Buffalo was inferior to the P-40 in every respect, particularly rate of climb and armament, where it carried only two .30-caliber machine guns against the four .30s and two .50s of the P-40. Finally RAF taunts grew too pointed to ignore, and a dogfight was arranged between Erik Shilling, of Washington, D.C., and an RAF pilot in a Buffalo. Much to everybody's astonishment, Shilling flew rings around his opponent. Later when the Americans saw the Buffaloes drop like flies under the Japanese onslaught over Rangoon, P-40 stock rose until finally AVG pilots refused an RAF offer to trade Hawker Hurricanes for P-40s.

Before I left the United States in the summer of 1941 I asked a few friends in Louisiana to watch the newspapers and send me any clippings about the AVG. Now I was being swamped with clippings from stateside newspapers, and my men were astonished to find themselves world famous as the Flying Tigers. The insignia we made famous was by no means original with the AVG. Our pilots copied the shark-tooth design on their P-40s noses from a colored illustration in the *India Illustrated Weekly* depicting an RAF squadron in the Libyan desert with shark-nosed P-40s. Even before that the German Air Force painted shark's teeth on some of its Messerschmitt 210 fighters. With the pointed nose of a liquid-cooled engine it was an apt and fearsome design. How the term Flying Tigers was derived from the shark-nosed P-40s I never will know. At any rate we were somewhat surprised to find ourselves billed under that name. It was not until just before the AVG was disbanded that we had any kind of group insignia. At the request of China Defense Supplies in Washington, Roy Williams of the Walt Disney organization in Hollywood designed our insignia consisting of a winged tiger flying through a large V for victory.

FIREWORKS BEFORE THE 4TH

by Colonel Robert L. Scott, Jr.,
USAAF

. . . "You're absolutely right, every place except in your date," (said General Chennault).

He was looking at me now, kind of pinning me up against the wall with his eyes.

"Just your date's wrong, that's all. Don't wait for the Fourth. Get them on the day before—hit them July 3—go set up the planes."

I almost committed a serious mistake. I caught myself just about to say that we couldn't do that, that we wouldn't actually be an official part of the Army Air Forces until the Fourth of July. I remembered just in time. What the devil did official activation mean to guerrillas like us "paid killers, bandits, Hollywood playboys?" We'd beat them to it by a whole day.

This would be a real trap. I thought of all those amateurish traps I had tried to set with my P-40. I hadn't been ready then. Was I ready now? Well, General Chennault was setting this trap, and he must know. And he set it in secret too. The Old Man had learned the hard way that you didn't trust anything to encoding and decoding, that most of the times there were leaks, no matter what precautions you took. He didn't go to the trouble of giving me a written order; he just sat there at the cooncan game and told me to load up every flyable P-40 I could find. He said that a few of the experienced AVG had agreed to stay over just for him and that they'd go with me. We'd infiltrate the field of Kweilin five hundred miles eastward and not go barreling in there in formation and thereby warn the enemy that we were up to something unusual. I called in the maximum force from all three squadrons. We mustered twenty-nine planes.

We gathered our skeleton group of old ships, with new kids and myself and a scattering of other veterans—six, to be exact. Then on July 2 we left the field at Kunming, a couple of ships at a time, and flew leisurely along to the east, landing by single ships and by twos without even circling the town of Kweilin. No need to advertise the fact that we were there—spies would get the word through soon enough. From there we could strike either Hong Kong, Canton, or Hankow, but this time we were to strike none of those areas. We were going to sit tight and supposedly wait to be struck.

We hid our ships under camouflage nets, scattered at random in the boondocks and in the shadows of the strange-looking mountains bordering the Kwangsi field. In the slots beside the runway, where we'd have normally parked our fighters, the Chinese quickly placed dummy P-40s to bait the trap. These pseudo-airplanes were really very crude, made of light wood in the general shape of a Tomahawk P-40, covered with canvas, and then painted to resemble the actual fighter. Grinning shark teeth, wooden props, and the insigne of the Chinese Air Force completed the job. From aloft they fooled a close observer. I'd noticed them on other fields, and, until I had landed and was taxiing in close to them, I had thought they were actual fighters. They were so convincing that sometimes in the half-light of dawn and in the excitement of a jing-bow normally sharp-eyed pilots, fooled by the planned gag of the Chinese mechanics, would jump onto the wing of a dummy, thinking it was his ship.

That night, to bait the trap further, Chennault sent some of the old hands into town with instructions to visit certain establishments and "accidentally" pass out fake information that he wanted to reach the Japanese. As they drank wine and acted as though they had drunk too much, the men talked louder and louder for the benefit of the informers. They called rather boisterously that they were newly arrived and that Chennault had sent them to the nearby field to practice. The squadron would be kept at Kweilin for a day or so and then fly back to Chungking to defend the capital.

We hoped the acting had been good. Even if the enemy came in too early they'd probably get only the dummies.

July 3, 1942. We sat there on the alert in the operations cave at Kweilin and played cards. The hours dragged by, and I kept watching the action of the Chinese warning net, for the plotting board was situated right there in the cool, damp cave.

The net had been showing action ever since early morning, all around the main bases from which we could expect the enemy—Kai-Tak at Kowloon, Tien Ho near Canton, and farther north all around Hankow and Nanchang. At exactly 2 p.m. the atmosphere of the cave suddenly became charged, as though by electricity. The little Japanese flags on pedestals were shoved out across the plotting board. Starting at the danger points, they formed a straight line that pointed directly at us there in the cave. They showed the forma-

Bob Scott, a would-be Flying Tiger, flew as an outsider with the AVG and became their commanding officer when they were absorbed into the USAAF. He later authored the best-seller, God Is My Co-Pilot, *and retired a General.* **(Bill Hess)**

tions to be crossing the outer circle. Twenty-four were airborne from Kai-Tak, similar number from White Cloud. My hopes rose, but so did my nervousness, and the tension in the cave increased. Again I wondered whether I was ready. Were any of us? Somehow I just wished I hadn't heard that radio announcement from Tokyo Rose. I wished we'd waited for July 4. It was a whole day away.

At two forty-five the waiting was over. General Chennault signaled for me to scramble with my new command. There we went, an imaginery outfit taking off for combat the day before we were born. Maybe we would never be officially activated now. Going out to meet ninety-six planes with a piddling twenty-nine, the last words I heard the Old Man say were that the enemy was a hundred miles away and we were not to come down from our altitude until he told me to, that, no matter what happened, we were to maintain strict radio silence and he'd tell me when to attack!

I ran toward my ship, past the Chinese operations people playing with the little flags on the plotting board, where tiny red meatballs stared threateningly at me in the dim yellow glow of a twenty-five-cycle bulb. We saddled up then, took off in a cloud of red dust, and climbed as fast as we could to twenty-one thousand feet, an altitude simple to remember since it was as high as the 40s would go, and some of them had a tough job getting even that high. My orders kept running through my mind so vividly that it was as if they were being repeated to me over the headset in my flying helmet. "Orbit west of the field—radio silence—nothing, but nothing, to make you break that silence—high in the sun. Stay there, circling and watching to the southeast low down—attack *only* when the word comes. No matter what the enemy does—you watch and wait."

I circled and strained my eyes, drying the sweating palms of my hands on the legs of my flying suit. I could hear the crackle of static, the drone of my engine. And suddenly there was a new sound, the strange, high Japanese voices calling to one another on our own frequency. They surely weren't observing radio silence. They were probably out on a holiday flight and telling each other what they were going to do to the unsuspecting Americans. Their overconfidence worried me one moment and chilled me the next. Then there they were—just flashes at first, flashes of windshields in the sunlight—and we were between them and the sun. I could make out black dots, twenty-odd here and another twenty-odd and another—there must be hundreds. My throat had been dry with the excitement, and now suddenly my tongue seemed to stick to my teeth. I found it difficult to swallow. Good Lord! I wondered how it would be when we went down among all those—and we had to go. There was no getting out of this now. I'd argued myself into a mess like this once too often. I looked around in the other direction to rest my neck. We kept circling, circling, circling. My neck soon ached on that side too, and my eyes burned. I could see dots all over the sky in every direction. I tried to count the air armada, and then I tried to keep my eyes focused somewhere else so I couldn't count them. But my eyes kept being drawn back. I had to look. I counted my own formation, hoping that somehow it would grow in number. I remembered Tokyo Rose's words, and I had to agree with her; this just might be our first and last flight together even though we had changed the date.

At three-ten the enemy formation was over the town of Kweilin. I could count them with ease now; and when they turned and the sun was at a certain angle I could see the big red meatballs on the wings and fuselages. They dove down for the ships they saw waiting for them on the field, the Chinese dummies.

I wanted to go down and get it over with. Over my shoulder I looked at my formation and wondered why Chennault didn't give the word. We were so outnumbered that it didn't matter when we went. *Oh, General Chennault, call me down. I'm ready. We're ready. As ready as we'll ever be!* The sky above our field was filled with circling, diving, strafing enemy fighters, although some of them stayed up high to form "top cover" for the strafers. When the fake P-40s were blazing and it was apparent to the Japs that they had caught the green Yankees on the ground with their pants down, even the top cover couldn't resist. They, too, came down to strafe and try to dive small frag bombs into the mouth of the operations cave. They must have been overjoyed that none of the ships on the ground had started an engine, that not one of the Americans had tried to take off.

Back and forth the Jap Zeros went. I could see the phosphorescent lines of their tracers arching across the Kweilin aerodrome from mountaintop to jagged mountaintop. The fires in the dummy planes looked most realistic, for the Chinese had placed a small can of gasoline inside each fake P-40. Now, wrapped in the flames, they looked so real I was a little sorry to see them burn. Why didn't the Old Man pass the word? Maybe the radio was out. Perhaps one of those bombs they had lobbed at the cave had gone inside. My hand moved to the top of my throttle to press the throat-mike button a dozen times, but it never quite got pressed. Circle, circle. We kept circling and watching and waiting.

The air was filled with smoke and the enemy's arrogant ships. They looped and rolled and chandelled off the runway above the burning dummies. High in the sun waited the real P-40s. Every now and then I'd note that my altimeter was unwinding. By some reflex I'd let the pressure of my hand push the nose of my ship down. The formation would follow me. But each time I'd remember in time and win it back and return to orbiting. Finally the decoys were nothing but ashes, and the pall of smoke had thinned out and risen so high that I could smell the fires. Then the word we'd been waiting for came, tersely, dramatically.

"Take 'em, Tigers, take 'em! They're ripe and waiting. Take 'em, Scotty!"

Down we went, no verbal orders, just a flip of the rudder and a dipping of my wing for direction. Behind me the various flight leaders relayed my signal. In a flash we were closing in on them. All the Zeros were pulled into tight formation by their leaders, and they were practically parading over the city of Kweilin. They loomed in my gun sights a thousand yards away, and I fought the temptation to open fire. We'd waited a long time, and this first pass had to be good. I'd forgotten how outnumbered we were. I'm very happy now that I did. But it was such a relief to get the word and end the suspense and go down from that incessant circling that perhaps we'd have been relieved to attack twice the number. Their formation was so perfect and so close we couldn't miss. Even the new kids remembered not to shoot at the whole formation but to concentrate on one ship at a time, with short bursts, then skid to another. Hang on aim, then fire—always short bursts! They didn't see us until it was too late. Twenty or more of them were already going down, and those we didn't burn on the first pass broke and ran in all directions. After the first dive, when we'd climbed back into the sun for altitude, we broke, too, and took out after the stragglers. I followed one with my wingman all the way to Canton, two hundred miles southeastward, and shot it down when the pilot lowered his landing gear preparatory to landing on White Cloud aerodrome. That day we shot down thirty-four Jap planes in the victory, but, more than that, we became blooded combat men.

When I dragged in on the final approach I noticed my tanks were almost dry. My voice sounded strange and foreign in the side tone of my radio as I called for landing instructions. I sounded like another person, and maybe I was. And could I have heard the lament of Tokyo Rose that night it would have done me good, but she didn't come through, there in the mountains of Kweilin. Later on we received a report from the British Intelligence, hiding in the outskirts of Kowloon, saying that she had raised hell that night. She emphasized that we had continued in the cowardly tradition already established by the mercenary killers of Chennault and had shot down one innocent student pilot as he was

about to land at the aerodrome of Canton. She bragged about the forty-eight P-40s the Japanese had caught and destroyed on the Kweilin field. But no mention at all was made of the thirty-four ships we knew they had definitely lost. The Chinese in Kweilin and the surrounding rice paddies had gone out and brought in the evidence of these thirty-four planes to Chennault as proud testimonials. Tokyo Rose asserted that, by raiding the Japanese training base at White Cloud the day before our fighter group was officially activated, we had violated some covenant of the Geneva Convention. We were starting out in the same dastardly fashion with which the AVG had left off.

Coming in to land, I was more than careful that day, watching closely for bomb craters in the runway. But the Chinese had been out there almost before the strafing had stopped to repair those pockmarks as well as to remove all the debris. I parked my ship in the boondocks again, far away from the hot ashes, and by the time I had walked up to the cave I had had time to breathe deeply and compose myself. General Chennault, as usual, appeared younger than he had when I'd left him before the battle. He always relaxed after something he'd planned went off well. I found him Indian wrestling with one of the Tigers, a sport in which, to my knowledge, he was never beaten. When he saw me come into the mouth of the cave, he stopped his exercise to congratulate me. I couldn't help being happy, nor could I hide the joy I felt.

"See how easy it is, Scotty? Any questions?"

"Yes, sir," I said. "I do have a question. Please tell me why we waited so long. Why'd we keep circling all that time?" Since I didn't mean to question his judgment, I hurried to say that I had thought his radio might be dead, that maybe one of the bombs had hit it, or that mine was out.

He leaned down to rub Joe's ears and took a cigarette out of the pocket of his leather jacket.

"Now, Scotty," he finally said, "put yourself in the place of that Jap commander. What would you have been thinking about if you'd been sitting where he was instead of up there where you were? What would you have been thinking when you first arrived in sight of those fat dummies?"

Well, that was easy. He wasn't going to catch me with that one. "Thinking about how many I was going to burn up on the ground. I'd have been calculating those two lines of P-40s, one on each side of the runway. Catch them before they started their engines."

Chennault just kept rubbing Joe's ears, kneeling down there close to the little dog on the floor of the cave. Then he stood up and looked me right in the eyes, practically laughing out loud.

"That's just what that Jap colonel was thinking. After that you saw him dive and zoom and use up most of his ammunition and most of his gasoline and let his disciplined formation get kind of out of hand. All the time you were hiding up there he was becoming more and more uncertain about those dummies down below that burned so fast. Twenty minutes, thirty—and all the time he's getting more and more overconfident. But he's worrying too. In fact he's just about to conclude that things are not just the way they seem to be when I call you down. He looks up at the danger quarter, up in the high sun, but it's too late. He looked there when he began to be worried about something else. Know what that was, Scotty?"

Sure I did. The cunning old fox. I found myself feeling a little guilty too, but I was happy just the same.

"His fuel, General. I see it all now. I'd have been worrying whether or not I had enough to take me back to Kai-Tak or White Cloud or wherever it was I had to go."

He grinned all over and winked at me then. He'd seen all this so long before, so many times. And this afternoon he'd been down there in his lookout point thinking it all out while I orbited up there and wondered what in the world everybody was waiting for.

"That's why you shot down half his planes, son, and didn't lose a single one yourself. Remember it." And from that moment on I never forgot.

So the 23rd Fighter Group was born in combat a whole day before Washington said that it was to be activated. With the added confidence of the stalwarts of the AVG who stayed with us, few as they were, all those green American kids didn't stay green very long. We took on the aura of the real Flying Tigers . . . .

We Live in Fame (Or Go Down in Flame) USAAF

DICK BONG

by General George C. Kenney, USAAF

On January 20, 1944, a radio came in from Washington stating that Colonel Neel Kearby's Congressional Medal of Honor for shooting down six Jap airplanes in a single combat had been approved. Neel happened to be in my office in Brisbane when it came in. I immediately rushed him up to General Mac-Arthur and had the ceremony done by the Old Man himself. The general did the thing up right, and so overwhelmed Neel that he wanted to go right back to New Guinea and knock down some more Japs to prove that he was as good as MacArthur had just told him he was.

Neel, who had scored his first victory on September 4, 1943, during the operation to capture Lae, was now credited with twenty victories, just one behind Captain Dick Bong who was due back in a few days. I told Kearby not to engage in a race with that cool little Scandinavian boy. Bong didn't care who was high man. He would never be in a race, and I didn't want Kearby to press his luck and take too many chances for the sake of having his name first on the scoreboard. I told him to be satisfied from now on to dive through a Jap formation, shoot down one airplane, head for a cloud, and come on home. In that way, as he was an excellent shot and a superb flier, he would live forever, but if he kept coming back to get the second one and the third one he would be asking for trouble and giving the Jap top cover a good chance to knock him off. Kearby agreed that it was good advice but he would like to get an even fifty before he went home. When I suggested that I'd like to send him home now for a month, he said, "I've only one to go to tie Bong. If you send me home now I'll never catch up. Let me get fifty first." I said all right, but I wished he would try to settle for one Nip per week.

Lieutenant Colonel Tommy Lynch, who had led the P-38s in their first flight over Dobodura in December, 1942, had just returned and was anxious to go after the top score. Tommy had led the pack with sixteen victories when I sent him back on leave the previous fall but now he needed four to catch Kearby and five to tie Bong. I told him to take it easy, too, and not to get in a race with anybody. He left for New Guinea, promising to behave himself.

Bong, Kearby, and Lynch were the big three in the Southwest Pacific as February, 1944, began. Major George Welch, with sixteen to his credit, had gone home in November, 1943. Captain Daniel Roberts, who had knocked down fifteen Nips in eleven weeks, was killed over Finschhafen on November 9, 1943, and Major Edward Cragg, also credited with a score of fifteen, was shot down in flames over Gloucester on December 26 of that same year.

The nearest fighter pilots to the top three now were Major Gerald Johnson, Major Tommy McGuire, and Captain James Watkins, all crack shots, who were getting Japs at the rate of two or three in a combat and were in a triple tie at eleven.

By the middle of February, when Bong got back to New Guinea, Lynch had run his score up to eighteen. On Bong's arrival, General "Squeeze" Wurtsmith, the head of the Fifth Fighter Command, assigned Tommy to his staff as his operations officer, and Dick as Lynch's assistant. When they wanted to know if that meant they were out of combat, Wurtsmith said that while they were no longer assigned to a combat squadron, they could "free lance" together as a team, either alone or attaching themselves to any squadron in the command, whenever they could be spared from their staff duties. "Squeeze" ran the Fighter Command without too much help, so they figured they would get enough action so that they wouldn't forget how to fly.

In the late afternoon of February 27 we picked up and decoded a Jap radio message which gave the time of arrival at the Wewak aerodrome of a Jap transport plane carrying some staff officers from Rabaul. By the time we got the information, it was almost too late for an interception, but we gave the information to Bong and Lynch, who hurriedly took off and flew wide open all the way, arriving over Wewak about two minutes before the Jap plane was scheduled to land. The inconsiderate Nip, however, was ahead of schedule, had already landed, and was taxiing down the runway. Lynch dived to the attack but found that in his hurry to get away his gun sights had not been installed. He called to Bong to take the Jap. Bong fired one burst, the plane was enveloped in flames for a second or two, and then it blew up. No one was seen to leave it, before or after the attack. The two kids then machine-gunned a party of

Dick Bong, with forty Japanese aircraft to his credit, was the top U.S. ace in both World Wars and the Korean conflict. A skilled pilot but a poor marksman, Bong gained his victories by maneuvering so close to his enemies that he couldn't miss. (USAF)

at least a hundred Japs who had evidently come down to greet the visitors. Subsequent frantic radio messages passing between Wewak and Tokyo indicated that the victims were a major general, a brigadier, and a whole staff of high-ranking officers.

On their return, Bong and Lynch came over to my New Guinea advanced headquarters and told me the story. I wanted to let Bong have credit for an airplane destroyed in combat, but of course if it was on the ground it couldn't count on the victory scoreboard. We counted only wing shots in the Southwest Pacific. I asked Dick if he was sure that the Jap transport was actually on the ground when he hit it. Couldn't it have been just an inch or so above the runway? Maybe the plane's wheels had touched and it had bounced back into the air temporarily? Everyone new that some Japs were poor pilots. Lynch stood their grinning, and said that whatever Bong decided was okay with him. Dick listened seriously, as if it were a problem in mathematics, and then looked up and said simply, earnestly, and without a trace of disappointment, "General, he was on the ground all right. He had even stopped rolling."

Everyone was now watching the scores of these two and Neel Kearby. A few days after Bong's return from his leave in the United States, Kearby had shot down two Jap fighters, bringing his score up to twenty-two. Neel felt pretty good until he landed back at his home aerodrome where he was greeted with the news that Bong had shot down a Jap fighter that morning over New Britain. The score was now tied, but it was at twenty-two. A few days later each of the three leaders added another victory. With Neel and Dick each at twenty-three and Lynch with nineteen, Eddie Rickenbacker's old World War I record of twenty-six didn't look so far away now.

On March 4 Kearby decided to break the tie. With his group headquarters flight, of Major Sam Blair and Captains Dunham and Banks, Neel headed for the Wewak area and trouble. Just west of the village of Dagua, sighting a formation of fifteen Jap aircraft, he signaled for the attack. A quick burst, and a Nip plane went spinning to earth in flames. One ahead. Now for a little velvet for that lead position. Neel turned back into the Jap formation and, with a beautiful long-range shot from a sixty-degree angle from the rear, got his second victim with a single burst. As he pulled away, three jap fighters closed in from above and behind. Dunham got one. Banks got another. The third Jap poured a burst into Neel's cockpit from close range. The P-47 with twenty-three Jap flags painted on its side plunged straight down. It never came out of the dive and no parachute opened, as it kept going until it disappeared into the jungle bordering on the Jap Aerodrome at Dagua.

Somehow I felt a little glad that Neel never knew that Dick Bong had added two more to his score that morning, shooting down a couple of Jap bombers during a fighter sweep over Tadji, New Guinea. Lynch in that same flight had bagged a bomber and a fighter, bringing his total up to twenty-one.

On March 9, Bong and Lynch flew another mission over the Tadji area to see whether or not the Japs were filling up the holes in the aerodrome, which we had bombed heavily a few days before. They couldn't find any airplanes to shoot at in the air or on the ground, so looking for some kind of target, they spied a Jap corvette escorting a couple of luggers just offshore, heading west toward Hollandia. Burst after burst of .50-caliber guns of each plane poured into the Jap vessel, which responded with its own deck defense guns. Suddenly Bong saw Lynch pull around and head for shore. One of his engines was smoking. Then, just as he got to the shore line, Dick saw in quick succession a propeller flying off, Tommy taking to his parachute, and at almost the same instant, the plane exploding. Bong flew around for several minutes to see if he could discover any indication that by some miracle Tommy had survived. There wasn't a chance, and Dick knew it. The chute had burned up with the explosion and probably Lynch was dead before his body hit the ground.

Dick flew back and reported. I was afraid that seeing Tommy go might affect his nerve, so I ordered him to Brisbane to ferry a new airplane back to his squadron and sent a message to the depot commander there that if the airplane was ready to fly before another couple of weeks I would demote him at least two grades.

It turned out that I needn't have worried about Bong's morale. I came back to Brisbane after he had been there about ten days, eating a lot of good food, drinking gallons of fresh milk, and sleeping at least ten hours out of every twenty-four. He had begun to get bored with going out to the depot each day and being told that his airplane was not yet ready. For the past couple of days he had been working with a sergeant out there, designing and building an attachment to carry a couple of cases of Coca-Cola on each wing when he ferried the airplane back to New Guinea. He then collected his four cases of Coke and loaded them ready to go as soon as the airplane was pronounced ready to go. A little later he showed up at my headquarters and asked where he could get coupons to buy sheets, which were rationed articles. We asked him if he wanted them for his whole outfit, but, no, he just wanted four for himself. We gave him his coupons and sent a major on the staff who knew where to buy sheets along with Dick. With the Coke and the sheets, he now figured the trip to Australia was really worth-while. I took him up to General MacArthur's office for a visit. He was so impressed that he walked around as if in a daze for the rest of the day. I held him for two more days to let him recover and then told the depot commander to let Dick have the airplane. Just before he took off, I told him to fight the Japs in the air from now on and leave the strafing jobs to someone else. Besides, the liquid-cooling system of the P-38 was too vulnerable. Strafing against anyone that shot back should be done by a plane with an air-cooled engine.

On April 3 he got in a fight over Hollandia

General George C. Kenney, a World War I fighter pilot, commanded the combined 5th and 13th Air Forces in the World War II Pacific theater. Top aces Bong and McGuire were under his command. **(USAF)**

while with his old Ninth Squadron, escorting a big bombing raid on the Jap aerodromes there. A Jap fighter got into an argument with Dick and lost. Number twenty-five.

On April 12 we again raided Hollandia with one hundred and eighty-eight bombers and sixty-seven fighters. Twenty Jap fighters intercepted. Our P-38s shot down eight of them and listed another as probable. Two of the Nip planes that were definitely destroyed in combat were added to the score of Captain Richard I. Bong, making his score twenty-seven, one more than the record set by Eddie Rickenbacker in France in World War I. The one listed as probable was also one of Bong's victims. He told me that the Jap plane he had reported as a "probable" in the combat of April 12 near Hollandia had gone into the water in Tannemerah Bay about twenty miles west of Hollandia. The reason it had been called a probable was that no one except Bong had seen it go down and his camera gun was not installed that day. Under the rules, he could not get credit for it unless the victory was confirmed by an eyewitness, or the wreckage of the Jap plane was found where he claimed it had crashed. He showed me on the photograph of the area exactly where the plane went into the water and said that it was a single-seater fighter of the type we called an Oscar, that he had hit the left wing, the pilot, and the engine, but that the plane had not burned.

When we captured the Hollandia area, a couple of weeks later, I got a diver to go down where Dick had said the airplane went in. The diver located it almost instantly and we pulled it up. It was an Oscar. The left wing had eleven bullet holes in it, the pilot had been hit in the head and neck, two cylinder engines were knocked out, and there was no sign of fire. I put out an order giving Bong official credit for the victory—his twenty-eighth.

A couple of days later a radio came in from General Arnold— at least it was signed with his name. Later on I found that one of his staff had written and sent it without telling Hap about it. It read:

Concern is expressed over the high loss rate of fighter pilots who have shot down many enemy aircraft. Your comments are requested concerning the desirability of restricting from action combat flying or return to United States of this type of personnel. A case in point is Captain Bong, who is credited with twenty-seven enemy aircraft. Only very recently we have lost the invaluable services of Colonels Kearby and Lynch.

Although he had been back only two and half months since his last trip home, the Pentagon seemed so worried about him that while I didn't agree with their thinking in the matter, I decided that I would use Arnold's message as an excuse to send Dick home, let him see his girl back in Poplar, Wisconsin, and be acclaimed as America's leading air ace of any war. He had mentioned a gunnery course.

I wired Hap that I was taking Bong out of combat to run a gunnery course for the Fighter Command but that I believed he ought to get the very latest information in the United States. Accordingly, I asked that after two or three weeks' leave at home Dick take the aerial gunnery course and then come back to me. I would then have him instruct the rest of my fighter pilots.

After all, the race of the aces was over, at least for the time being. The nearest score to Bong's twenty-seven was Major Tommy McGuire's twenty.

TARGET, YAMAMOTO

by Lieutenant Colonel Thomas G. Lanphier, Jr., USAAF

Admiral Isoroku Yamamoto, Commander in Chief of the Imperial Japanese Navy, who was sure he would dictate peace terms in the White House, was, until he died at 9:34 a.m., April 18, 1943, a punctual man. His punctuality led to his death.

Riding one of his newest Mitsubishis at close to four miles a minute, eleven minutes out of the Kahili aerodrome on Bougainville in the Solomons, with a swarm of Zeros to protect him, he figured he was well beyond the range of American fighters.

The admiral did not know that he was exactly one minute from a spot in mid-air above Bougainville that had since 4 p.m. the previous day, been designated by the White House in Washington as the point at which he should die.

If he had glanced through the bomber window within sixty seconds before death came, he would have seen a pair of United States Army Air Force Lightnings bearing down. These two—and fourteen others—opened their guns against him at that time and place according to a split-second plan arranged in Washington.

The admiral had flown, according to his sternly kept schedule, about 400 miles from Rabaul to a point eleven minutes by air from the Kahili airstrip. The Lightnings had flown 435 miles from Guadalcanal with equal precision, banking on his punctuality.

The fact that Yamamoto was intercepted and shot down can be credited to the perfect cooperation of many persons, the most cooperative of whom was the Japanese war lord himself. Had he not been exactly on time he would not have returned to Tokyo in a funeral urn.

Somewhere, somehow, the United States Navy had obtained detailed information concerning every movement Yamamoto was to make on his mid-April inspection tour in the South Pacific. This information was conveyed to Maj. John W. Mitchell of Enid, Mississippi, and to me in a Marine dugout on Henderson Field, Guadalcanal, the afternoon of April 17, 1943.

As we walked into the dank and musty room, a Marine operations major handed us a cablegram printed on blue tissue, the kind used by the Navy to distinguish top-secret dispatches.

The message said that Admiral Yamamoto and his staff would arrive by air in the Kahili area next day. The exact moment of his arrival and departure from each place on his itinerary was included in the message, which concluded with the directive that "maximum effort" be made to destroy Yamamoto. The cablegram was signed "Knox"—Frank Knox, Secretary of the Navy.

Since surprise would have to be the basic operating factor in the strike, that surprise could be obtained only by long-range fighters. Kahili was more than 300 miles from Guadalcanal, our base, and an additional 100 miles would have to be flown circuitously at low altitudes to escape enemy radar detection.

Some of the naval officers favored our trying to catch Yamamoto while he was moving, at one stage on his journey, across Shortland Harbor on a submarine chaser. Mitchell and I opposed that. No one in our outfit was qualified to identify a submarine chaser among the many ships plying Kahili waters.

Our arguments were heeled and our alternate suggestion, a mild-air interception, was adopted. It was decided to make contact with the Yamamoto aerial formation at a point west of Kahili on the air line from Rabaul to the air base at Ballale.

We figured the admiral's average speed would be around three and one-half to four miles a minute, that he would fly at about 10,000 feet or under to avoid use of oxygen masks. Knowing his arrival at Kahili was scheduled for 9:45 a.m. next morning, we decided to meet him thirty-five miles from this destination.

We had only eighteen Lightnings available for the mission and they would look puny against the 100-odd fighters we anticipated would be milling about the Kahili skies to cover the admiral's approach and landing. We had to find him, hit him and get out fast if we hoped to vote in the next election.

We decided to divide our eighteen Lightnings into two sections, one attacking, one covering. The attackers were to wait for the admiral at 10,000 feet, get through his six escorting Zeros, by surprise if possible, by force if necessary. There were four of us in this attack group—myself, Lieut. Rex Barber, my wing man, Lieut. Joe Moore, second element leader, and Lieut. Jim McLanahan, his wing man. We were picked to put the bee on Mr. Y.

Our covering section of Lightnings was to be led by Major Mitchell, who would also lead the entire formation to the rendezvous. He would cover from 20,000 feet. It would be his job to ward off any of, or all, the Zeros we expected might be aloft to welcome Yamamoto at Kahili.

Yamamoto had been, from childhood, a hater of all things American. He had lived every hour of his vengeful life, even as attaché in Washington, in anticipation of the moment when he would lay down in that city the Emperor's dictates for American bondage.

A conceited and arrogant man, Yamamoto, with a face like a frog but with a calculating mind that functioned precisely, had a personal calendar for the conquest of Asia and America.

The treacherous attack on Pearl Harbor was his opening gun in that campaign. An easy man to hate, Yamamoto, and one it would be an honor to destroy.

Major Mitchell and I returned to our squadron area on Guadalcanal and broke the news of the Yamamoto mission to our Lightning crews.

We had more than forty pilots available for only eighteen aircraft, and every one pleaded for a chance to get in on the show. Major Mitchell, as commanding officer, had the unhappy job of appointing thirteen from these forty. He and I and the attack group already were picked.

To accompany us in the covering group he chose Maj. Louis R. Kittel and Lieuts. Julian Jacobson, Raymond K. Hine, Besby T. Holmes, Douglas S. Canning, Delton C. Goerke, Gordon Whittaker, Roger J. Ames, Lawrence Graebner, Everett Anglin, William E. Smith, Albert R. Long, and Eldon Stratton.

Major Mitchell briefed them. Take-off 7:25 o'clock next morning (April 18). One circle of the field to make formation. On course and under way at 7:30 a.m. Indicated air speed 210 miles an hour, first stage of flight thirty feet above the water, this to last two hours, semi-circle of 435 miles to get around Japanese positions at Munda, Rendova, Vella Lavella, Shortland, Kahili, radios silent all the way.

After two hours of wave-skimming to keep under Japanese radars, we're to head in towards southeastern Bougainville and climb to the rendezvous, scheduled for 9:35 a.m. No sooner, no later. We knew Admiral Yamamoto's rigid adherence to punctuality. Major Mitchell's covering Lightnings were to take up patrol at 20,000 feet, 10,000 feet above the rendezvous point.

Lieut. Joe McGuigan, USN, and Capt. Bill Morrison, Army, both of the Intelligence branch, gave us supplementary information for the mission—weather due to be cloudless, windless; location of new Japanese anti-aircraft batteries. Each pilot got a bag of English shillings to buy necessities from Solomon Islanders, if we crashed or were shot down.

Captain Morrison, who had lived more than half his life in Japan, assured us that, barring hurricane or typhoon, Admiral Yamamoto would run true to lifetime form; that he would be punctual to the split second.

Pre-combat stomach gnawed me when I taxied my Lightning to the runway for the take-off next morning. As I rolled past Rex Barber's parking revetment in the dust kicked up by Major Mitchell's group, Barber eased his ship into the taxiway behind me. He grinned and waved. His grin showed up a gap where he'd lost a tooth in an extracurricular brawl in Fiji.

We thundered down the take-off run and lumbered into the air, heavy with auxiliary gas tanks. I looked behind and saw Joe Moore taking off alone. McLanahan, his wing man, had blown a tire on the taxiway. We left McLanahan behind. That left only three of us in the attack group. We circled the field and set out alongside Major Mitchell on the first leg of our date with Yamamoto.

Two minutes later Joe Moore pulled up alongside and made dejected gestures. His belly tanks were not feeding his engines. He couldn't possibly make the target. He, too, had to abort the mission. I slid into position beside Major Mitchell and wig-wagged this information and he waved his second element, Lieutenants Holmes and Hine, to join me. I had never flown with them before.

Out of sight of land most of the time, hugging the water all the way, we maintained absolute radio silence throughout. We sped along under a blazing mid-morning Pacific sun for two hours, following Major Mitchell's slightest turn or change. Just at the time that silence and the sun's glare began to get on our nerves, we turned and headed north on the last leg.

Five minutes later we knew that with only compass and air-speed indicator for navigation, Major Mitchell had brought us 400 miles to pay dirt. As we neared Bougainville's southeastern shore and went into the climb out of the surf spray, I glanced at my dash board clock. It was 9:33 a.m. Perfect timing.

Would Yamamoto be on time? We had our answer within thirty seconds. It came from Doug Canning in Major Mitchell's section. He broke the radio silence. He said, quietly, "Bogey. Ten o'clock high."

I looked upward to where, thinking of the sky as a clock, the dial figure ten would be. I saw black specks several thousand feet up, and about five miles away. I made them out as two enemy bombers with six Zeros for escort.

Here, just as the White House cablegram had promised, came Isoroku Yamamoto, punctual to the split second. It was 9:34 a.m.

Without taking my eyes from the Japanese formation, I switched to my internal fuel tanks, dropped my belly tanks for greater speed and maneuverability. I didn't have time to look for Barber. I knew from experience he'd stay glued to me.

I climbed parallel to Yamamoto's course, engines wide open, to get in front of my quarry. Our tactical situation then was not encouraging. We had hoped to meet the Admiral at 10,000 feet, to get in on him with a fast dive out of the sun. By a scant few seconds we were below and in front, with only four aircraft to his eight.

Major Mitchell, I learned later, had to scramble for his assigned post at 20,000 feet. I angled across in front of Yamamoto's formation, straining to reach at least the same altitude as his formation before being spotted. Major Mitchell was in a rocketing climb, scanning the air for Japanese fighters from Kahili.

Neither Mitch's section, nor mine, was discovered by the Japanese in the tense two minutes after we sighted the enemy. During those two minutes, though, I lost Holmes and Hine. Holmes called out that he couldn't drop his belly tanks. He levelled off and went on down the coast, kicking and slewing his ship in frantic attempts to tear them off. Hine, as his wing man, was compelled to stay with him.

Still the seconds were ticking away toward the second when the enemy must surely discover us. If he had sighted us even thirty seconds sooner than he did, someone other than Yamamoto might have been the fall guy that morning. Why they didn't spot us down there I'll never know.

Barber and I got to a point two miles to Yamamoto's right, and about a mile in front of him before his Zero cover saw us. They must have screamed the warning into their radios because we saw their belly tanks drop—a sign that they were clearing for action—and they nosed over in a group to dive on us, on Rex and me.

We closed in fast. Three Zeros which had been flying the seaward side of the Yamamoto formation came tearing down between it and us, trying to intercept us before we could reach Yamamoto's bomber.

Right behind them were the three Japanese Zeros from the inshore side of the formation.

Holmes and Hines were way off, down the beach, out of sight, and Mitch and his group were out of sight, too, climbing with throttles wide toward what they had every reason to believe would be the biggest fight of all, top Japanese cover from Kahili.

Rex and I were left free to finish our mission, the destruction of Yamamoto's two Mitsubishis and their swarm of protecting Zeros.

I was afraid we'd never get to the bomber that Admiral Yamamoto rode before the Zeros got us. I horsed back on my wheel to get my guns to bear on the lead Zero diving toward me.

Buck fever started me firing before I had my Lightning's nose pointed in his direction. I saw the gray smoke from his wing guns and wondered with stupid detachment if the bullets would get me before I could work my guns into his face.

He was a worse shot than I was, and he died. My machine guns and cannon ripped one of his wings away. He twisted under me, all flame and smoke. His two wing men hurtled past and I wasted a few bursts between them. Then I thought I'd better get my job done and go away before I got hurt.

I kicked my ship over on its back and looked down for the lead Japanese bomber. It had dived inland. As I hung in the sky I got an impression, off to the east, of a swirl of aircraft against the blue—a single Lightning silhouetted against the light in a swarm of Zeroes. That was Barber, having himself a time.

Excitement in a fight works wonders with a man's vision. In the same brief second that I saw Rex on my right, and saw the Zeros I had just overshot, I spotted a shadow moving across the tree tops. It was Yamamoto's bomber. It was skimming the jungle, headed for Kahili.

I dived toward him.

I realized on the way down that I had picked up too much speed, that I might overshoot him. I cut back on my throttles. I crossed my controls and went into a skid to brake my dive.

Two Zeros that had overshot me showed up again, diving towards Yamamoto's bomber from an angle slightly off to my right. They meant to get me before I got the bomber. It looked from where I sat as if the bomber, the Zeros and I might all get to the same place at the same time.

We very nearly did. The next three or four seconds spelled life or death. I remember getting suddenly very stubborn about making the most of the one good shot I had coming up. I fired a long steady burst across the bomber's course of flight, from approximately right angles.

The bomber's right engine, then its right wing, burst into flame. I had accomplished my part of the mission. Once afire, no Japanese plane stopped burning, short of blowing up. The men aboard the bomber were too close to the ground to jump.

The two onrushing Zeros saw it, too. They screamed past overhead, unwilling to chance a jungle crash to get me. In that second I realized that my impetus would carry me directly behind the Mitsubishi's tail cannon.

My Lightning's belly was scraping the trees. I couldn't duck under the Mitsubishi and I hesitated to pull up over its line of fire because I already was going so slow I almost hung in mid-air, near stalling speed. I expected those Zeros back, too.

Just as I moved into range of Yamamoto's bomber and its cannon, the bomber's wing tore off. The bomber plunged into the jungle. It exploded. That was the end of Admiral Isoroku Yamamoto.

Right about then, though, I got scared. I'd slowed so much to get my shots at Yamamoto's bomber that I was caught, so to speak, with my pants, and my heart, down around my ankles. My air speed indicator coldly told me I was doing only 220 miles an hour, or less than cruising speed, and I had only ten feet of altitude.

For the first time on the mission, I pushed my mike button and called Mitchell. I asked him to send down anybody who wasn't busy. The two Japanese Zeros were diving at me again, almost at right angles, to my left.

I hugged the earth and the tree tops while they made passes at me. I unwittingly led them smack across a corner of the Japanese fighter strip at Kahili, where Zeros were scrambling in the dust to take off. I made the harbor and headed east. With the Japanese on my tail I got into a speedy climb. At 20,000 I lost them. I was away with only two bullet holes in my rudder. Nothing more, except a year or two off my life.

Mitchell and his flight, responding to my call, came pile-driving down out of the sky and dispersed the Zeros. Contrary to all expectation, Mitch's covering section had met no resistance. Not one Zero had poked its nose any higher than 500 feet that day.

Mitchell, who was leading Solomons ace at that time, got only a snap shot or two in the brief melee when Barber, Holmes, and Hine were jumped by a gang of Zeros, Unfortunately, in this melee, one Lightning was seen in a long glide toward Shortland Island, its left engine smoking. Ray Hine was the only pilot who didn't get back from the Yamamoto mission, so it must have been his plane. No one has heard from Ray since.

Going home, Mitchell called out to all pilots. The mission had been accomplished. Everyone in top cover had seen the two bombers crash in the jungle in flames. There was no doubt of their complete destruction.

As we left Kahili, I relaxed. I heard the other pilots calling each other over the radio. Barber wanted permission to go back after a couple of Zeros he had sighted trailing him, but Mitch cooled Rex off and told him to head home at once. Our order had been explicit:

"Destroy the target (Yamamoto) at any cost, then break off and return to base, evading all further action."

We had complied to the letter.

A little over a month later the Japanese officially admitted the Fleet Admiral Isoroku Yamamoto had been "killed in combat with the enemy" in April. Subsequent reports fixed the scene "near Kahili aerodrome on southern Bougainville." He had burned to death in his twin-engined Mitsubishi, clutching his ceremonial sword.

Pilots, Man Your Planes: Marine And Navy Fighter Pilots

FIVE AT A CLIP

**by Stanley Johnston and Lieutenant Commanders John Thach
and Edward "Butch" O'Hare, USN**

"Six of us were in the air," Thach began. "Six other fighters who had just been relieved were almost down to the *Lexington*, when the first Japanese planes were sighted. I was at 10,000 feet and the six planes about to alight were ordered to climb right back to me. O'Hare was then on the deck of the *Lex.*

"The enemy consisted of nine twin-engined bombers flying in three vees of three. When first seen they were 12 miles out at 12,000 feet flying in a slight dive toward the 10,000-foot level. These were land-based planes. We discovered later that they were fast—able to do over 300 miles an hour—and almost identical to the Army's Martin B-26s.

"They had guns in the turtle back in the tail position, and in the nose—machine guns and 20mm cannon.

"In a running fight Lieuts. Noel Gayler, Walter Henry, Rolla Lemmon, and Ensigns Edward Sellstrom and Dale Peterson singled out and destroyed one each. I too got one. Each time one caught fire it would drop its bombs harmlessly into the sea because they were still too far from the *Lex.*

"This fight continued right into range of the ship's antiaircraft curtain, but our fighters stuck with them regardless. Two that we

damaged were finished off by antiaircraft fire from the ship. The ninth and last, in a crippled condition, turned away and tried to escape.

"A second enemy formation had been reported while we still were milling around with the first one. Six ships on deck, including Butch, were sent up to intercept them.

"Six of us in that first fight still had gas but the group that had been recalled at the last minute had to return for more fuel.

"This left us pretty well split up, and we were scattered widely as a result of the fight anyway. The new Jap group, another nine flying in three vees, was 60 miles behind the first lot which meant that none of us could see them yet.

"The six, including O'Hare, spread out to find and intercept these second raiders, climbing as they went. It happened that Butch and his wing man saw them first. They sounded the alarm and went into attack, beginning their dive 12 miles out. Here we had a bad break because O'Hare's companion found that his guns wouldn't fire. That left Butch there alone.

"The rest of us were heading his way, climbing up toward the oncoming Jap bombers, but we all knew we could not intercept them before they reached the bomb-dropping position."

Explaining the ensuing fight to me O'Hare said:

"I knew my wing man had dived away, but there wasn't time to sit and wait for help. Those babies were coming fast and had to be stopped. In the first run I fired into two, the two trailers in the last vee. I had to pull up to let them fall away.

"I had fired at the starboard engine in each ship and kept shooting each time till they jumped right out of their mountings. This caused both these planes to veer round to the starboard and fall out of the formation.

"I then crossed to the other side of the formation. I fired into the port engine of that plane and saw it jump out. I pulled away slightly while this third plane skidded violently and fell away, then went back in and fired the trailer of the middle vee, still shooting at the engines.

"The same thing happened again. It seems as if all you need to do is to put some of these .50-caliber slugs into the Jap engines and they come all apart and tear themselves right out of the ships. The engine fell out of this fourth plane, too, and I could see the plane commence to burn.

"By this time the Japs, still in formation, were right on top of the release point (the place where bombs aimed at the carrier would be dropped). They *had* to be stopped any way at all: there were five of them still. I came in close, shot into the fifth one till he fell away and then gave the remaining four a general burst until my ammunition was exhausted."

All this happened in a space of four minutes. During those four minutes Thach and several of his original group of six had turned and with wide-open throttles were boring down on the diminishing Japanese formation.

"As we closed in I could see O'Hare making his attack runs with perfect flight form, exactly the way that we had practiced. His shooting was wonderful—absolutely deadly. At one

David S. McCampbell was the top Navy ace of World War II, with thirty-four victories and a Medal of Honor. (USN)

time as we closed in I could see three blazing Japanese planes falling between the formation and the water—he shot them down so quickly.

"How O'Hare survived the concentrated fire of this Japanese formation I don't know. Each time he came in, the turtleback guns of the whole group were turned on him. I could see the tracer curling all around him and it looked to us as if he would go at any second. Imagine this little gnat absolutely alone tearing into that formation.

"Just as O'Hare got his fifth machine, we were within range and took over the fighting. We collected two more and shot up the other two. They staggered away losing height."

Back on the *Lexington's* deck, the plane-handling crews, the Admiral and his staff, Captain Sherman and his staff, and pilots of the bombers and dive bombers had been watching this show, although they had had a few moments of their own.

Out of the first formation the leading plane

was struck by antiaircraft fire while still several miles away. The damage seemed to have been loss of the left or port engine. The Jap pilot with desperate courage and great skill retained control of the bomber and made a suicidal attempt to crash into the *Lexington*.

With his starboard engine wide open he came down in a swooping dive toward the *Lex's* stern. He flew across a destroyer, then over the cruiser line. As he lost altitude he came within range of the small machine-gun cannons on the fleet's vessels and they all poured their fire up at him. But still he kept on coming. Lower and lower, closer and closer.

Finally, when he was down to a height of no more than 300 feet, the 1.1-inch and 20-mm. fire from the *Lexington* seemed to really take effect. The nose of the bomber began to come up, the speed to diminish. While still 200 yards behind the *Lexington's* zigzagging stern, the bomber finally stalled in the air. Its wings ceased to carry its weight and the nose dropped in a precipitate dive into the sea. An instant later only a huge pillar of black smoke marked the grave of the bomber and its crew.

Some of the most remarkable motion pictures taken in the Pacific, recorded this incident from the *Lexington's* rear deck. Stills taken from this film show clearly the intent of the Jap pilot, the condition of his ship, and the final stall and dive.

While this was going on O'Hare began his attack. The surrounding skies seemed to be full of planes falling from the first group of nine and from the formation further out. We lost two fighters in the engagement. One making an approach was hit on the engine with a 20-mm. shell. The engine quit and the pilot made a dead-stick landing near a destroyer which quickly picked him up. The second loss involved both plane and pilot.

Hardly had the skies cleared from the initial combat, when the four Japanese planes that had survived O'Hare guns, reached bombing distance and released their projectiles at the *Lexington*.

Capt. Sherman standing on the bridge was watching this formation closely. He saw the bombs fall away from the enemy planes and momentarily judged their probable course.

"Hard aport," he directed the helmsman. As the big ship, now traveling 25 knots or better, commenced its swing the Captain still kept his eyes on the falling bombs. But he evidently decided the *Lexington* was in the clear for he suddenly turned his back on the bombs and in a quiet voice ordered the navigating officer to bring the ship back to her course. With hands clasped behind him, he walked to the opposite side of the bridge to watch his fighters finish off the remaining Japanese planes.

Remember the ninth plane in the first formation? It had slid away damaged and disappeared over the horizon. But that is not the end of the story. Scout Pilot Lieut. Edward Allen saw this ship 30 miles away from the *Lexington* as he was returning from patrol. Turning after it he gave chase in his SBD which had a top speed of about 240 miles an hour.

Under ordinary circumstances the bomber could have stepped away from Allen's plane, but the damages sustained in the fight near the *Lex* had slowed it down so that it was doing no more than the little scout. Allen found that by careful trimming he could gradually creep up to within gun range of the bomber. At first machine guns from three or four emplacements fired at him as he came in close.

Allen fired back, using the two .30-caliber weapons in his nose. The recoil and rocket effect of his guns firing slowed him down a mile or two an hour allowing the Jap plane to pull ahead again. Allen would stop shooting, re-trim his ship, and slowly creep up to within range once more. Again he was met with machine-gun fire, this time not so much. He fired again and once more dropped back.

This seesawing and shooting was repeated for an hour, over a distance of almost 200 miles, before Allen's diminishing fuel forced him to break off and head back toward the Lexington. He reported that when he last saw the Japanese plane it was flying on, wobbling and recovering almost as though there was no hand at the controls. He said that the machine-gun fire directed at him ceased, and he believed he had killed or wounded all the crew.

Of the two of the last nine bombers that went wobbling away one is believed to have crashed. Another scout saw a damaged Japanese bomber fall into the sea some 30 miles away from the *Lexington,* and reported it had probably been fatally shot apart near the carrier but flew on for this distance before finally crashing.

Lieut. Commander Thach told me the encounter had taught him and his men a lot. It had given them a close look at enemy fliers and enemy aircraft.

"Those Japs came in with great determination. The first lot went right for the *Lex.* They never hesitated a second, despite our attack, until their leader was shot down. Then there was an apparent momentary uncertainty, that might have been, however, because of the heat of the assault they were subjected to. The second nine never faltered and came right on in to the bitter end, even though O'Hare was

eating them up behind and we were coming in from ahead.

"The morale of the Japs was shown by their ability to hold formation and keep their line headed toward the *Lex* without maneuvering defensively in any way. Also, they did not drop their bombs and try to get away when we closed in. They held on to their bomb loads until they were shot up or burning or beginning to fall. Another thing, none of them attempted to leave their burning planes by parachute.

"O'Hare's firing was a real record. We figured that he used only about 60 rounds to each of the planes he knocked down. That, of course, is deadly shooting. To knock down five planes with one load of ammunition is something that only a fighter pilot can appreciate. I don't suppose shooting like that has ever been seen before in the air.

"It also showed us that the only real defense for a carrier or any other vessel against air attack is an airplane. We're beginning to believe you must meet the attackers with at least plane for plane. It did show that the defending pilots have to be the best men procurable."

BLACK SHEEP

by Lieutenant Colonel Gregory "Pappy" Boyington, USMC

On the way to a new base, the Russell Islands, I was doing some tall hoping, for if this conglomeration that I called a squadron didn't see some action shortly, my combat-pilot days were over. I knew it. Age and rank were both against me now. Lady Luck just had to smile upon me, that's all.

The afternoon of our arrival in the Russell Islands I was called by Strike Command. Our first mission was scheduled for a 7:00 a.m. take-off the following morning, September 16, 1943. I had little sleep that night. For to-

morrow, I imagined the ghouls would be watching and hoping to see the poor little ole squadron flub its duff.

No one, I believe, noticed how concerned I was. Probably this escaped the officers in Strike Command, because I did nothing more than smoke one cigarette after another. This was not unusual. Besides, I smelled good, because I had refused all bourbon the previous night.

Not that combat worried me, for it didn't. My great concern was that the squadron might fall flat on its face or do something ridiculous. We had had little more than three weeks together—most squadrons were trained for months in the United States before they were sent out to a combat zone—and only three of my pilots had a taste of combat previously.

It was a temporary relief to get to hell out of the briefing shack and away from the officers in Strike Command. "Moon" was waiting patiently in one of the jeeps to drive Stan, myself, and a couple of the others down to the end of the strip, where our mighty Corsairs awaited like sleek, silent steeds. Truly a picture of beauty, in my opinion, were these new ships, the Corsairs.

Twenty Corsairs—five flights of four from our squadron—and of course twenty pilots were to escort three squadrons of Dauntless dive bombers and two squadrons of Avenger torpedo planes, totaling 150 bombers in all.

The mission was to wipe out Ballale. A small island west of Bougainville, heavily fortified, and all airfield, not unlike La Guardia. The main difference was that we knew the traffic was going to be much more conjested than the New York area is today, without the aid of Air Traffic Control directing our flight patterns. Besides the lack of A.T.C., as we know and depend upon it now, our traffic would be further distorted by antiaircraft fire, and God only knows how many Zeros.

And again, I don't believe that I gave a second thought to the fact that we had to fly six hundred miles round trip as the crows fly, up and down the old "Slot," sparsely dotted with tiny islands, most of these islands being Japanese held. The main worry was whether our seams would hold together as a squadron.

Our first problem was to get 170 aircraft off a single strip closely enough together, in time, that is, so that we would have adequate fuel to complete the trip yet leave ourselves a half hour's or more fuel for a fight at full throttle. A P&W 2000-HP engine at full throttle uses the old petrol much the same as if it were going through a floodgate.

Gregory "Pappy" Boyington became the leading Marine Corps ace with twenty-eight victories, after an unspectacular start with the Flying Tigers. He survived a Japanese prison camp and was later awarded the Congressional Medal of Honor. (USMC)

Wandering around our aircraft, getting a nod, or seeing a wave that each one after the other was in readiness calmed me down rapidly. Soon we received the start-up engine signal. One by one the shotgun starters audibly fired out black smoke. Each engine would go into a few convulsive coughs, afterwards smoothing out into a steady roar. Everything seemed much smoother, smooth as the perfect Venturi form of water vapor formed in misty silhouette about each ship, caused by the propeller and the extremely high humidity of the island air.

Take-off time—the last Dauntless had wobbled lazily into the air, starting to turn in one gigantic join-up circle. We took off in pairs down the snowy white coral strip at about twenty-second intervals, which was a feat in itself, because none of us had more than approximately thirty hours in these powerful new speed birds.

As we climbed, in shorter radii than the bombers, we gradually came abreast of the bomber leader, pulling up above and behind him. Radio silence was in effect. We had no intention of broadcasting our departure to the Japanese. The squadron was spread out like a loose umbrella over the bombers by use of hand signals. A reminder to lean out and reduce prop r.p.m. was passed along to all hands, in order to conserve precious fuel.

We settled down to the monotony of flying herd on the bombers. Our huge paddle-blade propellers were turning so slowly it seemed as if I counted each blade as it passed by. Hour after hour, it felt. The magnetism of counting those blades was so great I was tempted on several occasions to blurt out over the radio: "Who could ever believe this damn ocean could be so damn big!"

The group commander, leading the bombers, was responsible for the navigation. I didn't have that worry. Finally the monotony was to be broken up, because we were flying above fleecy layers of stratus that demanded all my concentration to hold the shadowy forms of the bombers below in sight. Actually, the reason we had this cloud separation was that the bombers had to fly between stratus layers too. There wasn't enough space for us to fly in the visual part of the sandwich and still remain above the bombers.

Thoughts of how we might louse up the all-important rendezvous after take-off were far behind. We had made that. And the rendezvous ahead, after our mission was accomplished, certainly couldn't have bothered me. For the Brass couldn't possibly see that, only the Nips could. And I don't believe I gave too much thought to them.

A new worry took its place. The clouds being the way they were, no Nip planes could find us. No action. The high command would undoubtedly have us all back as replacement pilots, and there I'd be directing traffic once again. I thought: "Damn the luck . . . Why

do I persist in planning the future when I know I can't?"

Hardly had I gotten through feeling sorry for myself when I noticed the dive bombers had all disappeared from sight.

"What in hell goes? We must be over the mission." I thought: "Jee—sus, if I lose these bombers, never showing up back at home base would be the best fate I could hope for."

I lowered the squadron through a thin layer of stratus to try to find the bomber boys. Upon breaking clear, the noise from my earphones almost broke my eardrums. One thing was for darn sure. There was no more radio silence in effect. After a few sensible words like: "Stop being nervous. Talk slower." Words came back more shrilly and faster: "Who's nervous? You son of a bitch, not me-ee." Then communications settled down to a garbled roar.

Avengers and Dauntlesses, which appeared to be streaking downward in dives at all angles, were making rack and ruin upon what, I realized suddenly, was Ballale. Some had already pulled out of their dives. Others were just in the process of pulling out. And still others were in their dives.

Huge puffs of dirt and smoke started to dot the tiny isle. A white parachute mushroomed out amid the dirty grayish puffs. Of course I realized it was at a higher altitude. Then a plane crashed. Avenger or Dauntless? How was I to know?

There were enough thick clouds over nearby Bougainville so that I did not expect any Nippon Zeros to intercept us from there. I don't know what I was thinking right at that particular moment. Or what I was supposed to be doing. Maybe, as the proverbial saying goes: "I sat there—fat, dumb, and happy." Perhaps I was watching the boys below in much the same manner as I witnessed the Cleveland Air Shows many times. Anyhow, for certain, high cover was about as close as I ever expected to get toward heaven. So we started down.

To add to my bewilderment, shortly after

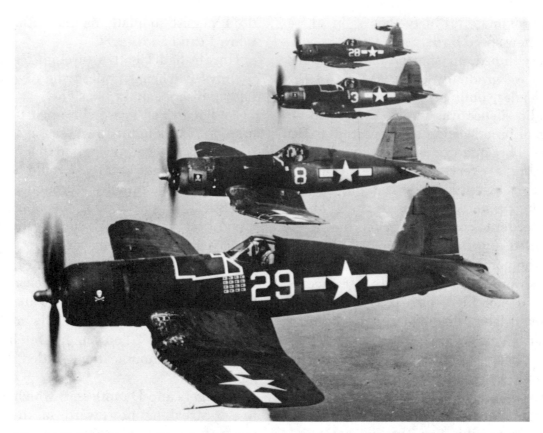

The F4U Corsair, readily identified by its gull wings, was a powerhouse. Flown primarily by Marines like "Pappy" Boyington's "Black Sheep," Joe Foss, and others, it was also one of the few prop-driven planes to see action in Korea. (Bill Hess)

we cleared the last bit of fluff, I saw that we were right in the middle of about forty Jap fighters. As for us, we had twenty planes that day.

The first thing I knew, there was a Japanese fighter plane, not more than twenty-five feet off my right wing-tip. Wow, the only marking I was conscious of was the "Angry Red Meat Ball" sailing alongside of me. But I guess the Nip pilot never realized what I was, because he wobbled his wings, which, in pilot language, means join up. Then he added throttle, pulling ahead of my Corsair.

Good God! It had all happened so suddenly I hadn't turned on my gun switches, electric gun sight, or, for that matter, even charged my machine guns. All of which is quite necessary if one desires to shoot someone down in the air.

It seemed like an eternity before I could get everything turned on and the guns charged.

But when I did accomplish all this, I joined up on the Jap, all right. He went spiraling down in flames right off Ballale.

The bursts from my six .50-caliber machine guns, the noise and seeing tracer bullets, brought me back to this world once again. Like someone had hit me with a wet towel. Almost simultaneously I glanced back over my shoulder to see how Moe Fisher, my wing man, was making out, and because I saw tracers go sizzling past my right wing-tip. Good boy, Moe—he was busy pouring an endless burst into a Nip fighter, not more than fifty yards off the end of my tail section. This Nip burst into flames as he started to roll, minus half a wing, toward the sea below.

In these few split seconds all concern, and, for that matter, all view of the dive bombers, left me again. All that stood out in my vision were burning and smoking aircraft. And all I could make out were Japanese having this trouble. Some were making out-of-control gyrations toward a watery grave.

A few pilots I had run into before, and some since, can relate every minute detail about an enemy aircraft they came in contact with. But I'll be damned if I can remember much more than round wing-tips, square tips, liquid-cooled, air-cooled, and of course the horrifying Rising Sun markings.

After a few seconds of Fourth-of-July spectacle most of the Nip fighters cleared out. Then we streaked on down lower to the water, where the dive bombers were re-forming for mutual protection after their dives prior to proceeding homeward. We found a number of Nip fighters making runs on our bombers while they were busy reforming their squadrons.

While traveling at quite an excessive rate of speed for making an approach on one of these Zeros I opened fire on his cockpit, expecting him to turn either right or left, or go up or down to evade my fire after he was struck by my burst. But this Zero didn't do any of these things. It exploded. It exploded so close, right in front of my face, that I didn't know which way to turn to miss the pieces. So I flew right through the center of the explosion, throwing up my arm in front of my face in a feeble attempt to ward off these pieces.

I didn't know what happened to my plane at the time. Evidently my craft didn't hit the Nip's engine when his plane flew apart. But I did have dents all over my engine cowling and leading edges of my wings and empennage surfaces. With this unorthodox evasive action Moe and I were finally separated, as by this time, I guessed, everyone else was. Certainly this wasn't the procedure we followed in the three-week training period.

Something else entered my mind after the initial surprise and fright were over, something I realized much more keenly than any of the pilots accompanying me on this mission. I am positive, for I had been involved in this deadly game with Mars for two long years. What I knew only too well was that the average pilot gets less than one chance in a hun-

dred missions of being in a position to fire a killing burst. And furthermore, when this rare chance comes, the one in a hundred, nine out of ten times the pilot is outnumbered, which cuts down his chances still further. Insight into these odds came to me very vividly, for I had tried my best for over two years. Yet my score to date was six. A great number of my previous mistakes suddenly came before me. Realizing that there was meat on the table that might never be there again, as far as I personally was concerned, I was determined to make hay while the sun shined.

Long after the bombing formation had gone on toward home, I found a Zero scooting along, hugging the water, returning to his base after chasing our bombers as far as he thought wise. This I had gotten from the past. When an aircraft is out of ammunition or low on fuel, the pilot will hug the terrain in order to present a very poor target.

I decided to make a run on this baby. He never changed his course much, but started an ever-so-gentle turn. My Corsair gradually closed the gap between us. I was thinking: "As long as he is turning, he knows he isn't safe. It looks too easy."

Then I happened to recall something I had experienced in Burma with the Flying Tigers, so I violently reversed my course. And sure enough, there was his little pal coming along behind. He was just waiting for the sucker, me, to commence my pass on his mate.

As I turned into this pal, I made a head-on run with him. Black puffs came slowly from his 20-millimeter cannons. His tracers were dropping way under my Corsair. I could see my tracers going all around this little Zero. When I got close enough to him, I could see rips in the bottom of his fuselage as I ducked underneath on my pass by. The little plane nosed down slowly, smoking, and crashed with a splash a couple seconds later, without burning or flaming.

Efforts to locate the other Zero, the intention of my initial run, proved to be futile. In turning east again, in the direction of our long-gone bombers, once more I happened on a Zero barreling homeward just off the water. This time there was no companion opponent with the plane. So I nosed over, right off the water, and made a head-on run from above on this Japanese fighter. I wondered whether the pilot didn't see me or was so low on fuel he didn't dare to change his direction from home.

A short burst of .50s, then smoke. While I was endeavoring to make a turn to give the *coup de grâce*, the plane landed in the ocean. When aircraft hit the water going at any speed like that, they don't remain on the surface. They hit like a rock and sink out of sight immediately. For the first time I became conscious that I would never have enough fuel to get back to home base in the Russell Islands, but I could make it to Munda, New Georgia. Ammunition—well, I figured that must be gone. Lord knows, the trigger had been held down long enough. Anyhow, there would be no need for more ammo.

But the day still wasn't ended, even though this recital of the first day's events may start seeming a little repetitious by now. And God knows I was certainly through for the day, in more ways than one. Yet when practically back to our closest allied territory, which was then Munda, I saw one of our Corsairs proceeding for home along the water. I tried to join up with him.

And just then, as if from nowhere, I saw that two Nip fighters were making runs on this Corsair at their leisure. The poor Corsair was so low it couldn't dive or make a turn in either direction if he wanted to, with two on his tail. There was oil all over the plexiglass canopy and sides of the fuselage. Undoubtedly his speed had to be reduced in order to nurse the injured engine as far as possible.

In any event, if help didn't arrive quickly, the pilot, whoever he was, would be a goner soon. I made a run from behind on the Zero closer to the Corsair. This Zero pulled straight up—for they can really maneuver— almost straight up in the air. I was hauling back on my stick so hard that my plane lost speed and began to fall into a spin. And as I started to spin, I saw the Zero break into flames. A spin at that low altitude is a pretty hairy thing in itself, and I no doubt would have been more concerned if so many other things weren't happening at the same time.

It was impossible for me to see this flamer crash. By this time, I was too occupied getting my plane out of the spin before I hit the water too. I did, however, shoot a sizable burst into the second Zero a few seconds later. This Zero turned northward for Choiseul, a nearby enemy-held island, but without an airstrip. The only thing I could figure was that his craft was acting up and he planned upon ditching as close to Choiseul as he could. Anyhow I didn't have sufficient gas to verify my suspicions.

Also, I was unable to locate the oil-smeared Corsair again. Not that it would have helped any, or there was anything else one could do, but I believe Bob Ewing must have been in that Corsair. For Bob never showed up after the mission. And one thing for certain, that slowed-down, oil-smeared, and shell-riddled Corsair couldn't have gone much farther.

This first day of the new squadron had been a busy one, all right. It had been so busy I suddenly realized that my gas gauge was bouncing on empty. And I wanted so badly to stretch that gas registering zero to somewhere close to Munda I could taste it.

I leaned out fuel consumption as far as was possible, and the finish was one of those photo ones. I did reach the field at Munda, or rather one end of it, and was just starting to taxi down the field when my engine cut out. I was completely out of gas.

The armorers came out to rearm my plane and informed me that I had only thirty rounds of .50-caliber left, so I guess I did come back at the right time.

But I was to learn something else, too, in case I started to think that all my days were to be like this one, the first one. For this first day—when I got five planes to my credit— happened to be the best day I ever had in combat. However, this concerned us nought, for one would have thought we won the war then and there.

Opportunity knocks seldom. But one thing for certain, people can sense these opportunities if they are halfway capable of logical thinking, and, of course, are willing to take the consequences if things go dead wrong.

Lengthy delay in arrival of relief squadrons from the States plus my ability to con Colonel Sanderson into making a squadron out of thin air were the necessary ingredients—and bluff. This was the shady parentage of my new squadron. Born on speculation. An operation strictly on credit had been approved: Air-planes, pilots, and even our squadron number, 214, were borrowed.

That night, I recall vaguely, the quartet of Moe Fisher, Moon Mullin, George Ashmun, and Bruce Matheson harmonizing on the cot next to mine. Tomorrow, the future, meant little to me then. Not even the possibility of a hairy hangover bothered me the slightest. So I took aboard a load of issue brandy, which our flight surgeon, Jim Ream, had been so kind to supply. I took this load of brandy, along with yours truly, to another world.

Sandy couldn't possibly have known that our first mission would work out this way—or could he?

INTO THE DRINK

by Major Joseph J. Foss, USMCR

"It was on November 17, 1942. Some Japanese destroyers were said to be approaching Guadalcanal, so they loaded 100-pound bombs under the wings of our F4F Wildcats. Eight of us took off. Soon we jumped eight Zeros and got involved with six of them. We managed to get 'em but lost one of our boys.

"Then we pulled up to the base of an overcast and spotted the destroyers. I decided to go in last and as the boys were peeling off I noticed the float of an enemy plane poke down through the overcast. I swung behind and when he dropped clear I made a pass. But I came in so fast—he must have cut his throttles back—I thought I'd run into him and couldn't shoot. As I went by at about 25 feet a guy in the back seat with a free gun turned that old baby on me and shot.

"The line of bullets stitched right up the cowling and I pulled my head back because I thought I was going to get it in the teeth. One bullet went through the canopy past my left temple. The plane seemed okay so I dived down, came up and got him with a belly shot. Then a second one jumped me and I got him the same way.

"About the time I was going to rejoin the bombing the engine of my old plane went *boom*! It was missing badly and that was the beginning of the end. I got on my radio but it was shot out. The other planes rendezvoused on the far side of the destroyers and couldn't see me. I headed home, trying to keep my altitude. The engine kept backfiring and cutting out.

"I flew into a rainstorm and kept losing altitude. Finally I broke into the clear near an island. I decided to make a water landing and came in a mile or so from the beach. The plane quit cold. I opened the canopy but forgot to lock it open. I got my parachute loose and forgot to unbuckle my leg straps.

"The plane hit a big swell and *wham!* the canopy slammed shut. She nosed up and sank. Water rushed in. I took a deep breath—

Joe Foss destroyed more enemy aircraft with the Marines than Boyington, who scored six of his victories with the AVG. After the war, Foss rose to command South Dakota's Air National Guard and later became the state's governor. (USMC)

mostly sea water. This thing went down, down, down, and I felt that something was crushing me. The water was cold. Maybe that cleared my head.

"I got the canopy open again. My leg caught but my buoyant 'chute pulled me up and finally I got free. I hit the surface like a cork and floated fanny up, head down because I'd forgotten to unbuckle the 'chute. I got out of it and came up spitting water like a whale. Then I got the parachute worked around under my belly and inflated my Mae West and started paddling toward the island.

"A strong tide carried me out to sea. It kept on raining and got dark. I'd been paddling around for maybe three hours when I suddenly saw a light nearby and a boat appeared coming right for my head. I ducked under and came up by its outrigger. The mumbo-jumbo of voices sounded like Japs so I kept quiet and they didn't see me and went on by.

" 'Let's look over here,' I heard someone say. I let out a beller. The light went out.

"Next thing, I was encircled by war canoes. Someone turned on a light and I saw all these dudes with big clubs raised over my head. I

The Grumman F4f Wildcat, together with the Flying Tigers' P-40, was among the first U.S. fighters able to face the Japanese Zeros. "Butch" O'Hare downed five Japanese aircraft in a single action in a Wildcat. (Grumman)

began yelling, 'Friend! American! Birdman! Aviator!'

"A canoe came close and I grabbed a hand that belonged to Father de Stuyvesant from the mission of Malaita, this Jap-held island in the Solomons. One native had seen my plane ditch. I'll never know how they found me 'way out there in the pitch dark.

"I spent the night at the mission. Next morning a flier saw my 'chute drying and sent a seaplane to pick me up. I was back in combat the next day. Whenever things slowed up a little I'd fly by the island and drop a bundle of magazines, cigars, candy, razor blades— stuff like that. The trees in the jungle literally swayed as the natives headed for the package.

"Father de Stuyvesant is now the Bishop of Guadalcanal. He writes that they're still using parts of my parachute as cloths in the mission."

The Lone Eagle Flies Again

THOUGHTS OF A
COMBAT PILOT

**by Colonel Charles A. Lindbergh,
Civilian Technical Representative**

Guns charged and ring sights glowing, our four Corsairs float like hawks over enemy-held land. Below us are the jungle hills of New Ireland; ahead, the purple volcanoes of Rabaul. Elsewhere, our eyes see a wilderness of cloud, sky and blue Pacific water.

We are cruising at 8000 feet, on a marine patrol, to cover the morning's strike, to make sure that Japanese Zeros don't interfere with American bombing crews. Our planes are from VMF 223, based on a rolled-coral strip in the Green Islands—200 miles east of New Guinea—four degrees south of the equator.

This is my first combat mission, and therefore unlike all other flights. My senses are peeled of the calluses formed by everyday routine. They awoke this morning with new awareness, crying out that I'll go forth to kill, and to run the risk of death; that, like man of primitive times, I'm both the hunter and the hunted. Inside this sun-browned skin that covers me, civilized perception and barbaric instinct are melting into some not-yet-tested-out alloy. Ever since my ears heard the noises of daybreak, all things around me—the air I breathe, the ground I walk on, the very trees of the jungle—seem to have taken on new qualities of beauty and of danger.

There was the graceful curve of my fighter's wing, as I climbed into the cockpit before take-off, testifying to the godlike creativeness of man. There was the awkward bulk of my pistol, digging into my chest, reminding me of our satanical destructiveness. I watched the bunched heads of coconut palms streaming past as my landing gear retracted and my air speed rose; they were followed by antiaircraft cannon at the strip's end. After that, the power of 2000 horses pulled me skyward to aviation's supermortal view, until a voice in my receiver shouted, "Clear your guns!"

Now, we are spread wide—the four of us—in combat formation, so we'll have room to maneuver in attack. At the foot of those hills below, hidden in that thick jungle mat of leaves and branches, are our enemies—men of different language and ideas, but with bodies and brains quite similar to ours. We know that their glasses are now trained upon us, that their loaded batteries will anticipate our course. At any moment puffs of black may shatter this crystal air. We are like the animals in that jungle—nerved to spring upon our prey; alert lest we be sprung on. One shot, and a Corsair may fall, like a feathered bird to an expert marksman. One swoop, and a dozen Japanese may lie dead in a badly camouflaged position.

Sixteen hundred rounds I carry, of .50-caliber ammunition, and I can spew them out at the rate of 5000 rounds a minute. Suddenly the grace of flight is gone. I see with war-conditioned eyes—these are wicked-looking planes we fly, manned by ruthless pilots, built to kill, trained to kill, hoping to kill, as we approach the heavily defended fortress of Rabaul.

At 10,000 feet, we tilt our wings and circle the bomb-pocked city. I see that its harbor is reefed with sunken ships—monuments to strikes that came before us. A single burst of ack-ack, high and wide, announces our arrival. The enemy is not wasting ammunition on patrolling fighters, and it's doubtful that he has enough Zeros left to put a squadron up. We range over the nearby Japanese airstrips; a few planes are in the revetments, but we see no sign of activity on the ground.

Army B-25s are bunched closely in the sky above us. Navy torpedo-bombers are coming in from the west. Flights of P-40 fighters fly high cover. The strike has begun. Airacobras, at much lower altitude, dive on their targets. Black puffs of ack-ack spatter the air.

One of our Corsair reports a "bogey" at seven o'clock, low. We bank, nose down and arm our guns. It's a twin-engine plane, American, the circled star is clear upon each wing. We pull out of our dives, spiral upward. I see an outskirt of Rabaul erupting like a new volcano—bombs from the B-25s have hit. The radio is full of chatter: a life raft has been reported on the water, fighters are already circling above it, and a "Dumbo" flying boat is coming in to rescue the downed man.

We swing southward. Columns of smoke and flame from magnesium clusters mushroom up in a grove of coconut palms—an enemy fuel dump was there. I see a TBF making its get-away, low over the water, while a shore battery's splashes follow it out from the coast. Another bogey is reported. We dive. It's only a P-39, strayed from the flock, somewhat nervous lest we mistake it for a Zero.

The B-25s have disappeared. Several fork-tailed Lightnings pass above us. I watch the torpedo-bombers reforming out at sea. A trail of smoke marks one which has been hit; it will probably have to ditch on the way home.

The strike is over; the air above Rabaul de-serted; old ack-ack bursts grow large and haze away. On the ground a dozen fires are burning. Now our secondary mission will begin. Since our ammunition boxes are still full, we have targets to strafe—long wooden buildings surrounded by palm trees. The flashes of guns were reported near them during a previous raid. We take up an angular course which may throw the defenders off guard, fly on beyond, whip into position, set our trim tabs for a dive. I reach down and purge my wing tanks.

Seven thousand feet . . . 5000 feet . . . 4000 feet . . . I wonder how many guns are shooting at us . . . 3000 feet . . . perfect range, but a Corsair is too close to my line of fire . . . 2000 feet . . . buildings and palms rush up at me . . . 1500 feet . . . the Corsair ahead pulls away, and I squeeze the trigger.

Six guns clatter in my plane as tracers

Charles A. Lindbergh, world famous for his first solo flight across the Atlantic, is less well-known for his combat exploits. As a civilian technical representative, he flew fighter missions in Corsairs and Lightnings, shooting down several of the enemy. (USAF)

streak from wings to roof, and walk the building's length. I level out twenty feet above the tree tops at 400 miles an hour. All this is forbidden land, just over a wing span beneath me, apparently deserted by life; actually full of watching eyes, and hands that would gladly feel a bayonet pierce through my belly. An airstrip lies ahead—probably bristling with machine guns. We bank toward the sea, flash past the shore line, hold low until we are out of range of antiaircraft cannon.

It's almost eleven o'clock. In eight more minutes a patrol of freshly fueled Corsairs will appear overhead to relieve us. Our assigned missions are completed, but we have plenty of ammunition left—that means we'll drop in on the Duke of York before returning home.

The Duke of York is an island lying in the channel between New Britain and New Ireland. A Japanese airstrip has been built on it. Near the strip are several small villages in which, our intelligence reports, enemy troops are quartered. Patrol planes have been instructed to keep these villages well strafed and to be on the alert for ground guns. How about the natives? "They took to the hills long ago. Besides, they're all unfriendly on New Ireland. Don't forget what happened to those pilots they turned over to the Nips."

We come in low above the palms and zoom 500 feet to start our runs. I get a row of huts in my sight and rake through them as I pull my nose up . . . dust rising . . . fragments flying . . . incendiaries ricocheting at all angles . . . watch the palms . . . easy to hold a dive too long when you're moving at five miles a minute . . . level off . . . bank left . . . hug the ground so Japanese guns can't follow you.

We break formation. Now each plane is on it own, to harass the enemy.

My heading takes me out to sea. I swing back toward the coast. At thatch-walled structure perches on a cliff; beside it are steel barrels. I let my bullets rip through air until I'm 100 yards away . . . chandelle to miss the palm tops . . . bank left . . . another row of huts . . . nose down . . . too close . . . only a short burst before I have to pull the stick

back . . . circle toward the airstrip . . . two Corsairs diving on my right . . . dust . . . tracers . . . incendiaries.

I climb to locate my position . . . dive to evade enemy machine guns . . . center a building in my sight . . . squeeze the trigger- . . . no . . . a steeple! . . . a church! . . . hold fire . . . ease back on the stick. . . pick out another target . . . dive . . . fire . . . ammunition almost gone . . . only one machine gun answers . . . Corsairs are rendezvousing out at sea. I join them.

"Onyx 12—Onyx 12." That's our radio call. The message comes in clearly, "Sweep St. George Channel for a rubber boat." We spread out 1000 yards apart and fly 500 feet above the water. A moment ago our mission was to kill; now it is to rescue. Some American plane is missing, and some report said it was last seen above this channel. We find nothing—take up our homeward course. Flying boats will continue the search.

We tighten to parade formation as we approach the Green Islands. Right echelon for peel-off . . . one . . . two . . . three . . . four. Watch intervals for landing . . . gear down . . . flaps down . . . canopy wide open. My wheels touch ground at 12:20, local time; it's been a three-hour-and-forty-minute mission.

Other planes warm up as we taxi in. A new strike is getting under way.

Leaf points of a coconut palm spear into the Southern Cross. A Marauder bomber drones off through distant night. The roaring fury of our war is replaced by damp, tropical silence. I smear bug repellent around my neck, and sit down on a grenade box. I can't wipe the vision of that church from my mind. Steeples don't fit into gun sights. Thoughts of God are antagonistic to the thoughts of war.

"I almost shot up a church today," I told my young Marine captain after we landed. "I just recognized what it was in time."

"Oh, you mean that little church on the Duke of York?" He laughed. "We strafe it on every mission. The Nips used to use it for their troops."

Sons of Heaven

A LONG WAY HOME

**by Chū-i (Lieutenant) Saburo Sakai,
Imperial Japanese Navy**

Nakajima called for order. "You are going to fly the longest fighter operation in history," he warned us. "Don't take any unnecessary chances today. Stick to your orders, and, above all, don't fly recklessly and waste your fuel. Any pilot who runs short of fuel on the return from Guadalcanal is to make a forced landing at Buka Island. Our troops there have been instructed to be on the lookout for our planes.

"Now, to fly to Guadalcanal and return to Buka means covering roughly the same distance as we flew from Tainan to Clark Field in the Philippines, and return. I am positive that we can fly that distance without trouble. Returning to Rabaul is another matter. You should be able to make it, but there may be trouble. So I repeat my warning: don't waste fuel."

(Commander Nakajima told me in Tokyo after the war that the admiral wished him to take to Guadalcanal on August 7 every Zero fighter at Rabaul which could fly. Nakajima protested, and offered instead to take the twelve best pilots in his wing, because he expected to lose at least half of his men during a mission of such extreme range. A bitter argument raged between the two men until they reached a compromise on the figure of eighteen fighter planes, with the understanding that the stragglers who landed on Buka were to be picked up later.)

As soon as we had our orders, the pilots broke up into trios. I told Yonekawa and Hatori, my two wing men, "You'll meet the American Navy fliers for the first time today. They are going to have us at a distinct advantage because of the distance we have to fly. I want you both to exercise the greatest caution in every move you make. Above all, never break away from me. No matter what happens, no matter what goes on around us, stick as close to my plane as you can. Remember that—don't break away."

We ran out to our planes and waited for the runways to be cleared. Twenty-seven Betty bombers thundered down the airstrip before us. Commander Nakajima waved his hand over his cockpit. By 8:30 a.m. all the fighters were airborne. The maintenance crews and the pilots who were not flying that day lined both sides of the runway, waving their caps and shouting good luck to us. The weather was perfect, especially for Rabaul. Even the volcano was quiet; its eruptions had ended in June, and only a thin streamer of smoke drifted to the west.

We took up our escort positions behind the bombers. I was surprised to see that the Betty's carried bombs instead of torpedoes, the usual armament for attacking shipping. The bombs disturbed me; I knew the problems of hitting moving targets on the sea from high altitude. Even the B-17s, despite their vaunted accuracy, wasted most of their bombs when attacking the shipping off Buna.

We gained height slowly, then flew to the east at 13,000 feet for Buka Island. About sixty miles south of Rabaul, I noticed a particularly beautiful island on the water. Brilliantly green and in the shape of a horseshoe, the atoll was listed on the map as Green Island. I had no idea that the eye-catching qualities of the colorful atoll would later prove the key to saving my life.

Over Buka the formations turned and flew south along Bougainville's west coast. The sun beat down warmly through the canopy. The heat made me thirsty, and, since we still had some time before reaching the enemy area, I took out a bottle of soda from my lunchbox. Without thinking I opened the bottle; I had forgotten the altitude. No sooner had I made a slit in the cork than the soda water geysered violently, the pressure escaping in the rarefied air. In seconds the sticky soda water was over everything in front of me; fortunately, the strong cockpit draft dried it almost immediately. But the sugar in the soda water dried on my glasses and I was unable to see! Disgusted with my own stupidity, I rubbed the goggles. I could see dimly.

For the next forty minutes I struggled to clean not only my goggles but the windscreen and the controls as well. I had never felt more ridiculous. My fighter wandered all over the formation as I scrubbed with increasing irritation. By the time I could see clearly in all directions we were already over Vella Lavella, about midway between Rabaul and Guadalcanal.

Over New Georgia we went for higher altitude and crossed Russell at 20,000 feet. Fifty miles ahead of us Guadalcanal loomed out of the water. Even at this distance I saw flashes of yellow flame against the blue sky over the disputed island. Apparently battles were already under way between Zero fighters from bases other than Rabaul and the defending enemy planes. I looked down at Guadalcanal's northern coastline. In the channel between Guadalcanal and Florida hundreds of

white lines, the wakes of enemy ships, crisscrossed the water. Everywhere I looked there were ships. I had never seen so many warships and transports at one time.

This was my first look at an American amphibious operation. It was almost unbelievable. I saw at least seventy ships pushing toward the beaches, a dozen destroyers cutting white swaths through the water around them. And there were other ships on the horizon, too far distant to make out in detail or to count.

Meanwhile the bombers swung slowly for their runs. Dead ahead of them small clouds drifted at 13,000 feet. To our right and above was the sun, its blinding glare blotting everything from view. I was uncomfortable; we would be unable to see any fighters dropping from that angle. My fear was soon realized. Without warning six fighter planes emerged from that glare, almost as if they had suddenly appeared in the sky. A snap glance revealed that they were chubbier than the other American planes we had fought. They were painted olive green, and only the lower sides of the wings were white. Wildcats; the first Grumman F4F fighters I had seen.

The Wildcats ignored the Zeros, swooping down against the bombers. Our fighters raced ahead, many of them firing from beyond effective range, hoping to distract the enemy planes. The Wildcats plunged into the bomber formation, rolling together, and then disappeared in dives. Over the water just off Savo Island, the bombers released their missiles against a large convoy. I watched the bombs curving in their long drop. Abruptly geysers of water erupted from the sea, but the enemy shipping sailed on undisturbed.

It was obviously stupid to try to hit moving ships from four miles up! I could not understand the failure to use torpedoes, which had proven so effective in the past. Our entire mission had been wasted, thrown away in a few seconds of miserable bombing inaccuracy.

(The following day the bombers returned, this time carrying torpedoes for low-level attacks. But by then it was too late. Enemy fighters swarmed all over the bombers, and many fell blazing into the ocean even before they could reach their targets.)

The bomber formation banked to the left and picked up speed for the return to Rabaul. We escorted them as far as Russell, beyond the enemy fighter patrols, and turned back for Guadalcanal. It was about 1:30 p.m. We swept over Lunga, the eighteen Zeros poised for combat. Again bursting out of the blinding sun, Wildcats plunged against our planes. I was the only pilot who spotted the diving attack, and at once I hauled the fighter up in a steep climb, and the other planes followed me. Again the Wildcats scattered and dove in different directions. Their evasive tactics were puzzling, for nothing had been gained by either side. Apparently the Americans were not going to pick any fights today.

I turned back to check the positions of my wing men. They were gone! Things weren't as obvious as they seemed; the enemy would fight, after all. I looked everywhere for Yonekawa and Hatori, but could not find

them. Sasai's plane, the two blue stripes across its fuselage, regained formation, several other fighters moving up to position behind him. But not my wing men.

Finally I saw them, about 1500 feet below me. I gaped. A single Wildcat pursued three Zero fighters, firing in short bursts at the frantic Japanese planes. All four planes were in a wild dogfight, flying tight-left spirals. The Zeros should have been able to take the lone Grumman without any trouble, but every time a Zero caught the Wildcat before its guns the enemy plane flipped away wildly and came out again on the tail of a Zero. I had never seen such flying before.

I banked my wings to signal Sasai and dove. The Wildcat was clinging grimly to the tail of a Zero, its tracers chewing up the wings and tail. In desperation I snapped out a burst. At once the Grumman snapped away in a roll to the right, clawed around in a tight turn, and ended up in a climb straight at my own plane. Never had I seen an enemy plane move so quickly or so gracefully before; and every

The Japanese Navy Mitsubishi Zero was way ahead of its time, superior to most U.S. fighters at the war's beginning. American technology soon caught up, however (for instance, the Zero did not have the protective armor carried by U.S. planes), and surpassed it. (Monogram)

second his guns were moving closer to the belly of my fighter. I snap-rolled in an effort to throw him off. He would not be shaken. He was using my own favorite tactics, coming up from under.

I chopped the throttle back and the Zero shuddered as its speed fell. It worked; his timing off, the enemy pilot pulled back in a turn. I slammed the throttle forward again, rolling to the left. Three times I rolled the Zero, then dropped in a spin, and came out in a left vertical spiral. The Wildcat matched me turn for turn. Our left wings both pointed at a right angle to the sea below us, the right wings at the sky.

Neither of us could gain an advantage. We held to the spiral, tremendous *g* pressures pushing us down in our seats with every passing second. My heart pounded wildly, and my head felt as if it weighed a ton. A gray film seemed to be clouding over my eyes. I gritted my teeth; if the enemy pilot could take the punishment, so could I. The man who failed first and turned in any other direction to ease the pressure would be finished.

On the fifth spiral, the Wildcat skidded slightly. I had him, I thought. But the Grumman dropped its nose, gained speed, and the pilot again had his plane in full control. There was a terrific man behind that stick.

He made his error, however, in the next moment. Instead of swinging back to go into a sixth spiral, he fed power to his engine, broke away at an angle, and looped. That was the decisive split second. I went right after him, cutting inside the Grumman's arc, and came out on his tail. I had him. He kept flying loops, trying to narrow down the distance of each arc. Every time he went up and around I cut inside his arc and lessened the distance between our two planes. The Zero could outfly any fighter in the world in this kind of maneuver.

When I was only fifty yards away, the Wildcat broke out of his loop and astonished me by flying straight and level. At this distance I would not need the cannon; I pumped 200 rounds into the Grumman's cockpit,

watching the bullets chewing up the thin metal skin and shattering the glass.

I could not believe what I saw; the Wildcat continued flying almost as if nothing had happened. A Zero which had taken that many bullets into its vital cockpit would have been a ball of fire by now. I could not understand it. I slammed the throttle forward and closed in to the American plane, just as the enemy fighter lost speed. In a moment I was ten yards ahead of the Wildcat, trying to slow down. I hunched my shoulders, prepared for the onslaught of his guns. I was trapped.

No bullets came. The Wildcat's guns remained silent. The entire situation was unbelievable. I dropped my speed until our planes were flying wing-to-wing formation. I opened my cockpit window and stared out. The Wildcat's cockpit canopy was already back, and I could see the pilot clearly. He was a big man, with a round face. He wore a light khaki uniform. He appeared to be middle-aged, not as young as I had expected.

For several seconds we flew along in our bizarre formation, our eyes meeting across the narrow space between the two planes. The Wildcat was a shambles. Bullet holes had cut the fuselage and wings up from one end to the other. The skin of the rudder was gone, and the metal ribs stuck out like a skeleton. Now I could understand his horizontal flight, and also why the pilot had not fired. Blood stained his right shoulder, and I saw the dark patch moving downward over his chest. It was incredible that his plane was still in the air.

But this was no way to kill a man! Not with him flying helplessly, wounded, his plane a wreck. I raised my left hand and shook my fist at him, shouting, uselessly, I knew, for him to fight instead of just flying along like a clay pigeon. The American looked startled; he raised his right hand weakly and waved.

I had never felt so strange before. I had killed many Americans in the air, but this was the first time a man had weakened in such a fashion directly before my eyes, and from wounds I had inflicted upon him. I honestly didn't know whether or not I should try and finish him off. Such thoughts were stupid, of course. Wounded or not, he was an enemy, and he had almost taken three of my own men a few minutes before. However, there was no reason to aim for the pilot again. I wanted the airplane, not the man.

I dropped back and came in again on his tail. Somehow the American called upon a reserve of strength and the Wildcat jerked upward into a loop. That was it. His nose started up. I aimed carefully at the engine, and barely touched the cannon trigger. A burst of flame and smoke exploded outward from his engine. The Wildcat rolled and the pilot bailed out. Far below me, almost directly over the Guadalcanal coast, his parachute snapped open. The pilot did not grasp his shroud lines, but hung limply in his chute. The last I saw of him he was drifting in toward the beach.

The other three Zero fighters quickly reformed on my wings. Yonekawa grinned broadly at me as he slid into position. We climbed and headed back for the island in search of other enemy planes. Antiaircraft shells began to burst around us. Their aim was sporadic, but the fact that heavy flak guns were already on shore, only hours after the invasion, was upsetting. I knew that our own forces required at least three days following a beach landing to set up their antiaircraft weapons. The speed at which the Americans moved their equipment ashore was astounding.

(Long after the day's flight was over, Commander Nakajima filled me in on what had happened to the other fourteen Zeros. The enemy Navy fighters held a constant advantage over Guadalcanal. They kept diving in groups of six and twelve planes, always from out of the sun, raising havoc with the Zero formations. Never before had Nakajima and his men encountered such determined opposition or faced an enemy who would not yield. Again and again the plunging Wildcats shredded the Zero formation.

Every time the Wildcats dove, they fired, rolled back, and disappeared far below, refusing to allow the Zeros to use to their own advantage their unexcelled maneuverability.

The tactics were wise, but the Americans' gunnery was sadly deficient. Only one Zero fighter fell before these attacks.

It was Nishizawa's day to shine. Before his ammunition ran out, the astounding ace in incredible maneuvers which left his wing men hopelessly far behind him had shot six Grumman fighters out of the sky.

For the first time Nakajima encountered what was to become a famous double-team maneuver on the part of the enemy. Two Wildcats jumped the commander's plane. He had no trouble in getting on the tail of an enemy fighter, but never had a chance to fire before the Grumman's teammate roared at him from the side. Nakajima was raging when he got back to Rabaul; he had been forced to dive and run for safety. And Nishizawa and I were the only two pilots in the entire group to down any enemy planes during the day's fighting.)

Meanwhile I returned to 7000 feet with my three fighters behind me. We flew through broken clouds, unable to find any hostile planes. No sooner had we emerged from one cloud than, for the first time in all my years of combat, an enemy plane caught me unawares. I felt a heavy thud, the scream of a bullet, and a hole two inches across appeared through the cockpit glass to my left, only inches away from my face.

I still had not seen any other planes in the air. It might have been ground fire which hit me. Then I caught a glimpse of an enemy bomber—not a fighter—which had caught me napping. The Dauntless hung on its wing, racing for cloud cover. The audacity of the enemy pilot was amazing; he had deliberately jumped four Zero fighters in a slow and lightly armed dive-bomber.

In a moment I was on his tail. The Dauntless jerked up and down several times, then dove suddenly into a cloud. I wasn't giving up that easily; I went right in after him. For a few seconds I saw only white as we raced through the billowing mass. Then we were through, in the clear. I closed in rapidly and fired. The rear gunner flung up his hands and collapsed over his gun. I pulled back easily on the stick and the shells walked up to the engine. The SBD rolled repeatedly to the left, then dropped into a wild dive. Yonekawa saw the pilot bail out. It was my sixtieth kill.

Back at 13,000 feet, we searched for but failed to find the remainder of our group. A few minutes later, over the Guadalcanal coast, I spotted a cluster of planes several miles ahead of our own. I signaled the other fighters and gunned the engine. soon I made out eight planes in all, flying a formation of two flights. Enemy. Our own planes did not form up into flights in their formations. I was well ahead of the other fighters and kept closing in against the enemy group. I would take the planes on the right and leave the others for the three Zeros following. The enemy group tightened formation; perfect! They appeared to be Wildcats, and tightening their formation meant that I had not been sighted.

If they kept their positions I would be able to hit them without warning, coming up from their rear and below. Just another few seconds . . . I'd be able to get at least two on the first firing pass. I closed in as close as possible. The distance in the range finder shrank to 200 yards—then 100—70—60 . . .

I was in a trap! The enemy planes were not fighters, but bombers, the new Avenger torpedo-planes, types I had never seen before. From the rear they looked exactly like Wildcats, but now their extra size was visible, as were the top turret with its single gun and the belly turret with another 50-caliber gun.

No wonder they had tightened their formation! They were waiting for me, and now I was caught with eight guns aiming at me from the right, and an equal number from the left. I was on engine overboost, and it was impossible to slow down quickly.

There was no turning back now. If I turned or looped, the enemy gunners would have a clear shot on the exposed belly of the Zero. I wouldn't stand a chance of evading their fire. There was only one thing to do—keep going, and open up with everything I had. I jammed down on the firing button. Almost at the same moment every gun in the Avenger formation opened up. The chattering roar of the guns and the cough of the cannon drowned out all other sound. The enemy planes were only twenty yards in front of me when flames spurted from two bombers. That was all I saw. A violent explosion smashed at my body. I felt as though knives had been thrust savagely into my ears; the world burst into flaming red and I went blind.

(The three pilots following me reported to our commander the they saw both Avengers falling from the sky, along with my plane. They stated further that the enemy planes were trailing fire and smoke; there were officially credited to me as my sixty-first and sixty-second air victories. But an official American report of the battle denied any losses of Grumman TBF Avengers operating from the three aircraft carriers southwest of Guadalcanal. Perhaps the two planes made it back to their ships. As my own plane dove, with me unconscious in the cockpit, the three Zeros followed me down. They abandoned their chase when my fighter disappeared into a low overcast.)

Several seconds must have passed before I regained consciousness. A strong, cold wind blowing in through the shattered windshield brought me to. But I was still not in control of my senses. Everything seemed blurred. I kept lapsing back into waves of darkness. These swept over me every time I tried to sit up straight. My head was far back, leaning against the headrest. I struggled to see, but the cockpit wavered and danced before my eyes. The cockpit seemed to be open; actually, the glass had been shattered, and the wind streamed in to jar me back to semiconsciousness. It struck my face; my goggles were smashed.

I felt . . . nothing but a soothing, pleasant drowsiness. I wanted to go to sleep. I tried to realize that I had been hit, that I was dying, but I felt no fear. If dying was like this, without pain, there was nothing to worry about.

(EDITOR'S NOTE: Badly shot up, wounded,

nearly blind, bloody, partially paralyzed, and fighting unconsciousness, his plane a shambles, Sakai did the impossible. Flying many hundreds of miles over the vast Pacific, he managed to return safely to his base at Rabaul.)

BATTLE OVER PALEMBANG

by Chu-i (Lieutenant) Hideaki Inayama, Imperial Japanese Army

"Enemy Corsairs approaching the airfield!" The ground staff whipped away the wheel chocks; I eased open the throttle and as the note of my powerful radial changed to a deep-throated roar, my Nakajima-built Shoki (Demon) fighter began to move forward in swirling clouds of reddish dust.

As I reached the take-off point, out of the corner of my eye I could see the ground personnel hurriedly pushing aircraft into sandbagged dispersal pens, and about ten miles to the southeast a column of oily black smoke was spiralling into the sky. The Palembang refineries!

My comrades had now lined up behind me; I raised my arm, opened the throttle fully, and I was gathering speed down the runway. Five seconds, ten seconds . . . tail up. The sun, immediately behind me, turned the airscrew into a shimmering arc, blinding me as I glanced over my shoulder.

Suddenly, the sun was momentarily blotted out. A stream of small bright lights flashed past my starboard wing-tip. I was being strafed! As I glanced up, I caught the momentary flash of two dark blue Corsairs. Jerking back the stick, I jumped my Shoki into the air, retracted my undercarriage and simultaneously jabbed at the button operating the flaps, skimming along the tops of the coconut trees. No smell of burning! No unnerving knocking! My engine roaring smoothly! How those British pilots could have missed such a sitting duck I could not imagine, but I could thank my lucky stars that I was not already buried in the blazing funeral pyre of my faithful Shoki.

For a year, my squadron, the 87th of the Imperial Japanese Army Air Force, had been based on a former Dutch airfield, one of four fighter squadrons based within a radius of forty-two miles of the vitally important Palembang oil refineries. My squadron had received new Nakajima Shoki fighters, known to our enemies as Tojos, late in 1943, and our airfield, forty miles southwest of the refineries, comprised dusty red strips, three wooden hangars, and a collection of huts.

Some thirty Shoki fighters were always at a state of readiness on the airfield, but by the beginning of 1944 tension was mounting, for the enemy was heading in our direction. Squadrons of Nakajima Hayabusa (Oscar) single-engined fighters and Kawasaki Toryu (Nick) twin-engined fighters were moved in to strengthen our defenses, and then, on January 4, the aircraft from a British carrier task force had made a sweep over the oilfields in northern Sumatra.

The morning of January 24 dawned with a thin mist lying over the field. A thin layer of cloud hung at about a thousand feet, and the sun-burned mechanics were busily completing minor checks and refuelling the fighters. The sun rose on a hive of activity. I walked over to my aircraft and chatted to my chief mechanic while the sun dispersed the last vestiges of mist.

After a few minutes I crossed to the duty hut and began to chalk up details of the day's patrols. At that moment the air-raid siren shrilled out. With a shout of "Get airborne" to the pilots grouped around the duty hut, I grabbed my chute harness and flying helmet, and ran hell for leather to my Shoki. All round the airfield engines were starting up, belching their pale exhaust fumes. I clambered into my cockpit, opened the throttle a little to raise the revs, quickly checked my instruments and simultaneously plugged in my radio leads and oxygen mask, hooked on my parachute and buckled my safety belt.

All switches-on. Airscrew in fine pitch. I held the stick tightly and opened the throttle. Everything satisfactory! A glance told me that the other Shoki fighters of my flight, the 3rd Flight which sported blue markings, were taxiing into take-off position. My headphones crackled and I was told, "Enemy-fighters attacking neighboring airfields. Strength unknown!" Two or three minutes later I was to learn that they were also attacking *our* airfield!

After running the gauntlet of the strafing Corsairs I began a shallow climb as soon as my airspeed indicator read 220 m.p.h. How had my comrades fared? Did they get off the runway safely or were they hit? I made a tight climbing turn to port, and as I burst through the layer of cloud I saw other Shoki fighters climbing. If my own Flight had taken off successfully there was no sign of my comrades as none of the other fighters attempted to formate on me. I was certainly worried about their non-appearance, but my task was the defense of the refineries, so I opened the throttle fully and headed for Palembang in a steady climb.

Scattered cloud like torn cotton wool floated in the azure sky but as yet I could see no sign of the enemy. I depressed my R/T button. "Hullo, Musashi, hullo Musashi. Kamikaze calling. Any information?" The fighter controller answered immediately. "Approximately one hundred enemy fighters and bombers have just passed over Peton and are now penetrating the refinery area." By now my altimeter indicated over 12,000 feet,

and I switched on my oxygen, its sweetish smell immediately filling my face mask.

At 15,000 feet over the refineries I encountered fifteen or sixteen of our fighters circling in formation. The surprise attack by the Corsairs had evidently reduced our strength seriously. I started a slow turn to port, casting a look at my instruments as a pre-combat check. I flew across the Moesi River, and was turning towards the west when I spotted black mushrooms of antiaircraft fire between layers of scattered cloud at about 6000 feet. Voices crackled in my headphones but they were too garbled for me to get the gist of what they said. At that moment I spotted an enemy formation; nine aircraft in a trio of close vics of three slap in the middle of the antiaircraft bursts. Above them was a formation of Corsairs with Hellcats providing top cover.

Our Shoki fighters screamed down on the enemy. I dived through the two layers of escort fighters like a bat out of hell, heading straight for the bombers which were now within a stone's throw of the refineries. I was closing fast, too fast. I throttled back and lined my Shoki behind the starboard plane of the last trio of bombers. The Grumman Avenger danced in my gunsight, Its bomb-bay doors were already agape.

Steady, steady, fire! I squeezed the firing trigger and four 13-mm. machine guns pumped streams of bullets into the luckless Avenger. I broke away and as I made a sharp climbing turn I saw my quarry burst into flames and spin into the dark green carpet of jungle below. The remaining eight Avengers, unaware of their comrade's fate, and ignoring the antiaircraft barrage, had entered a shallow dive and were dropping their bombs slap on their target.

I had to admit to admiration at the way those Avengers pressed home their attack. Stick after stick of bombs fell squarely on the refineries which were soon belching flame and smoke, and through this pall climbed the indomitable Avengers.

I could not see any of my comrades. For all

I knew I was the only Nipponese fighter in the sky! An enemy aircraft momentarily crossed in front of my Shoki. I fired but missed. I pulled back the stick and zoomed up into the sky, taking another look at the scene of devastation below. The pale blue storage tanks were erupting in flame, one by one, and the pall of oily black smoke was thickening rapidly. Suddenly, a Hellcat flashed past my starboard wing-tip, intent on escorting the Avengers. I didn't follow it down as throughout the combat the fighter controller had been repeatedly instructing us to concentrate on the bombers and avoid combat with the escorting fighters.

I scanned the sky for more Avengers. Below, to port, a cumbersome grey barrage-balloon burst into flames and fell into the inferno of the refineries. Chains of red fireballs from the antiaircraft batteries hidden in the jungle were now getting uncomfortably close, and I was just deciding that discretion was the better part of valor when, "Hello Kamikaze, hello Kamikaze. Musashi calling. The second enemy wave is now approaching your position!"

I was flying at 3000 feet, and as I started to climb, a glance at my fuel gauges told me that my fuselage tank was getting low. As I gained altitude I anxiously scanned the surrounding sky for my comrades. Columns of black smoke rising on both sides of the Moesi River marked the last resting places of friends and foes alike.

Two aircraft were in a tight turn below me. I strained my eyes to identify them . . . one of our Nakajima Hayabusa fighters with a Hellcat on its tail, following every maneuver of the frantic Nipponese pilot as if the two aircraft were joined by invisible cables! Tracers were zipping past the Hayabusa and it was obviously only a matter of time before the pilot of the Hellcat would be able to paint up another "meatball" beneath his cockpit! I half rolled and dived after the Hellcat whose pilot was oblivious to anything but his target.

The Hayabusa and the Hellcat were now in a tight turn to port. The Hellcat was in my gunsight momentarily as I skidded around on its tail. I loosed off a burst which narrowly missed, and I was now overshooting my target. For a fraction of a second I was flying

The Navy's F6F Hellcat, succeeding Grumman's earlier Wildcat, became more than a match for the Zero, which saw no comparable improvements. (Bill Hess)

level with the Hellcat on its starboard side, and I glimpsed a look of surprise on the face of the British pilot. I pulled the nose of my Shoki up, intending to full loop on to his tail, but the British fighter broke to starboard, dived under my fighter's belly and was daisy-cutting over the jungle at full speed. The pilot of the Hayabusa performed several rolls to signal his appreciation of my intervention.

I climbed steadily to 9000 feet, performing lazy turns over the burning refineries. My forward visibility was now partly obscured by oil splashes on my windscreen, but I recognized two Shoki fighters flying some 3000 feet below me at ten o'clock, but as I descended towards them, I spotted the second attacking wave to the south. There appeared to be about a hundred aircraft with Avengers forming the bottom step of the wave at about 6000 feet. Some three hundred antiaircraft guns around the refineries opened up at that moment, and one Avenger immediately exploded, and another shed a wing and spun in.

The top cover of Hellcats now broke formation, spreading into small combat groups. Keeping a wary eye on them, I headed for the Avengers, barrel-rolling up beneath them, loosing a burst at the nearest machine and climbing through their air formation. Four escorting Hellcats were immediately on me, and I turned sharply to port, two of the Hellcats overshooting.

The Shoki was fast and had an excellent climb rate, but it was no match for the excellent little Grumman in maneuverability. I pulled maximum *g* which forced me down into the cockpit. The blood rushed to my head and I nearly blacked out. Glancing over my shoulder I saw that the nearest of my pursuers was 400 yards away. I flung my Shoki into another vertical turn to port. The leading Hellcat opened fire, but he could not bring his guns to bear effectively on my wildly turning fighter. I knew that my minutes were numbered, and then the unexpected happened. A burst of antiaircraft fire landed slap in the middle of the Hellcats and they immediately broke to starboard!

I started to climb again, but the air battle seemed to be over. The Avengers had dropped their bombs and had turned back southwestwards. I hastily checked my remaining fuel and gave chase at full throttle. At 1500 feet two Avengers were flying southwards, their leader trailing smoke. Sitting ducks! I carefully turned in behind them, concentrating on the damaged Avenger, which still had its bomb doors open. Probably his hydraulics had been damaged.

Six hundred yards . . . five hundred yards . . . suddenly its ball turret gunner opened fire. Red tracers slipped past my Shoki, but I held my fire. Two hundred yards . . . I could clearly see the gunner in the ball turret. Now I was flying in the wash of my quarry and my aircraft was bouncing around like a mad thing. Steadying the Shoki I fired at point-blank distance. The bullets from my four 13-mm. guns ripped into the Avenger, its "greenhouse" canopy bursting into fragments like leaves in a gale. Flames seared back from the port wing root, and the Avenger rolled over on to its back and then fell away into the jungle below.

I now turned my attention to the second Avenger which appeared to have been damaged by antiaircraft fire, for there was a large hole near the starboard wing-tip, and the skinning was fluttering like a fan. We were now down to 500 feet and, although I doubted that it would ever make it back to its carrier, I had to finish it off.

I could not see any gunners in its turrets, and I throttled back and sat on its starboard wing. The British pilot stared at my Shoki, with its circular red Hinomaru insignia and black-painted upper surfaces, and I could only guess his thoughts. He obviously had very limited control over his sorely damaged aircraft, and could do nothing but wait for the inevitable. My curiosity was to prove my undoing, however, for I pushed the throttle forward and climbed above him, intending to take him in a diving turn, but the delay was just enough to enable the crippled Avenger to reach some scattered cloud. I didn't have a chance to fire, and by this time I had only just enough fuel to get me back to my base.

I could see columns of smoke rising from the direction of the airfield, and as I circled the base at low altitude, I could see that a hangar and several aircraft were burned out. After landing, my chief mechanic and armorer ran across to my Shoki with worried expressions on their faces. I greeted them cheerfully, saying, "Everything worked perfectly. No trouble at all."

It was then that they told me that all my comrades had been prevented from taking off by the strafing Corsairs. The 87th had lost no less than seven pilots and twelve fighters! Another day like that and. . . !

KAMIKAZE

by Gocho (Corporal) Yasuo Kuwahara, Imperial Japanese Army

Somehow the remaining time passed. It was as if there had been a blank space, then I found myself standing on the airfield, suited up, waiting to fly. There were sixteen pilots all told—four of us escorts, the remaining dozen never to return. The twelve had just grouped for final directions before an officer with a map.

We all stood at attention, respectfully listening to the commanding officer now—his parting words. A short distance away I could see Tatsuno, but he didn't look real—just a fascimile. His spirit . . . It had already gone like the wind among the lanterns.

Around the shaved skull of each *Kamikaze* was bound a small flag, the crimson rising sun over his forehead. These departures were never conducted in a perfunctory manner. There was much ceremony, much show, toasts and valiant speeches—most of which I had already learned by rote.

Boys and girls, drafted from school to work on the base, were allowed to assemble with the squadron on these occasions. Among the fringe of onlookers a knot of girls began to weep, and then grew quiet. It was time for the commanding officer's speech.

Yes, the same words, the words I had heard so often on this runway during the past weeks—the voice droning nasally for several minutes, and then the conclusion: "And so,

valiant comrades, smile as you go. . . . There is a place prepared for you in the esteemed presence of your ancestors . . . guardian warriors . . . *samurai* of the skies. . . ."

And at last it was time to sing the battle song:

The Airman's color is the color of the cherry blossom.
Look, the cherry blossoms fall on the hills of Yoshino.
If we are born proud sons of the Yamato race,
Let us die fighting in the skies."

Then the final toast. The *sake* glasses were raised and the cry surged: *Tennoheika Banzai!* (Long live the Emperor.) The *Kamikaze* were saying *sayonara* now, laughing and joking as they climbed into their obsolete planes—antiquated fighters, even trainers. The old planes didn't matter, though. It was a one-way trip. The smiles? They might remain on some of these faces to the very last. For others, those smiles began to fade as they settled into their cockpits. Maybe for a few the fear cloud would not settle until the enemy convoy loomed. And what was courage? I never knew. Who was the most courageous—the man who felt the least fear or the man who felt the most? But just then I could think of only one man.

There he was with Nakamura, walking toward me. He didn't look real. That was right; the spirit had left already. His body would mechanically fulfill the duty. What a strange smile carved on that waxen face. *Tell him! Tell him you'll cover him all the way that you'll die with him. But no, he doesn't want it, and something, something strangles all words. Your time will come soon enough, Kuwahara.* Yes, by repeating those words, I could ease the sensation of guilt. I was no friend; I hadn't been for weeks. And never once had he presumed to suggest that we see each other more often.

The lead slab in my chest was heavy now, weighing me down, crushing the words. "Tatsuno . . . I . . ." Our hands met in an icy clasp. Nakamura stood by, looking down. Nakamura, a better friend than I, was giving me this final moment.

"Remember . . ." the words came, "how we always wanted to fly together?" I looked into his eyes and bowed my head.

"I will follow you soon," I whispered.

Then he gave me something. "Here," he said, "take care of this for me. It's not much to send, but take care of it."

Quickly I looked away. Tatsuno had just given me his little finger. Our doomed men always left something of themselves behind, a lock of hair, fingernails, an entire finger—for cremation. The ashes were sent home to repose in the family shrine. There, in a special alcove, the ashes would reside with the pictures of ancestors. Once yearly, a priest would enter that room to pray.

The first motors were beginning to rev, and I held onto Tatsuno as if by holding on I might preserve him. "*Sayonara*, Yasuo," he said. We fell toward each other embracing.

Without looking back, I broke away and stumbled to my Hayabusa. Not knowing how I got there, I found myself seated, fastening my safety belt, feeling the controls, adjusting my goggles. The whole base was grumbling in final preparation.

I checked the prop mixture, then pressed the starter button. One cylinder caught, a high coughing explosion, then another and another. . . . The motor blared, and shifted into a steady grumble. We were moving out—lethargic, winged beasts coming to life. Uno, a veteran with five kills, was in the lead; I was close behind him—signals coming from the control tower. Already the onlookers were in another world, withdrawn. A ring fading from the prop blasts hurled back the air, sand, bits of straw and paper.

The commanding officer, students, other pilots, the mechanics who had come to bid

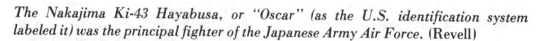

The Nakajima Ki-43 Hayabusa, or "Oscar" (as the U.S. identification system labeled it) was the principal fighter of the Japanese Army Air Force. (Revell)

good-by to the ships they had nurtured—all began shrinking as the strip sank beneath us.

It was good flying weather. The seasonal rains had subsided, leaving a clear dome of blue. Within minutes, we had left the mainland behind, left the mountains, and I was thinking how Japan itself is little more than a conglomeration of mountains, great, rolling remnants of the past, when islands reared and sank like stricken monsters, when fires burst from nature's hidden furnaces. We left the shores. The shores of four islands, and the slopes that house over seventy million people—in the crust of black-brown dwellings.

There was the refueling stop at Kagoshima on the island of Kyushu, about an hour after take-off. For twelve men, the last glimpse of their homeland. For twelve men, the three-hour flight to Okinawa would be their last hours on earth. Oka and Yamamoto had left three weeks ago.

A few minutes off Kagoshima we spotted a flight of B-29s escorted by Grummans, traveling toward Shikoku. Altering our course slightly, we faded into a skein of wispy cirrus clouds, and cruised on at a moderate speed. Below, the Pacific rolled, a deep, scalloped green, glinting further out under the sun, like a billion holiday sparklers.

I thought of many things during that flight to Okinawa. Home was a dream, an old wound that throbbed faintly, and not so often as it had. Toyoko? I saw her countless times, in countless ways. Sometimes just a silver face, unreal in the garden moonlight—or glowing softly beneath a lantern gateway. Sometimes the clear eyes, as they had looked at me on our first meeting. Little movements—the way she walked in her tight *kimono*, such dainty steps, one foot placed directly in front of the other.

But always there was a great void within me, and I kept hearing Nakamura's fateful augury from a few hours back in the other world; "Today we will fulfill our obligation to the emperor. I have a feeling in my bones." Nakamura, the recruit who had first be-friended me during the beginning days of basic—those frightening times, my loquacious friend, a practical man and a strong one.

I remembered a day long, long ago when Tatsuno and I had run laughing through the streets of Onomichi, swatting at each other with our caps. Always the pensive one, Tatsuno, the rare friend in whom one could always confide, whose understanding went so far below the surface. "Tatsuno, Tatsuno . . ." I repeated the name, and moved on in a dream.

The waters turned back, and far ahead the clouds were merging. "One hour left," Uno's words crackled in the intercom. I glanced at him, ahead, off my right wing, and signaled acknowledgment. Uno was a squat, sinewy sergeant in his early twenties, who had known only a farmer's life and had been transformed into a cunning sky fighter. Soon, if he was lucky, he would be an ace.

Ahead, the clouds were heavier, cutting off the sparklers beneath them. Off somewhere amid that darkening water. . . .

Our *Kamikaze* were traveling in wedges of three—lethal arrows slicing toward the American ships. On and on, we cut deeper into the day. The time was close at hand and, as it drew nearer, the dry, plaster feeling in my mouth increased—something that always happened. My hands were clenching and opening—the inevitable sweating. "You're too taut, Kuwahara," I kept saying. Quick glimpses of Toyoko again. "Wait for me, Toyoko. Wait for me."

Strange how so many irrelevant thoughts kept pecking at me. They were part of my defense mechanism—sedatives against fear. Soon these last sedatives would wear off.

Long since, we had passed the small islands of Yaku and Togara, and now with Amami fading in our wake, we looked ahead. Okinawa! It was looming before us, brooding, and a throbbing in my head had started. I craned my neck, then came the jolt. Sergeant Uno waggled his wings. Far off, I saw the swaths of the first American ships. I began counting those water trails—*ichi, ni, san, shi*—twenty-five in all, and there, no bigger than seeds for the moment, in the center of that task force was our quarry, four carriers, guarded by battleships and a perimeter of destroyers.

Uno signaled again and our twelve *Kamikaze* crept ahead of us at full bore—moving into the strike at ten thousand feet. The four of us climbed slightly, following. Moments sliding by, the ships growing . . . growing . . . growing. They were beginning to open up!

At last the waiting was over. I even welcomed the fear. It would all happen fast now. Then we could return and make our reports as usual. It would be no more dangerous than ever.

Tatsuno was leading the last V in an all-but-defunct navy plane—a Mitsubishi, Type 96.

Already the twelve had opened their cockpits, and fluttered their silk scarves in the wind. Always the wind—the divine wind. Ahead and beneath them the first flak was beginning to burst in soft, black puffs, and the tracers were red lines reaching for the heavens.

Now . . . we seem to be almost on top of them! I am sweating, watching. The lead *Kamikaze* dives, dropping vertically into a barbed-wire entanglement of flak. He'll never make the carriers; that seems obvious. Instead, he's heading for a cruiser near the fringe. For a moment it looks as if he'll make it. But no—he's hit, and it's all over. His plane is a red flare fading, dropping from sight.

Everything is a blur now—a mixture of sound and color. Two more of them go the same way, exploding in mid-air. A fourth is luckier. He screams unscathed through the barrage, leveling inside the flak umbrella near the water. A hit! He's struck a destroyer right at the water line. A bellowing explosion, then another and another. It's good! It's good! The ship is in its death throes. It can't stay afloat—water plunging over the bow, stifling it. It upends and is gone.

Now I'm losing track of the flights. They've been scattered. The two trailing formations are forging in through the lethal blossoms. Everywhere, incredible sound and confusion. One of our planes is skimming low across the water, gunfire kicking up a thousand spouts around him. He's closing the gap, aiming straight for a carrier. Straight in—he'll score a direct hit. No, no, they got him. He's bashing into the stern, inflicting little damage.

The defense is almost impregnable. Only a gnat could penetrate that firescreen now. Two more suicides stab at the same carrier and disintegrate, splattering the water. Others have dropped like firebrands into the sea. Impossible to keep track at all now. So far I can be certain that we have sunk only one ship.

Already, only a few planes left. It's hard to discern some of them against the murky horizon. Two planes, an advanced trainer and a Mitsubishi fighters, have swerved back toward us. We circle above them, watch them complete their arcs and head back in. That Mitsubishi! It's Tatsuno! Yes, I'm positive. He was in the last V—the only navy plane!

The two of them are diving, knifing for the convoy's core. Suddenly the trainer plane next to him is hit, virtually clubbed from the sky. His wing and tail rip off, and he corkscrews insanely away, out of my line of vision.

Tatsuno is alone now, still unhit, making a perfect run, better than they ever taught us in school. Tatsuno! Tatsuno! Fire spouts from his tail section, but he keeps going. The orange fingers reach out. His plane is a moving sheet of flame, but they can't stop him. Tatsuno! A tanker looms, ploughing the leaden liquid. They're closing! A hit! An enormous explosion rocks the atmosphere. For a curious instant embers seem to roll and dance. Now a staccato series of smaller bursts and one mighty blast, shaking the sea like a blanket. The tanker is going down. Gone. No trace but the widening shroud of oil.

That was my friend.

The *Kamikaze* were all gone now, so far as I could tell. We had sunk a destroyer and a tanker, wounded a cruiser and (though I didn't learn it till later) severely damaged a battleship. But I had no time to ponder our success. The Hayabusa ahead of me waggled its wings in warning. A flock of Grummans was preparing to pounce on us.

I had seen them streaking from the carrier—hornets angered at having their nests disturbed. Then I had lost track of them in the melee. Now, swiftly, two Hellcats were on my tail, three hundred yards off, firing bursts. Two more were moving up fast, maneuvering into firing position. Lead began to chew my stabilizer, and a 50-caliber slug pierced the canopy inches above my head.

Instinctively the four of us broke hard in a tight turn, Uno rolling like a leaf in the wind. The next instant we were on their tails. Uno thumped off a cannon burst, and one of the Hellcats tumbled off sidewise, sputtering, belching smoke. Near by, to my left, Nakamura's wing guns glittered. I saw this out of the corner of my eye.

Vainly I was trying to draw a bead on one of the enemy, but we were on opposite ends of a teetering balance scale. Now! I was tracking him! I sent one crushing out from the cannon and missed. Angrily I opened up with my guns, but wasn't really aiming.

Three Hellcats discernible now, and four Hayabusas. The Americans fanned in opposite directions, twisting frantically. From the corner of my eye again, I saw Nakamura opening up, saw him hit home! A Hellcat sprouted fires all along the fuselage and broke apart, chunks of it hurtling back in the slip stream. Two and two! Nakamura and I were even now. I shook my fist at him, but he didn't see me.

What a fool I was! My own foe would get away! He was bidding for altitude. I nosed after him from below, and there was his unprotected belly. I cut loose.

Realizing his predicament, the Grumman started a loop, cutting back sharply—an unwise maneuver had I not been so close. As it was, however, my bullets ate empty space behind his tail, and I looped after him firing

from a ridiculous upside-down position. Astounded, I saw pockets of smoke. A surge of proud satisfaction swept over me, but he was still game, running for the clouds.

I executed an Immelmann, righting at the top of my loop just in time to see the Hellcat explode into nothingness. Uno cut a high, crying arc along the cloud fringe. He had clouted it dead center with his 25-mm. cannons. Victim number six for Uno, and I felt cheated.

"Run for it!" his words came. "No more games today!" At least a dozen, perhaps two dozen, of the enemy were milling hungrily about. They had spotted me, and in every direction I could see the blue wings and white stars, the blunt snouts. My friends had vanished, and I shoved the throttle on overboost, swirling away toward the clouds.

But it was a bad move. Four or five of the enemy were roaring toward me head-on and my heart wrenched. To fight would mean swift destruction now. Instinctively I hit the stick, rolling to the left. All of them overshot, losing me. Just then, however, a lone Hellcat was dropping in a vertical spiral only a hundred yards above. A crackling sound. I'd been hit! Still, no discernible damage. I rolled once more, dropping off hard, rolling, rolling—saw sea and ships gyrating on a giant turntable, then hit a straight dive. I was dropping like a rock, knowing instinctively that several of the enemy were following.

This was my only escape now. Long hours of suicide practice would give me an advantage, and most of them would not go all the way with their faster, but less maneuverable, craft. But now, intent upon escaping the air enemy, I found myself a clay pigeon for the convoy below. Miraculously I streaked through the flak, and leveled barely above the waves. A tenacious Grumman was not so lucky! He was blasted by his own ships, hurled into the sea. A geyser was his burial marker.

Egging every molecule of strength from my Hayabusa, I roared across the water, the air around me full of death. Then I climbed, looking toward my homeland. I'd thrown most of the Americans. If I could only make the clouds . . . The outer ships were still salvoing at long range, the clouds just ahead, building into black mountains.

Just then there came a jolt, and loud clank. My plane was staggering. One lone Hellcat was closing the distance, firing like a madman from nearly six hundred yards. I'd been hit! And for a moment I was paralyzed.

I waited for the smoke, for the explosion, as the motor faltered, and began to grind—then, blessedly, caught hold. The Hellcat was closing, a ravenous shark, ripping away with his fifty-calibers. Faster, Kuwahara, faster! The clouds . . . another few seconds. . . . Then I was caught up in the mantle of a cloud. I'd make it! The enemy had tried everything in his power—everything he had on the ocean, everything he could send into the sky. The enemy had failed.

I grinned grimly into the gathering gloom. Ahead, lightning fractured the sky, and the air walls came back together with an ominous slam—something more powerful than all the ships could offer. But at least, I told myself, the elements were impersonal.

My cockpit was gradually being filled with a burning odor, and I wondered again just how much damage I'd suffered. Soon I forgot about that, though. Another problem—perhaps a much greater one. Rain was lacing my wings, coming fast. And then, a sudden deluge blotted out my vision entirely for an instant before giving way to flashing, neon spiderwebs. And every crackle was followed by a stunning jar, as if truck loads of lumber were being dumped against my frail shelter.

I had flown through wind and rain before, but never had I seen such a storm as the one mounting before me. Just ahead clouds converged at all angles in a sooty maelstrom, and the rain was lashing harder. Already, water sluiced through the holes in my windshield, while the winds grew more savage. Once my motor coughed, and I held my breath, until it sounded healthy again. The burning smell had abated, perhaps because of the torrent.

My temples throbbing, I squinted through the gloom. Off somewhere lay the day, but there near the storm's gullet it was almost night. With each flash, thunder numbed the sky with reverberating concussions. Soon I was unsure of my directions, yes, completely unsure. My compass was waggling like a scales pointer under sudden pressure, and with a shock, I noted that both my gyro horizon and my turn-and-bank indicator were out of commission. No matter what awaited me out in the day, I had to leave that inferno—fast!

But which way? Angling off to the left was a sick smear of yellow. I clutched my controls and nosed toward it—a moth to light. It was increasing a little when the belly of my plane seemed to drop from under me—a downdraft. In an instant I had slipped a hundred feet, my prop clawing helplessly. It was like a blow in the stomach. The motor rattled as if at any minute it would tear loose.

Then the pressure lifted, and I was blasted upward, shaken and rolled. I emerged from that one, groggy, my head spinning. No rational means of piloting my Hayabusa now. Cut my rudder to the left, and I could just as easily be hurled off to the right. Cut my elevator upward, and I might be slammed toward the sea.

With instruments dying, the motor steadily growing more asthmatic, I was desperately tired. Only moments before, I'd grinned in the storm's face, but now my hands and arms were growing numb. I'd been flying too long. I was too tense. Even the inside of my plane revolved dizzily now, and my vision was so blurred that it would be hard to tell whether the rain ever let up or not.

All sense of time was gone. Once when the winds abated, I found myself drifting aimlessly, blinking at the blue flashes, hearing the reverberations. Like an automaton, I was flying with only one purpose—to keep going, on and on, until the great light would shine again.

Then the winds came raving back to assault me. The flashes lit a vast cloud face, its mouth breaking into a leer. My ship began to shudder and drop as though bouncing down a flight of invisible stairs. No longer were the elements impersonal. The lightning was not crackling; it was laughing. The thunder shouted, hammering with its fists. The wind, most of all, hated me—cursing, buffeting, wrenching. Was even nature with the enemy?

Suddenly a volcanic eruption of air and cloud caught beneath my wing, hurling me end over end. With no more control than a dried leaf I went spinning down a cone of blackness. Yes, this—death and oblivion!

But even in death I remembered . . . . Somewhere down the sky's long hallway, something willed the battered, shuddering metal back, exerted effort against strange controls.

I was flying level, the leaden waves curling at my belly, scudding with froth. As from a distance, sounds of the motor rose and fell, and my ship seemed to jump along. It seemed I was back with my first glider, being towed across the turf at Onomichi High School.

Even lower I settled. Low, so low! Just a dipping of one wing, just a few degrees, and the ocean would have me once and for all. Why fight it? It always got what it wanted. Only a matter of moments, a matter of degrees. . . . But there was still a perverse spark within me. No, I wasn't afraid. I would taunt the ocean, dipping my wings never quite far enough—tantalizing the waves. They knew how to hypnotize, so well, and they would take me soon. But not until I had laughed—as the lightning had laughed at me.

Suddenly the water flashed green. An instant later it had turned white-hot, blinding me, I kept blinking, till the pain eased. I was in a world of burnished gold.

Nothing now but water and sky. I climbed to a thousand feet, and droned ahead, soaking up light. It took a while for the awareness to come. I was alone—the only man in this strange, beautiful world—lost amid the lonely reaches of sun and sea.

The motor sputtered, and I glanced at my fuel gauge: only twenty-five gallons—little time left. Apprehensively, fearing the American ears that would now be listening beyond the horizon, I began to signal. No answer. I waited and tried again. Still, no reply. My fighter kept winging ahead, staunch once more—wonderful creature! But now, after everything else to run out of fuel—to expire slowly, like a strong man with his wrists cut. It seemed hopeless—but there was the faintest . . . I cut the air control valve to its thinnest mixture, cut the propeller cycles down—below 1800 rpm's. Much less, and I'd be in for a stall.

I signaled again, caught my breath and waited. An answer! China! "This is Nanking. . . ." The message was coming! I had made connections.

A few degrees left, and straight ahead was Formosa. In less than twenty minutes I would be there. Soon. . . . Yes, I could see it, seeming to rise and fall like a great ship. The motor purred, steady, true.

Once I looked back. I had a feeling that I shouldn't, but I looked back. Somewhere off in the golden afternoon was Okinawa. Somewhere lurked the enemy task force—only twenty-three ships now, instead of twenty-five. Somewhere, drifting in the sea, were the remains of Tatsuno, and the others. No pain anymore—not for Tatsuno.

And there—hanging slumbrous now, far behind—was the storm. "The divine storm" had saved me, as it had saved my people centuries before.

PART FIVE

FIRST JET WAR—KOREA

The MiG Killers

FIRST JET ACE

by Captain James Jabara, USAF

I had begun to think I never was going to get that fifth MiG. I got my fourth on April 22 but the pickings had been pretty lean since that time. Then, about five o'clock in the afternoon of May 20, 14 of our F-86 Sabres from the 4th Fighter Interceptor Group were jumped by 50 Commie jets over Sinuiju, near the Yalu River.

I was in the second wave of 14. I tacked on to the three MiGs at 35,000 feet, picked out the last one and bored straight in. My first two bursts ripped up his fuselage and left wing. At about 10,000 feet the pilot bailed out. It was a good thing he did because the MiG disintegrated.

Then I climbed back to 20,000 feet to get back into the battle. I bounced six more MiGs. I closed in and got off two bursts into one of them, scoring heavily both times. He began to smoke.

Then when my second burst caught him square in the middle he burst into flames and fell into an uncontrolled spin. All I could see was a whirl of fire. I had to break off then because there was another MiG on my tail.

That was my bag for the day and it made me feel pretty good to know that I was the first jet ace in the history of aerial warfare.

We fight a private little war up in MiG Alley—maybe the first time in history that two fighter outfits have engaged in such a peculiar type of warfare. On our side of the Yalu River is the 4th Fighter Interceptor Wing. On the other side are the Red MiG-15s.

The capabilities and general characteristics of the two airplanes are just about the same. The battle tactics of the enemy are quite similar to our own. And he holds many advantages which I'll discuss later in some detail.

Here's where the puzzle comes in. We've knocked down or damaged several score of MiGs—exactly how many I honestly don't know. We've lost exactly one of our planes to enemy action and one from causes unknown.

James Jabara, champion of "MiG Alley." A veteran of World War II, Jabara became the first jet ace when he downed five Communist MiG-15s in Korea. His total for the conflict was fifteen. (USAF)

We're not magicians. We're just average fighter pilots with some previous combat time, sound tactical training and a little patience to wait for the other guy to make a mistake. But the score is lopsided and I guess the enemy is wondering why.

I'm not going to tell him, except in general terms, for this test between the best jet planes in the world is only in its first phase. The end isn't in sight yet, and the score could change. But I don't believe it will.

We're in Korea for one main reason—I'm speaking of the F-86 Sabre jets. That's to shoot down as many MiGs as we can, to help retain air superiority for our side and protect our battling ground troops from enemy air attacks.

But there are a few ground rules in this private war of ours. We have to go up to their ball park—MiG Alley, in far northwestern Korea, near the Yalu River that splits North Korea and Manchuria—or the enemy won't play. That means a one-way trip of 250 miles or more, depending on where we're based. That's a lot of distance, measured in jet fuel. And any fan can tell you the home team has a big advantage.

While we're burning up a third of our fuel on the trip to MiG Alley, we have to save the amount to get home again. That leaves us a third to stay in the area, hunt for the enemy, and fight him. And dogfights really eat up fuel, whether you're diving, climbing, or just maneuvering at high speed.

And we have all the normal worries: "flame-outs" (engine failures), weather, and surprise by an enemy who knows when we're on our way through his early-warning radar or GCI (Ground-Controlled Intercept).

He has all these advantages, plus the fact that he almost never fights more than 50 miles from his base. He is near friendly territory in case he gets shot down or bails out, and he can cruise at high speeds at all times, with no extra fuel tanks to slow him down.

But the biggest ground rule of all is his sanctuary in Manchuria, across the Yalu River, where he can run any time the fight gets too hot for comfort. The traffic light changes to red the minute he darts across the river, and it never changes to green no matter how long we wait.

Our Sabre is a shade faster, but not enough to make a big difference. Sometimes I've wished it had a little more speed. We can outdive the MiG at any altitude. The radius of turn is about the same, but we seem to execute it with more finesse.

The MiG has a slight superiority in rate of climb, and heavier firepower, with its three cannon. Fortunately they don't seem to be able to hit us with it. Note please that I say *heavy* firepower—not *rate* of fire.

In general characteristics, the planes are similar and both damn good. It's hard to tell one from the other in our 600-mph plus dogfights, and we have to use R/T (radio telephone) and code words to maintain air discipline.

The Sabre is slightly larger and heavier, and carries six .50-caliber forward-firing machine guns with a total of 1800 rounds of ammo. The MiG carries one 36-mm. cannon, and two of either 20- or 23-mm. When the caliber of a gun increases, the rate of fire usually decreases. Maybe that's one reason the MiGs haven't been able to hit us. But the puffs of smoke from their guns scare hell out of me.

The MiG is rugged, make no mistake. It can soak up a lot of battle damage. I still don't know why some of the planes I damaged didn't go down. I could see the armor-piercing phosphorus-loaded incendiary bullets sparkle on impact as they hit the wings and fuselages. I guess it's almost as rugged as our Sabre, and next to the Sabre I would rather fly the MiG than any other fighter.

I can't get too technical about tactics, for the game is still going on and the team that gives away its signals usually doesn't win. But I can discuss a few general points, especially what we've learned from their tactics.

Early in the air war—we were fighting the MiGs back in December—they would split up into elements of single planes, unprotected

The F-86 Sabrejet was the victor in the world's first jet war: Korea. Evenly matched against the Soviet MiG-15 at the war's beginning, improvements on the Sabrejet later gave it the edge. (USAF)

and generally at our mercy. Maybe they had no planned tactics, for they were certainly easy pickings.

Now they generally stick closer together, and we have to bounce twos instead of singles—unless they get panicky and forget the direction of their Manchurian sanctuary. If desperate they loop, roll, and split S.

When we're fighting on the deck, they frequently try to lure us across the North Korean flak areas hoping their ground gunners will pick us off like geese on the wing. That's an old Luftwaffe trick I learned to avoid while flying two tours in F-51s in Europe with the Eighth and Ninth Air Forces.

At times we see the MiGs pulling vapor trails. Then they duck below the contrail level and we can't see them. They hope we think they've left the area. Actually they're waiting to bounce us. We haven't fallen for that trick so far and I can tell them now we don't intend to.

The escort work we've done for FEAF Bomber Command B-29s has presented tough problems in tactics, as on April 12, when there were more than 225 planes, friendly and enemy, in the air at one time. The Superforts were leveling their demolition bombs on the important rail bridge at Sinuiju on the North Korean side to slow down Red resupply.

That day the MiGs showed that they are more aggressive against B-29 formations than against fighters. We were at a disadvantage because of slowing down for proper escort. By the time we drop our external tanks and get up speed, a MiG can be roaring through the bomber formation with his cannons blazing.

We counter this by keeping four plane elements together and take our chances on superior gunnery. The MiGs feint, hoping we'll follow and leave the bombers unprotected. We stick. And shoot. In that April 12 battle our F-86s, plus escorting F-84s and the B-29 gunners, got eight MiGs for sure, probably destroyed seven and damaged 18. We lost some Superforts but no fighters.

We had good air discipline in that fight and flew a good solid formation. The wing men protected the element leaders who did the firing. The enemy made mistakes and we capitalized on them. We only had seconds to

The Republic F-84 Thunderjet, together with the F-80 and F-86, comprised the USAF jet team over Korea. (USAF)

do this, so we moved fast. But the tactics when we're escorting B-29s aren't exactly typical.

Consider a fighter vs. fighter mission. We take off in four-plane formations and enter the target area, maybe 30 minutes later. We patrol MiG Alley, the Yalu River area. The enemy spots our calling card on his GCI and can bounce us first. He initiates the bounce about 70 percent of the time and our tactics naturally evolve around this fact. We try to spot the MiG and anticipate his actions. Fortunately our group commander, Col. John C. Meyer, and my squadron commander, Lt. Col. Glen T. Eagleston, are a couple of the shrewdest fighter-pilot tacticians in the world.

They figure out our tactics for us and we stay alive by following orders.

We drop our extra fuel tanks as we sight the MiGs so we can gain speeds almost up to Mach one. Then we maneuver to get into firing position. After all a fighter is simply an airborne gun platform. The pilot must turn, dive, and climb to get into position to fire. At the same time he was to watch for other planes, both his own and the enemy's.

The fight usually starts at 35,000 to 40,000 feet. It can wind up 50 feet above the ground. If the MiGs strike first, and we're not in firing position, we break hard to the left or the right, and down, so we can maneuver for a better position. A wing man covers each element leader.

The wing man doesn't fire unless he has specific instructions, or gets separated. It's a tough assignment and as far as I'm concerned half my victories should go to good wing men like Lieutenants Gill Garrett, Roy McLain, Bill Yancey (who also has done some fine shooting himself while flying element leader), and Dick Becker.

When I'm concentrating on my sights, trying to handle the Sabre smoothly, and following the enemy's gyrations, I don't have time to look around and protect myself. The wing man acts as an extra set of eyes for me. He watches for MiGs and friendly planes, and gives me radio warnings or signals. To me he's worth his weight in .50-caliber ammo.

If we're outnumbered, or the fighting gets

too rough, then we maneuver around and wait for the enemy to make a mistake. Thank God he makes more than his share of them.

Like the one he made in the big scrap on April 12. I was at 25,000 feet and he was 5000 feet beneath me, heading for the B-29s. That advantage in altitude was my break and I used it to get speed. I caught him just as he was in range of the B-29s. The bullets saddle-stitched his fuselage, but he went into loops and rolls. He was badly crippled. Another burst got his engine and I saw him crash trying to leg it across the Yalu.

The numerical odds were against us on April 22, when our 12 Sabres were outnumbered three to one. With Capt. Norbert W. Chalwick flying protection for me, I took my time about getting behind a couple MiGs and hit them both with short bursts. I had to pop my dive brakes to keep from running into one. I was still firing as he rolled on his back. I followed him down but I didn't realize how close to the ground I was until he crashed. I had a hell of a time pulling out of my dive. The cockpit dial showed nine *g*s before I blacked out. Fortunately my eyes focused in

about three seconds and by instinct, I guess, I was headed upward.

That was my fourth kill. The first one was on April 3, when Becker was flying wing man. We were two against two. We saw the MiGs first at 7000 feet and I used 1200 rounds, damaging the engine of one MiG that flamed out and crashed about ten miles from its home field. I damaged the other.

On April 10 we were MiG hunting again in the Alley. We let down from 36,000 feet through the undercast and broke out in the clear at 10,000. We saw six of them at 5000 and bounced them from the seven o'clock position. Four of the MiGs broke up into the overcast and two broke down toward the ground. They just shouldn't have done it. I took after them. The leader scampered away, leaving his wing man wide open. After three Lufberys (360-degree turns) I scored hits on the wing man. I used up my 1800 rounds of ammo but stayed with the MiG for about 30 seconds, meanwhile radioing my wing man, Lt. Otis Gordon, to start shooting.

This proved unnecessary, as the enemy pilot suddenly bailed out about 30 miles south

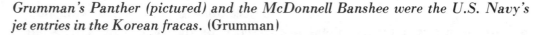

Grumman's Panther (pictured) and the McDonnell Banshee were the U.S. Navy's jet entries in the Korean fracas. (Grumman)

of Sinuiju. I was flying almost at the speed of sound and couldn't see much, but he had a light blue parachute, black helmet, and light grey oxygen mask.

All of us would like to know who's actually flying the MiGs. It's good bull-session material, especially after a mission. The consensus is that the enemy has two teams. The first team, a lot of people think, is made up of highly-trained Communists and ex-Luftwaffe pilots. The second stringers are Chinese and possibly North Koreans. To me they're all tough. The best ones are aggressive, they can maneuver the MiG, and they usually know what to do in case of trouble.

I learned some lessons early in the game in MiG Alley. I flew seven missions between December 23 and January 2 and didn't get a crack at the enemy until the fifth one, when I bagged a probable kill. I was flying Lt. Comdr. Paul E. Pugh's wing (he's a Navy pilot flying with us on the interservice exchange program, and has two victories over the MiGs). He took out after the leader of a flight of four. An enemy plane got on Pugh's tail and I radioed him to break as he was being attacked from six o'clock. I didn't know it until later, but his radio receiver wasn't working.

The fight had gone down from 35,000 to 1500 feet. There was nothing to do but try to get the MiG off Pugh's tail. I started shooting from 1500 and had plenty of strikes on the wings and tail section by the time we reached 800, with the enemy making no evasive maneuvers. Suddenly he did a split S. Two MiGs were after me from the stern position and I couldn't watch the crippled plane any longer. I almost laid myself wide open, and never made the same mistake again.

What does all this add up to? To me, we've come a long way and done a lot of good in the Korean air war since being alerted back to New Castle, Delaware, last November. We've done our bit to keep enemy air off the backs of our ground troops.

I'm glad to be in combat again. I like to fly jets at high speeds, although it takes something out of a guy—even at 27.

I don't get nervous anymore. I outgrew that in the last war. But the strain is greater now because of the high speeds, split-second timing and the fact that the Sabres and MiGs look alike. To me fighting for 30 minutes in the F-86 is equivalent to ten times that in an F-51.

We have good equipment, superior leadership and training, and I know our pilots are better than theirs, whomever they may be. As Colonel Meyer says, the nucleus of our wing is composed of the champions of the greatest air battles of history—between the US and Germans in World War II. There are at least 11 aces among us and our wing had the highest score in the last war, 1016½ enemy planes destroyed.

Colonel Meyer says we're the champs of that war, and I guess that applies to this one, too. At least the score thus far would indicate as much.

SABREJET LEADER

by Colonel Harrison R. Thyng, USAF

Like olden knights the F-86 pilots ride up over North Korea to the Yalu River, the sun glinting off silver aircraft, contrails streaming behind, as they challenge the numerically superior enemy to come on up and fight. With eyes scanning the horizon to prevent any surprise, they watch avidly while MiG pilots leisurely mount into their cockpits, taxi out onto their runways for a formation take-off.

"Thirty-six lining up at Antung," Black Leader calls.

"Hell, only twenty-four taking off over here at Tatungkou," complains Blue Leader.

"Well, it will be at least three for everybody. I count fifty at Takushan," calls White Leader.

"I see dust at Fen Cheng, so they are gathering up there," yells Yellow Leader.

Once again the Commie leaders have taken up our challenge, and now we may expect the usual numerical odds as the MiGs gain altitude and form up preparatory to crossing the Yalu.

Breaking up into small flights, we stagger our altitude. We have checked our guns and sights by firing a few warm-up rounds as we crossed the bomb line. Oxygen masks are checked and pulled as tight as possible over our faces. We know we may exceed eight *g*s in the coming fight, and that is painful with a loose mask. We are cruising at a very high Mach. Every eye is strained to catch the first movement of an enemy attempt to cross the Yalu from their Manchurian sanctuary into that graveyard of several hundred MiGs known as "MiG Alley." Several minutes pass. We know the MiG pilots will become bolder as our fuel time limit over the Alley grows shorter.

Now we see flashes in the distance as the sun reflects off the beautiful MiG aircraft. The radio crackles, "Many, many coming across at Suiho above forty-five thousand feet." Our flights start converging toward that area, low flights climbing, yet keeping a very high Mach. Contrails are now showing over the Antung area, so another enemy section is preparing to cross at Sinuiju, a favorite spot.

We know the enemy sections are now being vectored by GCI, and the advantage is theirs. Traveling at terrifically high speed and altitude, attackers can readily achieve surprise. The area bound by the horizon at this altitude is so vast that it is practically impossible to keep it fully covered with the human eye.

Our flights are well spread out, ships line abreast, and each pilot keeps his head swiveling 360 degrees. Suddenly MiGs appear directly in front of us at our level. At rates of closure of possibly 1200 miles an hour we pass through each other's formations.

Accurate radar range firing is difficult under these conditions, but you fire a burst at the nearest enemy anyway. Immediately the MiGs zoom for altitude, and you break at maximum *g* around towards them. Unless the MiG wants to fight and also turned as he climbed, he will be lost from sight in the distance before the turn is completed. But if he shows an inclination to scrap, you immediately trade head-on passes again. You "sucker" the MiG into a position where the outstanding advantage of your aircraft will give you the chance to outmaneuver him.

For you combat has become an individual dogfight. Flight integrity has been lost, but your wing man is still with you, widely separated but close enough for you to know that you are covered. Suddenly you go into a steep turn. Your Mach drops off. The MiG turns with you, and you let him gradually creep up and out-turn you. At the critical moment you reverse your turn. The hydraulic controls work beautifully. The MiG cannot turn as readily as you and is slung out to the side. When you pop your speed brakes, the MiG flashes by you. Quickly closing the brakes, you slide onto his tail and hammer him with your "50s." Pieces fly off the MiG, but he won't burn or explode at that high altitude. He twists and turns and attempts to dive away, but you will not be denied. Your 50s have hit him in the engine and slowed him up enough so that he cannot get away from you. His canopy suddenly blows and the pilot catapults out, barely missing your airlane. Now your wing man is whooping it up over the radio, and you flash for home very low on fuel. At this point your engine is running very rough. Parts of the ripped MiG have been sucked into your engine scoop, and the possibility of its flaming out is very likely. Desperately climbing for altitude you finally reach forty thousand feet. With home base

Commander of the 4th Fighter Interceptor Wing in Korea, Col. Harrison Thyng was a veteran of both WW II theaters and became a two-war ace. His Sabrejet wing ruled "MiG Alley." (USAF)

now but eighty miles away, you can lean back and sigh with relief for you know you can glide your ship back and land, gear down, even if your engine quits right, now. You hear over the radio, "Flights reforming and returning—the last MiGs chased back across the Yalu." Everyone is checking in, and a few scores are being discussed. The good news of no losses, the tension which gripped you before the battle, the wild fight, and the *g* forces are now being felt. A tired yet elated feeling is overcoming you, although the day's work is not finished. Your engine finally flames out, but you have maintained forty

thousand feet and are now but twenty miles from home. The usual radio calls are given, and the pattern set up for a dead-stick landing. The tower calmly tells you that you are number three dead-stick over the field, but everything is ready for your entry. Planes in front of you continue to land in routine and uninterrupted precision, as everyone is low on fuel. Fortunately this time there are no battle damages to be crash landed. Your altitude is decreasing, and gear is lowered. Hydraulic controls are still working beautifully on the pressure maintained by your windmilling engine. You pick your place in the pattern, land, coast to a stop, and within seconds are tugged up the taxi strip to your revetment for a quick engine change.

This mission is the type most enjoyed by the fighter pilot. It is a regular fighter sweep, with no worries about escort or providing cover for fighter-bombers. The mission had been well planned and well executed. Best of all, the MiGs had come forth for battle. Our separate flights had probably again confused the enemy radarscope readers, and, to an extent, nullified that tremendous initial advantage which radar plotting and vectoring gives a fighter on first sighting the enemy. We had put the maximum number of aircraft into the target area at the most opportune time, and we had sufficient fuel to fool the enemy. Our patrolling flights at strategic locations had intercepted split-off MiGs returning toward their sanctuary in at least two instances. One downed MiG had crashed in the middle of Sinuiju, and another, after being shot up, had outrun our boys to the Yalu, where they had to break off pursuit. But they had the satisfaction of seeing the smoking MiG blow up in his own traffic pattern. Both instances undoubtedly did not aid the morale of the Reds.

The Other Side of the Parallel

RED FLIER

**by Senior Lieutenant Kum Sok No,
North Korean Air Force**

My assignment to go into combat on the Korean side of the Yalu came as a surprise. Until then, all our air bases had been confined to Manchuria because of the constant B-29 raids on North Korea.

In November, 1951, Uiju, where I reported after finishing MiG training, was the only operational communist airfield in North Korea. The others were abandoned, bombed-out concrete strips. Kim Il Sung and Air Force Gen. Young Wang were banking on the propaganda value of the first North Korean jet division "defending" our country from Korean soil. Before that, the Russian and Chinese MiG pilots based in Manchuria had been the only jets fighting the UN.

But the experiment was doomed from the start. One morning soon after I arrived, I saw eight MiGs on the apron, pilots ready in the cockpit. General Wang and our Russian adviser were talking in front of headquarters. Suddenly, seemingly from nowhere, I saw two American Sabres—more than 200 miles from their home base—swoop low over the field. I hit the ground just as a trail of .50-caliber bullets started tearing up the dirt. From the corner of my eye, I could see General Wang and the Russian do the same.

But the pilots were trapped in their MiGs. When the Sabres left, we counted our casualties: Senior Lt. Yontae Chong killed in his cockpit, one MiG destroyed in flames, and two pilots wounded.

On November 15, 1951, I faced the Americans in the air for the first time. I took off early from Uiju in a formation of eight MiGs headed south. I had no desire to fight the

Top ace of the Korean action was Captain Joe McConnell, Jr.; with sixteen kills. (USAF)

211

Americans, but I had no choice. The squadron commander kept up a spirited series of orders and words of encouragement over the intercom, but I scarcely heard what he said. I kept remembering the words of our political officer: "The cowardly Americans will flee and desert their comrades to certain death." With my survival at stake, I guess I hoped the Reds were telling the truth for once.

My old-style MiG-15A, was, I believe, a better fighting instrument than the F-80 or F-84, but no better than the old Sabre which most UN pilots were flying. Fortunately, the ferocious new Sabre, the F-86F, had not yet appeared in Korea.

We met the Americans near Pyongyang. They, too, were flying a close formation, feeling us out. Suddenly they broke for the attack and quickly split our inexperienced group. The fighting was over almost before it began, and we turned and raced northward for Uiju.

There were no casualties, but the battle taught me another lesson about Red propaganda. The Americans were not cowards. The Sabres attacked with more courage than my fellow MiG pilots, and they understood cooperation. When one of our MiGs got on the tail of a Sabre, three of the Americans risked their lives to shake him off. In all the time I flew for North Korea, I never once saw a Red pilot try to save another's life.

The fighter scrambles at Uiju were inconclusive. During the next six weeks we lost three of our 30 MiGs and shot down one South Korean propeller P-51 and an American F-80 jet.

The American bombing of Uiju took a greater toll. I slept with my clothes on every night; at least half a dozen times after dark B-29s droned overhead and plastered our field. Whenever I heard the alert, I raced for the mountains a mile away. My MiG wasn't equipped for night fighting; the Russians had refused to give us or the Chinese their radar-equipped night fighters. They didn't even want us to see them. A suspicious Russian mechanic once shooed me away from a parked radar MiG. Occasionally, the Russians sent night fighters from Manchuria to meet the B-29s over Uiju, but they usually failed to make contact in the darkness.

The Russians kept a monopoly on their radar fighters. I can safely say that every B-29 shot down in night raids during the Korean war was the handiwork of Russian pilots.

After six weeks we had reached the limit of our endurance. Our runway, gutted with twenty-foot bomb craters, kept our MiGs virtually grounded. On December 15, 1951, the decision was made to abandon Uiju. Immediately 5000 civilians, including women and children, were put to work repairing the runway with basketfuls of stones and earth. When it was done, I and the other MiG pilots happily took off across the Yalu for the sanctuary of Antung, Manchuria, not to return until after the truce.

Almost immediately the complexion of the air was changed. Antung, headquarters for 210 MiGs of three communist air divisions—one Russian (Kozhedub had gone there from Anshan), one Chinese, and our North Korean—became the focus of that war.

In January, 1952, the United States Air Force switched to a new Sabre. Until then the jet fighting had been almost a draw. The new Sabre was at least a ton heavier than the MiG and had a faster rate of descent. It could break the sound barrier in a dive. Our latest MiG-15B could not exceed Mach .98—that is, 98 per cent of the speed of sound at a given altitude—in a dive and Mach .95 in level flight. One Russian pilot once tried to push his MiG through the sonic barrier, but his wings collapsed and he crashed to his death.

The new Sabre, although heavier and better armored, was more maneuverable than our MiG. We were so hopelessly outclassed by the new Sabre and the better-trained American pilots that it became virtual suicide even for the new MiG-15B to take one on single-handed. We were told to maintain large, tight formations, never to get below a Sabre in a fight, and to attack only in much greater strength.

The Russian pilots were jaunty at first. At

The Soviet-made MiG-15 was flown by the North Korean, Soviet and Communist Chinese Air forces against the UN services. It was designed by the noted Russian engineering team of Mikoyan and Gurevich. (USAF)

mess, which we shared with them, one of them boasted to me, "The Americans are all right, but we are better. No one can outfly our new MiG."

Kozhedub's division had received a host of commendations from Stalin himself for shooting down propeller P-51s, B-29s on daylight raids, F-80 Shooting Star jets and British-built MK8 jets. With only a few months left to their Korean combat tour, they were impatiently waiting to return to Moscow in honor.

Then the new Sabres appeared over the Yalu. Every clear flying day from January, 1952, until the truce in July, 1953, the alert sounded in my barracks at four a.m. By five o'clock the regimental bus would have brought us to Antung field.

At the second alert we'd run to our planes and wait for the signal to take off. Approximately thirty Sabres, forming a loose circle composed of little clusters of two and four planes, would come and we'd send up 100 or more MiGs to meet them. On the average we lost four to five MiGs a day, many of them piloted by Russians. Some days we lost as many as ten planes. I saw one disabled MiG after another splash into the Yalu or crash-land on the runway, engulfed in flames. Sabre losses, on the other hand, were very light.

I had my first close brush with the Sabre on the morning of January 25, 1952. Sixteen of us took off early and crossed the Yalu into North Korea, flying at 8000 meters. Ahead of me I saw the inevitable groups of two and four Sabres coming toward Antung. In my earphones I heard orders to climb above the Sabres and wait to attack. The MiG's only advantage is that it can climb higher and faster than the Sabre.

I started to climb with the formation when suddenly I heard the staccato of machine-gun bullets. We had wandered into the middle of the scattered Sabre groups by mistake and overlooked two Americans in a deadly position, above and behind us. The Sabres—two against sixteen—made their pass in a near-sonic dive, guns blazing, then dived out of range.

The fight was over in an instant. I nervously assessed the damage. My plane seemed all right, but I could see three flaming MiGs hurtling toward the ground. Only one parachute opened. The formation was badly scattered, so I turned and raced thankfully the forty miles toward home.

The total Red air strength was a little over 900 MiGs: 400 Russians, 400 Chinese, and our two North Korean divisions of 125 MiGs. There were divisions stationed at Antung, Anshan, Tat'ungho, Ta Hua Shan, Taepo, North Mukden, West Mukden, East Mukden, Liaoyuan, Kwantien, Tientsin, and Chingtao. In addition, the North Korean Air Force had 100 operational propeller planes in

Manchuria and forty IL-28 jet bombers training at Kungchuling that never saw combat.

Before the war was finally over the Reds had lost more than 800 MiGs and pilots—400 Russians, 300 Chinese, and 100 North Korean—almost a 100 per cent turnover. My division of seventy MiGs lost thirty, none of which were replaced. I personally survived sixty missions unscathed, and without any Sabres to my credit.

By May, 1952, when Kozhedub's pilots were ready to go home, their cockiness was gone. My old instructor, Captain Nichenko, had been killed by a Sabre. The few months of warfare with the new Sabre had cut their ranks in half.

The night before they left, I heard them singing Russian folk songs and carousing drunkenly in their barracks. The next morning one of them told me it had been no victory celebration, but one of thanksgiving by those who had come through alive.

Their replacements were not so fortunate.

Two new Russian divisions, one to replace Kozhedub's and another to go to Tat'ungho, arrived from Europe heady with home-front propaganda tales of Red air victories. But within two months both Soviet divisions were almost entirely wiped out by the new Sabre jets. The Russian commander of the replacement division at Antung was sent back to Moscow in disgrace.

Their propaganda still boasted about the MiG's superiority, but we pilots knew the truth. After dinner, the 100 grams of wine we drank to make sleep easier loosened the stubbornest Red tongues. "I had 100 Sabres after me today," one worried Russian pilot exaggerated. Another, a World War II ace, confessed that he was mortally afraid of the Americans, who really were "air murderers," as the party claimed.

But our political officers would admit only that "the American mercenaries have more flying hours." (I had gone into combat with only fifty jet hours.) They rationalized their

Piloted by Lt. Russell J. Brown, an F-80 Shooting Star was the victor in the first all-jet dogfight, downing a MiG-15 on November 8, 1950. (USAF)

defeats: "We are not fighting for money and women, but for our country, communism, and our people."

Our air defeats were demoralizing in themselves. In addition, we were subjected to political harrassment at our own bases. A pilot in my outfit, Lt. Yun Chul Sin, was discharged in disgrace when the security officer learned that his brother had fled to South Korea. Other pilots were executed for little more. Col. Tal Hion Kim, the popular commander of the 11th Division, which consisted of propeller-driven YAK-9s and IL-10s, stationed at Feng Cheng, Manchuria, was accused of defecting to the West. He was executed without a trial.

I had ignored politics in my first year in the air force, but during MiG training in 1951, I realized that the most suspicious thing about my career to date was not joining the Communist Party. I was afraid my aloofness would invite a fatal investigation of my background.

I conceived an entirely new plan of survival. I joined the Communist Party and assumed the role of a supercommunist. I had observed that the most fanatic Reds, those who shouted the slogans loudest, were the most trusted men.

I surrounded myself with good communists. Fortunately, my only living relative was a Red—Air Force Maj. Ki Un Riu. I told my superiors that my mother had been killed in a raid, but actually I had lost track of her. Riu had joined the party in 1946 and he believed I had been converted to communism. My battalion security officer, Captain Ho, was from my home town, and outwardly we, too, became friends.

For the next two years I played the communist zealot. I got top grades in Marx-Leninism and became an active Youth Organization committeeman. I spoke up against American "imperialism." My political officers were impressed. I was even called upon publicly to read statements from Kim Il Sung and Stalin.

I worried day and night for two years that my insincerity would be discovered, but no one ever suspected me. In fact, I was rewarded for my work. In July, 1952, I was made vice-chairman of my battalion Communist Party and, in August, promoted to *Sanwi*—senior lieutenant—and named squadron leader of four MiGs.

Soon after I became active in the party I discovered "public denunciation." This is a clever variation of the Russian practice of "self-criticism," which Stalin once called "our greatest weapon." Of the 100 men in my battalion, sixty belonged to the Red cell. At least ten times during every meeting someone would get up and emotionally denounce a fellow member for some "shortcoming"— anything from sloppy flying to deviationist ideas. It was bad communist taste to defend oneself. Charges were to be accepted as the truth, and an attempt was made to reform. Serious charges were passed on to the all-powerful security officer.

A dreadful pall of fear hung over our field. We all carefully weighed every spoken word. No one had any real friends. People kept to themselves. Each man, in a sense, became my enemy. I learned to strike first, to search out other people's shortcomings and to cover my own faults. As vice-chairman I was expected to make frequent denunciations, and I played the role to the hilt, even though it turned my stomach. I tried to limit my attacks to top communists. One day an especially important Red, Maj. Chun Tuk Lee, lost our field in bad weather and crashed his MiG while landing at Chin Chou, a Chinese air base. The next week I dramatically faced a major at our party meeting.

"Comrade Lee outwardly appears to be a good communist," I began my denunciation, "but this farce shows him as a lazy man who does not care about his expensive equipment. Perhaps he does not hate the enemy enough or doesn't love our glorious leader, Kim Il Sung."

He listened with his head down, staring at the floor. After that night, Major Lee was openly hated by everyone and his value as a communist diminished. My stock, however, went up considerably.

Not even rank stood in the way of a skillful denouncer. I once denounced our chief of staff, Col. Kil Yon Chae, because he had a warm stove in his room while the men froze, and because he didn't keep our parachutes in a specially heated room. I myself was denounced twice, once by a mechanic, who called me a "harsh officer."

I led a Spartan existence in the North Korean Air Force. I worked seven days a week, from four a.m. until bedtime. When the Russians weren't flying they courted Chinese girls or had vodka parties in the barracks. In contrast, we North Koreans were compelled to attend an endless series of Youth Assembly, Communist Party and propaganda meetings. As vice chairman, I was busier than most. I represented my battalion at divisional party meetings and supervised the work of pilot "spies" who checked on other men.

I earned 260,000 Chinese yuan, or $8.50, a month. Food was my only luxury. We shared the Russian officers' mess, where I ate anything I wanted—chicken, caviar, beef, pork, ice cream, cognac. But I never had a furlough, an overnight pass, or even a full day off. Every few months I got into Antung on a Sunday, but we were forbidden to dance or drink liquor in public. Marriage was prohibited during wartime and a single man could not even correspond with a girl. As Lt. Kuk Yul Oh, a trusted Red who had studied in Moscow, once whispered to me, we overdid our communism.

For two years I slept uneasily every night, my rest disturbed by horrible nightmares. Playing the communist so long had badly frayed my nerves. Before going to bed I often thought about my mother, whom I had given up for dead. I worried about all the people I had denounced, and whether I had done the right thing.

I was sick and tired of the Red deceit. I decided to escape to South Korea in my MiG. Kim Il Sung had warned that the family of any defector would be punished, but I had no one to worry about except my Red uncle.

Escaping by air to South Korea would not be easy. An IL-10 propeller-plane pilot had made it in 1950, before the war, but my base was a good 200 miles from the American lines. There was a good chance I'd be shot down by a hunting Sabre or even a MiG before I crossed the 38th parallel. If I reached South Korea I'd still have to worry about more Sabres and American AA batteries. Would the Americans believe I was anticommunist if I was shot down? Perhaps I would be put in PW camp. The communists had told us that the Americans used prisoners as human guinea pigs in their Pacific A-bomb tests.

I decided on a less risky alternate plan. At night I pored over my flight maps, and memorized a course from Pyongyang, North Korea, to Kimpo airfield outside Seoul, the main American fighter base. I decided, however, to wait until I was stationed in North Korea closer to the 38th parallel. I calculated the distance, the time, and fuel required, and the course heading, and filed this information in the back of my mind.

Meanwhile, the communist air situation was getting desperate. The top Chinese MiG outfit, the 3rd Division, had only twenty-five planes and pilots left out of an original seventy. They couldn't train pilots fast enough to replace those shot down. The Russian replacement divisions had also been cut to pieces.

Our frightened Red commanders resorted to desperate schemes. In June, 1952, my battalion—ten planes—was suddenly yanked out of the front and sent back to Anshan for a secret training mission. The day we arrived, my division CO, Gen. Tae Yong Kang, called us together to explain.

"Much of the American Sabre strength is at Kimpo," he said. "We are here to train to destroy the Sabres before they get into the air."

We were to do by strafing what we couldn't do in the air. During the next two months we prepared for this mission. From my study of maps and models I got to know Kimpo as well as any Sabre pilot. Red fliers normally crossed into South Korea only at night when our flimsy, single-engine, wood-and-canvas PO-2 "bombers," stationed at Sariwon, flew over South Korea and dropped grenades and small fire bombs by hand on oil dumps and other targets. According to our plans, the Americans would be completely unprepared for a daylight raid.

But at the last moment, the mission to Kimpo was canceled. Our officers decided we'd end up losing our ten MiGs. Instead we were sent on four strafing missions to eastern South Korea, where we faced the weaker propeller-driven planes of the South Korean Air Force.

The situation became so bad in early 1953 that the Reds tried to save face with fictitious claims of success. Every day, as the Sabres destroyed more and more MiGs, General Wang would joyously announce that five or six Sabres had been downed. Commanders were told to pad their weekly reports. I had never heard such lying in my life. One officer, Col. Kuk Song Tae, vice commander of the 2nd Division, took credit for shooting down two Sabres, for which he got the Hero's Medal. But I had flown with him that day and I knew his claims were a lie.

Then the last spring before the truce, the Reds announced a desperate *kamikaze* suicide plan. The American Navy had been shelling the east-coast Wonsan area very heavily, and our generals feared an American invasion.

"Now that General Eisenhower is President of the United States," the chief political officer of the air force told us, "we can expect an allied invasion any day. He is a master of amphibious landings. Skilled flying will not be enough to stop the American devils. When that day comes, each of you must dive your body and plane into the American Navy and landing craft."

A deathly hush fell over the audience. I looked around at the stunned, fear-smitten faces of the other pilots. Although a few of the fanatic Reds would have obeyed such an order, most of us refused even to consider committing suicide for the communists. For days afterward almost everyone on base walked around sullen-faced.

The Red air defeats had put the Russians in an especially bad position. They'd started the war with puppet North Korean man-power, but by June, 1953, they were rapidly losing their own MiG divisions and their best pilots. We Koreans had a saying, "The Soviet is holding the tiger's tail." If they withdrew their planes and pilots, the Chinese and North Koreans would lose their faith in their ally. And if they stayed, it meant that the American Sabres would continue to bleed the Russian Air Force white. We heard rumors that the Russians had a new supersonic fighter, the MiG-17, but it never appeared in Manchuria.

A truce was the only way out. At Russia's insistence, negotiations were resumed at Panmunjon and it was signed in July. But for the sheer superiority of the American Sabre jet, I'm sure the Korean war would still be going on today.

A week before the signing, our air force vice commander, Gen. Han Jun Kim, spoke at our base. He told us that according to the truce terms it would be illegal to bring weapons or men into North Korea after midnight on July twenty-seventh. We had to transfer our entire air force from Manchuria back to North Korea before then. Everything was to go to Uiju, which was being repaired again by the Chinese soldiers and forced laborers.

"What about night B-29 raids before the truce goes into effect," I asked after the general was finished. "Won't they destroy our MiGs on the ground?"

General Kim said we would have to take our chances. "The Soviet Union can always supply us with MiGs," he added. "The border between China and Korea is long and the Neutral Commission cannot be everywhere."

From July twenty-third to July twenty-sixth we went back and forth and landed 100

MiGs on the bumpy grass strip alongside the still-pitted runway at Uiju. But my premonition proved correct. The B-29s came there every night that week and destroyed more than twenty planes on the ground.

General Wang suddenly switched tactics. He decided it would be more practical to break the truce than take further losses. On the twenty-sixth and twenty-seventh, everyone at Antung—Russian, Chinese, North Korean pilots, mechanics, commanding officers—worked around the clock dismantling and crating MiGs. On the night of the twenty-seventh, the field was lit like day while we worked frantically. About three hours before the deadline, my battalion was finished and large tractors loaded our crated MiGs onto river barges for shipment across the Yalu.

We arrived in North Korea the next morning, nine hours after the truce deadline. During the next week the rest of our planes and pilots returned from Manchuria. As late as August I saw crated MiGs on railroad flatcars coming from China in violation of the truce.

I stayed at Uiju a few days, then was transferred to Kusong in Western North Korea. I stayed there until September, when I was transferred to Sunan, the partially rebuilt main base near Pyongyang.

While we had been fighting, the Reds kept telling us how fine air-force life would be in peacetime. Yet, during August and September, even though there was no war, there was no letup in our rigorous life, except for the regulation on marriage. I finally realized that communist countries are always at war. When they speak of peace, they really mean peace in 50 to 100 years—whey they expect the whole world will be communist.

My assignment to Sunan was just the chance I had been waiting for. It was only fifteen kilometers from Pyongyang and only seven minutes' flying time to the 38th parallel.

On the afternoon of September twentieth, after not flying since my arrival at Sunan, I learned that I was scheduled for a training flight at 9:05 a.m. the following day. I decided I would never return.

Early the next morning I checked my parachute and made sure I had my four colored flares. If I couldn't find Kimpo, I planned to land at Suwon, another Sabre base.

Before take-off I called together the two other pilots assigned to fly with me that day. "Don't wait for me," I told them. "I'll be up a little longer today, so you land first."

They took off, and a few minutes later I followed. I flew in the vicinity of the field for seven minutes, until one of them had landed and the other was going in. I looked down at the ground, then rechecked the heading and the other figures I had memorized. I hesitated, but I knew that if I didn't go now I would spend my whole life under the communists.

I turned the plane sharply to the right and took a 170-degree heading for Kimpo.

Just before I reached the parallel I heard the voice of my CO at Sunan calling me on my radio, "No 77. Where are you?" He kept this up for a few minutes, but I never answered. Up to the last minute, they never suspected their "faithful Red pilot," Kum Sok No, was escaping.

Soon after I crossed the parallel, I spotted a few Sabres below and ahead, but they ignored me, apparently not recognizing me as a member of the Red Air Force. I lowered my landing gear as a sign that I was friendly. I kept rocking my wings as a friendly signal to the AA batteries below.

A few minutes later I saw Kimpo ahead. I recognized it from the maps and models I had studied at Anshan. Four Sabres were training nearby, but they went on with their work as I passed. I started to drop altitude, shooting off a colored flare every few thousand feet.

I think the tower recognized me then, for I heard some garbled English words on my radio. I approached the field contrary to the usual landing pattern. I didn't want to risk being shot down while circling the field, so I decided to land immediately—in the wrong direction. I came in low and just missed a head-on collision with a surprised Sabre that was landing on the other side of the same runway. I rolled to a stop next to a group of parked American jets.

About thirty American pilots came rushing to meet me. I opened the canopy of my plane and the last thing I did as a member of the Red Air Force was smash the glass over the picture of Kim Il Sung that sits over the instrument panel of every North Korean plane. I was free.

A tall American extended his hand as I jumped down. Soon I was surrounded by the others. They shook my hand, jabbered away in a strange language, and looked over both me and my plane very carefully. These smiling, soft-spoken fellows were not at all the devils I had pictured Sabre pilots to be. A few seconds later I was whisked away to the operations hut in a jeep.

I had quite a few surprises waiting for me in the free world. I heard for the first time that Gen. Mark Clark had offered $100,000 to the first Red pilot who delivered a MiG-15B into allied hands. Hostilities were over, but the Pentagon ruled that I was to be paid the money. Since then I understand that an offer for subsequent MiGs has been withdrawn. My mother was alive and well and I was reunited with her in Syngman Rhee's home. She had been evacuated from Hungnam to South Korea after the Chinese invasion in the winter of 1950-1951. . . .

PART SIX

VIETNAM—
MISSILES IN ACTION

Sock It to "Uncle Ho"

DOGFIGHT OVER 'NAM

by Colonel Robin Olds, USAF

This is how two MiG-17s became the victims of Col. Robin Olds and his pilot, 1st Lt. Stephen B. Croker. These were aerial victories three and four for Olds, making him the leading MiG-killer at that time in Southeast Asia. An ace from World War II, the 8th TFW commander was battle-tested and experienced. Olds termed the events of 20 May "quite a remarkable air battle." According to his account:

F-105s were bombing along the northeast railroad; we were in our escort position, coming in from the Gulf of Tonkin. We just cleared the last of the low hills lying north of Haiphong, in an east-west direction, when about 10 or 12 MiG-17s came in low from the left and, I believe from the right. They tried to attack the F-105s before they got to the target.

We engaged MiG-17s approximately 15 miles short of the target. The ensuing battle was an exact replica of the dogfights in World War II.

Our flights of F-4s piled into the MiGs like a sledge hammer, and for about a minute and a half to two minutes it was the most confused, vicious dogfight I have ever been in. There were eight F-4Cs, twelve MiG-17s, and one odd flight of F-105s on their way out from the target, who flashed through the battle area.

Quite frankly, there was not only danger from the guns of the MiGs, but the ever-present danger of a collision to contend with. We went round and round that day with the battles lasting 12 to 14 minutes, which is a long time. This particular day we found that the MiGs went into a defensive battle down low, about 500 to 1000 feet. In the middle of this circle, there were two or three MiG's circling about a hundred feet—sort of in figure-eight patterns. The MiGs were in small groups of two, three, and sometimes four in a very wide circle. Each time we went in to

Colonel Robin Olds, an 8th Air Force ace of World War II with twelve victories, increased his score in Vietnam by knocking down four MiGs. He commanded the 8th Tactical Fighter Wing in Vietnam, and following the war served as Commandant of Cadets of the USAF Academy, holding the rank of Brigadier General. (USAF)

engage one of these groups, a group on the opposite side of the circle would go full power, pull across the circle, and be in firing position on our tails almost before we could get into firing position with our missiles. This is very distressing, to say the least.

The first MiG I lined up was in a gentle left turn, range about 7000 feet. My pilot achieved a boresight lock-on, went full system, narrow gate, interlocks in. One of the two Sparrows fired in ripple guided true and exploded near the MiG. My pilot saw the MiG erupt in flame and go down to the left.

We attacked again and again, trying to break up that defensive wheel. Finally, once again, fuel considerations necessitated departure. As I left the area by myself, I saw that lone MiG still circling and so I ran out about ten miles and said that even if I ran out of fuel, he is going to know he was in a fight. I got down on the deck, about 50 feet, and headed right for him. I don't think he saw me for quite a while. But when he did, he went mad, twisting, turning, dodging, and trying to get away. I kept my speed down so I

wouldn't overrun him and I stayed behind him. He headed up a narrow little valley to a low ridge of hills. I knew he was either going to hit that ridge up ahead or pop over the ridge to save himself. The minute he popped over I was going to get him with a Sidewinder.

I fired one AIM-9 which did not track and the MiG pulled up over a ridge, turned left, and gave me a dead astern shot. I obtained a good growl. I fired from about 25 to 50 feet off the grass and he was clear of the ridge by only another 50 to 100 feet when the Sidewinder caught him.

The missile tracked and exploded 5 to 10 feet to the right side of the aft fuselage. The MiG spewed pieces and broke hard left and down from about 200 feet. I overshot and lost sight of him.

I was quite out of fuel and all out of missiles and pretty deep in enemy territory all by myself, so it was high time to leave. We learned quite a bit from this fight. We learned you don't pile into these fellows with eight airplanes all at once. You are only a detriment to yourself.

MiG SWEEP
by Major John T. Correll, USAF

All during the Christmas holidays the lights burned late in the operations complex at Ubon Air Base in northeastern Thailand. A bold plot was being hatched. Only a handful of men knew about it yet, but if it worked, a task force of American fighters would lure North Vietnam's new MiG-21s up from their sanctuaries and destroy them.

It was December 1966, the 23rd month of the air war over North Vietnam. The war had recently entered a more aggressive phase. The North Vietnamese pilots, now flying MiG-21s as well as the older MiG-17s and -19s, had stepped up their attacks on American fighter-bomber formations.

Late in December, Seventh Air Force ordered the first fighter sweep of the war against the MiGs in the Red River Valley north of Hanoi. It was to be called "Operation Bolo," and there had been little debate about

who should plan and lead it.

"We gave the job to the man most likely to succeed," an Air-Force general would later tell the New York *Times*. "We gave it to Olds, of course."

"The phrase is a good description of Col. Robin Olds," the *Times* commented: "All-America tackle and captain of the football team at West Point; husband of Ella Raines, the actress; quadruple ace in World War II; full colonel at 30 years of age; and now at 44, everybody's choice as the hottest pilot of the Vietnam war."

The wing he commanded was hot, too. So far in the war, American pilots had shot down 27 MiGs, and 14 of those were by Olds's 8th Tactical Fighter Wing—the "Wolfpack"—at Ubon.

Their success in "Operation Bolo" would hang on a classic deception: could they mislead the enemy into thinking that their F-4C Phantoms were bomb-laden F-105s and thereby get Hanoi Air Defense Command to commit its MiGs against what appeared to be an irresistible target?

The mission was laid on for Monday, January 2.

Advance word on "Operation Bolo" was on a strict need-to-know basis. Every pilot in the wing was put into intensive training for the role he would play in the MiG Sweep, but great care was taken to make this seem part of a more general training program. Air crews who would fly "Operation Bolo" were not told about it until Sunday morning. Ground crews knew only that something big was coming as they labored to get the airplanes into peak condition.

"They didn't know what was afoot, but every man felt the sense of urgency," Colonel Olds would write later in *Air Force* Magazine. "I found one crew chief hobbling about his bird on crutches, his broken leg dangling in a cast. He told me he didn't know what was going to happen, but he was making blankety-blank sure his bird was ready for it."

As for Colonel Olds, he divided his time between preparations at Ubon and shuttling back and forth to brief other Southeast Asia wings selected to participate in "Operation Bolo."

The MiG Sweep was going to be a surprise in an air war that hadn't seen many surprises. Day after day, the Thuds and Phantoms flew into Route Pack Six, the heavily defended area around Hanoi. They could strike only at a limited number of approved targets, which were located in a relatively small geographical area. There were only so many approach routes. Moreover, the rules of engagement prohibited them from going after MiGs on the ground. And even if the MiGs did come up from their airfields, the American fighters could not pursue them if they retreated across the border into China. The North Vietnamese were well aware of these rules of engagement, and were of course familiar with the typical characteristics or "profile" of the bombing missions.

During this early part of the war, most of the Route Pack Six bombing missions were being flown by F-105s out of Korat and

A pair of F-4 Phantoms prepare to refuel over Vietnam. The F-4 was the principal tactical fighter of both the USAF and the USN. (USAF)

Takhli. The Thuds had greater range than F-4s, but when loaded down with bombs, they had to operate at lower altitudes. The Thuds also refueled lower and farther to the west than the Phantoms.

Route Pack Six was guarded by a large number of radar-guided surface-to-air (SAM) missiles. For protection against these, the Thuds had begun to carry ECM (electronic countermeasures) pods to jam the SAM sighting radars. The F-4s did not have ECM pods yet.

But the SAMs were not the only threat to the fighter-bomber formations. Even the Stateside news media were commenting on North Vietnam's growing fleet of MiGs.

"U.S. intelligence has now photographically pinpointed the number of Hanoi's jet planes based in North Vietnam or across the border on Red China's airfields," *Newsweek* reported. "The total count now runs to 15 of the supersonic MiG-21s, 96 of the older MiG-17s and -15s, plus eight IL-28 light jet bombers. All of the advanced MiG-21s are located at Phuc Yen air base near Hanoi. The rest are about evenly dispersed between fields near Hanoi or in staging areas in Red China."

Increasingly, the Thud flights were being "bounced" by MiGs. It was a harassing tactic, designed to force the F-105s to jettison their bomb loads short of target. The Thud was far from an ideal air-to-air dogfighter, but it had a nose-mounted cannon, sometimes carried a Sidewinder missile, and once free of its bombs, could put up a presentable fight. Furthermore, while it could not maneuver with either the F-4 or the MiG-21, it had the speed to outrun both of them at low altitude.

It was against this backdrop that 8th Wing planners conceived "Operation Bolo."

The Phantoms would fly every leg of their mission just as the F-105s would. To put the icing on the cake, they would, for the first time, be carying ECM pods. Instead of bombs, they would be armed with heat-seeking Sidewinders and radar-guided Sparrows.

Monday at Ubon was tense, and the tension grew when, during aircrew briefings, the order for an hour's weather hold on the mission came through from Seventh Air Force. Then, finally, the word flashed from Saigon to execute "Operation Bolo."

"O.K., you Wolfpack, let's get 'em," Colonel Olds shouted. The pilots suited quickly and climbed into their waiting airplanes. Almost every flyable airplane in the wing was going. Phantoms, strung out in seemingly endless file, waited their turn to wheel onto the runway. Then they were off, two by two, into the afternoon sky. Even the spares, those aircraft standing by to fill in for last minute aborts, went.

It was an awesome air armada. There were 14 flights of Phantoms: seven from the Wolfpack, seven from elsewhere. In addition, six flights of F-105s would accompany them in and strike at SAM sites in Route Pack Six.

Colonel Olds's call sign, chosen with a sense of humor by someone on the operations staff at Seventh Air Force, was "Olds Lead." He flew the first ship in the first flight. All of the Wolfpack flights had automobile call signs. Three minutes behind Olds came Ford Flight, led by Col. Daniel "Chappie" James, the 8th Wing deputy commander for operations. The flights were spaced out to put wave after wave of F-4s into the battle area, so the MiGs would get no rest.

"We were trying our best to look and act like Thuds," said Maj. Phil Combies, who was flying Rambler Four. "Normally, fighter pilots don't talk much to each other in transit, but we put out a few radio calls to simulate Thuds making checks and so forth."

Rambler Flight was the third in the formation, three minutes behind Ford.

Across the Black River they swept, on the typical F-105 ingress route. Below them was an unbroken floor of clouds. Their center-line auxiliary fuel tanks ran dry and were dropped. Olds Flight increased speed and crossed the Red River. Phuc Yen airfield was six minutes, 23 seconds ahead. The cloud deck below hid the peaks of Thud Ridge, so

MiG-15s taxiing for take-off position. (USAF)

named by the F-105 crews for whom it was a favorite landmark and navigation aid.

At the southern end of Thud Ridge lay Phuc Yen airfield and the MiGs.

Meanwhile, Hanoi radar was tracking the inbound formation of airplanes. Everything the North Vietnamese knew about how the Americans operated indicated that this was a large strike force of F-105s.

The American flyers had hoped for better weather. With clouds stretching all the way to the horizon, the Hanoi air defense commander might not commit his MiGs, even if he fell for the deception. He might figure that the undercast would so limit the effectiveness of visual bombing by the Thuds that it was not worth the risk to try stopping them. Furthermore if the MiGs did come up, the clouds would offer them a place to hide from the F-4s.

About two minutes from Phuc Yen, Colonel Olds's back-seater, Lt. Charles Clifton, momentarily picked up a radar blip, possibly a low-flying MiG, but lost it. Olds Flight passed Phuc Yen and circled back. Still no MiGs. Ford Flight arrived and hurtled by, a thousand feet away.

"Olds!" called out Capt. Everett T. Raspberry in Ford two. "You have MiGs at your six o'clock!"

This was it.

Colonel Olds saw MiGs pop through the clouds off his wing, and looking over his shoulder, saw the one Raspberry had seen, coming at him from behind. Olds broke his flight to the left.

"Olds babe, you've got one right on your—!" Olds two sang out.

Colonel Olds tightened his turn. Now the MiG could not bring its guns to bear, and Olds shifted his attention to another MiG, this one in front of him. Clifton obtained a radar lock-on, which would guide the Sparrow missiles toward the MiG's fuselage. The missile leaped forward, guiding true, but the radar broke lock. Olds quickly fired a heat-seeking Sidewinder, but that missed, too, and the MiG disappeared into the clouds.

Rambler Flight, coming in along the east side of Thud Ridge, heard over their headsets the crackling exchanges between Olds and Ford Flights in the battle area.

"Olds, where are you?" queried Capt. J. B. Stone in Rambler Lead.

"Find your own," came the answer from someone.

By now, MiGs were not that difficult to find. As Maj. Phil Combies would later recall, "There were MiGs all over the sky."

Olds and Clifton, headed southwest, saw another MiG come up through the clouds, going east. Olds broke sharply in pursuit, and advanced power to full afterburner. He and Clifton prepared to attack with Sidewinders.

Gun camera sequence showing the death of a MiG-15. (USAF)

All set, Olds pulled the nose of the Phantom up nearly vertical and vector-rolled hard right. The F-4 responded beautifully. As the nose sliced the horizon at the completion of the roll and came down toward the cloud deck, it was obvious that they had gained position inside the MiG's turn. Olds lined up on him, got a good growl from the Sidewinders, and squeezed the trigger twice.

The first Sidewinder hit the MiG, tearing the wing away in a bright red flash. The MiG tumbled, end over end, and fell through the clouds.

Olds, Ford, and Rambler Flights had now engaged the enemy, and the battle, punctuated with orange explosions and smoke, covered 30 miles of sky. Phantoms and MiG-21s had tangled before, but never in so major a battle as this. The smaller MiGs, red stars gleaming on their silver wings, could maneuver more tightly than the F-4s, but the Phantoms were doing all right. Several MiGs were down, and not a single Phantom had been hit.

A lone MiG decided to jump Ford Flight's right flank. If he could bring either his 30-millimeter gun or his Atoll missiles to bear, he was in excellent position to make a kill. Ford Three and Four broke hard right, and the MiG hurtled by, overshooting them.

Colonel James in Ford Lead and Captain Raspberry on his wing had seen the MiG's attack develop, and had something more than escape in mind. As the MiG drew nearer, they broke right, but recovered with a barrel roll to the left, causing the MiG to overshoot. This put them directly behind the MiG—who only a few moments ago had been the attacker. Raspberry squeezed off a single Sidewinder. It hit the MiG's cockpit and exploded.

Phil Combies in Rambler Four had a MiG in his sights. "Lock on!" he told Lt. Lee Dutton in his back seat. Combies fired his first Sparrow, saw it go wide, fired another, and watched the MiG blow up in an orange fireball.

"I was startled to see his chute hanging there," Combies said later. "How could he get out of the airplane before the explosion? I suppose he saw the missile coming and ejected. He could have seen the rocket fire coming out of the Sparrow's tail."

Momentarily, Combies found himself lining up on another MiG. The North Vietnamese pilot, who had been after Combies but lost him, rolled out, rocking his wings and looking for the Phantom as he climbed. Combies launched his last two Sidewinders. They were about halfway to the MiG and looking good when the warning came.

"Suddenly," Combies said, "one of our F-4 pilots came on the air yelling *'F-4C, I don't know your call sign. Break left. Break left.'* Cripes, every F-4 up there broke left. Later, we learned he was warning J. B. Stone, who had a MiG-21 firing at him, but who evaded and knocked one down. I cleared myself and rolled back, to the right where my MiG was. No MiG, just a guy hanging in a chute. His airplane and mine were the only two in that

A North Vietnamese MiG-21 "Fishbed" in flight near Hanoi. (USAF)

particular piece of the sky that I knew about. The MiG probably blew up or fell through the clouds. I put him down as a probable."

No single crew on the MiG Sweep would be credited with more than one confirmed MiG kill today.

Olds, Ford, and Rambler Flights, running low on ordnance and fuel, headed out. Colonel Olds passed command to Maj. Fred Crow in Lincoln Lead. But the battle was over for the MiGs, too. They had retreated into the clouds, and would not rise again. The shooting part of the MiG Sweep had involved only the first three flights of Phantoms.

A crowd was gathered on the ramp at Ubon. The first F-4 touched down and taxied in. As it passed the wing command center, the pilot in the front seat raised his hands and clasped them together, indicating that the mission was a success.

One by one, the planes returned and were counted. "There's two, three, four. . . ." And when the last aircraft landed, a yell of "all safe" drew a tremendous cheer.

Colonel Olds herded his pilots off to debriefing. As yet, no one had an accurate count on how many MiGs had been shot down.

"Okay," said Olds. "Let's have one at a time, starting with lead flight." Gradually, they pieced the story together.

They had shot down seven MiG-21s—of which North Vietnam had but 15.

"It was quite a day," said Phil Combies, "but you should have seen the night. My head hurts thinking about it."

Colonel Olds missed the evening's celebration. He was in Saigon, making a personal report that brought a broad smile to the face of Gen. William W. "Spike" Momyer, the nail-hard fighter tactician who commanded Seventh Air Force.

The MiG Sweep created quite a clamor in the press. It had, said *Time* Magazine, "chopped Ho Chi Minh's air arm off at the elbow."

When Colonel Olds met with reporters, somebody asked him what he thought of MiG-21 pilots.

"I think," said the master of the MiG Sweep, "they are very aggressive. I think seven of them made mistakes."

A FIGHTER PILOT
IN VIETNAM

by Major Gerald D. Larson, USAF

Normally, when the statement is made, "I am a fighter pilot, and I fly F-4s," some F-105 pilot says, "How can a pilot who flies an airplane with two engines, two throttles, two cockpits, and an anticollision beacon ever possibly call himself a fighter pilot?"

I've recently returned from a short temporary duty tour with the 555th Tactical Fighter Squadron at Ubon Royal Thai Air Base, in the eastern part of Thailand, and I would like to discuss some of our Southeast Asia facilities, the out-country air missions, and some of the operational support activities.

Our missions at Ubon included both day and night flying activity and, as you might expect, this caused a few problems. The billeting arrangements had to be coordinated for day sleepers and night sleepers. Billeting facilities were entirely adequate though and, when compared to some of the South Vietnam bases, were absolutely first class. We operated the messing facilities on a twenty-four-hour basis to support the day-and-night flying operation. Breakfast, lunch, and dinner were served simultaneously around the clock, and it always seemed strange to enter the Officers Mess at 5:00 in the morning for breakfast and find people at the next table eating their dinner after finishing night-flying activities.

Since we worked around the clock, seven days a week, other problems developed. For instance, the Chaplain wondered why no one came to church on Sunday. Well, he finally figured out that it was because no one ever knew when Sunday arrived. He solved the problem by posting signs on Saturday, "TO-MORROW IS SUNDAY, GO TO CHURCH."

Some of the other base facilities included a library, a base exchange, some hobby shops, and even a swimming pool. As you can see, our facilities were totally adequate. We occasionally had a water shortage or power loss. However, these were rare inconveniences.

At Ubon, with F-4C aircraft, we were responsible for many different types of missions. I would like to expand on a few of the more frequent types and discuss some of the details associated with each.

• *The strike-type mission* is an attack against a predetermined, fixed target. The target may be a bridge, railroad yard, petroleum storage, truck park, etc. The aircraft are, for this type of mission, configured with bombs, wing tanks, Sparrow and Sidewinder missiles. The strike-type mission is accomplished both during the day and night. Day strikes in the North are considered fairly exciting missions. The night strikes there are even more so because, as you might expect, at night you can see all the flak coming up, and the Delta area during a night strike resembles a Chinese New Year's celebration.

• *The armed reconnaissance mission* is configured in the same manner as the strike, that is, fuel tanks, missiles, and bombs. The armed recce mission involves reconnaissance of a predesignated area or route segment. Targets of military significance are attacked and destroyed. Typical targets are trucks, barges, troop concentrations, etc. This armed recce mission is also accomplished both day and night. The night work involves an element of two aircraft operating as a team, using flares for illumination and rockets or bombs as ordnance. Finding a target or even finding the right road segment under flare illumination is fairly exacting, and the requirement for precise navigation is apparent.

The F-4, with two crew members, is ideally suited for the night operation. Four eyeballs are better than two for finding targets, and the capability to have one set of eyes on the aircraft instruments at all times while maneuvering for an attack and during the attack is highly desirable. When the flare burns out, the attacking air crew may be suddenly left in a very uncomfortable situation—that is, complete blackness, no horizon, and with the aircraft in an extreme attitude close to the ground as required for a bomb run or during target pull off. There is a disorientation problem that you can't imagine. With the backseater, and that guy in back is called the GIB—guy in back—he is constantly on the gauges once an attack starts and recovers the aircraft to straight and level flight when the situation becomes hairy. It was our technique to automatically have the GIB initiate recovery if the airspeed dropped below 300 knots, angle of bank exceeded sixty degrees, or the aircraft was apparently going to descend below a prebriefed minimum altitude.

• *The combat air-patrol mission* requires only drop tanks and missiles. The purpose of the combat air patrol is to kill MiGs and protect the main strike force, which may be several flights of F-105 aircraft. Naturally, the combat air-patrol mission is very desirable. Everyone wants a MiG, so everyone is eager to go.

• *The escort mission* involves the protection of a slower type aircraft from MiG activity. The aircraft configuration is the same as that for combat air patrol—fuel tanks and missiles. We always visually identify a suspected hostile aircraft before attack. Therefore, we have a close-in manuevering engagement, and I am, needless to say, very happy to see the M-61 Gatling gun and computing optical sight installed in the F-4E model.

The daily frag order lays on the operational missions for the next twenty-four-hour period. This frag is received by teletype late in the afternoon and contains a description of the targets for the next day's missions, air-refueling areas and rendezvous times, call signs, etc. From this frag order, the squadron operations officer assigns his flights to specific missions. Flight commanders then assign aircrew names. By early evening, the pilots can check the flying schedule for the next day's operation and start serious mission planning work.

Assuming a strike mission has been scheduled, the planning starts at the intelligence section, where the air crew receives target photographs to study. From these photos, the pilot will pick the most distinctive recognition features in the target area. He will note the position of the enemy defenses, that is, which AAA and SAM sites will affect his mission. He will also note the terrain and general topographical layout in the target area. The air crew will note the entire strike force composition which is operating in his *and* the adjacent target areas during the time his strike mission is in progress.

The last stop for the night in this planning phase is the weather forecaster in an attempt to determine probable weather conditions affecting the mission. From this information, the flight leader and air crew compile their flight profiles from take-off to refueling, to target area, and back home. Once this is accomplished, it is then back to the BOQ for a restful night's sleep. I might add, it's necessary for the air crew to plan not only for the primary target, but also for secondary and tertiary targets in case a weather divert is required, so each strike flight can execute a go on any one of three preplanned targets.

The next morning before take-off a general briefing is conducted by Intelligence and Operations sections. Once again, the topics covered include target description and location, time on target, forces involved, refueling schedule, enemy defenses, etc. Latest weather is also thoroughly briefed at this time. In case weather in the primary target area precludes a successful attack, the secondary or tertiary target go is executed.

After this general briefing concludes, individual flight briefings are accomplished. These flight briefings are concerned with specific details of the mission. Take-off, join up, tanker rendezvous, and refueling procedures are briefed. The air-refueling portion of the mission is given very close attention, since expeditious refueling is mandatory. It is desirable to arrive in the target area with the maximum amount of fuel possible. The technique then is for the wing man to drop off the tanker last, because, as you know, wing men burn more fuel staying in position than lead and element lead.

After the refueling is covered, the formations and tactics are briefed. It is very important for every flight member to know the precise tactics to be used when attacking the target. Our dive-bombing techniques reduce our exposure time to enemy defenses to the minimum. During the planning phase, it is necessary to find each enemy SAM and AAA site which would affect the flight during the mission. If possible, the flight leader avoids the enemy defenses; however, in the Delta area this is not possible, and optimized tactics must be used to put the bombs on the target.

It is mandatory to keep the flight of four aircraft together as a fighting unit for mutual support. When outbound from the target area after the bombs are off, the flight is then closed up and organized for a possible MiG engagement.

The F-4s remain in the target area as long as possible to provide MiG CAP for the F-105 strike force. It develops that most strikes by F-4 aircraft are really strikes with MiG CAP backup.

The enemy defensive posture is formidable—it includes MiG-15s, MiG-17s, MiG-21s, SAMs, and antiaircraft artillery of the 37- to 57-mm. size and the heavier 85- to 100-mm. guns, and gun-laying radar positions. There are also countless numbers of small arms used against low-flying attack aircraft.

The enemy defense radar system very closely integrates the SAMs, AAA, and MiGs. Some days it appears that when the SAMs and the AAA are active, the MiGs will not be up. However, as soon as the pilots count on this, SAMs, AAA, and then MiGs will all be encountered within a very short period of time. The North Vietnamese defense-control system is outstanding, and they have very effectively integrated their entire defense structure.

Support elements that are used with a North strike mission include the SAM suppressor flights. These flights play a very interesting cat-and-mouse game with the missile sites to kill or suppress them. This concept has proven to be effective. It is a very risky job, which is performed outstandingly well by F-105s.

The photo-reconnaissance support is superb. RF-101 and RF-4 aircraft do a really fine job in obtaining quality, timely photographs of the target area, both for target-study purposes and for bomb-damage assessment. The photo-recce units operate day and night. Their motto is, "We Kill'em and Fil-m." They have a very unenviable task, since they operate unescorted, day and night, in the most highly defended enemy environment.

The SAC tanker units—the air-to-air refuelers—provide notable support for the fighters. Tanker air crews will do everything possible to assist fighters, particularly as they come out of the target area. There have been cases where the KC-135 tanker crews have stayed with a crippled fighter, transferring fuel to him, right down to the final approach at the closest recovery base. There is not a fighter pilot in South Vietnam or Thailand who wouldn't gladly buy a box of the finest stogies for every KC-135 tanker crew involved in the Southeast Asia air operations.

The search-and-rescue operation also deserves mention. HH-3 helicopters, or the "Jolly Greens," as they are called, extend to their maximum range, when necessary, to recover downed air crews. At time they pick up downed crewmen under most intense enemy ground fire, and their record for successful air-crew recoveries has been commendable.

The A-1 escort aircraft which accompany the "Jolly Greens" do an outstanding job in suppressing ground fire for the rescue choppers. They deserve a lot of credit, because they, too, are very vulnerable and press to the limit if any hope exists for a successful rescue pickup.

In summary, fighter aircraft are being used very effectively in the war in Vietnam. The F-105s are ideally suited for the strike role, and the F-4 has proven to be extremely versatile, performing equally well in the escort, air-to-air, and air-to-ground role.

The Southeast Asia air war is unique in that we are constraining our airpower to a level which will produce our desired goal. Airpower is effectively reducing the enemy's will and capacity to fight in Southeast Asia.

USAF F-5s refueling at the belly of a KC-135 tanker over Vietnam. The F-5 was also flown by the RVN Air Force.

VAMPIRES, TAKE IT DOWN!: "WILD WEASEL" IN ACTION

by Captain Don Carson, USAF

"Sam's at two and five . . . guns at three," my Bear,* Don Brian, cooly calls over the intercom, telling me where the threat is located.

"I light up the afterburner, and our speed approaches 600 knots. I turn toward the SAM site which is looking at my flight of four Weasels with his radar. We have the green light in the outboard weapons-pylon buttons, indicating that when we're in range and position, we are armed and ready to fire our AGM-45 Shrike antiradiation missiles.

"SAM's at twelve o'clock . . . a three-ringer." My Bear now has the SAM battery off our nose and is getting very strong signals on his indicating equipment. We press in, pull up our F-105 at the proper range, and hose off a pair of Shrikes just as the SAM site fires at our flight. My skin crawls as the rattlesnake sound in my headset and the flash of the warning-gear light tell me it is for real this time.

"Valid launch . . . twelve o'clock," yells my Bear.

"Vampires . . . take it down," I call to my flight as I nose over and unload. "Taking it down" is the standard Wild Weasel maneuver of rapidly diving in full afterburner and picking up speed to avoid the SAMs being guided to your aircraft. Sometimes by descending you can even lose the SAM radar tracking you, or force the SAM to overshoot and pass harmlessly by. If this does not work, at least you have one heck of a lot of airspeed you can use to make a break at the last moment and maybe make the SAM miss your aircraft. Even today when you see a fellow Weasel, the greeting is "Take it Down."

But now I see the clouds of dust and the "telephone poles" trailing fire as they climb.

*Friendly nickname for "Guy in Back."

Our Shrikes are still guiding directly toward the radar van which controls those SAM missiles. It is located in the center of the SAM ring, surrounded by the missile launchers.

"Guns at four o'clock," says my Bear. "Move it around. They are really on us." I don't, because SAM is our main concern at this particular moment. Suddenly, however, the SAM's appear to go unguided and streak off well above our flight. This meant the radar-control van had shut down in hopes of foiling our Shrikes, but it doesn't work. Our Shrikes impact the radar-control van, and dust and smoke rise to make the target area clearly. We can "jink" at last to keep the guns which are still hammering heavily at us from having a steady target.

Climbing back to gain altitude for a dive-bomb pass, I arm up my bombs and check for the green lights in the centerline weapon-station indicator. It looks good. I roll our F-105 over on its back and pull the nose through the horizon until the burning SAM-control van fills our gunsight combining glass . . . at 45 degrees of dive. I roll the wings level and put the pipper on the SAM launcher, just beyond the control van—550 knots, passing through 6000 feet—it looks good.

"They are really hammering us with the 37mm. from the east side of the site," calls my Bear. I see the red streaks passing over the canopy. There is not much that we can do. "Hang in there, Super Bear," I tell him, as I depress the pickle button on the control stick. We can feel the six 750-pound bombs leave the aircraft.

Lighting the afterburner, I honk back on the stick and get crunched down in the seat by the weight of 7 gs. I work the rudders and start another "jinking" turn, to throw the gunners off. I read somewhere that 90 percent of all fighter pilots pulled off a target to the right, so I almost always pulled off to the left. Lucky thing, today, at least because three more guns had opened up and were lighting the sky off my right wing as we turned left. Had I turned right, we would have been in the middle of the flak. There is a tremendous explosion as a ball of fire and dust rises from where a SAM on a launcher had been just moments before. We continue climbing as we watch our flight devastate the remaining missiles and launchers of this once-deadly SAM complex. This is one SAM that will not come back to "stuff" us or our friends.

The surrounding guns are still extremely active and I feel that we are very lucky to get out without having anyone hit that day. We rejoin our flight of four and head southwestward to find our tanker and some much needed fuel.

Once we cross the river, we spread out and I reach back beside the headrest and pull out the rubber hose which connects to a thermos bottle full of the best ice water in the whole world. I will be eternally grateful to Republic Aviation for installing this magnificent piece of equipment in the Thud. After a couple of hours with the hot Southeast Asian sun beating down through the canopy, you feel like a wilted stalk of celery in a hothouse. The tension and heat of the battle often leave your mouth so dry it seems full of cotton. It's funny how you remember little things . . . even today a glass of cold water on a hot day brings back the vision of reaching for that water-bottle hose.

Other memories came back, too, SAMs, Bears, Vampires, Shrikes, Thuds. Strange sounding names? Not to a Wild Weasel crew. Oh yes! The Weasel I'm talking about weighs 54,000 pounds. It's not the world's largest animal. It's a specially equipped two-place F-105 Thunderchief that performs one of the most daring combat missions ever imagined.

Wild Weasels have operated from both Takhli and Korat RTAFB under several squadron designations. The last of the F-105 squadrons of the many that once were stationed in Thailand is a Weasel Squadron: the 17th Tactical Fighter Squadron at Korat RTAFB.

Birth of the Weasels

In the late 1960's, the Weasel Squadron at Korat was called the 44th TFS Vampires. "Rolling Thunder," was the code name for the air war in North Vietnam, and it was in full swing. The SEA skies were filled daily with flight after flight of fighter-bombers pounding targets in North Vietnam. Unfortunately, these same skies were also filled with the heaviest concentrations of radar-controlled antiaircraft guns (AAA), MiGs and Surface-to-Air Missiles (SAMs) ever seen.

The strike flights were made up of F-4s and single-seat models of the F-105. Heavily laden with bombs, they were easy targets for SAMs when they went North. If targets were to be hit within the protective SAM rings which surrounded any major target area, it became obvious that some form of SAM-suppression tactics were necessary. F-100s, became the first "Weasels" in this role, but the greater armament, speed and range of the F-105 proved far better suited to the unique mission.

Capable of speeds in excess of 900 miles an hour on the deck, the F-105 could easily walk away from the more maneuverable MiGs which also roamed the skies of North Vietnam, ready to strike the unwary.

A Weasel pilot and his Bear (electronic warfare officer) fly as a precision team. Each understands and trusts the other's abilities completely. There is no time to ask questions when a Bear yells "SAMs at three o'clock . . . . take it down!" You react instantly—and even that may be too late.

"Bears" are a strange breed of aviator. Their fantastic ability to interpret the radar scope's electronic messages and warnings in the back seat inspires admiration not only for their ability but their sheer fortitude in combat. I will never, for the life of me, understand

F-105 Thunderchiefs taking off. (USAF)

how anyone could be brave enough to sit there during a hairy combat mission and not grab the stick or throttle!

I guess they had as much faith and trust in their pilots as we had in them.

Weasels always flew as a crew. It was much better to fly with the same person everyday. You soon worked out a private code system which could say more with less words than you ever thought possible. This became important when there were 20 strike aircraft sharing the same radio frequency as your Weasel flight and there were SAMs and MiGs in the area. The radio could get so full of chatter that it was a small miracle to get a word in edgewise. Through the din, you and your Bear not only had to keep each other informed on what was happening, but you also had to keep the strike flights advised. Especially you had to warn them when SAM came up.

It would be difficult to heap too much praise on the Thunderchief. It is definitely a pilot's and Bear's aircraft. The cockpit is large and quite comfortable for a fighter. It has lots of leg and elbow room, even for some-

one like me who is 6 feet 6 inches. With a full load of ordnance, the old Thud would weigh in at 54,000 pounds, and on a hot day at Korat, would take a cross-country trip on the ground before getting airborne.

Once in the air, however, the machine was a pure delight to fly. You could trim it up and go supersonic 50 feet above the trees without holding the stick. It was the most stable and honest aircraft a pilot could ever ask for. After flying the Thud, I personally doubt that any pilot would ever be completely satisfied with another aircraft. I have flown faster and more maneuverable fighters, but they are just not the same as the F-105. Do I sound prejudiced? I am, and proud of it. I am also still in love with the F-105. Try and find a Thud driver who isn't!

Ryan's Raiders

In 1967, while the Weasel program was in full swing, a special group of six F-105s (Weasels) were modified with an improved radar bombing system, first tested at Yokota AB, Japan. Men like Majors Ken Furth, Stan

Lockley, Captains Larry Huggins, and Paul Hanson, some of the most experienced F-105 pilots in the USAF, were the initial instructors in this pioneer program. They developed the tactics and expertise to give the Air Force its first accurate all-weather night-fighter bombing capability.

The back seaters were ex-radar bombardiers who were now part of this elite program named "Ryan's Raiders" for the man who spearheaded it, Gen. John D. Ryan. This highly specialized mission, while not exactly the Wild Weasel mission, was so closely dependent upon Weasel support that we considered it all part of the Weasel operation. Officially known as *Commando Nail*, it became part of the 44th TFS mission, and select crews would fly nightly bombing missions against targets deep into North Vietnam. The Raider pilots and Bears would spend hours studying radar predications and target-area maps to determine the best approach. They then flight-planned together for additional hours to assure precision to the nth degree.

Raider missions were flown while most of the pilots at Korat were at the O' club singing fighter-pilot songs, or asleep in their hooches resting for a 4:30 a.m. take-off. Many mornings you taxied back from your mission, and saw the morning-strike flight readying for take-off in the predawn semilight.

What were these Raider missions like? You've never lived until you've battled the Southeast Asia weather at night. There, thunderstorms can build all day, reaching unbelievable ferocity late at night. The problems of making a rendezvous with your tanker, who gave you fuel both going to and coming from your target, became far greater than during a day mission. A night thunderstorm tanker join-up and aerial refueling—with the lightning and St. Elmo's fire crackling around your canopy and pitot tube until they glowed with an eerie purple light—could be more frightening than the arcing red balls of 37- or 57-mm. guns.

Weather was a factor most of the year, yet somehow you always found your tanker and always got your fuel. It still amazes me what man can do when he must. To fly under such conditions nightly and not lose more aircraft to natural causes alone is remarkable.

The one thing that always bothered me was what would happen if a bolt of the lightning, which was everywhere, were to hit the armed bombs which were strapped to the belly of my aircraft? To my knowledge, this never happened to anyone and somehow the worry became less important the closer we got to our target area and the more the NVA guns began finding us in the darkened sky. However, I still wonder.

Once into North Vietnam, you cut off all external lights and headed toward your IP (initial point), from which you would turn toward your target run-in. Flying at a carefully preplanned altitude and speed, you watched your radar scope, while your Bear gave you minute corrections from his larger expanded radar picture.

"We're on time, how's it look?"

"One degree left, target dead ahead at 25 miles," he would answer. As another flight provided cover in regular Weasel birds, you pressed in and delivered your nightly surprise packages to Ho's boys when they least expected it.

You never became complacent. Even if you managed to slip into the target area without too much trouble, you could be certain that the moment your bombs impacted the ground, every gunner in that portion of North Vietnam would be after you. The sky would light up like the Fourth of July.

Despite the knowledge that every "Roman candle" was aimed at putting your aircraft out of business, the sight of 37-mm. tracers arcing up in graceful curves with the illusion of increasing speed as they approached you, was still beautiful in a strange way. Of course, the farther away they were from your aircraft, the more beautiful they became! When they were all around you, lighting up the instrument panel so brightly that you didn't need the cockpit lights, they were downright ugly.

It was easier to see a SAM or AAA at night, so you had more warning time in which to react. This balanced out the handicap of operating in darkness.

As you headed southwest once again, you often looked back to see the explosions and fires of the target you had just hit. It always gave me a good feeling to know that there was another load of munitions or supplies that would not be used to kill people in South Vietnam.

Weasels of Note

The men who flew the Wild Weasel missions are some of the greatest men I have ever known. Many will go down in the historical accounts of the Southeast Asian conflict alongside great names from aviation's past. Men like Majors Mike Muscat, and his Bear, Kyle Stouder, credited with knocking out five SAM sites. Now both lieutenant colonels, they light up with pride when you ask them about their days as Weasels. When asked what he liked most about being a Weasel, Colonel Muscat said, "It was a clear case of providing support for the strike forces and attacking highly professional military complexes of the enemy. There was no question of a SAM site being a civilian target."

Col. Robert S. Beale, now at the flight-test center at Edwards, was a young major when he led many of the great raids up North. His flight of Weasels paved the way for the strike flights which followed. "As a Weasel, I knew that the strike force's success depended on how well I did my job. I did everything possible to get the SAMs to shoot at me and not at the strike flight. The beauty of being a Weasel was that you were on your own and had a great deal of flexibility in hunting, finding, and destroying SAMs."

Always the first ones into the target area and the last ones to leave, Weasels never failed to get their piece of the action. Bob Beale got even more than the normal Weasel's share. Credited with destroying half a dozen SAMs and an untold number of guns, he wears the Air Force Cross, Silver Star, two DFCs and 12 Air Medals in testimony of his deeds.

Then there are Weasels like Chuck Horner, Nick Donelson, Mike Gilroy, Billy Sparks, Jim MacInerney, Leo Thorsness, Meryln Dethlefsen, and many others. The list includes SAM killers, MiG killers, Medal of Honor winners, and just great fighter pilots.

If it were not for the Weasels, there is little doubt but that the bombing campaign of North Vietnam would not have been as successful as it was. Neither would losses have been as low as they were for the agile fighters and powerful B-52s who braved the heaviest defenses ever known in aerial warfare. In my book, that makes the Wild Weasel operation pretty damned important! I'm glad I was there.

"STEVE" RITCHIE
BECOMES AN ACE

by Captain Richard S. Ritchie, USAF
and Captain Charles
DeBellevue, USAF

Air-to-air warfare in Southeast Asia began on April 3, 1965, when a U.S. Navy strike force of four F-8Es bombing the Thanh Hoa Bridge, approximately 33 nautical miles south of Hanoi, was attacked by MiG-17s. One Navy aircraft was damaged during the engagement. Enemy aircraft did better the next day when an Air Force attack force, bombing the same target, was jumped by MiG-15s and MiG-17s about 76 miles south of Hanoi; two F-105 Thunderchief fighter-bombers were shot down by MiG cannon fire. Until 17 June, on which day a U.S. flight of F-4Bs downed two MiG-17s with Sparrow missiles, aerial engagements had been infrequent. One month later, a flight of four F-4Cs of the 45th Tactical Fighter Squadron faced two MiG-17s. Both fell victims to the deadly Sidewinder heat-seeking missiles. By mid-1965, the air-to-air contest was well underway.

The aerial battles in Vietnam bore little resemblance to the dogfights of World War II or even Korea. The equipment had become so sophisticated and the speed of aircraft so incredibly increased that it took coordination and teamwork to kill a MiG. Every air-to-air encounter involved the ability and training of many people—support personnel, ground crews, strike and protective flight air crews, and the airborne and ground-radar operators. Unlike the air-to-air engagements of previous wars, in which a single pilot pitted his aircraft against a single opponent, some modern aircraft required two-man crews, working as an integrated and well-disciplined team.

Captain Richard S. (Steve) Ritchie, the first USAF pilot to down five MiGs in Southeast Asia, achieved this distinction as one member of a team. On his fifth kill, for example, he needed the aid of his backseater, Capt. Charles DeBellevue; he relied on the support of his flight; and he coordinated his techniques with those of the other flights in the area, as they all blended their skills for the mutual assistance necessary to fight as a team. Moreover, it would have been impossible for him to score his victories without Red Crown and Disco, the two supporting radars that pinpointed MiGs and friendlies in the skies of Vietnam. They provided Ritchie and the F-4s with flawless coordination and exact information.

How important this interaction proved to be can be illustrated in the following radio transmissions recorded in Ritchie's fifth kill. Cockpit communications are identified as "Ritchie (intercom)" and "DeBellevue (intercom)." Transmissions between Ritchie and other aircraft and radar are identified as "Buick," "Olds," "Vega," and "Radar." "Bullseye" was a reference point in North Vietnam known to aircrews and ground agencies. Bullseye located the MiGs without the MiG pilot knowing that the U.S. transmissions referred to him.

Radar:	Buick, Bandits 240/30, Bullseye.*
Buick:	Copy 240 at 30.
Ritchie (intercom):	What in the hell are they [the MiGs] doing down there?
DeBellevue (intercom):	What's our fuel?
Ritchie (intercom):	11.2.
DeBellevue (intercom):	OK.
DeBellevue (intercom):	I've got some friendlies and some MiGs. The MiGs are behind the friendlies right now.
Buick:	Buick shows MiGs 10 miles behind friendlies.
Buick:	Stand by for position.
Olds:·	Olds 90 right [Olds Flight is also turning toward the MiGs].
Radar:	This is Red Crown. Bandits at 253/37, Bullseye.
Buick:	Copy that.
Ritchie (intercom):	Bandits on the nose.
DeBellevue (intercom):	It looks like two of them at least.
Buick:	Buick flight, fuel check.
Olds:	Olds, 90 left.
Radar:	This is Red Crown. Bandits 252/51, Bullseye.
Buick 3 (The element lead	

*Enemy fighters at 240– and 30 miles from Bullseye

responsible for protecting Capt. Ritchie's airplane):	Buick 4, this is 3. Can you read me? We've got bogies [unindentified aircraft] off to the left at 10 o'clock, way out.
Buick 4:	Tally.
Radar:	This is Red Crown. Bandits 251/57, Bullseye.
DeBellevue (intercom):	Roger, I've got 'em.
Ritchie (intercom):	I can't believe we're not getting a SAM [surface-to-air missile] shot at us.
DeBellevue (intercom):	Me either.
DeBellevue (intercom):	Bandits. We're running in.
DeBellevue (intercom):	He's at 1 o'clock right now. [At this point, Buick Flight is converging head on with the MiGs. Olds and Vega Flights are chasing the MiGs, ground radar is telling everyone where the MiGs are. All the F-4s are using radar, eyeballs, and everything else to try to get to the MiGs, and the MiGs are trying to run away from everyone and get home.]
Ritchie (intercom):	Keep giving it to me, Chuck.
DeBellevue (intercom):	OK.
Buick:	Disco, do you have an altitude on them?
DeBellevue (intercom):	Looks like the MiGs are 160 [degrees] from us.
Radar:	This is Red Crown. Bandits 250/67, Bullseye.
DeBellevue (intercom):	1 o'clock [the MiGs are just to the right of the nose] Two of them at least.
Radar:	Vega, they are 255/62, Bullseye.
Vega:	Roger.
DeBellevue (intercom):	Two sets looks like. May be 4 MiGs.
Radar:	Vega, Disco. They are 248 for 53 [miles].
Buick:	Say altitude of MiGs.
Radar:	Buick, they are 266 for 32. Heading 080. Speed point 7. [Capt. Ritchie now knows their position, heading, and speed. Speed is seven-tenths of the speed of sound, or point seven mach. Now all he needs is their altitude.]

Captain Steve Ritchie, the USAF's first Vietnam war ace, standing beside his F-4 Phantom. (USAF)

Captain Jeff Feinstein, the USAF's third ace, mounts his Phantom at Udorn Air Base, Thailand. (USAF)

Major Bernard Fisher earned the Medal of Honor while flying a prop-driven A-1E Skyraider. With an 800-foot ceiling, surrounded by 1500-foot mountains, and under heavy ground fire from 2000 North Vietnamese regulars, he landed to rescue a downed fellow airman, and flew him out. (USAF)

Buick:	Say their altitude.
DeBellevue (intercom):	22 miles dead ahead.
Buick:	Say altitude please.
Buick:	Anybody know their altitude?
DeBellevue (intercom):	25. We're locked. [The bandits are at] 25,000 [feet], 15 miles dead ahead.
Buick:	Buick flight, reheat. [Capt. Ritchie is now starting a climb from 15,000 feet to get up to the MiGs.]
Ritchie (intercom):	We want to get a visual first. [Because of all the friendly airplanes converging, Capt. Ritchie wants to see the MiGs before he fires.]
DeBellevue (intercom):	They are dead ahead going right to left. They're about 1130. You're in range.
DeBellevue (intercom):	Come left a little.
DeBellevue (intercom):	Come left a little.
DeBellevue:	About 11 o'clock. Three and one-half miles ahead. Turning left. 3 miles, 2½. They are off the scope. Hurry it up!
Ritchie (intercom):	I've got'em. I've got'em, I've got'em [visual].
Buick:	Buick's got a tally ho. [He sees them.]
DeBellevue (intercom):	Three miles — 3½ miles, 2 o'clock. [Capt. Ritchie is in a hard climbing turn, attempting to get behind the MiGs. He fires his first missiles, which miss.]
DeBellevue (intercom):	You got min overtake. OK, you are out of range. You are out of range. [At this point, Capt. Ritchie has turned and is directly behind the MiGs. He fired and missed during the turn, but is now accelerating and closing on the MiGs from behind.]
Ritchie (intercom):	They are 12 o'clock straight ahead.
DeBellevue (intercom):	You're in range. You're in range. Fire. [Captain Ritchie fires again.]
Ritchie (intercom):	He's conning way high [the MiG is making a contrail].
Buick:	Splash! I got him! Splash!
DeBellevue (intercom):	Good show, Steve!

FIRST TRIPLE OVER
VIETNAM

Official U.S. Navy Report

On May 10, 1972, two Navy Fliers, Lt. Randy Cunningham (pilot) and Lt. jg William Driscoll (radar-intercept officer), became the first American fliers to qualify as aces solely as a result of Vietnam air action. The two, in their F-4J Phantom II, downed their third, fourth, and fifth enemy MiGs before their aircraft was hit by an enemy surface-to-air missile and went down off the Vietnamese coast. Both men were quickly rescued from the water and returned to their ship. They had earlier downed their first MiG on January 19, and their second on May 8. In addition to becoming the first Vietnam aces, the two men are the first "Team of Aces," the first to score a triple kill over Vietnam, and the first U.S. all-missile aces. The two airmen were members of Fighter Squadron 96 operating aboard *USS Constellation* (CVA-64), and both had been awarded Silver Star medals prior to their triple kill. On the same day as their triple kill, other Navy pilots downed an additional four MiGs and Air Force fliers downed three, to bring the day's total kill to 10, also a new Vietnam record.

The following official Naval messages describe Cunningham and Driscoll's five victories:

Z 0 190809Z Jan 72
FM CTG SEVEN SEVEN PT FOUR

TO NMCC
CINCPACFLT
CINCUSARPAC
CONSEVENTHFLT
COMUSMACV
CTG SEVEN SEVEN PT ZERO
SEVENTH AIR FORCE/INODM/DUPF

CINCPAC
CINCPACAF
COMNAVAIRPAC
COMUSNAVPHIL
CTF SEVEN SEVEN

INFO CNO
CTG SEVEN SEVEN PT FIVE
CTU SEVEN EIGHTP PT ONE PT ONE
CINCSAC

COMNAVAIRPAC
CTG SEVEN SEVEN PT SIX

An artist's conception of Lt. Cmdr. Swartz's A-4 Skyhawk downing a North Vietnamese MiG-17. (McDonnell-Douglas)

SECRET/JPCCO/JOPREP JIFFY/PINNACLE/USS CONSTELLATION/OPREP-3/

005/
H.   MIG 21 KILL
H1. NO VOICE REPORT DUE CLASSIFICATION
H2. 190558Z JAN 72
H4. AT 190558Z JAN 72, DURING AN IMMEDIATE PROTECTIVE REACTION
     STRIKE IN SUPPORT OF AN UNARMED RECONNAISSANCE MISSION OVER
     QUAN LANG AIRFIELD, NVN, F4J SHOWTIME ONE ONE TWO FROM VF-96
     SHOT DOWN ONE MIG-21 WITH TWO SIDEWINDER MISSILES. POSITION
     WAS APPROXIMATELY 19-03N, 105-17.5E. SHOOTDOWN CONFIRMED BY
     WINGMAN. PILOT LT RANDALL H. CUNNINGHAM, USNR, RADAR IN-
     TERCEPT OFFICER LTJG WILLIAM P DRISCOLL, USNR.
Z.   LAST OPREP-3 REPORT THIS INCIDENT. AMPLIFICATION TO FOLLOW BY
     GP-4
     GP-4

BT

SECRET/JPCCO/JOPREP JIFFY/PINNACLE/USS CONSTELLATION/OPREP-3/002/

FRESH BATH/SFASIA AIROPS/FOR 8 MAY 72 (U)
H.   MIG-17 KILL
H1. NO VOICE REPORT DUE CLASSIFICATION
H2. 080153Z MAY 72
H4. AT 080153Z WHILE PROVIDING MIGCAP FOR CONSTELLATION STRIKE
     GROUP AT SON TAY DRIVER TRNG AREA BEN: 0616KH0137, F4J A/C
     SHOWTIME 112 FROM FITRON NINETY SIX WAS ATTACKED BY THREE
     MIG-17 A/C. MIGS FIRED GUNS AND ONE ATOLL MISSILE AT SHOWTIME
     112 AND WINGMAN SHOWTIME 101. POSITION APPROX 2106N/11521E; 25

Like the F-4, the A-7E Corsair II was used by both the USN and the USAF in the Vietnam War. In the background is the U.S.S. Enterprise. (LTV)

NM NORTHWEST OF HANOI. SHOWTIME 112 ENGAGED MIGS FIRING TWO SIDEWINDER MSLS AT ONE OF THE MIG-17 A/C. MIG OBSERVED TO PITCH OVER AND IMPACT IN KARST RIDGE. SHOWTIME 112 AND WINGMAN SHOWTIME 101 BOTH OBSERVED IMPACT AND EXPLOSION/FIREBALL. PILOT OF SHOWTIME 112 LT RANDALL H. CUNNINGHAM, USNR; RIO LTJG WILLIAM P. DRISCOLL, USNR. LT CUNNINGHAM AND LTJG DRISCOLL HAD SHOT DOWN MIG-21 ON 19 JAN 72 ALSO IN SHOWTIME 112

OPAGE THREE RUHGOEA085 SECRET
    (SAME CREW, SAME AIRCRAFT). CTG 77.4 OPREP-3 SER 005 JAN 72 REFERS.
Z.   REMARKS.
Z1. HP LOTS' DEBRIEF AT 080320Z MAY 72.
Z2.   LAST OP-3 THIS INCIDENT AMPLIFICATION TO FOL IN OPREP-4.
GP-4

BT

SECRET/JPCCO/JOPREP JIFFY/PINNACLE/CTG 77.4/OPREP-3/005/

ROLLING THUNDER/SEA AIROPS/FOR 10 MAY 72 (U)
H.   MIG ENGAGEMENT/MIG-17 KILLS
H1.   NO VOICE REPORT DUE CLASSIFICATION.
H2.   100600Z MAY-100610Z MAY 72
H4.   DURING CONSTELLATION STRIKE ON HAIDUONG RR YDS: BEN 0616-0066, 2057N/10620E, STRIKE GROUP ENGAGED BY AT LEAST SIX MIG-17 AND TWO MIG-21 A/C. WHILE PROVIDING TARCAP, F4J A/C SHOWTIME 106 ENGAGED A MIG-17 WHICH HAD ATTACKED AN A7E A/C OFF TARGET. THIS MIG ESCAPED. ST 106 ENGAGED SECOND MIG-17 OVER TGT AND FIRED TWO SIDEWINDER MSLS. THE SECOND SIDEWINDER HIT THE MIG WHICH BURST INTO FLAMES. MIG-17 PILOT OBSERVED TO EJECT OVER HAI DUONG WITH GOOD CHUTE. ST 106 THEN ENGAGED OBHIRD MIG-17 AND FIRED ONE SIDEWINDER WHICH KNOCKED OFF TAIL ASSEMBLY. MIG PILOT EJECTED OVER HAI DUONG WITH GOOD CHUTE OBSERVED. MIG OBSERVED TO FOLL LEFT, IMPACT WITH GROUND AND EXPLODE. PILOT OF SHOWTIME 106, LT MATTHEW J. CONNELLY, USNR, RIO LT THOMAS J. BLONSKI, USNR. THE CREW OF SHOWTIME 112 OBSERVED INITIAL MIG-17 PILOT LEAVE A/C AND SUBSEQUENT IMPACT AND EX-PLOSION. CREW OF SHOWTIME 110 OBSERVED/CONFIRMED SECOND MIG KILL INCLUDING IMPACT WITH GROUND.
Z.   REMARKS.
Z1.   STRONG POSSIBILITY EXISTS THAT ADDITIONAL MIGS WERE SHOT DOWN DURING ENGAGEMENT BY OTHER CONSTELLATION F4J A/C. POSSIBILITY OF ONE OR MORE KILLS BY LT CUNNINGHAM/LTJG DRISCOLL IN F4J SHOWTIME 100. CREW OF SHOWTIME 100 RESCUED AFTER BEING FORCED TO EJECT OFF COAST OF NVN. CTG 77.4 OP-3 SER 004 MAY DTG 100650Z MAY 72 REFERS.
Z2.   PILOT DEBRIEF COMPLETED 100730Z MAY 72.
Z3.   ADDITIONAL INFO TO FOLLOW BY OPREP-THREE.
GP-4

BT

SECRET/JPCCO/JOPREP JIFFY/PINNACLE/CTG77.4/OPREP-3/008/

ROLLING THUNDER/SEA AIROPS/FOR 10 MAY 72 (U)
H.   TRIPLE MIG KILL/TOTAL OF FIVE MIGS SHOT DOWN BY LT. RANDALL H. CUNNINGHAM, USNR (PILOT) AND LTJG WILLIAM P. DRISCOLL, USNR (RIO) SINCE 19 JAN 72.
H1.   CTG 77.4 OPREP-3 SER 005 DTG 100816Z MAY 72/SER 006 DTG 101016Z MAY 72.

An F8u Crusader is signalled for take-off from the U.S.S. *Forrestal. Note Sidewinder missiles on fuselage mounting.* (USN)

H2.   100600Z MAY-100610Z MAY 72.

H4.   F4J A/C SHOWTIME 100 ASSIGNED FLAKSUP MSN IN SUPPORT OF STRIKE GROUP AT HAI DUONG RR YARD (BEN:0616-0066). ST 100 WAS LAST ON TGT AT 0601Z, AND AFTER DELIVERING ORDNANCE, WAS ATTACKED BY TWO MIG-17 A/C FIRING CANNONS AT ST100'S SEVEN O'CLOCK POSIT. WINGMAN, ST 110 OBSERVED ATTACK AND CALLED FOR ST 100 TO BREAK. WHEN ST 100 BROKE, MIG OVERSHOT AND ST 100 REVERSED AND FIRED A SIDEWINDER MISSILE AT MIG WHICH BURST INTO FLAMES AND IMPACTED GROUND AT ESTIMATED POSITION 2055N/10623E. SIDEWINDER HIT, EXPLOSION, AND IMPACT OBSERVED BY ST 100, AND WINGMAN 110. NO CHUTE OBSERVED.

AFTER MIG KILL, SHOWTIME SECTION (110 AND 100) OBSERVED AN ESTIMATED EIGHT MIG-17S IN COUNTER CLOCKWISE ORBIT AROUND TARGET AREA BETWEEN TEN AND FIFTEEN THOUSAND FEET. AN ADDITION FOUR MIG-17S A/C WERE OBSERVED DIVING IN COLUMN FROM NORTHEAST.

ST 100 NOW 2-4 MILES SOUTH OF HAI DUONG AT APROX 12000 FT. ST 100 OBSERVED A MIG-17 ATTACKING ST 112, CALLED FOR ST 112 TO BREAK. MIG DISENGAGED 112 AND ST 100 FIRED SECOND SIDEWINDER MISSILE WHICH KNOCKED THE MIG'S TAIL OFF CAUSING THE MIG TO ROLL OUT OF CONTROL. MIG PILOT EJECTED. EJECTION AND CHUTE OBSERVED BY ST 110, ST 106, AND ST 102. SECOND MIG IMPACTED GROUND AT 2054N/10620E. IMPACT OBSERVED BY ST 110 AND ST 102 -5 -0049/ 0603Z. DURING THIS SECOND ENGAGEMENT, TWO MIG-19S WERE OBSERVED BY ST 112 TO BE FIRING AT ST 100 WHILE ST 100 PURSUED AND SHOT DOWN MIG-17. ST 100 AND 112 ALSO OBSERVED TWO MIG-21S PASSING OVERHEAD DURING THIS PORTION OF THE ENGAGEMENT.

ST 100 HEADED TO 170 DEG FOR FEET WET AND MET THIRD MIG-17 HEAD ON. TIME APROX 0605Z WITH STRIKE GROUP APPROACHING FEET WET EXCEPT FOR SEVEN SHOWTIME F4J A/C INVOLVED IN MIG ENGAGEMENTS IN TARGET AREA. THIRD MIG-17 WAS FIRING CANNONS AT ST 100. ST 100 PULLED UP INTO VERTICAL SCISSORS MANEUVERS WITH MIG. AFTER 2-3 MINUTES, MIG ATTEMPTED TO DISENGAGE AND ST 100 MANEUVERED TO MIG'S SIX O'CLOCK POSIT AND FIRED ANOTHER SIDE-WINDER. THE MIG PITCHED OVER AND IMPACTED THE GROUND WITH RESULTING EXPLOSION AND FIREBALL. MIG-17 IMPACT OBSERVED BY ST 106, ST 110 AND ST 100 AT APPROX POSIT 2053N/10622E.

SHOWTIME 100 AGAIN ATTEMPTED EGRESS OF TGT AREA AND WAS JUMPED BY A FOURTH MIG-17. ST 100 ATTEMPTED TO ENGAGE THIS MIG BUT DISENGAGED WHEN ST 106 CALLED FOUR ADDITIONAL MIGS AT 100'S SIX O'CLOCK POSIT. ST 100 BROKE AWAY AND ACCELERATED TOWARDS GULF OF TONKIN. WHILE A APPROXIMATE POSIT 2035N/10625E, AT 16,000 FT, ST 100 WAS HIT BY A SA-2 MISSILE FROM VICINITY OF NAM DINH. NO RHAW OBSERVED BY CREW BUT PILOT SPOTTED SA-2 MISSILE VISUALLY JUST PRIOR TO IMPACT AND RIO OBSERVED ORANGE CLOUD AFTER BURST. PROGRESSIVE LOSS OF HYDRAULIC SYSTEMS EX-PERIENCED AND CREW FORCED TO EJECT APPROX FIVE NM FEET WEST OF THE MOUTH OF THE RED RIVER AT 20-19N/106-40E. PILOT AND RIO RESCUED BY HELO FROM USS OKINAWA AND RETURNED TO CONSTEL-LATION VIA OKINAWA APPROX 101100Z. BOTH PILOT AND RIO UNIN-JURED.

AM ESTIMATED TOTAL OF TWELVE MIG-17, TWO MIG-19, AND TWO MIG-21 A/C WERE OBSERVED BY VF-96 SHOWTIME A/C DURING ENGAGEMENT. MIGS WERE OBSERVED TO HAVE ATTACKED AT LEAST TWO ATTACK (A7E/A6A) AIRCRAFT WITH NO DAMAGE TO ATTACK A/C.

Z.   REMARKS

Z1. TAPE RECORDING OF ENTIRE ENGAGEMENT ON BOARD CONSTELLATION.

Z2. SAR DEBRIEF AND RECONSTRUCTION COMPLETED AT 101500Z MAY 72.

Z3. THIS AMPLIFIES H1, AND IS FINAL OPREP-3 THIS INCIDENT.

Z4. ON THIS DATE, CONSTELLATION/AIRWING NINE FIGHTER CREWS DESTROYED FIVE MIG-17 A/C AND ONE MIG-21 CONFIRMED, PLUS ONE ADDITIONAL MIG-17 (PROBABLE) DESTROYED. SIX CONFIRMED AND ONE PROBABLE WERE RESULT OF AIRBORNE ENGAGEMENTS. CTG 77.4 OPREP-3's 003 DTG 100530Z, 005 DTG 100816Z, 006 DTG 101016Z, AND THIS OP-3 REFER.

Z5. THE PILOT OF SHOWTIME 100 LT RANDALL H. CUNNINGHAM, USNR, AND HIS RADAR INTERCEPT OFFICER, LTJG WILLIAM P. DRISCOLL, USNR ARE CREDITED WITH A TRIPLE MIG KILL ON 10 MAY 72 WHICH ALONG WITH THEIR MIG-21 KILL OF 19 JAN 72 OP-3 SER 005 DFG 190809Z JAN 72) AND THEIR MIG-17 KILL OF MAY 8 72 (OP-3 SER 002 DTG 080350Z MAY 72) TOTALS FIVE. CONSTELLATION ACCORDINGLY CLAIMS FOR THEM THE FIRST TRIPLE MIG KILL AND FIRST ACE STATUS OF VIETNAM WAR.

GP-4

BT

PART SEVEN

HOLY WAR

The Arab-Israeli Wars (1948–1982)

BATTLE FOR THE PROMISED LAND

**by Captain William Lichtman,
RAF, USAAF, Israeli Air Force**

Two days later the truce ended when an invading Arab army ruptured the peace, and we got our combat flying orders. Our task was to break up enemy troop concentration and a tank convoy at Mishmar Hayadin.

"Okay, boys," I told the fellows in my squadron. "We're aviating again. Now. The three B-17s will carry a full bomb load of 250-pounders. The Forts will have a 51-umbrella cover. We'll fly at about 18,000 feet. The meteorology report is clear and visibility good. The 51s will have a double job, as cover, and also to break up any enemy interlopers. The bombs will be all anti-personnel eggs. We'll clobber all hell out of them. Dave, you'll be my wing man."

I looked at the two Irishmen in the squadron. "And you two *goyim*," I grinned affectionately at them, "will fly 2 and 4 position. Dave and I will be 1 and 3. Raid is at first light. Okay, scramble!"

Funny, I thought, as I hopped out of the jeep to draw my chute, how all wars seem the same. You have a bunch of guys, nice guys, but that's all you know or care. Then suddenly you go into combat and each guy becomes an individual, someone separate and yet a part of a whole, a friend, a comrade, his blood your blood, his fears your fears, cemented by the hot lava of warfare. Suddenly, nothing seemed serious anymore, at least not that which had appeared so serious before. We might be laughing and cracking jokes, but none of us would dare say or even think that perhaps he might not be coming back. The mask of warfare, I was thinking, always wears a crooked grin. If Mars was shown in a hideous smile, it was not because he felt like laughing, but because he did not want others to know the fear that writhed and cut within him.

Right now it was cutting me until my bowels were complaining. It never failed. Just before combat fight, when it was difficult and I was all zipped up and ready to go, Nature made her demands. Why, I wondered. Was it her way to preserve me, so that my blood, my fibers, my nerves, every muscle and bit of strength be used to keep me alive instead of digesting food?

As always, the girls who handed out the chute packs to us looked at us with those mournful eyes, half sad, half worshipping. I suppose, to them, we were heroes. If they only knew how scared we were. Who said it . . . "There are no cowards, only men who are a little less afraid?"

The ships were coughing, then roaring into life as we approached them. Dave and I and Kelly and McDonald, the two Irishmen, walked together. As one of the 51s coughed louder, almost like a sneeze, Kelly remarked, in very bad Yiddish . . . *"A gezuht uff dir!"*

It was the traditional blessing given to anyone who sneezes.

"Nexten yuhr," McDonald quipped. *"Zul mir zein in Yerushilyim."* Where he had picked up another hoary Yiddish Hebraic hope, that next year we should be in Jerusalem, I don't know. But we thought it was uproariously funny.

"Okay, you potato-eaters," I said affectionately. "I only hope you fly better than you can talk Yiddish."

"There isn't a Jew-boy living that can outfly a son of the Ould Sod," Kelly grinned, getting into his cockpit.

I had to smile again. Here we were, calling each other names that would have drawn blood on the New York streets of my boyhood. But here on this field, preparing to fly off into battle, religion meant nothing, names meant even less. We were men, united, the same, brothers.

If there ever will be a true Brotherhood of Men, I pondered, it will have been forged in combat.

I walked around my own 51, inspecting it, giving it a fond pat on the nose before climbing in. This was my girl friend for my date. May she be good to me! I prayed.

There was an excitement about combat, a feeling that no other sensation could rival, not even that of entering a woman for the first time. It was a heady, light, intoxicating feeling, making everything seem clearer and brighter. You could get quite poetic about it, if you wanted to. Two men meeting, in death-dealing, complicated machines, against the big field of the open sky. One would lose, the other would win. For a time not even that was important.

There was no more time to think. There was work to be done.

For a time, the pattern was the same. The clouds, then the first sight of the target area. Then the bombers starting to drop. Down.

In the 1948 War of Independence Ezer Weizman flew this black Spitfire. (IAF)

Farther, gracefully, 10,000, 9000, 8000. Level off, Mustangs hanging right above them, watching, alert.

Then the puff-puff-puff, the breaking black mushrooms of the AA fire.

Way off.

Forty-millimeter stuff, but off. Way, way off.

Then the breaking pattern of the bombs below, the spurts of flame and dirt and earth and smoke.

"When the bombers get well out of the target area," I said over the radio, "and are on their way home, we'll stooge around here for a bit. Hit everything that moves."

The bombing was over, the B-17s were high-tailing it home. But we hung around, waiting, knowing that there would be opposition. It was Kelly's voice that sang out:

"Spits at six o'clock!"

"Ours?" I demanded.

"Can't tell. Too far away."

"Okay, I'll take a look," I said, making a sharp turn and breaking away. Dave was right behind me. Dave! Good old Dave! I thought. And he's the one who wanted seventy-five dollars an hour!

Then I heard an excited voice over the radio.

"Break, break! Wolf, wolf, wolf! Break . . . three bandits sitting right on top of you. Twelve o'clock high! Break! Wolf!"

There were four Spitfires above Dave and me. And two more under us at six o'clock. Kelly and McDonald would take care of *them*. The four Spits were Dave's and mine. And they were coming fast at us. I could hear the enemy voices over the radio . . .

"Here comes the Jew-boys!"

I grinned, wondering what Kelly and Mac would think of being called Jew-boys by the Egyptian pilots. Evidently, they didn't like it, for the two Irishmen tore into the Gyppos at once. Dave and I split up, each of us going after one of the enemy.

My Egyptian seemed either foolish or inexperienced, flying straight ahead for the deck. How green can you get? I wondered why this Gyppo made no attempt to get out of the way, but flew straight, with me on his tail, my 50-calibers ripping him to pieces. Two more shot bursts and the end came in a vivid explosion of flame and smoke.

It had been so easy that I felt ashamed of myself. Evidently I must have hit his tank. They were sending green kids against us, I thought, seeing the other Gyppo plane spiralling down, the flames licking him hungrily.

". . . and the shame of it!" I heard Kelly say over the radio, "him calling me a Jew-boy, and me a fine broth of an Irishman!"

That was all there was to the fight. With two of their Spits shot down, the other four Gyppos headed for safety behind their own lines. I had spent harder and more dangerous moments in training than in this fight.

As soon as I landed, the back-slapping started. "Leon, you got the first one! The very first one to shoot a Gyppo down in this war!" One of the ground crew ran up with the paint and brush and the wooden frame, painting the first red fez on the nose of my P-51.

But to me, once I was back on the ground, it was a dull and familiar business. I had lived through it before, gone through it hundreds of times. But for Kelly it was different. It was his first kill. A former test pilot (later, in the United States, he would be one of the few ever to fly a jet and try to break the sound barrier), he was exulting. With his Vandyke beard and his loud sport shirt, he looked like a Hollywood version of a flier.

Then, as it always does, the war became mechanical. Even the technique of killing can become routine and businesslike.

It was fly, fly, and fly again. Three missions a day. Sometimes four. Sometimes for two hours, sometimes for three hours. Shipping, railroads, and troops. Ground support. Places like Majdal, Rafa, Gaza, Faluja, El Arish, Beersheba, and Damascus.

Fifty missions a month. Sixty.

Three fez-insignia on my plane. Then four and five. Four men lost to the squadron. Sweet and Leich got it coming in for a low-level job at the fort of Faluja. Willie Cannon got it from ground fire. The Israeli ground troops later found his body and brought it back. The Arabs had mutilated it, disemboweling it, and savagely castrating the corpse as well. It was sickening. Willie had been the lovable clown of the outfit. I had to write the letter to Willie's folks. What could I say? I told them that Willie had died like a hero.

That was the way of war—you had to cover up. The whole truth was too stark.

But there were some things which could not be hidden or ignored. There was the time when I was lucky enough to shoot down three enemy fighters within sight of all of Tel Aviv, all of them going into the sea. One of the Egyptian fighters was rescued and the first thing he demanded was to meet the fighter who had downed him. This Gyppo was supposed to be their "ace."

This made us all smile. The Gyppo fighters were, to put it bluntly, lousy. Not a man in my group had ever been shot down by an Egyptian; most of our losses were from flak or groundfire. The plain fact was that the Egyp-

tians were badly trained and inexperienced, no match for our men who had been seasoned in combat. It was like shooting ducks in a rain barrel.

This Gyppo pilot demanded to meet me, and raised a big clamor and fuss in Tel Aviv, which the papers recorded. The Israeli brass found themselves in the embarrassing position of finally being forced to recognize the men at Ramat David and the work they were doing. The name of Leon Baker began to be known. I was asked either to come to Tel Aviv and get my pictures taken with the downed Gyppo or at least to talk to him over the phone, with the reporters listening in.

I agreed to the latter; it was better than going to Tel Aviv.

In the C.O.'s office I heard the Egyptian's voice; he sounded like a young, confident fellow. And he was speaking with a refined British accent.

"Mr. Leon Baker?"

"Yes, that's right?"

"I'm the Egyptian Air Force officer you shot down outside Tel Aviv."

"Okay. Glad you weren't hurt."

After the French cut off supplies of arms and aircraft to Israel, the Israel Aircraft Industries designed and built their own fighter—the Kfir (Lion cub). It is also used by the Argentine Air Force. (IAF)

"You're an American, aren't you?"

Here it comes, I thought ruefully. Into the phone, I said: "That's right. Born and bred in the USA."

"Then why do you Americans come over and fight my people?" he demanded, his voice rising with indignation. "This is no fight or concern of yours. Your people and my people are not at war. Why do you do it—for money?"

"But your people and my people *are* at war," I said. "It's true that I'm an American. But I'm also a Jew."

There was a long silence. "Oh," he finally said.

"Yes, oh," I mimicked. "I saw some of your people's work. When *you* were shot down, you were rescued and you're nice and safe now. But what happened to Will Cannon, one of the Canadian boys in my squadron, when he was shot down? Do you want me to tell you?"

"Please do," he said politely.

"Okay, you asked for it. His fingers were broken off at the knuckles. A brass spike was driven into his anus. His guts were cut and drawn. His testicles were ripped off with a pincers, red-hot, because they found burned flesh around his groin. Then his throat was cut. And Willie Cannon wasn't even Jewish! He was a Canadian!"

There was a longer silence. Then . . . "He deserved it! It was none of his business, and

The U.S. filled the void left by the French and supplied A-4 Skyhawks. (IAF)

none of yours either, to come over here and fight us. I am told that you were also one of the pilots who bombed Cairo. I want to tell you that you missed your targets. You did little damage to the government buildings. Instead, you hit a slum area, killing hundreds of innocent men, women, and children. You hit the slum district of El-Baramony. You butcher! You killer! You . . ."

I hung up on Lieutenant Thotmos Salem.

All he meant to me was that I could add another of the funny little Egyptian hats to the nose of my plane.

THE WAR THEY WON IN 2½ HOURS

by General S.L.A. Marshall, USAR (Ret) and the Editors of American Heritage Magazine and UPI

In that least likely of all hours for achieving military surprise, between 0745 and 0815, on Monday, June the 5th, when the enemy camp was certain to be wide awake if not watchful and waiting, Israel went all out to destroy the fighting power of Egypt.

To begin, her combat forces had that one aim. Most of her resources, the preponderance of her heavy weapons, were concentrated in the blow aimed towards Suez and the Nile; the Israelis had decided merely to fence with the threat elsewhere against the nation's borders.

The pressures that compelled the decision for war had been mounting for weeks. Egypt's army had massed next to Israel's borders in the Gaza Strip and had heavily fortified the Sinai Peninsula in the strength of seven divisions, two of them armored. Nasser's soldiers stood everywhere behind permanent works heavily structured in concrete. Barring all main roads into Sinai were systematically entrenched and mined hedgehogs running miles deep.

Opposite this array Israel's army had marshalled three divisions and two independent brigades. The divisions were in fact task forces of between two and five brigades each, the greater number being ar-

mored brigades, under command of a temporary division headquarters, activated for the emergency. The generals of division had been identified with their brigades only in the several weeks gone since the call-up.

Israel's justification for the strike against Egypt—the purported, immediate provocation—is on record in the words of Brigadier General Yeshayahou Gavish, chief of the Southern Command at Beersheba: "The attack of the Egyptians started with movements of planes toward Israel, which were detected by our radar, and with the shelling of villages along the Gaza Strip."

There is no claim that these pips on a radar grid, allegedly seen to the west over the Mediterranean, ever materialized as an air armada violating Israel's space. Of the bombardment of numerous frontier village, however, there is adequate proof. Artillery and mortar shelling from beyond her borders was an affliction

MiG-17s parked at an airfield. This is the scene the IAF encountered when they eliminated the Egyptian, Syrian, Iraqi, and Jordanian Air Forces with unerring airborne cannon fire in 2½ hours. (USAF)

with which Israel had had to live more or less patiently for nineteen years.

When patience ended, plan took over according to a timetable that reads like the work force in an industrial plant changing shift and punching the clock. Having been told by the Army Chief of Staff, Major General Itzhak Rabin, at 0800 that the Egyptians were coming, Gavish could report at 0815 that three of his divisions were already moving on enemy territory. One column was advancing towards the Gaza Strip; the second was moving against Umm Gataf, a main Egyptian fortress organized around successive sub-ridges anchored on both sides to much higher, unflankable dunes and ridges, 30 miles southeast of El Arish; and the third division was slicing in between them, headed straight west over raw desert, roughing it where no road lay. One independent brigade was sparring toward Kuntilla in the south of Sinai with no intention of getting mauled in full-scale engagement.

To get away that fast, these several formations had to be already drawn up in march order, echeloned according to what combat would require of the columns from front to rear. They must have trained hard at it for some days; an armored division on the road stretches out twenty-five miles. Even so, the abrupt departure of these heavy columns to invade Sinai did not kill the last chance for peace-through-negotiation. That dim prospect had been scrubbed thirty minutes earlier at 0745. The further fate of the men in the desert had to be, for the anxious men at Zahal, Israel's defense establishment, temporarily a secondary consideration.

An air-raid warning had sounded at 0755 over Tel Aviv, an alarm hardly portentous of where the extreme trials of that morning would fall. Not a reconquest of Sinai's armed and arid wasteland but the preserving of Israel's interior through the destruction of Egypt's air power had become for Zahal the primary, dominating objective. While the alarm went on, a radio newscaster continued his scheduled report, completed it, then on the stroke of 0800, added quietly: "We are at war." In that way some of the public got the word. Early morning in Tel Aviv was otherwise almost normally calm, except at military headquarters. The sky was bright and cloudless. Following the all-clear, men and women proceeded on their routine rounds. Motor traffic had kept rolling, disregarding the alert. Things were a little different with the children. School had recessed with the mobilization so that students could take over the tasks of delivering mail, digging ditches, harvesting, and performing other work appropriate to older hands now in military service. It was a romp to be out of school (the joy ended when school doors reopened in mid-July to make up for lost time).

So when the clock struck eight, only one thing was more certain than that a new war had come: it would not be like the last war, in 1956. After that year the balance of heavy armament in the Near East had shifted radically against Israel—through Soviet assistance to Egypt, Iraq, and Syria in the form of modern tanks and military aircraft. Arab strength in tracked fighting vehicles and mobile guns was a lesser menace, although Egypt alone could field more Stalin-3, T-34, T-54, and T-55 tanks than Israel could muster in matching armor. Dramatically altering the problem was the all-around threat from Arab air bases. They could put up enough jet bombers, such as the TU-16 and IL-28, along with MiG-21 transsonic fighters and MiG-17s, to outnumber Israel's comparable types, like the Vautour bomber-fighter and the Mirage 111C, by better than two to one. With four air bases in Sinai, two of them new, Egypt could put MiGs over Tel Aviv in seven minutes, the flight time from El Arish.

Surprisingly, for Israel, June 5 did not bring total mobilization. Somewhere between twenty thousand and thirty thousand people had not been called up. Excluded was the civil-defense organization, a highly significant omission.

North of Tel Aviv at 0745 that morning there began at the several air bases a great

The French-built Dassault MD-450 Ouragan saw service with the IAF in the 1956 Sinai campaign. (IAF)

The Ouragans were joined in the conflict by the swept-wing Dassault Mystère. (IAF)

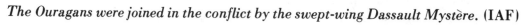

motion and stir: crews scrambling; fighting aircraft moving to the runways, some from underground hangars; planes taking off in formations of two, six, or eight,* the numbers varying according to the size and importance of the predesignated target. Such were the flight paths that farmers afield only a mile or so away might have wholly missed their going. The din and howl of this lift-off must have been deafening as group followed group low and to the west over blue water. But there was no confusion. All motion and tumult were directed toward one central purpose, little of which found echo in the nearby city. The people of Tel Aviv one month later still did not know at what time the air strike against Egypt was begun.

It was 0145 in New York and Washington when the attack order sent Israel's war planes winging toward the Nile, Suez, and Sinai— fifteen minutes before the armor was directed to roll for the borders. Those cities slept on, not knowing until 0330 that a new war was underway. By then its outcome was already virtually decided. There followed for Israel's High Command one suspense-filled hour, though not for her pilots.

First to take off was a formation of Vautour bomber-fighters of the deep penetration group. Theirs was to be the farthest journey, their target the bomber base at Luxor on the Nile, far to the southwest of Sharm-el-Sheikh and almost double the distance to Cairo. The key to the master plan was this: as to Egypt, it would be a synchronized attack, directed against eleven bases only. The lift-offs were timed and staged so that each formation fronting the first wave would go at its target in the same minute. Thereafter the same eleven bases would be pounded steadily for eighty minutes. Speed had been precisely measured against distance, without the aid of computers. Having tried and tested the mechanics of the staggered take-off, the Israelis knew it

could be done without fuss. There remained only the execution.

The eleven targeted fields whose destruction was expected to shock Egypt and superinduce in its air arm a state of near-paralysis were:

El Arish, Bir Gifgafa, Bir Tamada, and Jebel Libni in Sinai.
Abu Suer, Kabrit, and Fayid in the Canal zone.
Imshas, Cairo West, Beni Sueir, and Luxor in the Nile Valley.

All eleven were nominated and hit because they were the bases either for bombers or for MiG-21s, the hard core of the threat to Israel's interior. With the destruction of the fighter aircraft based on Sinai and the three fields of Suez, such MiGs as remained whole in Egypt would not have range enough to menace any city in Israel. The MiG is a short-legged aircraft.

Myth, often enough repeated, and especially when supported by arrows on a map, has a way of displacing fact. So it was that in the wake of the instant war, experts hypothesized about how Israel's airmen contrived the approach to Egypt to achieve full deception and accomplish total surprise. Most of the diagrams purporting to show the air strike have arrows indicating prolonged flight westward over the sea, then hooking back over the northeast corner of the Libyan Desert to approach the Nile from the west. Some show planes based on Beersheba hitting the Egyptian fields in Sinai.

None of this happened. There is an air base at Beersheba; its planes and pilots supported the armored attack into Sinai from the start. All the planes in the synchronized strike that smashed the eleven main bases took off from the runways near Tel Aviv. They flew west over the Mediterranean for a short distance. Those bound for the targets along the Nile then flew on a direct southwest course to their objectives. The Sinai-bound fighters, which are certain to have staged out last because of

---

*Gen. Ezer Weizman, in his book *On Eagles' Wings*, states that they flew in "foursomes." (Editor)

Israeli Vautour fighters. (IAF)

the short distance, flew almost due south.

So we might follow along a bit with the trail-blazing Vautours heading for Luxor some minutes before anyone in Tel Aviv's street crowd even knew there was a war. They moved out over a glass-smooth Mediterranean, which, for jets moving even at subsonic speed fifty to one hundred feet above the surface, is a far less friendly sea than one a bit choppy. They had to stay dangerously low lest they be picked up by enemy radar. At that level, a smooth sea means monotony, with the blending of water and sky, the loss of horizon, incessant strain in maintaining the proper altitude, and constant vigilance to avoid disaster in the form of ditching due to a slip in judgment.

The pilot leading that formation, an older colonel, in civilian life a specialist in aviation, selling his wares and ideas abroad, had been on a business trip to the United States when, on May 25th, he received an informal greeting relayed by his wife: "Come home, dear, defense needs you." With radios silent, the June 5th formation flew on toward Egypt. During the approach, as well as in actually striking at the target, the planes flew at maximum speed,

although none of the bombers or fighters flew at transsonic speed, since the war-loaded aircraft will not move that fast.

A few minutes past eight, and they were crossing the Egyptian coastline, rocketing along at tree-top level. Then should have come the first warning to the Egyptians, since, from that point on, direct observation of the Israelis' passage became unavoidable. Nothing happened. Without sign of any reaction below them, the planes flew on to Luxor without incident, rose five hundred feet in the air to bomb the runways and strafe the unbunkered TU-16s, which were neatly, evenly spaced on the apron and alongside the runways. These multimillion-dollar items—twin-jet medium bombers with a range of three thousand miles and a speed of six hundred miles per hour—blazed high right where the attackers had expected to find them. At Luxor the four 30-mm. cannon on the Vautours were the big killers of Egypt's Soviet-built aircraft. Much the same sort of thing was occurring at the other ten bases by the time the farthest-south Vautours were heading for home. At Israel's insistence, the French-built Mirages and Super Mystères had been modified to carry two 30-mm. guns instead of their original rockets. Thus, Israeli pilots beat Egypt's air force to death with cannon fire. It was so accurate that correspondents credited the devastation to a new secret weapon, something that smelled out the vulnerable heart of a sitting aircraft and went right to it. To attribute what happened to the magic of expert gunnery sounded much too simple.

Thus for eighty minutes, more of the same was delivered against the seven fields in the Canal zone and along the Nile. It was judged soon after the first strike that the MiGs based on Sinai were all burned to ash and wrecked metal. There followed a respite of perhaps twenty minutes. Then for eighty minutes more, the air force went at Egypt again.

Syrian and Iraqi bases went untouched through the morning. Only twelve fighting aircraft were left at the Tel Aviv bases to defend Israel. None was put up as a screen to the north or east, and when at last that was deemed advisable, only eight took to the air.

The mastermind of this plan, without doubt the greatest gamble with the largest payoff in the history of military aviation, sat in his unpretentious command post at Tel Aviv, supremely confident that it would work. At age thirty-nine, about one year earlier, Brigadier

General Mordechai Hod had taken command of an air force that weight-for-weight was probably the most effective fighting machine anywhere, made so largely by his predecessor, Brigadier General Ezer Weizman, now Deputy for Operations.* Weizman shaped the tools and trained the men. Hod was the man with the big idea.

Hod belonged to the first class of pilots ever to win wings in Israel, this on March 14, 1949. A third-generation Sabra (native-born Israeli), he had taken his first flight training in Czechoslovakia in 1948, then converted to jets in England. Married, the father of three children, this chief is anything but a martial type, despite his trim figure and erect bearing. A warm man, given to gentle humors, with a twinkle in his eye, especially when he speaks English as if he were not quite sure of himself, he participates keenly, agrees enthusiastically, and disagrees fairly. Hod would be good company in any circle. There is not a bit of side to him. He deals with people as if he enjoys them.

There were some simple reasons for his conviction that he could win the battle for

*Deputy of Operations of the entire Israeli Defense Force. (Editor)

A French Super Mystère B-1, similar to those acquired by the IAF. (USAF)

Israel over Cairo. He calculated that it would take the Egyptians one hour to assess what had happened and a second hour to agree on what could be done about it. He was convinced that when hit, they would not tell the truth to their allies. Instead, they would proclaim a victory, disarming in its effect. Syria and Iraq he could not take seriously; they were just an inconvenience. But he made one mistake. Instead of a lag of two hours, the Egyptians gave him four hours. Long before that it was all over. The planes of the first wave had all returned to home base by 0900. It was then that Hod put up the screen to the north. By the time the operation had been going for two hours fifty minutes, or at approximately 1100, he was able to report to Minister of Defense Moshe Dayan: "I am certain that there is not another bomber left in Egypt."

Yet he did so like a man walking in a dream. His intellect told him that his calculations must have worked out. His emotions simply refused to accept it. It was something too big for acceptance by his whole being at one time. Not until the following morning did it become matter-of-fact, past and proved.

During the days of strain before war's outbreak, as he braced for the problem, Hod had been almost alone in his high optimism. His political superiors, and some of the generals, looked askance. The plan was too bold; should it fail, ruin could result. They attributed its venturesomeness to the impetuosity of youth, which Hod at two-score took as a left-handed compliment.

Whereas people may ask if Hod is a genius, simplicity is his favorite word, the key to his system. He believes that modern air power has become oversophisticated; there is so much gadgetry that too little time is left for relentless schooling and practice in the fundamentals. His average pilot on that day was twenty-two and had begun his training in jets at eighteen, as a high-school graduate. Making the pilots' shooting more precise was a simple instrument Hod and his people had devised to keep the target in frame, an instrument they substituted for a French-made elec-

tronic wonder that came with the plane, rejected because testing proved that one factor had been overlooked. It was another simple calculation that at 0800 the Egyptians at the eleven air bases would have taken a break for a spot of tea. Leaving unscathed Egypt's additional fourteen bases was reckoned a safe enough risk by General Hod.

Knowing by 1100 that he had won the air battle in Egypt, Hod began shifting bombers and fighters to Sinai to support the attack by the armored columns. Around noon he began the air attack on the bases of Jordan and Syria and continued it through most of June 5th. But they were in effect finished after one hour. The only Iraqi base strafed was H-3,

General (Aluf) Ezer Weizman earned his wings with the RAF in a Spitfire during World War II. As commander of the IAF, he was the man most responsible for the growth training and over-all improvements in strength it has seen. He later served as Minister of Defense. (IAF)

General (Aluf) Mordechai Hod (left) commanded the IAF during the Six-Day War. Here, he is turning command over to General (Aluf) Benny Pelled, who headed the IAF during the Yom Kippur War. (IAF)

along the pipeline, just east of the border of the Jordan panhandle. One squadron of MiG-21s had set down there just in time to go out like a light. Habaniya, near Baghdad, was not attacked, being beyond range of Israel's bombers.

A third or more of Nasser's war planes remained in condition to fight. Well aware of it, Hod had no intention of renewing the assault on the bases. There had been no dogfights; not one MiG had risen to challenge a Mirage. So Egypt's pilots would always have an excuse for themselves: "We were given no chance to show what we could do." If their morale was to be shattered irreparably, it would have to be done in the air east of Suez. So here was the implicit invitation to come on and try. The air-to-air dueling started that Monday afternoon somewhat west of the Bir Gifgafa-Jebel Libni line and continued into Tuesday. There were growls and gripes from Israel's soldiers fighting below when the MiGs first appeared above them. Hod heard

rumbles like this: "Look, you said you destroyed their air force; it's still around." Until cured, it had to be endured. Egypt threw SAM missiles into the air fight from the park west of the Mitla Pass, a fact that went unreported. There are entries in the record; an Israeli pilot said casually: "Hey, one of those blazing telephone poles is after me." No harm was done by the SAMs; Israel's fighters were flying too low.

Some of the story is told in statistics. Hod's people flew only 492 sorties to kill 402 enemy planes on the ground. All told, Israel's forces destroyed 452 planes; some were gunned down by antiaircraft batteries. There were thirty-one dogfights near Suez and above western Sinai; five Egyptian planes were shot down, not one Israeli plane. Hod lost twenty-five pilots, twenty-four of them when their ships were shot down by ground fire; the other man died as a forward observer with the army. Yet the 492 sorties were the lesser part of the work load; airmen flew nearly a thou-

The French-built Mirage did valiant duty in practically annihilating the combined Arab Air Forces in the Six-Day War of 1967. (IAF)

French-designed and Israeli-built, the Fouga Magister flew combat missions despite its trainer status. (IAF)

sand sorties in support of the armored advance into Sinai.

Hod was above all elated by the performance of the Fougas. The Fouga Magister, built in Israel, is the basic trainer for jet pilots, and this relatively slow schooling craft had been souped up with two machine guns and thirty-six rockets to operate as a tank-killer over Sinai. Older men—El Al pilots and others from civilian life—had been called back to man this fleet. These turtles of the air force destroyed more than seventy Egyptian artillery pieces, took on the enemy armor wherever they found it, and softened the base camps before the armored spearheads came up. Their over-all contribution to quick victory is incalculable.

Hod learned that he had sorely underestimated the resources of his men and their machines. He had expected three to four sorties a day from the average pilot; he got an average of seven, and some went as high as ten. He figured the standard of gunnery established in peacetime training would drop during combat; instead, it rose. He anticipated that the serviceability of aircraft would slip steadily downward once fighting started. To begin, it was ninety-nine per cent, and it held that way through six days.

One young pilot shot down four enemy planes. In between number two and number three he was hospitalized for a wound, then ducked back to duty without permission. But for the wasted time, he might have become Israel's first ace.

The blow dealt Egypt by General Hod's men and machines on the morning of June 5th doomed President Nasser's hope for any military success against Israel.

Defense Minister Moshe Dayan, himself a dirt soldier, was quick to point out that decision was never in doubt thereafter. So there *was* something new under the sun: for the first time, air power had effectively won a war.

An IAF 2-seater, trainer model of the F-16. (General Dynamics)

THE RAMADAN WAR, 1973: *
The Arab Viewpoint

by Brig. General Hassan el Badri,
Egyptian Armed Forces
Brig. General Taha el Magdoub,
Egyptian Armed Forces
Brig. General Mohammed Dia el
Din Zohdy, Egyptian Armed
Forces

Never before had Egyptian pilots gone through an aerial war with Israel, for in the two previous rounds the enemy surprised our planes on the ground and destroyed them. British Canberra planes and French Mysteres, acting on behalf of Israel,** did this during the 1956 war. The incident was repeated in 1967 by the Israeli air forces.*** After both of these wars, our land and naval forces were in a most awkward position, devoid of air cover.

But the Ramadan War was totally different. † Aerial fighting was in full force from the very first moments of the war to the end. Operation Badr started by dealing the enemy a concentrated surprise blow by air. There followed a ferocious air battle, which increased in tempo until our air force had accomplished all of its assigned missions. The air force emerged stronger, more experienced,

*The Arab name for the Yom Kippur war.
**In the Sinai Campaign, the British and French were allies of Israel.
***This was the Six-Day War.

†Because the Arabs were well-armed with Soviet SAM-6 missiles.

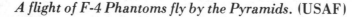

A flight of F-4 Phantoms fly by the Pyramids. (USAF)

Model of an Egyptian Air Force MiG-21. (Minicraft/Hasegawa)

and more capable. Behind this successful achievement was persistent work, started with great determination and resolution the moment the fires on Egyptian airfields were put out at the end of the Third Round.

At once preparations were made to increase the number of pilots considerably. This long and exhausting operation took five or six years. At the same time the number of air-force technicians, engineers, and ground-crew members was increased. This also took a long time. Then a great network of airfields was established all over Egypt to absorb the great number of planes and pilots.

The first lesson learned from the 1967 disaster was the necessity of protecting planes on the airfields. A large number of solid concrete shelters was built at every airfield and air base. Thanks to them, the watchful air-defense forces, and fighter protection, not one plane was hit on the ground in the Ramadan War. Planes took no more than two minutes to leave their concrete shelters and zoom skyward toward their objectives.

The second lesson was the necessity of training commanders to assess situations accurately, make sound decisions, and exercise strict control. To achieve this many exercises were held, studies were made, and many missions were sent abroad. As a result our armed forces in general had efficient commanders.

All of this took backbreaking effort and was carried out under the most difficult conditions. Fighting never really stopped, and the War of Attrition ate up quite a lot of effort. But the great success of the Ramadan War justified it.

Operation Badr started with a concentrated air attack, well-coordinated between the Egyptian and Syrian fronts and other services of the Arab armed forces. Our 250 aircraft soared eastward simultaneously toward their carefully selected objectives. Each air formation had both a primary objective and an alternative objective. Those to be destroyed included: the Meleez, Thamad, and Ras Nasrani airfields; ten Hawk surface-to-air missiles; two long-range artillery positions; three radar positions and direction and warning stations; two interference and jamming stations in the Sinai (Om Khushaib and Om Margam); three logistics areas; and the strongpoint east of Port Fuad.

At dawn on the seventh of October our fighters intercepted enemy air attacks on our airfields. Violent air battles took place on the seventh, eight, ninth, and tenth of October, north of the Delta, with sixty to seventy Israeli planes involved in each. Our planes, in cooperation with the air-defense system, succeeded in hitting and destroying many enemy planes and preventing them from achieving their objectives. They were obliged to dump their bombs and rockets in open spaces, except for a few that succeeded in reaching our airfields. They caused only minor damage, which required only a few hours to repair.

Between the seventh and the twentieth of October, the Israelis tried to attack ten Egyptian airfields: Qattamia, Mansourah, Salehiah, Tanta, Shebraweet, Gianaclis, Quesna, Abu Hammand, Beni Suef, and Bir Arida. In the first, and most important attack, on the seventh of October, they tried to attack seven airfields. Thereafter only one to four airfields were attacked each day, for the Israelis realized that they had totally failed to oust the Egyptian air forces from the battle. For instance, although they attacked Qattamia six times with 166 sorties, and Mansourah five times with 66 sorties, both continued to operate very efficiently throughout the war. As of October twenty-first the enemy stopped attacking airfields completely.

For twenty-two days our air forces successfully flew cover over our ground operations.

Then, with the development of the enemy enclave west of the canal, the Suez and Fayed areas were the scenes of desperate air battles. Over seventy fighter planes on each side participated in fatal and close fighting that in some instances continued for an hour or more. There were fifty air battles, of which eight were major ones. Approximately ninety enemy planes were downed over the northern part of the Delta, Port Said, Fayed, and Suez. Israeli pilot First Lieutenant Avee Hayeem Alkalai, taken prisoner by our forces, said, "I believe the Egyptian air forces have reached the highest level of efficiency. I never expected that Egyptian planes would attack ours. I observed one air battle in which three Phantoms were downed, leaving the Egyptian planes in full control."

From early morning of October 7 our air forces bombed the enemy's operational reserves, inflicting heavy losses in tanks, equipment, weapons, and personnel. Squadrons of Sukhoi fighter bombers, MiG-17s, and MiG-21s attained records in the rates of hitting and destroying enemy targets. They flew more than 1000 sorties.

Direct air support of both field armies was achieved with great skill and coordination. Approximately 3000 air support sorties were flown.

An Israeli Phantom coming in for a landing. (IAF)

A MiG-21 in flight. (USAF)

Egyptian helicopers also performed well. They dashed to their assigned missions of landing Ranger troops deep inside southern and northern Sinai. This surprised, confused, and paralyzed the enemy, impeding his maneuvers and blocking supply lines. Our helicopters continued to supply the troops so that they could continue fighting day and night under the most difficult and dangerous circumstances.

Our bombers dropped hundreds of tons of bombs and missiles over the Sedr and Tor airfields. They annihilated and scattered concentrated armored and motorized forces that infiltrated toward Deversoir, destroying bridges and command posts. Bombers also played a great role in protecting political and economic objectives, standing ready to check should the enemy try to bomb civil objectives, especially after President Sadat declared before the battle that it would be "an eye for an eye, interior for interior, and napalm for napalm."

The other air functions too were significant.

Recently furnished F-16s reputedly were used in the 1981 attack. (General Dynamics)

U.S.-built F-16 Eagles were also reportedly employed in the 1300-mile mission against the Baghdad reactor. The Israelis had to cross three enemy borders—twice. (IAF)

Reconnaissance formations accomplished many successful missions before, during, and after the war. They were of great value in following up enemy counter-operations, detecting and thwarting them. Air force technicians and engineers kept the planes at the highest level of efficiency. They succeeded in refueling and rearming planes with ammunition and bombs in no more than six minutes. But they did not boast of this as Israel did in 1967 when its technicians accomplished the same in seven and one-half minutes.

A measure of the extent to which the enemy was impressed with the threat of Egyptian air operations is the fact that Israel devoted approximately half its fighters to fly cover over Sinai. Of the total 10,322 combat sorties that the Israelis flew on the Egyptian front from the sixth to the twenty-second of October, 4098 were flown as air cover.

APPENDICES

The Top Aces of All Wars and All Nations

World War I, 1914–1918

THE ALLIES

American

A total of 117 Americans shot down five or more enemy aircraft to become aces. This includes victories gained while serving with the French and British, but only those who eventually served in the U. S. Air Service are listed.* Here are the first five:

	Victories
Captain Edward V. Rickenbacker	26
Lieutenant Frank Luke, Jr.	21
Major Raoul Lufbery	17
Lieutenant George A. Vaughn, Jr.	13
Captain Field E. Kindley	12

*For example Captain W. C. Lambert, an American, scored 22 victories with the RAF.

French

There were a total of 160 aces in the French Aviation Service. Following are those who head the list:

	Victories
Captain René Fonck	75
Captain Georges Guynemer	53
Lieutenant Charles Nungesser	45
Lieutenant Georges Madon	41
Lieutenant Maurice Boyeau	35

British

Some 550 British fighter pilots, including Commonwealth nations (Canada, Australia, New Zealand, Ireland, South Africa) downed five enemy aircraft each to qualify as aces. There were also nineteen Americans in their ranks. (Officially, the British did not recognize the designation, and in fact considered ten victories as the minimum.) These are the top five:

	Victories
Major Edward "Mick" Mannock	73
Lieutenant Colonel William A. Bishop (Canada)	72
Major Raymond Collishaw (Canada)	68
Captain James B. McCudden	58
Captain A. Weatherby Beauchamp-Proctor (South Africa)	54

North Vietnamese

Colonel Nguyen Tomb	13 +
Captain Nguyen Van Boy	7 +

Belgian

Tiny Belgium produced a total of five aces:

	Victories
Lieutenant Willy Coppens	34
Lieutenant Edmond Thieffry	10
Adjutant Andre de Meulemeester	10
Captain Fernand Jacquet	7
Lieutenant Jan Olieslagers	6

Italian

Among the forty-three Italian fliers who qualified as aces were:

	Victories
Major Francesco Baracca	36
Lieutenant Silvio Scaroni	26
Major Pier Ruggiero Piccio	24
Lieutenant Flavio Barracchini	21
Captain Fulco Ruffo di Calabria	20

Russian

Because of the Russian Revolution and the loss and destruction of official records, the total number of Russian aces will never be known. The following five head the list of those whose records remained or were reconstructed:

	Victories
Captain Alexander Kazakov	17
Captain P. d'Argueef	15
Lieutenant Commander Alexander P. de Seversky*	13
Lieutenant I. Smirnoff	12
Lieutenant M. Safonov	11

*Later commissioned Major in United States Air Service. Founded the company that produced the P-36, P-47, F-94, F-105, and A-10.

CENTRAL POWERS (THE ENEMY)

German

Heading the list of more than 300 German aces was *Rittmeister* Manfred von Richthofen, also known as the "Red Baron" because of his all-red Fokker and Albatros fighters. He was leader of the famous "Flying Circus" and was the ranking ace of both sides—friend and foe—in the First World War.

	Victories
Rittmeister Manfred *Frhr.* von Richthofen	80
Oberleutnant Ernst Udet	62
Oberleutnant Erich Loewenhardt	53
Leutnant Werner Voss	48
Leutnant Fritz Rumey	45

Austro-Hungarian

Like the British, the Austro-Hungarians considered only those with ten or more victories as aces. However, some thirty of their pilots downed more than five enemy aircraft apiece.

	Victories
Hauptmann Godwin Brumowski	40
Leutnant Julius Arigi	32
Leutnant Frank Linke-Crawford	30
Leutnant Benno Fiala	29
Leutnant Josef Kiss	19

Spanish Civil War, 1936–1939

REPUBLICAN (LOYALIST)

Colonel Andres Garcia Lacalle	11
Captain Jose Bravo Fernandez	10
Captain Zarauza Manuel Clavier	10
Captain Miguel Zamudio Martinez	10

NATIONALIST (INSURGENT)

Major Joaquin Garcia Morato	40
Major Julio Salvador Diaz	23
Major Angel Salas Larrazabal	22
Captain Manuel Vasquez Sagaztizobal	22

World War II, 1939–1945
THE ALLIES

United States Army Air Force

Major Richard L. Bong	40
Major Thomas B. McGuire	38
Colonel Francis S. Gabreski	31
Lieutenant Colonel Robert S. Johnson	28
Colonel Charles H. MacDonald	27

United States Navy and Marine Corps

Captain David McCampbell (USN)	34
Lieutenant Colonel Gregory Boyington (USMC)	28*
Major Joseph Jacob Foss (USMC)	26
First Lieutenant Robert M. Hanson (USMC)	25
Lieutenant Cecil E. Harris (USN)	24

*Including 6 with "Flying Tigers"

British

Squadron Leader Marmaduke T. St. J. Pattle (So. Africa)	41
Group Captain John E. "Johnnie" Johnson (British)	38
Group Captain Adolf G. "Sailor" Malan (So. Africa)	35
Wg. Cdr. Brendan "Paddy" Finucane (Ireland)	32
Flt. Lt. George F. Beurling (Canada)	31⅓

USSR

Grds. Maj. Ivan Kozhedub	62
Grds. Col. Aleksandr Pokryshkin	59
Grds. Cpt. Dimitriy Glinka	56

Grds. Cpt. Grigoriy Rechkalov	56
Grds. Cpt. Kirill A. Yevstigneev	56

China

Colonel Liu Chi-Sun	11½
Lieutenant Wang Kuang-Fu	8½
Major Kao Yu-Hsin	8
Major Kuan Tan	8
Captain Yuan Pao-Kang	8

France

Lieutenant Pierre Clostermann (RAF)	33
Capitaine Marcel Albert	23
Commandant Jean E. F. DeMozay (Oka Marloix)	21
Lieutenant Pierre LeGloan	18
Capitaine Edmond Marin la Meslée	16

Norway

Lieutenant Colonel Sven Heglund	15⅓
Lieutenant Colonel Werner Christie	11
Captain Helmar Gundt-Spang	10⅓
Colonel Kaj Birksted (Denmark)	10
Major Martin Y. Gran	9½

THE AXIS (THE ENEMY)

Germany

Major Erich Hartmann	352
Major Gerhard Barkhorn	301
Major Gunther Rall	275
Oberleutnant Otto Kittel	267
Oberstleutnant Walter Nowotny	258

Italy

Major Adriano Visconti	26
Lieutenant Franco Bordoni-Bisleri	24
Lieutenant Leonardo Ferrulli	20

Japan

C.W.O. Hiroyoshi Nishizawa (Navy)	104
Lieutenant Tetsuzo Iwamoto (Navy)	80
C.W.O. Shoichi Sugita (Navy)	80
Lieutenant Saburo Sakai (Navy)	64
C.W.O. Hiromichi Shinohara (Army)	58

Korean War, 1950–1953

United States Air Force

Captain Joseph McConnell, Jr.	16
Major James Jabara	15*
Major Manuel J. Fernandez	14½

Major George A. Davis, Jr.	14*
Colonel Royal N. Baker	13*

*Each is credited with additional victories from World War II.

U.S. Navy & Marine Corps

Major John F. Bolt (USMC)	6
Commander Guy P. Bordelon (USN)	5

The Vietnam War, 1965-73

United States

Captain Charles D. DeBellevue* (USAF)	6
Lieutenant Randy Cunningham (USN)	5
Lieutenant William Driscoll* (USN)	5
Captain Jeffrey S. Feinstein* (USAF)	5
Captain Richard S. "Steve" Ritchie (USAF)	5

*Weapons System Officer (WSO) or Radar Intercept Officer (RIO)

Top Planes of All Wars

First World War

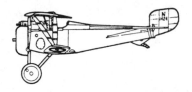
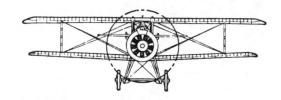
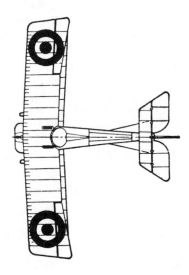

Nieuport 17

Wingspan: 27 ft.
Weight: 1,246 lb.
Length: 18 ft. 10 in.
Engine: 110-hp Le Rhone rotary
Speed: 107 mph at 6,500 ft.
Armament: 1 Lewis gun on upper wing or 1 fixed
Vickers machine gun on fuselage

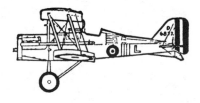
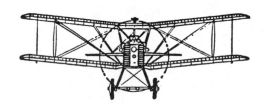
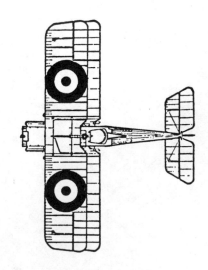

SE 5a

Wingspan: 26 ft. 7½ in.
Weight: 1,988 lb.
Length: 20 ft. 11 in.
Engine: 200-, 220-, or 240-hp Hispano-Suiza,
also 200-hp Wolsely W4a Viper Vee
Speed: 120 mph at 15,000 ft.
Armament: 1 fixed Vickers machine gun on
fuselage and 1 Lewis gun on
upper wing

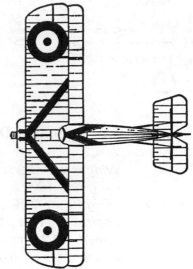

Sopwith Camel F 1

Wingspan: 28 ft.
Length: 18 ft. 8 in.
Weight: 1,453 lb.
Engine: 110-hp Le Rhone rotary or 130-hp Clerget rotary
Speed: 113 mph (Clerget) at 10,000 ft.
Armament: 2 fixed Vickers machine guns

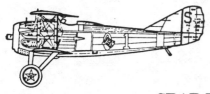

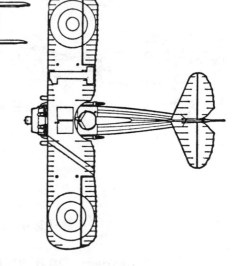

SPAD XIII

Wingspan: 26 ft. 4 in.
Length: 20 ft. 8 in.
Weight: 1,807 lb.
Engine: 220-hp Hispano-Suiza (1917) or 235-hp Hispano-Suiza (1918)
Speed: 134 mph (220 hp), 139 mph (235 hp) at 6,560 ft.
Armament: 2 fixed Vickers machine guns

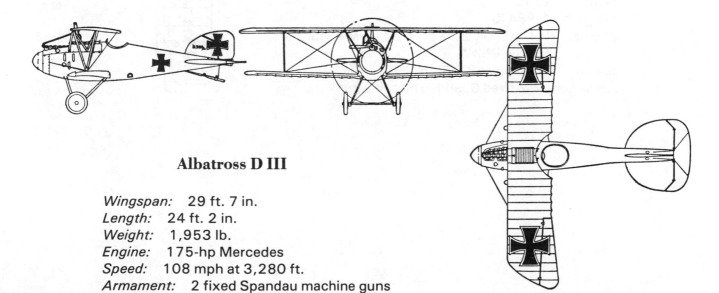

Albatross D III

Wingspan: 29 ft. 7 in.
Length: 24 ft. 2 in.
Weight: 1,953 lb.
Engine: 175-hp Mercedes
Speed: 108 mph at 3,280 ft.
Armament: 2 fixed Spandau machine guns

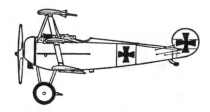
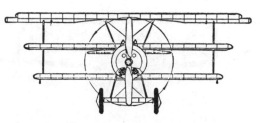
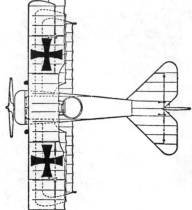

Fokker Dr I Triplane

Wingspan: 23 ft. 7 in.
Length: 19 ft.
Weight: 1,289 lb.
Engine: 110-hp Oberursel rotary
Speed: 122 mph at 8,900 ft.
Armament: 2 fixed Spandau machine guns

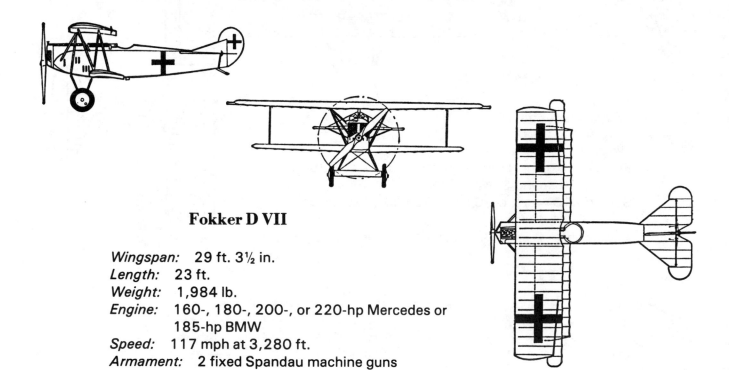

Fokker D VII

Wingspan: 29 ft. 3½ in.
Length: 23 ft.
Weight: 1,984 lb.
Engine: 160-, 180-, 200-, or 220-hp Mercedes or
              185-hp BMW
Speed: 117 mph at 3,280 ft.
Armament: 2 fixed Spandau machine guns

Spanish Civil War

  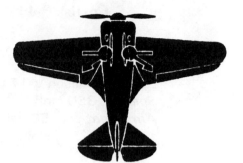

Polikarpov I-16 "Rata"

Wingspan: 29 ft. 6½ in.
Length: 19 ft. 11 in.
Engine: 480-hp M-22 9-cylinder radial
Speed: 224 mph
Armament: 2 7.62-mm machine guns, plus bombs

Fiat CR-32

Wingspan: 31 ft. 2 in.
Length: 24 ft. 5 in.
Engine: 600-hp Fiat A30
Speed: 233 mph
Armament: 2 12.7-mm machine
          guns

World War II

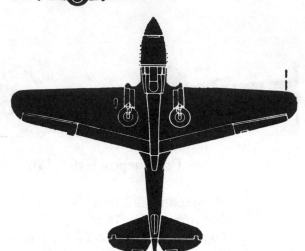

Curtiss P-40 Warhawk

Wingspan: 37 ft. 4 in.
Length: 31 ft. 9 in.
Engine: Allison V-1710-33/1,040 hp
Speed: 360 mph
Armament: 2 .50-caliber and 4 .30-caliber
machine guns

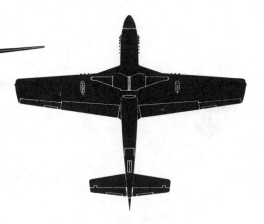

North American P-51 Mustang

Wingspan: 37 ft.
Length: 32 ft. 3 in.
Engine: Rolls Royce Merlin V-1650/1,495 hp
Speed: 437 mph
Armament: 6 .50-caliber machine guns

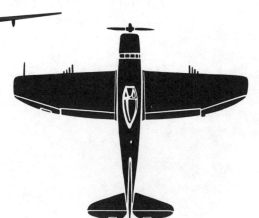

Republic P-47 Thunderbolt

Wingspan: 42 ft. 6 in.
Length: 36 ft. 1 in.
Engine: Pratt & Whitney R-2800/2,300 hp
Speed: 433 mph at 30,000 ft.
Armament: 8 .50-caliber machine guns and 1
bomb

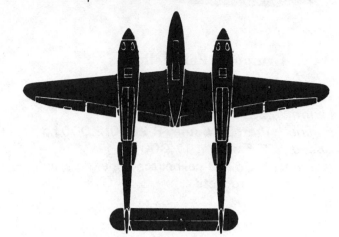

Lockheed P-38 Lightning

Wingspan: 52 ft.
Length: 37 ft. 10 in.
Engine: 2 Allison V-1710-89-91/1,425 hp each
Speed: 414 mph at 25,000 ft.
Armament: 1 20-mm cannon, 4 .50-caliber
machine guns, 2 1,600-lb. bombs
or 10 5-in. rockets

Bell P-39 Airacobra

Wingspan: 34 ft.
Length: 30 ft.
Engine: Allison V-1710-35 Vee/1,150 hp
Speed: 368 mph at 13,800 ft.
Armament: 37-mm cannon, 6 .30-caliber machine
guns, 1 500-lb. bomb

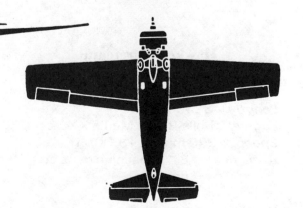

Grumman F4F Wildcat

Wingspan: 38 ft.
Length: 28 ft. 9 in.
Engine: Pratt & Whitney R-1830-76/1,200 hp
Speed: 330 mph at 21,000 ft.
Armament: 4 .50-caliber machine guns, 2 100-lb
bombs

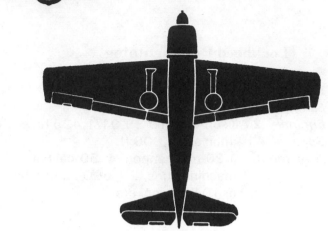

Grumman F6F Hellcat

Wingspan: 42 ft. 10 in.
Length: 33 ft. 7 in.
Engine: Pratt & Whitney R-2800/2,000 hp
Speed: 375 mph at 17,300 ft.
Armament: 6 .50-caliber machine guns and
                  rockets

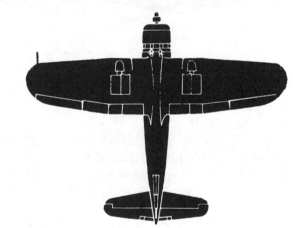

Chance Vought F4U Corsair

Wingspan: 41 ft.
Length: 33 ft. 4 in.
Engine: Pratt & Whitney R-2800/2,000 hp
Speed: 417 mph at 19,900 ft.
Armament: 6 .50-caliber machine guns

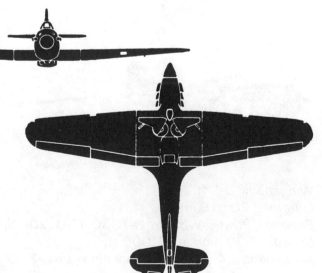

Hawker Hurricane

Wingspan: 40 ft.
Length: 32 ft. 2¼ in.
Engine: Rolls-Royce Merlin XX Vee/1,300 hp
Speed: 330 mph at 18,000 ft.
Armament: 8-12 machine guns or 4 20-mm
                  cannons

Supermarine Spitfire

Wingspan: 40 ft. 2 in.
Length: 31 ft. 4 in.
Engine: Rolls-Royce Merlin 64 Vee/1,710 hp
Speed: 408 mph at 25,000 ft.
Armament: 2 20-mm cannons and 2 .303-caliber
machine guns

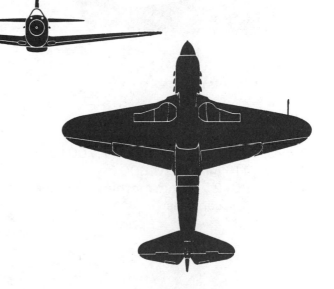

Yakovlev YAK-3

Wingspan: 30 ft. 2 in.
Length: 27 ft. 9 in.
Engine: Klimov M-105PF2/1,222 hp
Speed: 403 mph at 16,400 ft.
Armament: 1 20-mm cannon and 2 12.7-mm
machine guns

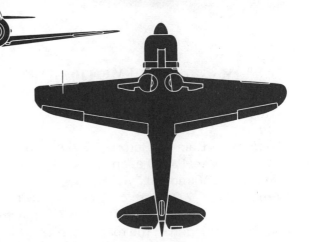

Lavochkin La-5

Wingspan: 32 ft. 2 in.
Length: 27 ft. 10 in.
Engine: Shvetsov M-82FN radial/1,650 hp
Speed: 402 mph at 16,400 ft.
Armament: 2 20-mm cannons and 6 132-mm
rockets or 2 331-lb. bombs

Messerschmitt ME 109

Wingspan: 32 ft. 4½ in.
Length: 28 ft. 4 in.
Engine: Daimler-Benz DB 601Aa inverted
Vee/1,150 hp
Speed: 370 mph at 22,000 ft.
Armament: 2 7.9-mm machine guns and 2 20-mm
cannons

Focke-Wulf F.W. 190

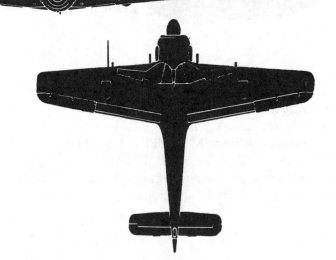

Wingspan: 34 ft. 5½ in.
Length: 28 ft. 10½ in.
Engine: BMW 801 D-2 radial/1,700 hp
Speed: 416 mph at 20,600 ft.
Armament: 2 7.9-mm machine guns and 2 20-mm
cannons

Messerschmitt ME 110

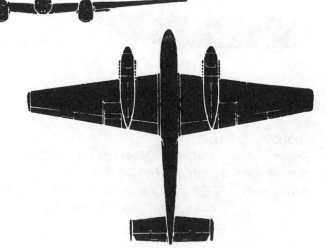

Wingspan: 53 ft. 4 in.
Length: 39 ft. 7 in.
Engine: 2 Daimler-Benz DB 601A-1 inverted
Vee/1,100 each
Speed: 336 mph at 19,685 ft.
Armament: 2 20-mm cannons, 4 7.9-mm machine
guns and 1 flexible 7.9-mm machine
gun in the rear cockpit

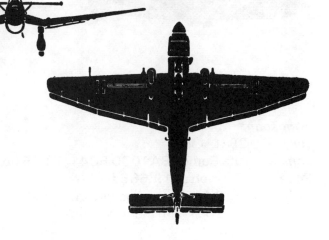

Junkers Ju-87 Stuka

Wingspan: 45 ft. 3 in.
Length: 37 ft. 9 in.
Engine: Jumo 211J-1 inverted Vee/1,400 hp
Speed: 255 mph at 13,500 ft.
Armament: 2 7.9-mm machine guns, 2 flexible
7.9-mm machine guns in rear
cockpit, 1 1,102-lb. bomb and 2 loads
of anti-personnel bombs

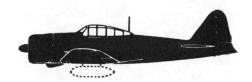
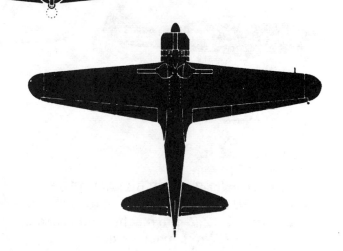

Mitsubishi A6M2 Zero (Zeke)

Wingspan: 39 ft. 5 in.
Length: 29 ft. 9 in.
Engine: Nakojimi Sakae 12 radial/940 hp
Speed: 332 mph at 14,950 ft.
Armament: 2 7.7-mm machine guns, 2 20-mm
cannons, and 2 152-lb. bombs

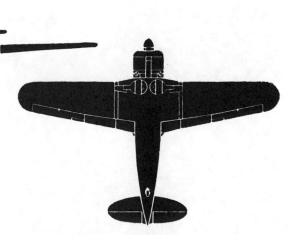

Fiat G-50

Wingspan: 35 ft. 9 in.
Length: 7 ft. 2 in.
Engine: Fiat A.74RC3P radial/870 hp
Speed: 302 mph at 19,685 ft.
Armament: 2 12.7-mm machine guns

Macchi MC-202

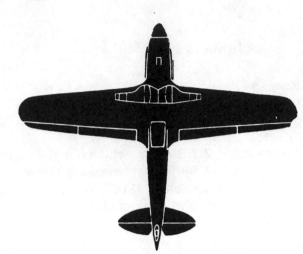

Wingspan: 34 ft. 8 in.
Length: 29 ft. 1 in.
Engine: Alfa Romeo RA1000 RC41/1,075 hp
Speed: 370 mph at 19,685 ft.
Armament: 2 12.7-mm machine guns and
2 7.7-mm machine guns

Reggiane RE-2001

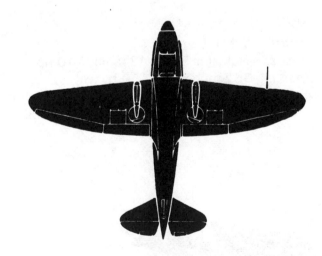

Wingspan: 36 ft.
Length: 27 ft. 4 in.
Engine: Daimler-Benz DB 601A/1,150 hp
Speed: 350 mph at 17,875 ft.
Armament: 2 12.7-mm machine guns and 2
7.7-mm machine guns

Korean War

At the start of the war the United States used piston-engine P-51's and Corsairs. The North Koreans and the Peoples Republic of China also employed Soviet World War II prop-driven aircraft.

Lockheed F-80 Shooting Star

Wingspan: 38 ft. 11 in.
Length: 34 ft. 6 in.
Engine: J33-A—23/4,250 lb. thrust
Speed: 512 knots at 10,000 ft.
Armament: 6 .50-caliber machine guns

North American F-86 Saber

Wingspan: 37 ft. 1 in.
Length: 37 ft. 6 in.
Engine: General Electric J47 single-shaft
  turbojet/5,000 lb. thrust
Armament: 6 .50-caliber machine guns

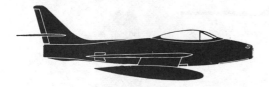

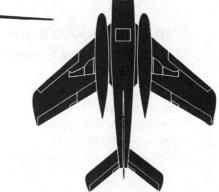

Republic F-84F Thunderstreak

Wingspan: 33 ft. 6 in.
Length: 43 ft. 3 in.
Engine: Wright J-85W/7,200 lb. thrust
Speed: 658 mph at 20,000 ft.
Armament: 6 .50-caliber 5-in. rockets

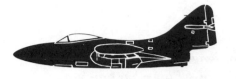

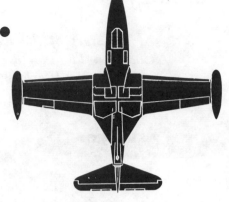

Grumman F9F-2 Panther

Wingspan: 38 ft.
Length: 37 ft. 8 in.
Engine: Pratt & Whitney J42P or J33A/5,750 lb. thrust
Speed: 526 mph at 22,000 ft.
Armament: 4 20-mm cannons

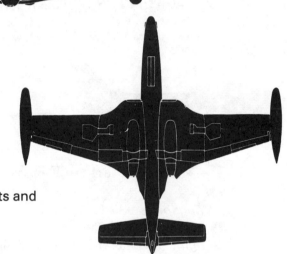

McDonnell F2H-Banshee

Wingspan: 41 ft. 7 in.
Length: 40 ft. 2 in.
Engine: 2 J34/3,250 lb. thrust each
Speed: 515 knots at sea level
Armament: 4 20-mm cannons, 8 5-in. rockets and bombs

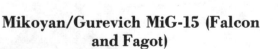
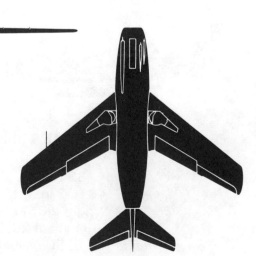

Mikoyan/Gurevich MiG-15 (Falcon and Fagot)

Wingspan: 32 ft. 2 in.
Length: 32 ft. 8 in.
Engine: VK-1/6,000 lb. thrust
Speed: 575 knots
Armament: 1 37-mm cannon or 2 23-mm cannons

Vietnam War

McDonnell Douglas F-4
Phantom II

Wingspan: 38 ft. 5 in.
Length: 58 ft. 3 in.
Engine: 2 General Electric J79-8 turbojets with
afterburner/17,000 lb. thrust each
Speed: 1,600 mph
Armament: 6–8 air-to-air rockets and a 20-mm
Gotling gun

Vought A-7 Corsair II

Wingspan: 38 ft. 9 in.
Length: 46 ft.
Engine: Pratt & Whitney TF30-6 double-shaft
turbofan/11,350 lb. thrust
Speed: 698 mph
Armament: Bombs, rockets

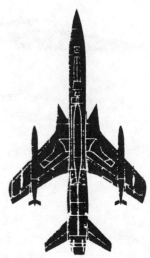

Republic F-105 Thunderchief

Wingspan: 35 ft.
Length: 64 ft. 3 in.
Engine: Pratt & Whitney J75-P-19W
Speed: 1,390 mph at 38,000 ft.
Armament: Varied loads of bombs and rockets

McDonnell Douglas A-4 Skyhawk

Wingspan: 27 ft. 6 in.
Length: 40 ft.
Engine: Wright J65-16A single-shaft
           turbojet/7,700 lb. thrust
Speed: 675 mph
Armament: Bombs, rockets, 2 20-mm cannons

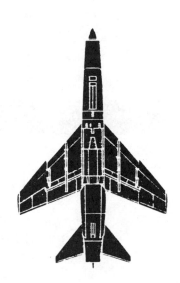

Vought F-8 Crusader

Wingspan: 35 ft. 8 in.
Length: 54 ft. 3 in.
Engine: Pratt & Whitney J57 double-shaft turbojet
           with afterburner/16,200 lb. thrust
Speed: 1,230 mph
Armament: 4 20-mm cannons, rockets, bombs

Northrop F-5 Freedom Fighter
(Tiger II)

Wingspan: 25 ft. 3 in.
Length: 47 ft. 2 in.
Engine: 2 General Electric J85-13 single-shaft
           afterburning turbojets/4,080 lb. thrust
           each
Speed: 925 mph
Armament: 2 20-mm cannons, varied

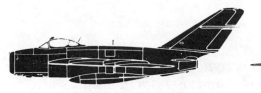

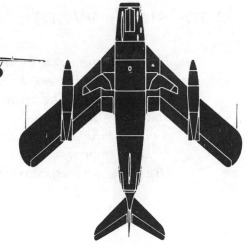

Mikoyan/Gurevich MiG-17
(Fresco)

Wingspan: 34 ft.
Length: 36 ft. 3 in.
Engine: Klimov VK-1 single-shaft centrifugal
   turbojet/5,952 lb. thrust
Armament: 1 37-mm cannon, 3 23-mm cannons,
   bombs, and air-to-air rockets

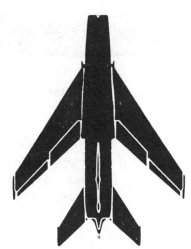

Mikoyan/Gurevich MiG-19
(Farmer)

Wingspan: 29 ft. 6½ in.
Length: 42 ft. 11¼ in.
Engine: 2 Mikuliu AM-5 single-shaft afterburning
   turbojets/6,700 lbs. each
Speed: 920 mph at 20,000 ft.
Armament: Rockets, cannons

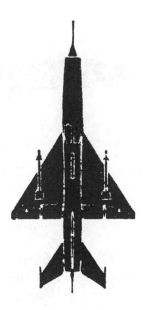

Mikoyan/Gurevich MiG-21
(Fishbed)

Wingspan: 23 ft. 5½ in.
Length: 46 ft. 11 in.
Engine: Turmonsky single-shaft turbojet with
   afterburner/11,240 lb. thrust
Speed: 1,285 mph
Armament: Rockets

Arab-Israeli Wars

Earlier in the Arab-Israeli conflicts the Israeli Air Force flew Messerschmitt Bf 109's, Spitfires, P-51 Mustangs, A-4 Skyhawks and F-4 Phantoms, among others. The various Arab air forces flew Soviet MiG 15's, 17's, 19's, and 21's. All of these are illustrated in other parts of this book. They represent the aircraft that participated in "Operation Peace for Galilee" (the Israeli incursion into Lebanon in pursuit of Palestine Liberation Organization terrorists) in mid-1982.

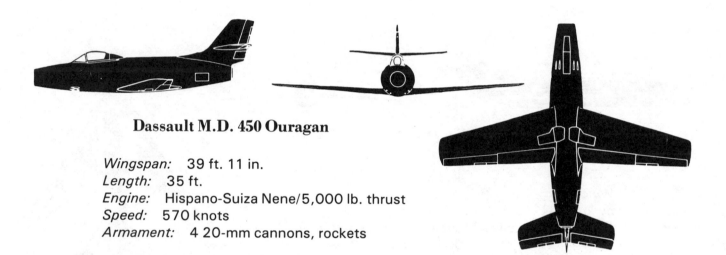

Dassault M.D. 450 Ouragan

Wingspan: 39 ft. 11 in.
Length: 35 ft.
Engine: Hispano-Suiza Nene/5,000 lb. thrust
Speed: 570 knots
Armament: 4 20-mm cannons, rockets

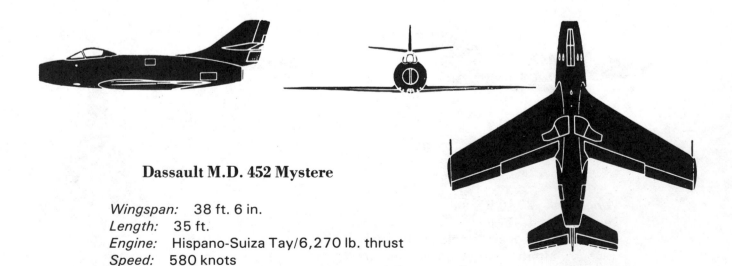

Dassault M.D. 452 Mystere

Wingspan: 38 ft. 6 in.
Length: 35 ft.
Engine: Hispano-Suiza Tay/6,270 lb. thrust
Speed: 580 knots
Armament: 4 20-mm or 30-mm cannons, 16
            rockets

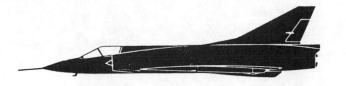

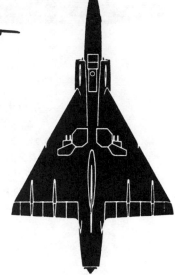

Dassault Mirage III

Wingspan: 27 ft.
Length: 50 ft. 10¼ in.
Engine: Snecma Atar 9B single-shaft
turbojet/13,225 lb. thrust
Speed: 863 mph
Armament: 2 30-mm cannons, bombs

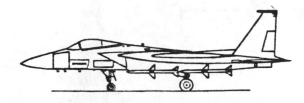

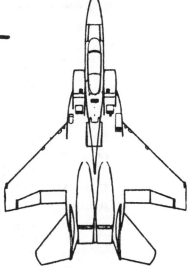

McDonnell Douglas F-15 Eagle

Wingspan: 42 ft. 9¾ in.
Length: 63 ft. 9¾ in.
Engine: A Pratt & Whitney F100-100 two-shaft
turbofans/14,871 lb. thrust
(23,810 lb. with afterburner) each
Speed: 1,650 mph
Armament: 1 20-mm multi-barrel cannon, 8 air-to
air rockets, and more

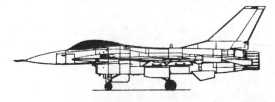

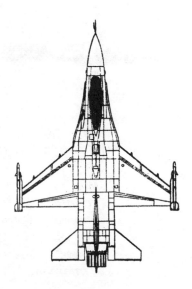

General Dynamics F-16 Falcon

Wingspan: 32 ft. 10 in.
Length: 46 ft. 6 in.
Engine: Pratt & Whitney F100-PW-100 two-shaft
afterburning turbofan/24,000 lb.
thrust
Speed: 1,300 mph
Armament: 1 20-mm multi-barrel cannon, 2
air-to-air rockets, and more

Hawker Hunter

Wingspan: 33 ft. 6 in.
Length: 42 ft.
Engine: Rolls-Royce Avon/6,500 lb. thrust
Speed: 640 knots
Armament: 4 30-mm cannons

Sukhoi SU-7 Fitter

Wingspan: 29 ft. 3½ in.
Length: 50 ft.
Engine: Lyulka AL-7F turbojet/15,430 lb. thrust
(22,050 with afterburner)
Speed: 1,055 mph
Armament: 2 30-mm cannons plus additional
weapons in wing pylons

Mikoyan/Gurevich MiG 23 Flogger

Wingspan: 47 ft. 3 in.
Length: 53 ft.
Engine: Turmansky R-29B/17,640 lb. thrust
(25,350 lb. with afterburner)
Speed: 840 mph
Armament: 1 23-mm twin barrel gun, rockets

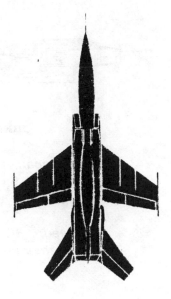

Mikoyan/Gurevich MiG 25 Foxbat

Wingspan: 46 ft.
Length: 73 ft. 2 in.
Engine: 2 Turmansky R-31 afterburning
turbojets/27,000 lb. thrust each
Speed: 2,100 mph
Armament: 4 air-to-air rockets

Other Conflicts (The Libyan Shootout, 1981; Falkland Islands War, 1982)

Additional aircraft that took part in the war for the Falkland (Malvinas) Islands, such as the Mirage, are shown elsewhere in this book.

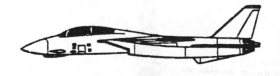
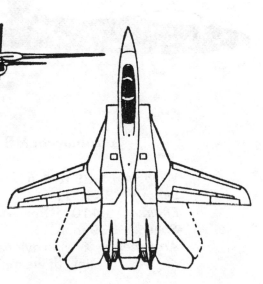

Grumman F-14 Tomcat

Wingspan: 64 ft. 1½ in.
Length: 61 ft. 2 in.
Engine: 2 Pratt & Whitney TF30-412A two-shaft
afterburning turbofans/20,900 lb.
thrust each
Speed: 1,564 mph
Armament: 1 20-mm multi-barrel cannon, 8–12
air-to-air rockets

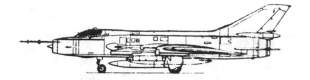

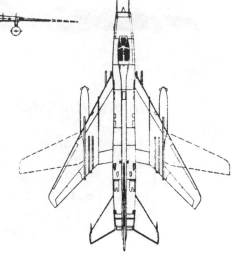

Sukhoi SU-22 Fitter J

Wingspan: 45 ft. 11½ in.
Length: 61 ft. 6½ in. (including nose probe)
Engine: Lyul'ka AL-21F-3 afterburning turbojet
17,200/24,700 lb. thrust
Speed: 800 mph
Armament: 2 NR 30 guns, 2 Atoll or Aphid
air-to-air missiles plus capability of
additional weapons

British Aerospace Sea Harrier

Wingspan: 25 ft. 3 in.
Length: 48 ft.
Engine: Rolls-Royce Pegasus 103 two-shaft
vectored thrust turbofan/21,500 lb.
thrust
Speed: 737 mph
Armament: 2 30-mm guns, 2 Sidewinder missiles
or other

Aeromacchi MB 326

Wingspan: 35 ft. 7 in.
Length: 34 ft. 11 in.
Engine: 3,410 lb. Rolls-Royce Viper Mk 540
Speed: 539 mph
Armament: 6 wing pylons can carry up to 4,000
lbs. of weapons

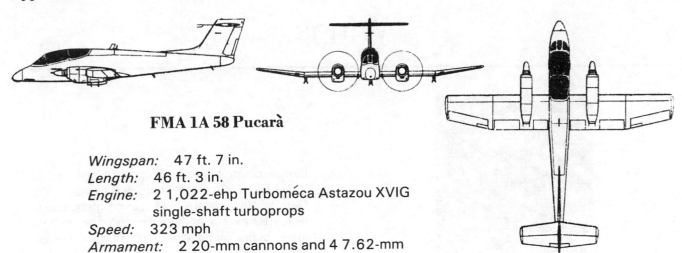

FMA 1A 58 Pucarà

Wingspan: 47 ft. 7 in.
Length: 46 ft. 3 in.
Engine: 2 1,022-ehp Turboméca Astazou XVIG
single-shaft turboprops
Speed: 323 mph
Armament: 2 20-mm cannons and 4 7.62-mm
machine guns

Wings

Badge of an Imperial German Army pilot of World War I. Of silver metal, it is similar to the German Naval pilot's gold-colored metal badge which has the sun near the top and a bird in flight in lieu of the Taube aircraft. (Der Dienst, Lowell, MI)

The RAF pilot's wings are embroidered and superseded the wings of the Royal Flying Corps which were the same except for the letters "RFC." The change took place during the First World War. These wings were also worn by American fliers of the "Eagle Squadron."

USAF pilots currently wear these silver metal pin-on wings. These were also the wings worn by United States Army Air Force pilots in World War II. During the First World War pilots of the United States Air Service wore wings embroidered with silver and gold thread. (Fox Military Equipment, Hinsdale, IL)

Navy "wings of gold" metal worn by naval aviators of the United States Navy, Marine Corps, and Coast Guard. These have been in use since the start of the Second World War.

Metal pilot's badge worn by members of the German Luftwaffe in World War II. It was silver metal tinted with gold around the edge.

Fighter pilots of the Imperial Japanese Air Service wore this bronze and silver metal pin-on badge during the Second World War. (Der Dienst, Lowell, MI)

Born in battle, the Israeli Air Force is considered the world's top fighting service today. Its fighter pilots wear these embroidered silver and blue wings featuring the "Star of David."

During the First World War, pilots of the United States Air Force wore wings embroidered with silver and gold thread. (Fox Military Equipment, Hinsdale, IL)

Medals

The award most coveted by German fliers in the First World War was the Pour le Mérite, more commonly known as ''The Blue Max.'' (Der Dienst, Lowell, MI)

Cast of bronze from Russian cannon captured during the Crimean War, the Victoria Cross is Britain's highest military decoration, with requirements for its award being similar to those for the United States Medal of Honor. (Der Dienst, Lowell, MI)

The United States Medal of Honor dates back to the Civil War and is the highest American military decoration. It is given for selfless heroism ''above and beyond the call of duty.'' Each of the United States armed forces has its own distinctive MOH with the same ribbon. This is the Navy version. (U.S. Navy Photo)

The Distinguished Service Cross was the decoration bestowed upon American fighter pilots, in World War I, for gallantry in action.

The French Croix de Guerre was awarded to Allied military personnel in both the First and Second World Wars. To distinguish between the two medals, the obverse had the dates of the particular war and they had different ribbons. This one, with palm, was awarded to Lt. Samuel H. Ulanoff in World War I. (He is this Editor's father.)

The Distinguished Service Order is awarded to officers of the British armed forces for distinguished wartime service. It can only be awarded to those "mentioned in dispatches."

The Military Cross was established early in World War I as an award to British Army officers and Warrant Officers for gallant and distinguished service in combat. It was also awarded to RFC and RAF fliers until the institution in June 1918 of the Distinguished Flying Cross (not shown here).

The first decoration awarded exclusively to American aviators was the Distinguished Flying Cross, instituted in 1926 for award to fliers of the United States armed services who distinguished themselves by heroism or extraordinary achievement in the air. It is a higher award than the Air Medal (not shown) which is roughly equivalent to the Army's Bronze Star.

Originally established by the King of Prussia in 1813, the German Iron Cross was awarded in both World Wars. The World War I medal had the date 1914 and the letter "W" with a crown above it, instead of 1939 and the Nazi swastika. (Der Dienst, Lowell, MI)

The United States Air Force Cross, authorized in July 1960, replaced the Army's Distinguished Service Cross, awarded to fighter pilots before the Air Force became a separate service.

Copyrights and Credits

ACE BOOKS, Inc. Excerpt from *Battling the Bombers* by Wilhelm Johnen. Copyright 1958 by Ace Books, Inc. Reprinted by permission of Ace Books, Inc. and William Kimber & Co., Ltd. All rights reserved.

AERO PUBLISHERS, INC. Excerpt from *The Red Baron*, by Von Richthofen. Copyright 1969 (second edition, 1980) by Stanley M. Ulanoff. Reprinted by permission of the editor, Stanley M. Ulanoff. All rights reserved.

AIR FORCE SPACE DIGEST "We Fly MiG Alley," by James Jabara; and "How a Fighter Pilot Sees the Air War in Vietnam," by Gerald D. Larson. Reprinted with permission from *Air Force Magazine*, the official journal of the Air Force Association.

AIRMAN MAGAZINE "MiG Sweep," by John T. Correll; and "Vampires, Take It Down," by Don Carson. Reprinted with permission from *Airman Magazine*, an official publication of the USAF.

AIR UNIVERSITY QUARTERLY REVIEW Excerpt from "Air to Air Combat in Korea," by Colonel Harrison R. Thyng, USAF. Reprinted by permission of the *Air University Quarterly Review*, Summer, 1953.

AMERICAN HERITAGE MAGAZINE Excerpt from "Swift Sword," by S. L. A. Marshall. Reprinted by permission of *American Heritage Magazine*.

ARCO PUBLISHING INC. Excerpt from *Winged Warfare*, by William A. Bishop. Copyright 1967 (second edition, 1981) by Stanley M. Ulanoff. Reprinted by permission of Stanley Ulanoff and Arco Publishing, Inc.

BALLANTINE BOOKS, INC. Excerpt from *Kamikaze*, by Yasuo Kuwahara and Gordon T. Allred. Copyright 1957 by Gordon T. Allred. Reprinted by permission of Ballantine Books, Inc. Excerpt from *Wing Leader*, by Group Captain J. E. Johnson. Copyright 1956 by Chatto & Windus, Ltd.; Copyright 1957 by Ballantine Books, Inc. Reprinted by permission of Chatto & Windus, Ltd. and Ballantine Books, Inc.

PETER BARRETT Excerpt from "The Great White Bears of Kotzebue," by Peter Barrett. From *True Magazine*. Copyright 1960 by Fawcett Publications, Inc. Reprinted by permission of the author.

ESTATE OF WILLIAM A. BISHOP Excerpt from *Winged Peace*, by Air Marshall William A. Bishop. Reprinted by permission of Mrs. William A. Bishop, Literary Executrix for the Estate of William A. Bishop.

CITADEL PRESS Excerpt from *Between the Star and the Cross*, by William Lichtman. Published by the Citadel Press. Copyright 1957 by William Lichtman. Reprinted by permission of the Citadel Press.

DOUBLEDAY & COMPANY, INC. Excerpt from *The Airmen Speak (Winged Words: Our Airmen Speak for Themselves)*, edited by Bentley Beauman. Copyright 1941 by Doubleday & Co., Inc. and British Crown copyright. Reprinted by permission of Doubleday & Co., Inc. and Her Britannic Majesty's Stationary Office. Excerpt from *Flying Tiger: Chennault of China*, by Robert Lee Scott, Jr. Copyright 1959 by Robert Lee Scott, Jr. Reprinted by permission of Doubleday & Co., Inc.

Index